*In the spring of 1940, as the clouds of war gathered over Europe, American newscaster Edward R. Murrow reported from London:*

> "The people here feel the machine is out of control, that we are all passengers on an express train traveling at high speed through a dark tunnel toward an unknown destiny. The suspicion recurs that the train may have no engineer."

*He was referring to Neville Chamberlain's Great Britain, but another and far more lethal train pulled out of the Berlin* bahnhof *during those same years.*

# THE NUCLEAR EXPRESS

# EXPRESS

## A POLITICAL HISTORY OF THE BOMB AND ITS PROLIFERATION

Thomas C. Reed and Danny B. Stillman

ZENITH PRESS

First published in 2009 by Zenith Press, an imprint of MBI Publishing Company, 400 1st Avenue North, Suite 300, Minneapolis, MN 55401 USA.

Zenith Press titles are also available at discounts in bulk quantity for industrial or sales-promotional use. For details write to Special Sales Manager at MBI Publishing Company, 400 1st Avenue North, Suite 300, Minneapolis, MN 55401 USA.

To find out more about our books, join us online at www.zenithpress.com.

Designer: Jennifer Bergstrom
Jacket Design: Brian Donahue

*Front cover image:* The fireball from the WILSON Event, 4:45 a.m. PDT, June 18, 1957, Yucca Flat, was photographed from a distance of about five miles within seconds after detonation. *Digital Vision/Getty Images*

Library of Congress Cataloging-in-Publication Data

Reed, Thomas C.
  The nuclear express : a political history of the bomb and its proliferation / Thomas C. Reed and Danny B. Stillman.
      p. cm.
  Includes bibliographical references.
  ISBN 978-0-7603-3502-4 (hb w/ jkt)
  1. Nuclear weapons—History.  I. Stillman, Danny B. II. Title.
  U264.R44 2009
  623.4'511909—dc22

                                    2008021384


Printed in the United States of America

# CONTENTS

To Amy, Carolyn, and Frank. — *T. C. R.*

To my wife, Ruth, and our children, David and Noelle. — *D. B. S.*

# PROLOGUE

The story that follows is a political history of nuclear weapons, from the discovery of fission in 1938 to the nuclear train wreck that may lie ahead. It is an account of where those weapons came from, how the technology surprisingly and covertly spread, who is likely to acquire those weapons next and, most importantly, why.

Nuclear weapons have always been instruments of terror. A half-century ago they jolted what remained of the Japanese government into surrender; they frightened East and West into backing away from Cuba; they convinced members of the Soviet *nomenklatura* to limit their ambitions as dreams of empire disappeared. A nuclear threat protected Allied access to Berlin, helped end the Korean War, precluded the further use of chemicals in Iraq in 1991, and convinced the contenders in various Mideast wars to call a halt before events ran out of control. Many an industrial megastate, confident of their patron's nuclear umbrella, decided to forgo nuclear developments of their own. Then the Cold War ended, the old protocols ceased to apply, and once-useful threats came to produce unintended consequences. While the Soviet gerontocracy and the Western democracies had a vested interest in survival, the mandarins of China and the insurgents of radical Islam may not be similarly constrained.

It was once thought there was a secret to the A-bomb and that a just and wise America would serve as the world's nuclear trustee during a peaceful reconstruction decade, but that is not the way history played itself out. Less than a quarter of the senior technical staff at wartime Los Alamos, New Mexico, were native-born American citizens. The Allies were well represented, some openly and some under cover. When the hostilities—and wartime alliances—ended, the technology began to spread. Soviet "representatives" helped their countrymen replicate the original Fat Man A-bomb within five years. British scientists, some of whom had flown as observers on the nuclear strike on Nagasaki, achieved the same results soon thereafter; within a decade of the Trinity event[1] the United States and the Soviet Union were transferring nuclear technology to their client states on a massive scale. They tolerated, and actually encouraged, cross-fertilization until it was too late to turn back.

---

1. Man's first nuclear detonation, in the New Mexico desert, July 16, 1945.

In the wake of the Suez crisis of 1956, France and Israel initiated a joint nuclear weapons program that marched hand-in-glove through Marcoule and Dimona[2] to the Algerian desert. With that first French test in 1960, two nations went nuclear with one shot.

Three years after Suez, Klaus Fuchs was released from his British prison. Fuchs, a German refugee, had fled to England in 1933, moved to wartime Los Alamos . . . in 1943, and while there spied for the Soviets. He was unmasked and sent to prison in 1950. Upon his release, in 1959, Fuchs did not retire. He fled to East Germany, where he met with Qian Sanqiang, China's chief A-bomb scientist, to whom he explained the inner workings of Fat Man. (Mao had made the decision to go nuclear four years before.) Fuchs may also have given the Chinese unique insights into the fundamentals of thermonuclear technology.

Five years after that conversation, in 1964, the Chinese went nuclear with a 22-kiloton shot in the Lop Nur desert. Two years later they tested their "export model," an ultra-simple A-bomb design, passed on to the Pakistanis and the master nuclear proliferator A. Q. Khan in 1983. In time, sketches of that weapon showed up in Libya.

During the 1970s, A. Q. Khan started pilfering uranium enrichment technology from Europe, the Indians fired a nuclear device made with plutonium extracted from an Atoms for Peace reactor, and radical Muslims began taking control of the world's petroleum supply. By the end of the 1970s, the nuclear secrets had spread, as had the petrodollars needed to support the nuclear habit.

With the coming of the 1980s, Deng Xiaoping's China apparently decided to actively promote nuclear proliferation within the Third World. In the decades that followed, Deng and his successors' governments trained scientists, transferred technology, and built infrastructure in furtherance of that policy.

By the end of the 1980s, the inefficiencies of the Soviet system were taking their toll. A nation that had gone nuclear with a vengeance was coming apart. The Soviet military was quite protective of its nuclear weapons, but the Soviet ministry charged with producing fissionable materials was not so meticulous. Plutonium and highly enriched uranium had been treated like so much coal. When the Soviet empire came to an end, chaos ensued. Successor republics found themselves awash with unlocked nukes and unaccounted-for materials. Most of those weapons and much of that material has since been rounded up, but the government of the Russian Federation has not been helpful in explaining some remaining nuclear anomalies nor in unveiling the biological warfare facilities created during that earlier era. The result is a Russian landscape still dotted with fissionable materials, biological fermenters, and

2. The plutonium-production reactors within France and Israel, respectively.

mysterious technologies awaiting their rendezvous with history under the control of a newly truculent quasi-tsar.

China stands astride this world like a young Colossus, a nation clearly supportive of nuclear proliferation. It entered the thermonuclear age with a speed that dazzled the West. Its collection of nuclear technology came not from super-spies, although it had a few; China collected its technology one graduate student at a time. The passing of Mao in 1976, the Tiananmen events of 1989, and the disintegration of the Soviet Union remade China into a fearsome global competitor with interests that could be well served by the devastation of Washington or New York, so long as that calamity was not directly attributable to Beijing.

Certain parts of the Chinese government may have decided it would be in their best interest to accept, or even encourage, multiple nuclear events (or wars) within the Western world: thus, the apparent Chinese tolerance of North Korean, Pakistani, and Iranian nuclear ambitions. China is a nation whose economic star is on the rise, with a prospective appetite for energy that will bid up the price paid in many ways. The only questions remaining: Who is to control China's ascent? And will that next generation continue to spread nuclear technology into the Third World?

Overlying all of this history is radical Islam's desire to destroy Western ways. This revulsion, ignored for decades, has now blossomed into armed conflict and nuclear ambition. The madrassa schools promoting this hatred have been funded by the West, addicted as it is to the profligate use of Middle Eastern crude oil. One Muslim nation, Pakistan, has gone nuclear, with many of her scientists and politicians welcoming the advent of a Muslim bomb. As the general in charge of that country during the 1980s put it, "We should acquire and share nuclear technology with the entire Islamic world." The current general's successor could well implement those thoughts during the twenty-first century.

"The detonation of a terrorist nuclear device in an American city is inevitable if the U.S. continues on its present course." Those are the words of Graham Allison, founding dean of the Kennedy School at Harvard and a former assistant secretary of defense. There is no doubt such a result could be achieved via an amateur device made from stolen Soviet-era fissionable material, by a weapon purchased from North Korea, or by a gadget assembled from Pakistani components. Few of our readers have seen a nuclear detonation; your authors have seen many. The effects of even a "primitive" A-bomb would not be inconsequential.

The September 11, 2001, attack on New York's World Trade Center is the event we all remember, but there was a similar attack eight years earlier that foretold the

*Opposite Page: UC Lawrence Livermore National Laboratory*

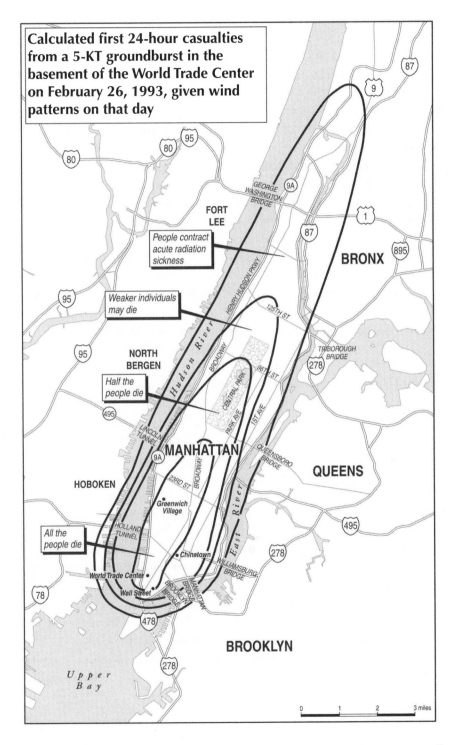

**Calculated first 24-hour casualties from a 5-KT groundburst in the basement of the World Trade Center on February 26, 1993, given wind patterns on that day**

People contract acute radiation sickness

Weaker individuals may die

Half the people die

All the people die

FORT LEE

BRONX

NORTH BERGEN

TRIBOROUGH BRIDGE

Hudson River

BROADWAY

HENRY HUDSON PKWY

125TH ST

CENTRAL PARK

96TH ST

PARK AVE

1ST AVE

GEORGE WASHINGTON BRIDGE

LINCOLN TUNNEL

MANHATTAN

QUEENS

QUEENSBORO BRIDGE

HOBOKEN

23RD ST

BROADWAY

Greenwich Village

East River

HOLLAND TUNNEL

Chinatown

World Trade Center

Wall Street

WILLIAMSBURG BRIDGE

MANHATTAN BRIDGE

BROOKLYN BRIDGE

BROOKLYN

Upper Bay

0    1    2    3 miles

5

future. On February 26, 1993, a Ryder truck loaded with homemade explosives was parked in the basement of those same Manhattan towers. The payload was 1,400 pounds of urea, nitroglycerin, and other combustibles, with sodium cyanide added to increase casualties. The mastermind of this attack was Ramzi Yousef, traveling on an Iraqi passport; his allies were radical Islamic conspirators financed by al Qaeda. The intent was to topple one of the World Trade towers onto the other amidst a cloud of cyanide gas. Fortunately, the targeted tower did not fall, and the lethal gas was consumed within the fire, but six people died and more than a thousand were injured as a result of that explosion.

Instead of fertilizer, suppose that Mr. Yousef had been able to place a primitive, five-kiloton nuclear weapon in the back of his truck. Since that vehicle had a one-ton capacity and three hundred cubic feet of drayage space, the very low-tech South African nuclear device developed during the 1980s would have fit nicely. After that February 1993 fertilizer attack, the U.S. nuclear weapons laboratories ran some calculations on the theoretical results of a five-kiloton explosion on the streets of lower Manhattan on February 26, 1993, given the wind and weather conditions on that day. The resulting fallout patterns are shown on the map on page 5.

The most frightening results of such an attack could have been:

- Most buildings south of Central Park destroyed, their inhabitants dead
- Millions of other New Yorkers, once living south of 125th Street, dying of radiation effects
- Millions more throughout the metropolitan area suffering acute radiation sickness
- Much of lower Manhattan, Brooklyn, and Hoboken set on fire

Unless we are attentive to history, a terrorist organization will soon be able to assemble and place such an A-bomb within a truck, ship, or container and deliver same to the heart of any number of U.S. cities. Even "small and inefficient" nuclear weapons could have a devastating effect on American society and its institutions. But is the simple raining of death and destruction on the West the only goal of these people? The jihadists and/or their patrons may have grander ambitions.

Perhaps they have in mind a takeover of U.S. governmental institutions modeled on Lenin's capture of St. Petersburg in 1917. After a few months of post-imperial turmoil, the Kerensky cabinet in the Russian capital was exhausted. It was a government in name only. Saint Petersburg, and eventually all of Russia, was ripe for takeover by a disciplined mob. In the twenty-first century, Muslim-extremist sleeper cells in the United States might hope to effect a similar coup amidst nuclear chaos. After nuclear detonations in, say, New York, Chicago, and Los Angeles, and with threats of more to come from hidden weapons, American civil society might well collapse.

Another terrorist aim might be the disruption of American financial power in the wake of a nuclear attack on its financial centers. Terrorists or their patrons might hope to trigger a currency crisis akin to that which afflicted Southeast Asia in 1997. America's reliance on massive overseas credit, its notes held principally by China and Saudi Arabia, makes this a real possibility.

Or, an Islamic dictator might just be seeking local hegemony, using the nuclear threat to topple nearby secular Arab governments in his march to regional power.

All these dark days are possible, but we think the most likely purpose of a Third World A-bomb will be as it was during the Cold War: deterrence. A Muslim dictator or a hegemonic Chinese chairman may simply wish to deter the United States from intervening as his state settles old scores. Unfortunately, such games of nuclear chicken, conducted with unsafe or inadequately secured weapons, can easily get out of control.

Ever since the Trinity event, nuclear politics have been challenging our ability to survive. If we are to make the right choices now, we need to understand how we got here. Where did these instruments of terror come from? How do they work?[3] What do they look like? Who has been helping whom? And what are the bottom-line strategic objectives of radical Islam and the People's Republic of China? As one century gives way to another, nuclear weapons are falling into less well-manicured hands, but their purpose remains the same: to effect a drastic change in the geopolitical status quo. It was once the surrender of Japan or the halting of Soviet expansion that Americans sought. It is now the eradication of Western culture or the abolition of the state of Israel that the Islamic extremists seek. A million lives may be lost along the way, but Armageddon is not necessarily the objective of these nuclear acolytes. We need to understand who they are and how they got to be so smart. That is the purpose of the pages that follow.

3. See appendix A for an introduction to the physics of nuclear weapons.

# BIG NEWS: NUCLEAR FISSION RELEASES NEUTRONS!

In the beginning, the headwaters of nuclear science lay in territories controlled by the European dictators. The discovery of nuclear fission in Berlin in 1938 triggered intense global interest, but Hitler and Mussolini did not understand what cards they held. They drove away the leaders of "Jewish physics" (i.e., quantum physics and relativity); they favored their own classical and more understandable "Aryan physicists."

In 1921, Albert Einstein won the Nobel Prize in physics for his discovery of the photovoltaic effect, but a decade later, on the eve of Hitler's coming to power, Einstein saw the handwriting on the wall. He fled Berlin, settling into Princeton for the rest of his days. Einstein provided the political spark for Roosevelt's decision to start work on a wartime A-bomb program.

In 1934, Edward Teller, Hungarian by birth, was pulled out of Göttingen, a small university town in central Germany, by a Jewish Rescue Committee. Teller first settled into George Washington University. Later, he moved to Los Alamos, New Mexico, where he, along with others, devised one key A-bomb concept, spherical implosion of a plutonium pit, and, in time, solved the central problem of H-bomb design.

Enrico Fermi was an Italian living with a Jewish wife in Mussolini's Italy. The intellectual climate at the University of Rome was stimulating, but the political atmosphere was growing heavy. On November 9, 1938, Hitler's Nazis unleashed the *Kristallnacht* terror in Germany. To Enrico and Laura Fermi, that was the last straw. The following week they traveled to Stockholm, picked up the professor's Nobel Prize for work on neutron bombardment of the nucleus, and then kept right on going, to New York. Two years later, Fermi initiated operation of the first chain-reacting nuclear pile at the University of Chicago, thereby opening the door to the production of plutonium and the explosion of Fat Man.

Lise Meitner was Austrian and Jewish by birth. In 1938, as a pioneering and isolated lady physicist, she was working alongside chemist Otto Hahn at the Kaiser

Wilhelm Institute in Berlin. Hahn was studying the chemical effects of neutron bombardment of the uranium nucleus. By 1938, Meitner and Hahn had enjoyed a thirty-year professional relationship.

That year started badly, with Hitler's virulent anti-Jewish policies penetrating even into academia; Meitner's file made it to the desk of SS chief Heinrich Himmler. In March, the Nazis annexed Austria in a bloodless (actually, highly acclaimed) *Anschluss*. Meitner's Austrian passport no longer protected her, since Austria was no longer a country. Her life was in jeopardy; lacking documentation, she found it difficult to emigrate. On July 12, 1938, with the covert assistance of a Dutch colleague and carrying but one suitcase, Meitner fled to Groningen, Holland, and thence to Sweden, leaving behind her long-time German associates and her beloved laboratory.

While living in Scandinavia, Meitner stayed in touch with her German colleagues. In November of 1938 she reconnected with Otto Hahn at a Niels Bohr–sponsored seminar in Copenhagen. Hahn, born in Frankfurt to "acceptable" German stock, had served in a chemical warfare unit during World War I. He remained securely behind, in Berlin, for the duration of the Hitler years.

At the time of their meeting in Copenhagen, Meitner urged Hahn to re-examine the products of his neutron bombardment of uranium. "You have it all wrong," she observed. "Your theories [of chemical reaction] make no sense." Hahn returned to Berlin, repeated his experiments, and on December 19 wrote to Meitner that he had found barium in the "reaction products." How could that be? Barium was far down the periodic table from uranium. "Perhaps you can suggest some fantastic explanation," he wrote. "Uranium really cannot break into barium."

Oh yes, it could.

Upon receipt of that letter, on December 21, Meitner and her nephew-physicist, Otto Robert Frisch, began to reflect on Bohr's model of the nucleus: a drop of liquid, held together by surface tension. If too big, it will pop apart. But how to account for the energy released in the Hahn experiments? According to Einstein's famous $E=MC^2$, that unexplained energy must have come from the tiny difference of mass, known as the "packing fraction," as one moves down the periodic table. The following day, Meitner responded to Hahn, advising that the nucleus must have split in two. To explain the phenomenon and the associated release of energy, she coined the word "nuclear fission".

Hahn received the letter on December 23, 1938, and published it soon thereafter. After the war, he and his virulently anti-Nazi coworker Fritz Strassman were awarded the Nobel Prize for the discovery of fission. Meitner spent the war years in Scandinavia, well out of Hitler's grasp. Her recognition only came decades later, in 1966, when Glenn Seaborg, chairman of the U.S. Atomic Energy Commission and a Nobel laureate himself, awarded the AEC's Fermi Prize to Hahn, Meitner, and Strassman for their "independent and collaborative contributions to the discovery of nuclear fission."

Niels Bohr was born in Denmark to a Jewish mother. In 1922, he won a Nobel Prize for explaining the structure of the atom. Seventeen years later, in early 1939, he visited the United States, carrying the news of the Meitner and Hahn discovery of fission and warning of the ongoing atom-splitting work continuing in Berlin. Bohr returned to Denmark in time for the Nazi invasion of western Europe in 1940, staying in Copenhagen until learning, in 1943, that he was about to be arrested. Bohr and his family fled to Sweden in a fishing boat. He and his son were then flown on to England in the bomb bay of a British Mosquito aircraft, traversing the German-controlled airspace over Norway along the way. In time, Bohr made it to Los Alamos, where his presence was so important that, even within the Los Alamos fence, he was given the code name "Nicholas Baker."

With the growth of Nazi animosity, this westward-flowing tide of nuclear-competent refugees worked its way to Paris, hosted by Irene Joliot-Curie, and New York, welcomed by Fermi. In March 1939, these assemblies of genius in the United States, as well as Soviet readers of the Hahn-Strassman paper in Moscow, confirmed that the lighter-weight fragments resulting from the fission of their parent nuclei needed fewer neutrons for stability. Thus, with every successful neutron bombardment of a uranium nucleus, two or three additional neutrons would be released.[1] A chain reaction was possible.

In March 1940, Rudolf Peierls and Otto Frisch, associates at Birmingham University in England, wrote a three-page paper that explained how a uranium fission bomb might be built using U-235. They could have written that paper for Hitler, since Rudolf Peierls had been born in Berlin to Jewish parents. But he fled Germany and immigrated to Birmingham when Hitler came to power. The Peierls-Frisch paper became the basis of the British MAUD Committee report and thus the Allied nuclear weapon program (the membership of the MAUD Committee and the delivery of the report is discussed in chapter 4). Peierls moved on to Los Alamos in 1943.

Wolfgang Pauli was born in Vienna in 1900 to Jewish parents. During the interwar years, he became a superstar in the world of quantum physics, devising the Pauli Exclusion Principle, which explains why all the universe does not collapse back upon itself. In the late summer of 1940, Pauli fled his Zurich enclave for

1. Joliot-Curie made this discovery in Paris; Fermi and Szilard at Columbia in New York. Flerov and Rusinov, working at Fiztekh, in Moscow, came to a similar conclusion in April 1939.

the security of Princeton and the company of Albert Einstein, leaving only his contemporary, Werner Heisenberg, in charge of the German nuclear weapon program. Pauli was awarded the Nobel Prize for physics in 1945.

Nine months after the discovery of nuclear fission, Hitler invaded Poland; World War II was on. The tide of refugees to the West began to flood; in time, much of that talent converged on Los Alamos and Chalk River.[2]

The Europeans were eager to settle their score with the dictators, inspired as they were by the arrival of yet another Jewish German refugee. Fritz Reiche, arriving in the United States in April 1941, advised his contemporaries that "a large number of German physicists are working intensively on the problem of the uranium bomb under the direction of (Nobel Prize winner) Werner Heisenberg."[3]

The mind boggles to think of how different the world might have been if those tyrants in Berlin and Rome had been more hospitable to their native scientific genius.

2. Chalk River, Canada, initially was the home of the Anglo-French nuclear weapons program.
3. As reported by Thomas Powers in *Heisenberg's War* (New York: Knopf, 1993).

# LOS ALAMOS: A FIRST, BUT NOT THE LAST

Until the middle of the twentieth century, most atomic and nuclear discoveries had come from European minds, including those of immigrants to the New World. The top seventy nuclear discoveries and innovations of those fifty years[1] (1897–1948) originated in:

| | | |
|---|---|---|
| U.S.A. | 26 discoveries | 37% |
| United Kingdom | 18 | 26 |
| Germany & Austria | 13 | 19 |
| Switzerland | 3 | 4 |
| France | 3 | 4 |
| Russia[2] | 2 | 3 |
| Netherlands & Denmark | 2 | 3 |
| Italy | 2 | 3 |
| Japan | 1 | 1 |
| TOTAL | 70 | 100% |

Note: China, Korea, and S.E. Asia    0

1. Source: Charles Murray, *Human Accomplishments* (New York: Harper Collins, 2003), 184–87, 203–204.
2. The Soviet Union became a closed society in 1917. Many discoveries thereafter may have gone unreported in the open literature.

| | | |
|---|---|---|
| Middle Eastern countries | 0 | |
| South Asia | 0 | |
| Southern Hemisphere | 0 | |

An examination of the Los Alamos technical staff roster from 1943 to 1945 shows the national origin of the twenty-four intellectual all-stars, i.e., the directors, division chiefs, and their deputies, to have been:

| | | |
|---|---|---|
| U.K. and Canada | 6 persons | 25% |
| U.S. | 5 | 21 |
| Germany/Austria | 5 | 21 |
| Hungary | 4 | 17 |
| Other European | 4 | 17 |

Thus, there never was an American nuclear cartel. Technology does not respect national borders, and in time, nuclear and atomic matters have ceased being even a European monopoly. We should not kid ourselves into thinking otherwise. By the summer of 1942, the European scientific diaspora had temporarily settled into Berkeley, Columbia, and the University of Chicago. Fearing Berlin's capabilities, these refugees and their American hosts were determined to beat Hitler to the nuclear punch.

In the beginning, nuclear cross-sections were at the heart of the puzzle. What was the probability of a given nuclear response to the bombardment of a nucleus by an incoming particle, usually a neutron? The answer came from experimental measurements. The standard unit of nuclear cross-section, $10^{-28}$ square meters, came to be known as a "barn," from the expression, "bigger than a barn door" (physicist humor, since the dimension was infinitesimally small). Once measured, cross-sections were then used to calculate the progress of a proposed nuclear assembly, chain reaction, or explosion. That data, in turn, was employed to calculate (correctly in the United States) the critical mass of uranium-235.[3] The Germans, in Berlin, miscalculated by a factor of ten, leading them to the conclusion that a portable bomb was not feasible.

In Chicago, Enrico Fermi was assembling a large pile of natural uranium (0.7-

3. The mass needed to sustain a chain reaction.

percent U-235) within a graphite matrix, which was necessary to slow down the cascading neutrons and thus promote their capture by the U-235 nuclei. On December 2, 1942, his "nuclear pile" went critical, producing slightly more neutrons than it consumed during each fission generation. Each neutron's gestation time was found to be about ten nanoseconds ($10^{-8}$ seconds), and thus that interval became the unit of time in nuclear work. It was given the name "one shake," as in "one shake of a lamb's tail."

Fermi had created the world's first chain-reacting nuclear reactor. The secret of his success was the use of ultra-pure graphite. In Berlin physicists were attempting a similar experiment, but they used commercial-grade graphite; their reactor never went critical.

In June 1942, as Fermi labored in Chicago, the German armaments minister convened a conference of scientists, army officers, and munitions experts to review Germany's nuclear options. Albert Speer wanted to hear about recent nuclear fission developments and then the prospects for an A-bomb on a time scale acceptable to Hitler. Physicist Werner Heisenberg, already a Nobel laureate, led the discussion. He was enthusiastic, but the others, hearing estimates of a nonportable weapon and given no evidence of a chain-reacting experiment, wished to pursue other avenues. Speer closed out the subject in discussions with Hitler on June 23. The Fuehrer preferred to focus on more immediate prospects: rockets and jet aircraft.

Even so, physicists in Germany continued to tinker with nuclear visions for another half year. It was only the destruction of the Norsk Hydro heavy water facility[4] in Norway by ten dedicated Norwegian Special Forces paratroopers in February 1943 and the mind-focusing German defeat at Stalingrad during that same month that led Speer to reconfirm, formally, the end of any nuclear weapons work within wartime Germany.

In March 1943, the Allied pace picked up, and the action moved to Los Alamos.[5] The scientists relocated to that isolated New Mexico mesa not only achieved awesome scientific breakthroughs, they did so with a breathtaking speed while the engineers at their sides brilliantly coupled those discoveries into the industrial infrastructure and then into the military machines needed to win the war.

Once gathered, the scientists of Los Alamos immediately recognized the possibilities of plutonium as a nuclear weapon material. That element had been discovered by American Glenn Seaborg in Berkeley in March 1941, but it had not even been named when the Los Alamos talent first considered its possibilities. It was clear that "Material 49,"

---

4. Germany's source of heavy water (deuterium oxide), needed as an alternative neutron moderator in lieu of impure graphite. In postwar interviews, knowledgeable German scientists confirmed that the elimination of the Norwegian heavy water production facility was the key factor in terminating German A-bomb research.
5. This was the case even though the University of California had no formal contract to manage the Los Alamos laboratory until April 15, 1943.

as it was then known, would be a more efficient weapon fuel. Less of it would be needed for a critical mass; more yield would result from a given mass. On the other hand, there were problems. Plutonium generated too many neutrons spontaneously; it could not easily be brought to supercriticality. The solution: a spherical implosion, driven by high explosives, to both rapidly assemble and compress the new metal.

The requirement to accurately implode a ball of fissionable plutonium led to the engineering, machining, and testing of very intricate high-explosive lenses in the canyons of New Mexico. One such partially assembled system is shown in the photo section of this work. High-explosive lens technology was one of the real "secrets of the A-bomb" later appropriated by Soviet spies and Allied scientists after World War II.

Engineers needed to learn the metallurgy of plutonium; no one had ever cast, machined, or even handled this very dangerous metal before. The scientists needed to figure out its equation of state: its hydrodynamics as highly compressed plutonium metal turned into superheated plasma during implosion and compression. Then came the pursuit of neutron generators, the devices needed to flood the assembling core of a nuclear weapon with thousands of initiating neutrons at just the right instant.

These were the cutting edges of A-bomb technology honed in Los Alamos. Equally astonishing was the speed with which those nuclear concepts were brought to tangible reality. It was only at the end of 1941 that governmental papers were signed reflecting a serious U.S. interest in A-bombs. General Leslie R. Groves was not put in charge of the Manhattan Engineering District (as the A-bomb project was called) until September 1942. Fermi's chain-reacting "nuclear pile" did not go critical until December 1942. Robert Oppenheimer and the first scientific staff members did not arrive in Los Alamos until March 1943. At the earliest, the autumn of 1942 should be considered the starting point for America's serious efforts to achieve a nuclear weapon. Yet within three years of that start, A-bombs were falling on Japan. Could we make such quick progress today? And what does that tell us about the speed with which others can join the nuclear club if they are serious about doing so?

Science was important during World War II, but equally startling were the muscular achievements of American industry in producing the critical materials—enriched uranium and plutonium—needed for America's weapons. It was not until General Groves was put in charge, in the autumn of 1942, that the Army Corps of Engineers began to acquire land near Oak Ridge, Tennessee. Construction of the Oak Ridge gaseous diffusion facility on a hundred-square-mile patch of the Tennessee Valley did not start until the end of that year. It cost $500 million[6] to build, employed twelve thousand workers, and began to produce weapons-grade enriched

6. Six billion 2008 dollars.

uranium within two years. Little Boy detonated over Hiroshima thirty months after groundbreaking at Oak Ridge.

Only after Fermi's chain-reaction experiment succeeded did work start on another, even larger materials facility, this one along the Columbia River in Hanford, Washington. A 780-square-mile site was to be the home of America's plutonium-production reactors and reprocessing facilities. The first reactor at Hanford went critical after midnight on September 27, 1944, but by dawn the power level had fallen to zero; the reactor had quit operating. DuPont's engineers[7] had foreseen the problem: xenon poisoning. That gas, a fission byproduct, had built up in the reactor during its early hours of operation, absorbing the neutrons needed to maintain the chain reaction. Bypass tubes, designed into the reactor's core by foresightful engineers, drew off the disruptive gas, and the reactor resumed operation. Within four months of going critical, plutonium metal was being delivered to Los Alamos. This mysterious disabling of a reactor, its reasons, and cure were among the secrets passed to the Soviets by their agents in the United States.

The first American plutonium-based bomb, Fat Man, was fired as the Trinity event in New Mexico on July 16, 1945, ten months after reactor criticality had been achieved. No followers in the nuclear parade have ever moved that fast, but it can be done.

The technology and industrial effort were impressive, but they still only addressed two legs of the wartime challenge: the third was weaponization. The "gadget"[8] had to be converted into a weapon that could fit into a B-29 bomb bay, could be maintained and armed by military personnel, could be transported safely from assembly point to target, and that would work reliably once it got there. While those requirements may sound mundane, they are not simple. Few weapon systems, from automatic rifle to A-bomb, have made the transition from tested concept to operational weapon in less than two years. The first American H-bomb was tested conceptually in October 1952, and a portable version was tested on a barge in February 1954, but an operational weapon was not dropped from an aircraft and fired until May 1956—three and a half years after the first test.

The warriors of 1945 dealt with the challenges of weapon maintenance and arming by sending no less than the senior military officers from Los Alamos, qualified weapons engineers, to accompany the gadget from New Mexico to the skies over the target. In the case of Little Boy, navy Capt. William Parsons flew aboard the *Enola Gay*. Because of

7. The Army recruited the DuPont Corporation to build and operate the facility at Hanford. The company continued to operate it safely for the duration of the war.
8. To maintain security, even inside the Los Alamos fence, Oppenheimer directed that the word "bomb" never be used. The world's first nuclear weapon was to be referred to as "the gadget."

Little Boy's linear design, Captain Parsons could arm it after takeoff and then assure its well-being until weapon drop. Similarly, navy Cmdr. Frederick Ashworth accompanied Fat Man from Tinian to target, but his mission was a little more dicey. Fat Man, being a spherically-imploded device, could not be armed en route; it was ready to fire as the host aircraft, *Bock's Car,* started its roll down the runway.

Safety was addressed simply enough: by being very careful. The first American (and Soviet) A-bombs were quite delicate and dangerous. As noted above, an aborted *Bock's Car* takeoff could have resulted in disaster. In a crash, the high explosive in Fat Man would have exploded, scattering plutonium across the island. Some nuclear yield might have resulted as well. The entire war in the Pacific rode on those four Wright Double Cyclone 2,200-horsepower propeller engines as that B-29 began its takeoff roll on that August morning, but those engines had been cared for meticulously—everything worked as planned.

Reliability rides on the seemingly trivial, easily overlooked by designers in the laboratory. For example, the environment in a B-29's bomb bay would change drastically en route to Japan. Temperatures would drop from the tropical August heat experienced on takeoff, to forty degrees below zero Fahrenheit during the four-hour ride to Japan. Fat Man's components would shrink; the rattling of the engines might jar loose a connection. Any misalignment between detonators and high explosive would have rendered Fat Man inoperable. Thus, seemingly minor adjustments were essential en route to the target. It was this concern for reliability that weighed heavily against any U.S. decision to stage a demonstration test with advance notice to the Japanese. President Truman's interim committee on bomb use, meeting in Washington on June 1, 1945, noted: "An atomic bomb is an intricate device, still in the developmental stage. Its operation will be far from routine. If, during the final [airborne] adjustments to the bomb, the Japanese defenders should attack, a faulty move might easily result in some kind of failure. Such an end to an advertised demonstration of power would be much worse than if the attempt had not been made at all."

As it was, Allied scientists and engineers, pilots, and crew chiefs pulled it off. As a team they were ready to strike Japan within weeks of the Trinity test, instead of two years.

In this new twenty-first century, intelligence officers and policy planners debate the time required for a given nation to develop a nuclear striking arm. This is not a new pastime. At the time of the first Soviet nuclear test, in August 1949, the U.S. intelligence community was publishing estimates of five years until the U.S.S.R. could go nuclear. Unfortunately, the Soviets had fired their first device the previous week.

There are a few morals to be drawn from the above tales:

1. Technology does not respect national boundaries; the word travels fast; nuclear secrets do not keep. (Nuclear cross-sections are published and available at the MIT bookstore. They accompany the nuclear weapon designs that now proliferate on the worldwide web.)

2. Any well-industrialized society with the intellectual firepower, economic resources, and government determination can join the nuclear club less than three years from "go." (Think Germany, Taiwan, Brazil, etc. It's a long list.)

3. This time span can be shortened if the society of interest has plutonium-producing nuclear reactors or uranium-enrichment machinery already in place as part of its energy economy. (Think Japan, India, or the Koreas.)

4. It may take a little longer if the would-be nuclear power lacks a full industrial base, but national will counts for a great deal. (We speak of Iran here as well as Pakistan and, once again, North Korea.)

CHAPTER 3

# THE RAIDS ON JAPAN

How did they do that? How could the wartime United States have entrusted the world's first A-bomb, a delicate and temperamental gadget, developed at staggering cost, to a novice B-29 crew? How could the United States be sure that Japanese fighters would not rise up to attack the unescorted *Enola Gay*? B-29s could operate at thirty thousand feet, but so could the new Japanese Zero interceptors. The answer to both questions is the same: practice. The United States lulled the Japanese defenders into complacency, and they trained their own American crews by making innocuous trial runs over a dozen Japanese cities during the summer of 1945. Repeated three-aircraft missions at first dropped only propaganda leaflets. Then came comparatively harmless attacks with single blockbusters known as "the pumpkin." It was only in August that the lethal U.S. nuclear attacks began.[1]

## ATTACK ON TOKYO

The crisis for Japan started on the evening of March 9–10, 1945, the night of the great Tokyo firebomb raid. During previous months, the U.S. Army Air Forces had made sporadic bombing attacks on the Japanese homeland, with minimal results. Industrial production had continued after perhaps a thousand deaths in Tokyo—tragic but manageable for the Japanese government. Then Maj. Gen. Curtis LeMay arrived. He was put in charge of the 73rd Bomber Wing based on Saipan. General LeMay devised a radically different approach to the destruction of Japan; it started with a massive, low-level incendiary attack on the nation's capital.

LeMay struck at midnight. Three hundred B-29s based on Saipan dropped 8,500 bombs that, in turn, dispersed a half-million canisters of incendiary fuel. By dawn, sixteen square miles of eastern Tokyo were completely destroyed, eighty-eight thousand people were dead, and the survivors were burned and disfigured refugees. War from the air would never be the same.

---

1. See appendix B for a full listing of the 393rd (Nuclear) Bombardment Squadron's missions over Japan.

In June, General LeMay began the step-by-step incineration of the entire Japanese homeland. Five hundred aircraft armadas of B-29s, now based in the Mariana Islands, made weekly attacks on the smaller and more remote cities of southern Japan. By the end of June, eighteen such municipalities had gone up in flames.

Given these dreadful and massive attacks, the Japanese air defense forces "learned" not to waste precious gasoline and pilots on the "harmless" three-aircraft mini-raids taking place elsewhere. The leaflets fluttering down from the sky were laughably bad translations into Japanese, and the pumpkin was just one bomb, although it was the size, shape, and weight of Fat Man. At 10,000 pounds, the pumpkin delivered a whopping 5,500 pounds of explosives to its target, but that was pretty insignificant to the Japanese when compared to LeMay's massive firebomb attacks. Yet, the American pilots were learning their routes on those flights. They were practicing release procedures with a dummy Fat Man. In early July 1945, Japanese Lt. Masataka Hakata entered these three-aircraft formations into his operations register. He noted their odd flights patterns: dropping one bomb, turning, and zooming away. To him and the Japanese air-defense hierarchy, they seemed harmless enough to be ignored.

## THE JAPANESE SCIENTISTS UNDERSTOOD

By the beginning of World War II, the Japanese had a modest nuclear program under way. As early as October 1940, as scientists in Britain were organizing their thoughts within the MAUD report, Colonel Suzuki of the Japanese Army and Professor Sagane of Tokyo Imperial University were producing a similar twenty-page paper for the army general staff based on the early fission discoveries in Europe. The Suzuki-Sagane paper concluded that the construction of an atomic bomb was possible and that Japan might have adequate uranium in-country to build one.

In May 1943, the project was given structure (Prof. Yoshio Nishina was put in charge) and a home (the Aviation Technology Research Institute in Tokyo). Professor Nishina was a world-class physicist, fifty years old at the beginning of World War II. During the prewar years, he had developed close relationships with Niels Bohr and Albert Einstein. The initial Japanese A-bomb venture was known as the "N Project" (for Nishina, not nuclear). The scientists involved settled on thermal diffusion as the means for collecting weapons-grade U-235.

Two tons of high-grade uranium ore would be needed for the N Project's research phase alone. Professor Satoyasu Iimori was to find it. His initial hopes lay within Japan's Fukushima Prefecture, but the uranium mines there turned out only small quantities of low-quality ore. Army commanders throughout the empire were given orders to look for better material. Professor Iimori even turned to the Germans for help. During the summer of 1943, as the Americans began to turn the tide in the

21

Pacific, this global search had produced enough uranium to start work. By the end of November 1943, Prof. Tadashi Takeuchi's isotopic separator was ready for its first test; by January 1944, Japan's N Project had produced a small, rice-sized crystal of uranium hexafluoride. By March, the thermal separator was ready to run, but the American B-29s were also closing in on the Japanese homeland. The first B-29 flew over Tokyo on November 1, 1944. The firebombing of that city four months later burned the entire N Project to the ground. Professor Nishina and his scientists escaped with their lives, but that part of Japan's nuclear weapons project came to an end.

Meanwhile, in another part of Japan, inter-service rivalry was assuring a second look at this problem. Earlier in the war (July 1942 to March 1943), the Imperial Navy's Research Committee on Nuclear Physics Applications had concluded that "It should be possible to make an atomic bomb, but probably difficult even for the U.S. to achieve during the war." At that time, the navy decided to turn its attention to radar, but later in 1943, as the war took turns for the worse, the Japanese Navy's Fleet Command returned to the A-bomb as a possible route to salvation. It sponsored the "F Project" (for fission) at the Imperial University of Kyoto. Professor Bunsaku Arakatsu was put in charge; high-speed centrifuges were his preferred route to U-235 separation. That was the right approach, as Pakistan's A. Q. Khan came to show a quarter-century later, but in 1944, the technical challenges were too great and the supply of uranium hopelessly small. Professor Arakatsu understood that his machines needed to spin at 100,000 rpm if they were to separate U-235 (in gaseous hexaflouride form) from U-238 effectively. The best he could achieve was 40,000 rpm. Professor Kiichi Kimura was put in charge of finding more uranium for the F Project, but he came up empty-handed.

Kyoto would become a safe haven during the war. American Secretary of War James Forrestal was a man of letters; he considered Kyoto, Japan's onetime imperial capital, to be a cultural treasure. Much to the chagrin of General Groves, Forrestal declared Kyoto to be off limits to bombing. But even with this free pass, no centrifuge at the F Project ever got up to speed, and no enriched uranium was ever produced.

Then came Hiroshima. On July 16, 1945, Fat Man was tested in New Mexico; on July 22, at Potsdam, President Truman and the Prime Minister Churchill made the final decision to use the A-bomb on Japan as soon as possible and without prior specific warning. On July 24, they advised Stalin of the Trinity test. His response: "I hope you make good use of it against the Japanese." On July 26, the leaders of the United States, Great Britain, and China issued the Potsdam Declaration, setting forth a demand for Japan's surrender. That document included a clear, but not A-bomb–specific, warning of "the utter devastation of the Japanese homeland" to come if the Allied demands for unconditional surrender were not met. The proclamation closed with the warning that, "The alternative for Japan is prompt and utter destruction." During the weeks that followed, there would be leaflets warning the population of target cities to evacuate, but otherwise the Japanese were taken by surprise.

At 2:27 a.m. on the morning of August 6, Col. Paul Tibbets taxied his B-29, the *Enola Gay*, onto a runway on Tinian Island, 1,500 miles east of the Phillipines. He and his two escort planes, one to photograph and the other with yield-measuring instrumentation, took off at 2:45 a.m. They assembled into formation over Guam and headed for Japan.

At 8:16 a.m., Little Boy detonated over the Aioi Bridge in Hiroshima. Destruction was beyond belief; it took well over twenty-four hours for the Japanese government in Tokyo to come to terms with what had happened. On August 8, the morning papers in Tokyo referred only to a "new type of bomb," but Professor Nishina knew better. On the previous day, Lt. Gen. Seizo Arisue had been put in charge of an investigating team to look into the attack on Hiroshima. His lineup would include Professor Nishina from the N Project in Tokyo and Professor Arakatsu from the F Project in Kyoto. Those scientists and their associates correctly identified the event as nuclear; they got the yield right by noting the distance of power-line insulation burnoff from ground zero; and, by examining bomb debris,[2] they identified the lethal ingredient: U-235. Unfortunately, a little knowledge can be a dangerous thing. The Japanese scientists knew of the huge infrastructure needed to separate U-235 from uranium metal. They had spent years trying to achieve this result, and thus they concluded (correctly) that the United States could only have one such weapon. By implication, Hiroshima was a one-shot demonstration. Too bad if you lived there, but the Japanese Empire should not take the event too seriously. The Americans could not have another U-235 A-bomb.

On August 9, as General Arisue's committee was assembling its report, Nagasaki was hit by Fat Man. Working in real time now, the scientists got the yield right, again based on insulation burnoff, but they found the bomb debris to be quite different from Hiroshima—it contained plutonium. Japanese scientists had read of this material, and they understood large quantities could only come from a nuclear reactor. They concluded (again correctly) the Americans must have a plutonium-producing reactor in operation. If there were one such weapon, there must be more because a reactor can churn out plutonium at a prodigious rate. The likely message, from scientists, through General Arisue, to the cabinet: "Better take this one seriously; better accede to American demands; there are probably more plutonium bombs."

---

2. The specific fallout measurements were made by Professor Kuroda; his papers now reside at the University of Nevada at Las Vegas.

Or perhaps it was the message taped to the side of an instrumentation canister, dropped on the outskirts of Nagasaki several miles from ground zero, in conjunction with the August 9 attack. Luis Alvarez, Phillip Morrison, and Robert Serber, all Los Alamos scientists, had relocated to Tinian for the bomb drops. They penned a one-page personal message to Prof. Ryokichi Sagane, a friend from their prewar days together in Berkeley. Professor Sagane had returned to Japan in 1940 to co-author the initial Japanese A-bomb study noted earlier. The Alvarez-Morrison-Serber letter urged Professor Sagane to use his influence "as a reputable nuclear physicist, to convince the Japanese general staff of the terrible consequences which will be suffered by your people if you continue in this war. . . . Unless Japan surrenders at once, this rain of atomic bombs will increase manyfold in fury. With best regards . . ."

The canister with message attached was dropped on August 9. It was recovered by Japanese Naval Intelligence, although the note was not turned over to Professor Sagane until after the war.

## THE END

On the afternoon of August 10, in the aftermath of Nagasaki, the emperor of Japan broke with history to call a true policy meeting of his cabinet. He would participate, not just preside, but there were no conclusions. The Japanese general staff continued to argue, and discussions dragged on for days. Fortunately, the American cryptographers were reading the minutes of those cabinet meetings, via the Magic intercepts, as soon as they were distributed to sub-cabinet officials. The Americans noted the emperor's unprecedented August 10 intervention. That afternoon, General Marshall, the army chief of staff, modified the U.S. Army's weapon-release authority. General Groves, manager of the A-bomb program, was no longer authorized to "drop bombs as made ready." By written message on August 10, General Groves was instructed "not to release [further A-bombs] over Japan without express authority from the president."

The next American Fat Man would have been available about nine days after the Nagasaki attack. On August 14, as a prelude and a prod, the Americans unleashed a seven-pumpkin raid on various parts of Aichi Prefecture (Nagoya and Koroma) in hopes the Japanese would take note. Such raids had immediately preceded the earlier nuclear attacks. Perhaps the Japanese got the message, for on the afternoon of August 14, the emperor again met with his cabinet. He ignored those military officers wishing to fight to the last Japanese man, woman, and child. The emperor commanded an end to hostilities; soon thereafter, he recorded a radio speech implicitly accepting the Potsdam Declaration.

At noon Tokyo time on August 15, 1945, the Japanese emperor's message was broadcast to his nation; it was picked up by U.S. listening posts in San Francisco.

President Truman immediately acknowledged receipt. With the insight provided by Magic, Truman considered the emperor's speech to be a full acceptance of the Potsdam Declaration. The war was over; surrender documents would be signed aboard the USS *Missouri* in Tokyo harbor three weeks later.

It is fortunate the Japanese leadership acted as it did, for it appears that another city-busting A-bomb would have been dropped within Aichi Prefecture, in the vicinity of Nagoya on Japan's main Honshu Island, on August 17 or 18. The weapon components and bomb casings were already on Tinian, only the plutonium cores were needed to implement that third nuclear attack.

After such a "strategic" assault on a major port city, America's General Marshall intended to then use his increasingly available A-bombs as tactical nuclear weapons in support of the planned November 1 landings on the Japanese homeland. The general had gone to New Mexico after the Trinity test to hear about A-bomb aftereffects. He concluded (incorrectly) that his troops would be able to function safely in the aftermath of nuclear attacks on the Kyushu beachheads. General Marshall would have had another nuclear weapon at his disposal *every week* during the September/October "softening up" time period. Fortunately, that maelstrom never came to pass.

With these events, mankind had crossed the nuclear threshold. The use of a few nuclear weapons, backed up with the threat of more to come, had convinced an exhausted government to do what the holders of the nuclear trump card wanted done.

# THE U.S.S.R. AND THE UNITED KINGDOM: UNINTENDED PARTNERS

Winters in Moscow are usually dark and cold, the stuff of Tolstoy, Zhivago, and Stalin, but December 1991 was different. During the summer of 1991, political thunderclouds had boiled to enormous heights over central Russia. Boris Yeltsin had been elected[1] to the presidency of a revitalized and sovereign Russian Federation. Mikhail Gorbachev, the teetering president of a sclerotic Soviet Union, had proposed an all-union treaty unacceptable to the communist establishment. The old guard attempted a coup, bungled it, then fluttered to the ground like so many autumn leaves. In the fall of 1991, the citizens of Leningrad voted to reassume their imperial name, and President Yeltsin banned the Communist Party. With the first snows came a true winter solstice. Youngsters were celebrating in the streets; the *nomenklatura* were planning their exit strategies; the grand old men were reflecting on their place in history.

There was no grander old man than Yuliy Borisovich Khariton. Born in the time of the tsars,[2] Khariton had been schooled in Russia, trained in Cambridge, and then returned to Moscow in 1931 at age twenty-seven to organize the Laboratory of Explosives as part of the Institute of Chemical Physics. In early 1939, Khariton and his fellow scientists read with interest the papers by Hahn and Strassman emanating from Berlin, the Meitner and Frisch explanations from Sweden, and then the Joliot-Curie's experiments from Paris. Khariton and his associates replicated the key research and then came to the same conclusions as their peers in Berlin, Paris, New York, and Chicago: a chain-reacting nuclear explosion was within the realm of possibility. In the summer of 1939, at a seminar

---

1. With over 57 percent of a reasonably bona fide vote.
2. In St. Petersburg, February 17, 1904.

in Leningrad, Khariton and his co-worker, Yakov B. Zeldovich, published three papers that set forth the steps needed to achieve an atomic bomb. Their laboratory director, N. N. Semenov, forwarded those conclusions to the Soviet minister of defense.

In early 1941, pursuing their earlier thoughts, Khariton and Zeldovich calculated the critical mass of U-235. They thought it would be about twenty-two pounds. Unbeknownst to the young Khariton, the KGB's Colonel Barkovsky was extracting a similar analysis of A-bomb prospects from the British War Cabinet files.[3] The British estimate of critical mass was twenty-five pounds of U-235. All indicators pointed to the same conclusion: a bomb, exploiting nuclear energy, was feasible. But then Hitler intervened. The Nazi invasion in June 1941 turned every Russian's attention to the survival of Moscow and Leningrad.

## REFLECTIONS

A half-century later, Yuliy Khariton could look back on a wartime of crisis, a postwar race to catch up, an era of breakthroughs, and a denouement of bankruptcy and collapse. As he reflected on the role of Soviet science in the twentieth century, Khariton was proud of the results; he only regretted the secrecy. He wanted recognition for all, including credit to certain Americans for unknowingly giving help, but he also wanted to mark the boundary between espionage and Soviet science, and he wanted to be the one who drew that line. To open this window to the West, Yuliy Khariton sent for Danny Stillman in late 1991.

On December 7 and 8, 1991, Boris Yeltsin and the newly elected presidents of Ukraine and Belarus were meeting at the Bison Forest Lodge outside Brest to abolish the Soviet Union. On that same evening of the 8th, Danny Stillman and an associate from Los Alamos[4] were preparing to board Yuliy Khariton's personal railcar at Moscow's Kazan Station. They were to begin a 240-mile trip through the Russian winter to a place where no westerner had ever been—the one-time monastery town of Sarov, now the heart of the Soviet nuclear weapons complex.

## EN ROUTE

Stillman and Krikorian were picked up at the Kazan Station by a security man who was a veteran of the Chernobyl disaster, accompanied by a gorgeous young female interpreter. They were a cheery and helpful pair, but the nighttime trip through the Russian winter—even in a Soviet hero's personal railcar—was grim. There were no dining facilities, although

3. Via his man in London, John Cairncross.
4. Stillman made it a practice never to travel overseas unaccompanied. On this trip to Russia, he was accompanied by Los Alamos chemist Nerses Krikorian.

escorts Demin and Kutyanina had brought the tea, wine, and cognac and the salmon, bread, and cheese needed to make it through the night. A Spartan restroom awaited all at one end of the car. The train superintendent, quite drunk, tried to evict Stillman and Krikorian into the winter snows outside Moscow, as *no* foreigners were allowed into the nuclear city hundreds of miles to the east. Fortunately, bureaucracy and rank prevailed.

At dawn, the train stopped ten miles outside its destination. There were the usual dogs, then the security checkpoint. Every train was emptied and thoroughly searched before proceeding through the fence line into Sarov. In time, Stillman, Krikorian, and their escorts were met by four men in a curtained van, backed up by an armed escort vehicle, for the ride to the institute's guest house. Although the facilities within Sarov were fairly new, built as a home for the cutting edge of Soviet technology, the city still felt like a prison. The guesthouse was equally Stalinesque in design and hospitality, with a watchful floor matron at one end of each hall, the communal shower at the other.

## THE ALL-UNION SCIENTIFIC RESEARCH CENTER FOR EXPERIMENTAL PHYSICS

On the morning on December 9, immediately after their guesthouse check-in and still recovering from a cold and sleepless train ride, Stillman and Krikorian were escorted to the House of Science, a beautifully built modern two-story building that served as the institute's hospitality center. It was located down the street from the personal residences of the director and other senior staff. None of those duplex cottages was particularly impressive. By U.S. standards, they were 1940s ranch houses, set incongruously amidst tall trees and the snows of central Russia.

Stillman and Krikorian were greeted with full honors upon their arrival at the House of Science. Academic Yuliy Khariton, a diminutive man of eighty-seven years and not more than ninety pounds, was there to meet them. During their entire stay Khariton would not leave their sides other than for sleep. Khariton could not have stood more than five feet four inches tall. He was a charming and gentle man, an introvert, but also a dedicated communist. He always wore a coat and tie, with no hint of the informality that characterizes the U.S. nuclear weapons complex. Khariton spoke perfect English with a strong British accent, the product of his years at Cambridge. He wanted to use his command of the language to tell his side of the story, the saga of Soviet scientific chrysalis. During the days that followed, whenever Khariton spoke in larger gatherings, the room invariably fell silent out of respect.

The proceedings started with a late breakfast, followed by a tour of the House of Science, then a long session in the second-floor conference room. Without delay and without a flood of vodka, it was there that the nuclear tsar of the Soviet Union began his *tour d'horizon*:

During World War II, Soviet scientists followed Western nuclear developments closely, thanks to excellent espionage efforts within the United States and Britain. In February 1943, as the United States opened its laboratory at Los Alamos, the Soviet Defense Committee initiated parallel work within Moscow at what became known as Laboratory No. 2.[5] On March 10, 1943, Igor Vasilevich Kurchatov, age thirty-six, was put in charge of that organization. He assigned to Yuliy Borisovich Khariton the responsibility for A-bomb design. Within a month, Kurchatov and Khariton were examining a first-class stream of intelligence data originating from agents within Los Alamos and Chalk River, Canada.

Until war's end, the Kurchatov project was mainly academic: engineering a natural uranium reactor suspiciously akin to the Fermi pile (neutrons moderated by very pure graphite, cooled with water). The team at Laboratory No. 2 undertook research on isotope separation, and they conceptualized U-235 and plutonium weapons, but only with the bombing of Hiroshima and Nagasaki did Stalin come to appreciate the political significance of those weapons. In August 1945, Stalin put his security chief, Lavrenti Beria ("a terrible man"[6]), in charge of a special committee[7] with orders to build the bomb as soon as possible.

Beria's assistant, Avrami Pavlovich Zavenyagin ("quite a decent man"), immediately visited the ruins of Berlin, extracting papers of interest from the Kaiser Wilhelm Institute and locating the German stash of uranium oxide (over fifty tons), acquired through Belgium and by then stored within eastern Germany. That find accelerated operation of the first Soviet nuclear reactor[8] by a year. It first went critical on December 25, 1946, and it was during April of that postwar year that Khariton's A-bomb project was moved east, out of Moscow to the more secure village of Sarov. The new institute had a formal name, the All-Union Scientific Research Institute for Experimental Physics, but as with all secret Soviet facilities, it was to be known only by its number: Arzamas-16. That code derived from the institute's post office address in the city of Arzamas, forty-five miles to the northeast. A host of other names were used interchangeably to confuse outsiders: "Design Bureau 11," "Base 112," "Moscow Center 300," "Site 500," and so forth. By 1991, Arzamas-16 and its associated production facility had subsumed the ten square miles of the old city of Sarov into a secure hexagon of over eighty square miles of laboratories, factories, homes, schools, and remote, high-explosive test facilities.

5. Typical of Soviet obfuscation, there never was a "Laboratory No. 1."
6. Khariton's words.
7. Full name: the Special Committee and Technical Commission on the Atomic Bomb.
8. The Fermi replica in Moscow, known as F-1.

Khariton gave full credit to Klaus Fuchs, a German refugee who had fled to Britain and thence to the United States, for supplying invaluable insight into the design of the U.S. Fat Man. This, in itself, was a significant admission, since on March 8, 1950, immediately after Fuch's conviction and sentencing, the Soviet news agency Tass stated that "Fuchs is unknown to the Soviet government, and no agent of the Soviet government had any contact with him."

In 1991, Khariton echoed the observations of other Soviet intelligence agents with whom we met and talked in the 1990s—that Fuchs operated out of ideology. He never received money or any other tangible benefit for his efforts. Fuchs was led to believe that the three Allied powers (United States, United Kingdom, and U.S.S.R.) had agreed in 1941 to share any and all new weapons technologies on a timely basis. In Fuchs' eyes, the American bureaucracy was only slowing the flow of the technology promised to their Soviet ally. Fuchs felt he was bypassing those hurdles in support of a partner in whose ideology he truly believed. Khariton confirmed that Fuchs, "a good communist," had sent, via the Greenglass-Rosenberg courier system, fully dimensioned drawings of Fat Man. Khariton received these documents even before the Trinity test, thus accounting for Stalin's nonchalance when informed of Trinity by President Truman at the Potsdam conference during July 1945.

But then the conversation took a strange turn; Khariton inaccurately denied the existence of any other agents within Los Alamos or elsewhere in the wartime United States. In actual fact, the United States was awash with communist sympathizers and planted Soviet moles. One example, Ted Hall, was exposed by authors Albright and Kunstel[9] in 1997.

Hall's treachery first became apparent upon the release of the Venona transcripts in 1996. These were the messages between the Soviet embassy in Washington and Moscow center during World War II. Having saved copies, American code breakers began to decrypt these communications in the late 1940s, leading to the immediate arrests of the Rosenbergs and Klaus Fuchs, among others. The texts were not released to the public until after the end of the Cold War.

Hall was a world-class expert on implosion at Los Alamos, but there were others. The Venona transcripts and supplementary sources[10] make it clear that another agent lay hidden deep within the Los Alamos fence, under the code name PERSEUS.

From the U.S. production facilities, other Soviet sympathizers provided a parallel flood of technical detail. Those at Hanford warned of xenon poisoning and

9. Joseph Albright and Marcia Kunstel, *Bombshell* (New York: Times Books,1997).
10. KGB operative Anatoly Yatsov, deathbed conversations with Lona Cohen, all fleshed out by several investigative authors. See the discussion of PERSEUS further on in this chapter.

other reactor problems; those at Oak Ridge helped with diffusion barrier design. On October 27, 2007, President Putin of Russia confirmed these arrangements when he awarded, posthumously, the title of Hero of the Russian Federation to Soviet intelligence agent Zhorzh (George) Koval a few months after that agent's death, in Moscow, at age ninety-four. Citations at the award ceremony made clear that Koval and his associates had successfully penetrated the American factories and laboratories turning out the plutonium, enriched uranium, and polonium needed for production of the American A-bomb. They had collected and transferred descriptions of those materials, the technology needed to produce them, and the quantities being turned out. As President Putin put it in 2007, Koval's work, "helped speed up considerably the time it took for the Soviet Union to develop an atomic bomb of its own."

Koval was the perfect spy. Born in the United States in 1913 to Russian immigrant parents, he returned to Russia after the revolution. Schooled at the University of Moscow in chemistry and trained by the Red Army's intelligence arm, the GRU, he was then re-inserted into American life at the beginning of World War II. Being American-born, with no foreign accent, Koval was then drafted into the U.S. Army at age thirty. Armed with phony documents that showed him holding an associate degree in chemistry from a local community college, Koval (Soviet code name, Delmar) was trained by the army in radiochemistry, then sent off to Oak Ridge, Tennessee, where he hit pay dirt in the collection of nuclear production technology. In time he was reassigned to other, more central Manhattan District facilities, which gave him insight into the entire U.S. nuclear materials production complex.

The postwar defection of Soviet code clerk Igor Gouzenko, in Ottawa, gave Koval cause for concern. The GRU urged him to stay in the United States, thereby running the risk of exposure, but in 1948 Koval was allowed to return home. He joined the faculty at the University of Moscow, taught chemistry, earned his Ph.D., and went on to enjoy a peaceful retirement.

Aside from the scientific facilities, Soviet espionage also penetrated the management of the American A-bomb program. A former AEC security official now confirms the presence of at least two GRU agents within the Manhattan District headquarters. As of this writing, one is still alive, living in Moscow and staying in discreet contact with his former competitors. The other is now deceased, but while alive he took credit for helping *both* wartime allies with their nuclear work.

It may be that Khariton was sincere in his disclaimers. Intelligence often makes its way to the user wearing a mask. Sources are seldom disclosed. One day an interesting memo shows up, or a senior official just seems to have a bright idea. Khariton admitted as much when he said Kurchatov often displayed "impeccable physical intuition." Thus, the Soviet claim that Fuchs "was our only spy" remains an article of Soviet cant, but it is not true.

The Fuchs A-bomb drawings were welcome, but the design was still carefully recalculated within the Arzamas-16 facility. Weapons boss Lavrenti Beria was suspicious of disinformation possibly fed into the Soviet system by U.S. counterintelligence. Beria made it clear to his underlings: a failed first test could only be the result of sabotage. He wanted the names of all responsible hands, in advance. That was the execution list in the event of failure.

## MAYAK

By his own admission, Khariton knew of the slave labor used to build Arzamas-16. "There was little joy in watching the columns of prisoners who built the installation," he said, but this indignity did not seem to bother Khariton's conscience. As a good communist, he viewed forced labor by political unreliables as simply the price of overtaking the imperialists.[11] Even so, it was not clear that Khariton understood the broader cost, the full price paid by the Soviet people to produce that ball of plutonium first placed into his A-bomb. Only later, in the mid-1990s, did many leaders of the Soviet nuclear empire even meet each other.[12] It is doubtful they communicated during the 1940s. Whether Khariton knew it or not, that ball of plutonium was terribly costly: millions of rubles, tons of concrete and steel, hundreds of thousands of lives.

In April 1946, as many of the people within Laboratory No. 2 were being moved to Sarov, another decision was made: to open a fissionable materials production facility in the southern Ural Mountains at a place called Mayak. This plant would be code-named Chelyabinsk-40, later Chelyabinsk-65, in connection with the nearest industrial city. Mayak would be home to the "A" plutonium-production reactor, the "B" reprocessing facility (to extract plutonium from the irradiated fuel rods), and the "V" metallurgical laboratory, intended to cast and machine plutonium parts. For two years, forty-five thousand workers and uncounted numbers of prisoners worked to build these facilities. They dug an acre-sized pit, more than a hundred feet deep, just for the reactor. Prisoners died by the thousands during the construction that followed; those who did not were returned to Siberia for "extended terms" so they could not disclose the secrets of Mayak.

The "A" reactor went critical on June 10, 1948. Xenon poisoning was anticipated and was not a problem. Irradiated fuel rods emerged six months later, in time producing the first fractional gram of Soviet plutonium.

---

11. There is no record of any of those prisoners ever leaving Arzamas-16 alive.
12. At the History of the Soviet Atomic Program conference held in Dubna, north of Moscow, in May 1996.

The prisoners were not the only ones expendable at Mayak. Most young professionals on the scientific staff were exposed to hundreds of times the radiation dosage now acceptable within the nuclear industry. Few have survived. They cleaned up plutonium oxide and corrosive acids without benefit of facemasks or gloves. Time was everything. The Nazi invasion was fresh in everyone's mind; the American imperialists were deemed to represent a similar threat. Every good Russian simply did what he had to do.

## FIRST LIGHTNING

By June 1949, Mayak had produced enough plutonium for RDS-1, the first Soviet A-bomb. (The initials stand for *Reaktivnyi Dvigatel Stalina*, "Stalin's Rocket Engine.") That device, internally an exact copy of Fat Man, was fired atop a steel tower west of Semipalatinsk[13] on August 29, 1949, fourteen months after the Mayak reactor first went critical. Once again, immediately before the test (known as First Lightning), Lavrenti Beria explained the stakes to Khariton. The scientific director of Arzamas-16 was to be executed if RDS-1 did not work. In later years, Khariton described Beria as "the personification of evil in modern Russian history," but he also gave Beria credit for being "a first-class administrator who could carry a job through to completion." Fortunately for Khariton, RDS-1 *did* work; it gave twenty-two kilotons, as did Fat Man.

When a nuclear device is detonated within the atmosphere, a plume of radioactive debris begins to spread, high in the atmosphere and downwind. An observer a hundred miles distant is in no danger, but an aircraft flying a thousand miles away, if properly equipped with filters and collection devices, can bring home samples. In the United States those samples go to the Air Force Technical Applications Center (AFTAC), where scientists and contractors pick through the debris to ascertain what was in the bomb and how it worked. Think of sampling your neighbor's chimney smoke; you can tell if he is burning firewood to stay warm, if he is cooking for his family, or if he is making steel. Similar analyses are possible from nuclear bomb debris. In 1949, U.S. Air Force weather aircraft, flying off the Kamchatka Peninsula, performed that collection; other bomb debris was found in navy rainwater collectors. Within a few days, both air force and navy scientists came to the same conclusion: the Soviets had tested a nuclear weapon on August 29. Wishful U.S. defense and intelligence officials did not want to hear that; they were forecasting a five-year hiatus before the Russians could test. The U.S. secretary of defense tried to claim a Soviet reactor had blown up. Thoughtful scientists at Berkeley proved otherwise. They confirmed the debris came from a bomb, utilizing

13. In eastern Kazakhstan.

plutonium, bred in a reactor that had been running for about a year. The debris was remarkably similar to that from the Nagasaki weapon. President Truman decided to rely on his scientific advisors, not the politicians; on September 23, 1949, he announced the Soviet test. The reactions, in East and West, were of earthquake proportions.

## THE EXPANDING SOVIET NUCLEAR HORIZON

Once freed of the execution threat, Khariton's staff moved out on a broad intellectual front. Within two years, they completed a new A-bomb design that was half the diameter, two-thirds the weight, far more efficient in its use of fissionable materials, and twice the yield of Fat Man/RDS-1. Known as RDS-2, it was successfully tested on September 24, 1951. In time the Khariton team came to build bombs "ten times lighter" and skinny enough to fit into artillery shells. There followed a dazzling array of nuclear tests; within a decade, the Soviet Union had pulled abreast of U.S. nuclear technology in some important respects.

Even before the first Soviet nuclear test, Stalin turned his attention to the production and deployment of his new weapons. On March 9, 1949, he directed the construction of a nuclear weapons production facility within the Arzamas-16 complex. As a factory, it came to be known as Avangard; sixteen buildings operated quite independently of the physics institute. Avangard could produce twenty nuclear weapons per year. Ten thousand people worked at this new weapons plant and twenty thousand at the physics center, with another fifty thousand people needed to run the town's infrastructure. Those who think the assembly (and disassembly) of a nuclear weapon is simple should bear this scale in mind. Stalin's first nuclear weapons came off this production line in December 1951. Yuliy Khariton conducted the final inspections on each as it was accepted into the Soviet inventory.

## THERMONUCLEARS

The first Soviet A-bomb was a great achievement, but even as Khariton and his associates were starting work in Moscow during that winter of 1945/46, the Soviet Special Committee was considering another possibility: thermonuclear weapons. Khariton was given the additional task of looking into the matter. His staff reported back in November 1947. They were unable to find an immediate solution to the problem of igniting a capsule of deuterium and tritium.

At that time, KGB agents were still meeting with Klaus Fuchs, as yet undetected by the West. He was living in England, working at Harwell. Fuchs provided no useful information about American H-bomb designs, but he did furnish critical thermonuclear cross-section data and perhaps much more. Based on those interviews, Khariton, Kurchatov, and their associates proposed a work plan for the development of a Soviet H-bomb. The Special Committee approved that arrangement in June 1948, eighteen months before Truman announced his intent to pursue similar technology in the United States. There is no evidence of any internal Soviet debate regarding the H-bomb decision. The new Soviet weapon-to-be was given the code name RDS-6. Competing groups were established at Arzamas-16 to pursue spherical "layercake" and linear "pipe" approaches[14] to the ignition of thermonuclear fuel.

In February 1950, immediately after the Truman announcement of a U.S. thermonuclear effort,[15] Yuliy Khariton was put in full charge of the Soviet thermonuclear program at Arzamas-16. Igor Kurchatov was his boss. Igor Tamm and Yakov Zeldovich were his deputies. Andrei Sakharov and other future weapons all-stars were, at that time, young assistants. Thus, Khariton would have been the logical recipient of any intelligence relating to the U.S. thermonuclear program.

In March 1951, Edward Teller and Stanislaus Ulam published their internal Los Alamos paper outlining the correct solution to H-bomb design (radiation implosion of a second stage). On June 17, the U.S. AEC approved that approach, authorized the assembly and test of a device employing those principles, and directed the production of the special nuclear materials needed.

On February 26, 1952, apparently unaware of the U.S. plan, the Soviet nuclear weapons ministry settled on the single-stage, spherically imploded RDS-6s concept as their best bet for achieving a successful H-bomb. The resulting design was to package layers of thermonuclear fuel (Li6D) around an improved fission core, and then implode the entire assembly with high explosive. In Sakharov's memoirs, these approaches are known respectively as "the first idea" (the use of Li6D as thermonuclear fuel, attributed to Vitaly Ginsburg) and "the second idea" (imploding a fission core and thermonuclear fuel as an integrated assembly, Sakharov's own invention.) Taken together, the package came to be known as the Layercake. RDS-6s, which was to be tested in June 1952, would require modest amounts of tritium and was expected to yield one megaton within a five-ton package.

The RDS-6s design process did not go well. On December 29, 1951, the Soviet council of ministers agreed to the postponement of the test date to March 1953. Significantly more tritium was allocated to the device in an attempt to offset falling calculated yields.

---

14. The former was given the name RDS-6s, for "spherical"; the latter RDS-6t, for "tube"
15. On January 31, 1950.

On October 31, 1952, the United States detonated Mike, a two-stage thermonuclear that produced 10.4 megatons of yield. Within a day, the fact of that test was known to Stalin. We believe he also learned of the approximate yield.[16] Beria and Kurchatov were not able to offer Stalin any explanation of how the American device worked. Since they did not know, they started to guess. A month after the Mike event, Beria wrote a memorandum to his associates (Kurchatov, et al.), noting, "Information has reached us that the USA has conducted experiments with articles [like Layercake]. . . . Tell [the staff at Arzamas-16] to put all their effort into ensuring the successful completion of the research and experimental design work connected with RDS-6s." But Mike was *not* a Layercake device; Beria had misdirected his scientific staff. In time this led to Beria's ultimate dilemma.

The Soviet leadership knew there had been a significant U.S. nuclear event in the Pacific; we believe they understood it to have been a multi-megaton detonation. At the same time, Beria's scientific staff was painting an ever-darker picture of the possibilities for RDS-6s—a growingly small fraction of Mike's yield consuming ever-larger quantities of tritium. If Stalin learned of all this, the Soviet nuclear weapons boss Beria would be a dead duck.[17] But then, in March 1953 two things happened: Beria postponed the testing of RDS-6s to the summer of 1953, and Joseph Stalin died under most mysterious circumstances at his dacha ten miles outside Moscow. Beria's fingerprints were all over the case.[18]

On June 15, 1953, physicists at Arzamas-16 signed off on the final design of RDS-6s, but those were Beria's last days of authority.[19] As device assembly and test preparations were underway, Beria's competitors in the post-Stalin struggle for power[20] brought about his arrest, imprisonment, and, on December 23, his execution.

RDS-6s was tested on August 12. The device performed as designed, delivering a yield of four hundred kilotons, but that was only 4 percent of Mike's yield. RDS-6s derived only 15 to 20 percent of its yield from fusion reactions, yet it had used up most of the tritium in the Soviet inventory. There was a great deal of Soviet crowing in public about "the first H-bomb dropped from an aircraft." That was Khariton's

16. Russian historians disagree. They claim the Soviets were unable to measure American test yields until 1954.
17. There were other reasons for Beria to fear for his life. Stalin's paranoia meant purges were always in the air.
18. See Thomas C. Reed, *At the Abyss* (Ballantine Books, 2004), 21–27.
19. Beria was arrested and imprisoned by his peers on June 26 and was then held in an army, not KGB, prison.
20. Malenkov, Bulganin, and Khrushchev were the competitors for power. Army Marshal Zhukov reported to Bulganin and effected Beria's arrest.

boast to his dying day, but in private, the physicists at Arzamas-16 had the feeling that RDS-6s was an expensive dead horse. As Sakharov wrote in his memoirs, "This device had run its course." The autumn of 1953 was a gloomy time at Arzamas-16.

Seven months later, on March 1, 1954, the United States conducted the Bravo event, kicking off the Castle test series in the Pacific. Bravo gave fifteen megatons, substantially larger than Mike and almost forty times the yield of RDS-6s. In his December 1991 conversations with Stillman, Yuliy Khariton admitted the Soviets collected yield data and bomb debris from the Castle tests in 1954, but the results, he said, were of no help. The only fact that emerged was that multi-megaton thermonuclear explosions were possible, and the Americans knew how to do it.

During the ensuing month, March 1954, scientists at Arzamas-16 broke into a frenzy of brainstorming. Frank-Kamenetsky proposed the use of two primaries, to blast the secondary capsule from each side (the "razor" design). Zavenyagin, a bureaucrat, not a physicist, proposed a dozen or more primaries. That approach came to be known as "the candelabra." Neither made much sense. Then, one day in late March or early April 1954, Khariton says his deputy and long-time physics partner, Yakov B. Zeldovich, "Threw open his office door and joyously exclaimed, 'We have to do it differently; we'll release radiation from a spherical device!'" But there is a strange contravention to this statement. In later conversations, Lev Feoktistov (whom we will come to in a moment) said, "I never did hear from Zeldovich a direct confirmation of this account, nor did Sakharov, by the way."

By the end of April 1954, the physicists in Khariton's thermonuclear division at Arzamas-16 were fully focused on the correct solution: imploding a secondary capsule with radiation from a primary, and then lighting the highly compressed thermonuclear fuel. Within eight months, a conceptual design was on the table; in February 1955, the initial design was complete, and the device was given a name: RDS-37. Nine months later, the weapon was air-dropped from a Tu-16 bomber, giving a de-rated[21] yield of 1.6 megatons. Windows were shattered in the nearby city of Semipalatinsk, with two fatalities, one soldier and one young girl.

Was Zeldovich really that smart? Was he the father of the Soviet H-bomb? We think not. To this day, the origins of that Soviet two-stage thermonuclear technology remain unclear. Khariton maintained it was a spark of insight at Arzamas-16, but until a credible Soviet scientist steps forward to claim credit—as their counterparts have done in the United States, United Kingdom, France, and China—we revert to our earlier observation about the "impeccable physical intuition" displayed by

---

21. By replacing some uranium components with inert material to limit radioactive fallout.

those seated at the far end of the intelligence pipeline. We believe the Soviets did not discover radiation implosion on their own—they had help. The only question remaining: whence cometh that help? It is our belief that the Soviet agent then still at Los Alamos provided the missing piece.

The "secret of the H-bomb" does not involve blueprints and drawings. Whereas A-bomb success depends on the technology of materials manufacture and high-explosive lens design, the key to the H-bomb lies in one sentence, two little words actually ("radiation implosion"), if the listeners are sophisticated scientists who have been reflecting on the problem and who enjoy significant computational support.

## PERSEUS

Numerous authors, researchers, and archivists posit the existence of a yet-unidentified Soviet agent within wartime Los Alamos.[22] In 1942, this agent was given the code name PERSEUS by his New York recruiter and controller, Morris Cohen. Other experts on Soviet wartime espionage (for example, Albright and Kunstel) consider PERSEUS to be a myth, generated by the KGB to cover their tracks or to cover the work of three separate agents: MLAD (Ted Hall), STAR (Saville Sax), and PERS (unknown). We are of the view that PERSEUS was a real communist sympathizer/agent; he joined the Los Alamos Scientific Laboratory at its inception and remained there for decades until his retirement. In the mid-1990s, Stillman reported his suspicions as to the identity of PERSEUS to the FBI's special agent in charge of its Santa Fe office. Stillman reviewed the files and the supporting evidence with the Bureau's counterintelligence expert, but within weeks that agent was reassigned to the Wen Ho Lee case, and then became ill and was transferred to another site. Both the PERSEUS and Wen Ho Lee investigations died, botched beyond recognition, until the latter case returned to public scrutiny a few years later.

Since the man we consider to have been PERSEUS is now deceased, and since he can neither defend his family name nor refute our arguments, we identify him only by the initial code name given him by Morris Cohen: "Arthur Fielding." Until the Soviet KGB files are opened, no "smoking gun" is likely to appear. The actual identity of PERSEUS does not matter—his fingerprints are what count.

Mr. Fielding was born in the United States, but his parents soon emigrated, and he spent his younger years out of the country. Fielding returned to the United States to attend university, then left again to continue his academic life elsewhere. During

22. See the Venona transcripts, released in 1996; the Mitrokhin Archives; Michael Dobbs' interview with Anatoli Yatskov, *Washington Post*, October 4, 1992; Pavel Sudoplatov, *Special Tasks* (Boston: Back Bay Books, 1995), among others.

those difficult Depression years, as a contemporary of the Rosenbergs, he fell in with the young academic/intellectual crowd that saw communism as the most promising cure for society's ills. As World War II broke out, Fielding, too old for the draft, returned to the eastern United States to start work at a U.S. Navy facility. He soon joined one of the leading physics institutes in the United States and then, as Robert Oppenheimer was organizing the Los Alamos Laboratory, he was recruited to serve there. It was at that time, in 1942, that Fielding volunteered his services to Soviet recruiter Morris Cohen. Fielding worked and built an excellent reputation at wartime Los Alamos as a leader in the field of experimental physics. Like Klaus Fuchs and Ted Hall, Arthur Fielding initially served the communist cause out of ideology; all three feared an imperial U.S. nuclear monopoly at the end of the war.

Fielding stayed at Los Alamos as others returned to academia. He assumed significant responsibilities while his political loyalties remained murky. It may be the postwar Stalinist excesses and expansionism bothered him, or it may be the 1949–50 arrests of David Greenglass, the Rosenbergs, Klaus Fuchs, et al. gave him cause for concern. In 1950, Fuchs confessed and was sentenced in Britain to fourteen years in prison. At the same time, PERSEUS controllers, Morris and Lona Cohen, vanished from New York. (They turned up in the Soviet Union; their portraits now hang on the walls of the KGB museum in Moscow.) During 1950, Harry Gold, a member of the Rosenberg-Los Alamos spy ring, pleaded guilty and agreed to testify at the Rosenberg trial, and thus avoided execution; he got thirty years. David Greenglass, another courier, also copped a plea, agreed to testify, and got fifteen years. Ethel and Julius Rosenberg, along with Morton Sobell, went on trial in federal court in March 1951. All were found guilty. Sobell got thirty years; the Rosenbergs were sentenced to death.[23]

We believe that with these Cold War developments, with the arrest and conviction of so many of Arthur Fielding's fellow spies, and with the rupture of the courier chain connecting him to Moscow, Fielding suspended his Soviet connections. He turned his attention inward instead, to the new frontier of thermonuclear physics.

In January 1950, President Truman directed the U.S. AEC to proceed with a full thermonuclear program. Fielding was deeply involved in the hunt for ideas within the Los Alamos community. He exchanged memoranda and held discussions with Edward Teller, Stanislaus Ulam, Lab Director Norris Bradbury, and other heavy hitters of the thermonuclear world as those ideas took shape. On June 16 and 17, 1951, at a meeting of the AEC's General Advisory Committee, held at Princeton

---

23. The Rosenberg case remains contentious, though the Venona transcripts of Soviet wartime messages from the United States to Moscow leave no doubt as to their involvement. Whether they deserved the death penalty is another matter.

University, that committee, the AEC commissioners themselves, and a few outside gurus converged on the decisions needed to proceed:

1. Design, build, and fire an experimental device that would use the Teller-Ulam radiation scheme to implode a canister of liquid deuterium.

2. Start the production of lithium deuteride as quickly as possible.

3. Pursue a specific schedule.

Prior to the October 1952 Mike event, Fielding was appointed to a senior position within Los Alamos. From that roost he would be privy to every detail of the Mike event as well as the details of the subsequent 1954 Castle test series. He remained in place for years thereafter.

The question is, why did Fielding not provide the Soviets with details of Mike? Why did they spend so much time in the thermonuclear wilderness if they had such a good source within Los Alamos? The apparent answer: at that time they did not have such a source. Fielding was not a willing agent. During 1950, as the brutal face of communism became evident, we believe Fielding turned his back on that world. It was a time when another Soviet spy, Whittaker Chambers, came to a similar conclusion. Perhaps Fielding read and was touched by Chambers' best-selling memoirs.[24] Or on another level, the arrests of Fuchs, Rosenberg, et al. may have given Fielding great pause. Seeing his fellow spies disappear into federal prisons and execution chambers must have concentrated his mind. We believe that by 1950, Arthur Fielding had terminated his Soviet connection, until recalled to active duty.

As we have seen, after the Mike event, in December 1952, Beria sent his physicists barking up the wrong tree. On June 26, 1953, Khrushchev, Malenkov, et al. imprisoned and soon killed Beria to protect their own skins, but Beria's successors at the KGB surely remained puzzled, paying ever-greater attention to the secret of Mike. On March 1, 1954, the Americans conducted the Bravo event— fifteen megatons, with fallout everywhere. The radiochemistry from Bravo would have made it clear: that device bore no relationship to Layercake. The Americans had achieved a full multi-megaton event from a portable device . . . but how?

We believe a KGB asset made contact with Fielding during late March 1954. One approach might have been to his ego: "You are a bright guy, Fielding. You now have a bigger job at Los Alamos than Teller, and you were involved in his thermonuclear

24. *Witness* (Random House, 1951).

concepts. Surely you do not want Teller and Ulam to get all the credit in the history books. How did you do it?"

Another approach might be from the Dark Side: "We have a lot of history together, Mr. Fielding. The Cohens are our guests in Moscow. It could be quite embarrassing if they start to talk in public. We would like one small favor before we close the books on PERSEUS. Los Alamos did great things out in the Pacific last week. How did you do it?"

And/or the Soviets may have waved the tangible inducements that turned other U.S. citizens later in the Cold War. Fielding appears to have died a wealthy man; money may have been the clinching inducement to return (briefly) to the world of espionage.

For whatever reasons, Fielding's reply to his KGB contact could have been one simple sentence: "Edward Teller, Stan Ulam, and I thought up the idea of using radiation pressure to compress, and then light, thermonuclear fuel within an opaque capsule." That's all it would take. A short, top-secret, and highest priority message would make its way back to Moscow and thence to the desk of Yuliy Khariton. We believe that is how Edward Teller, inadvertently, came to be the father of *both* the U.S. and the Soviet H-bombs.

## THE SILENT SOVIET SCIENTISTS

In thinking this matter through, we have come to rely on the statements—and non-statements—of three intellectual and moral titans of the Soviet nuclear world. The first is Andrei Sakharov, one of the most brilliant men of modern Soviet science. He frequently claimed credit for RDS-6s, the Layercake, but he has never claimed credit for originating the idea of two-stage, radiation-imploded, thermonuclear technology. (He was supportive once the idea was proposed, and that carried great weight.) Sakharov became a Soviet dissident, sent into internal exile for years, but in the 1980s, he was released. He served in the first freely elected Russian parliament until his death in December 1989. Neither of your authors had the good fortune to meet Sakharov, but the man left behind a trail of memoirs and a talented biographer, Gennady Gorelik, who has been most helpful in clarifying the nuclear aspects of Cold War history.

Our second source is German Goncharov, one of the bright young physicists and device designers at Arzamas-16 in the 1950s. He is still there, leading the theoretical physics department, but he is also the principal investigator of, and reporter on, Soviet nuclear history. *Physics Today*, the lead publication of the American Physical Society, turned to Goncharov to provide the Russian account of the historic Dubna Soviet nuclear history conference in its November 1996 issue.

Our third source is Lev Feoktistov, the designer of the first Soviet series-manufactured thermonuclear weapon, the man who was drafted from Arzamas-16 to open a second Soviet weapons lab at Snezhinsk (Chelyabinsk-70), and who was later admitted to the Soviet Academy of Sciences. Every Russian we asked said that Feoktistov was the defining tower of integrity in the Soviet nuclear world. Before his death in February 2002, Feoktistov wrote a small book, *Nukes Are Not Forever*,[25] that reflected on his life's work.

During March 1997, in the aftermath of the Dubna Conference, these three, among others, were invited to visit the Lawrence Livermore National Laboratory. On March 15, at the conclusion of a long and most productive week, those gentlemen, plus Livermore Lab Director John Nuckolls, spent an evening at co-author Reed's home. The resulting insights into Soviet nuclear history were illuminating.

What did these gentlemen have to say about the origins of the Soviet two-stage H-bomb? Sakharov, in his memoirs and biography, says, "Several associates of our theoretical divisions apparently came to the [radiation implosion] idea simultaneously." He then goes on to use the words "apparently," "it seemed to me," "possibly," and "it may be that," but Sakharov never identifies the originator of the idea. Biographer Gorelik confirmed that Sakharov never took credit for what came to be known as "the third idea" himself.

Goncharov corroborated this. "Sakharov clearly ascribes priority to himself [for Layercake] and Ginsburg [for the use of Li6D], but he disclaimed any credit for [radiation implosion]." In our dinnertime conversations, Goncharov went on to speculate that, after the Bravo results became known, "Khariton retired to his office and emerged a wiser man." Goncharov believes that wisdom came from a re-examination of Klaus Fuchs's 1948 intelligence paper, for, as recently disclosed by Goncharov, that paper does contain the first seeds of the radiation implosion idea: Fuchs refers to the possibility of a ten-fold compression of thermonuclear fuel due to radiation. Gorelik concurs in the view that the Fuchs 1948 paper contained the seeds of "the third idea," but we do not believe that was the only source of Soviet wisdom.

Feoktistov was more categorically skeptical. "We had neither drawings nor accurate data from the outside, but . . . we were prepared to catch hints and half-hints. I can't shake the feeling that in those times, we were not completely independent."

We believe Soviet agents reconnected with PERSEUS, received a few key words, and passed them on to Moscow, thence Arzamas-16, and thence to Yuliy Khariton. That very intelligent leader of the Soviet thermonuclear program reflected on them, a light went on in his talented mind, and at the next brainstorming session, he suggested "the release of radiation from a spherical source to implode a secondary," while attributing this insight to a deputy—who would never accept the credit. We have to

25. Published as part of the "Abolition 2000" campaign in Russia in 1999.

further conclude that Khariton's 1991 invitation to Stillman and Krikorian was part of a campaign to mask the very extensive and continuing role of technical intelligence in the Soviet nuclear weapons program. The Soviet nuclear veteran wished to build a bogus wall a half-century in the past. "Fuchs was our only spy" was the Khariton mantra, but to quote from Hamlet's queen, as a murder inquiry was hitting close to home, "Methinks [he] doth protest too much."

## PARTING COMPANY

After their meetings in the House of Science drew to a close, Khariton escorted Stillman and Krikorian around his facility. What had once been an isolated Russian farm town, the site of an abandoned monastery, was now a bustling city of eighty thousand people, totally enclosed and utterly inaccessible to the outside world. As Stillman toured the town, his original impression did not change. It was a vast prison with marginal amenities for the privileged few. While they toured, Khariton reiterated his enormous pride in the scientific talent at Arzamas-16. He spelled out the achievements of each individual, and on bidding his guests farewell, he repeated his opening lines: "Never before has this history been told to any foreigner; the time was right to let the world know about the origins of the Soviet nuclear program." Then the mantra: "Except for some opening help from Klaus Fuchs, we did it all ourselves."

Khariton also understood that "the atomic age has come to define history," and, although he did not spell out the specifics, his handiwork set the stage for the war in Korea. This was a tale left for other Russian insiders[26] to tell five years later, but in summary, on August 29, 1949, the Soviet Union tested RDS-1 and thus became a nuclear power. A month later, Mao Zedong completed the communist takeover of China. In December of that year Mao came to Moscow, met with Stalin, discussed Korea, and sought agreement for Stalin to meet with Kim Il Sung, the leader of North Korea. Within a few weeks, the date was set; in late March, 1950, Kim Il Sung came to Moscow. During April the two men met and, after discussions with his generals, Stalin approved Kim's plan to invade South Korea. Stalin declined to commit troops to that venture, but he would allow the Soviet general staff to plan the attack. Stalin expressed confidence in his newly acquired bomb; it would give him immunity from U.S. retaliation. Two months later, on June 19, 1950, North Korea invaded South Korea. That war did not go as either Stalin or Kim planned. Stalin died before it ended; so did thirty-six thousand Americans, a

26. Vladislav Zubok and Constantine Pleshakov, *Inside the Kremlin's Cold War* (Cambridge: Harvard University Press, 1996).

million Koreans,[27] and another million Chinese,[28] all drawn into the Korean sinkhole as the Stalin-Kim plans went awry. When it was all over, the boundary between North and South remained essentially unchanged.

In his farewells, Khariton also neglected to mention Khrushchev's decision, in April 1957, to pass on Khariton's sophisticated nuclear technology to the People's Republic of China (P.R.C.) an aid package that was to include an actual atomic bomb.

## MEANWHILE, IN THE UNITED KINGDOM

Within months of the 1938 and 1939 discoveries of nuclear fission and chain reactions, scientists were gathering throughout Europe and the United States to think through the next step: the possibility of a nuclear weapon. In Britain, reflections started in the spring of 1940 as Europe dozed through the so-called Phony War. Then came the May 10 Nazi invasion of France. With the arrival of a Churchill government on that same day, scientific investigations of nuclear weapons took on serious purpose. The MAUD report,[29] "On the Use of Uranium for a Bomb," was delivered to the war cabinet in June 1941. Colonel Barkovsky of the Soviet KGB picked up his copy three months later.

With the Nazi invasion of western Europe, the fall of France, and the Battle of Britain, all in the summer of 1940, the core of the British nuclear program relocated to Chalk River, Canada. Other parts moved to New York as elements of a "trade mission." Then, once the United States was militarily engaged, many of those scientists moved to Los Alamos, heart of the Allied nuclear weapons design effort.

British and Canadian scientists dominated the roster at Los Alamos, and their observers flew with the Nagasaki mission, so when the war ended, the British were privy to all the key nuclear weapon design concepts. On the other hand, they had not been involved in materials production. They had been promised otherwise, specifically at the Hyde Park conference in 1942 and in the Quebec Agreements between Churchill and Roosevelt in August 1943. Given Britain's initial leadership in the field of nuclear science as well as its unilateral transfer of that technology to the United States in 1940–1941, the government of Great Britain felt entitled to the secrets of uranium enrichment, plutonium production, and weapons assembly, but that was not to be. Franklin Roosevelt had entered into the Hyde Park and Quebec Agreements with Churchill during the war, but by the time of the Hiroshima bombing, both men had been removed from the world stage.

27. 415,000 South Korean and 520,000 North Korean military and civilian dead.
28. David Halberstam, *The Coldest Winter* (Hyperion, 2007).
29. Prepared by Sir George P. Thomson, Chair. Members: Marcus Oliphant, Patrick Blackett, James Chadwick, Philip Moon, and John Cockroft.

In the summer of 1945, upon the surrender of Germany and seeking a mandate to rebuild the postwar world, Winston Churchill called for new elections in Great Britain. None had been held for ten years; a British coalition government had joined hands to fight the war. The election of 1945 was conducted on July 5; the votes were not tallied for three weeks, but when the results came in, Winston Churchill had been swept from office. On July 26, 1945, Churchill's wartime coalition partner and deputy prime minister, Clement Attlee, took the reins of power. He brought with him a belief in the embryonic United Nations (formed in June of that year) and a fear of nuclear weapons as instruments of sovereign power. On October 24, the war's victors ratified the UN charter, and on November 9, Attlee came to Washington to meet with President Harry Truman and Prime Minister Mackenzie King of Canada to discuss international controls on atomic energy. A week later, the conferees published an agreed declaration calling for the UN to take control of atomic energy matters, to assure only peaceful uses, and to eliminate nuclear weapons from national armaments. Those ideas did not sit well with U.S. opinion leaders and were anathema to the U.S. Congress. Within months, legislation was drafted precluding the sharing of U.S. nuclear secrets with any other nation.

During those same postwar months, during February 1946, a code clerk defected from the Soviet Embassy in Ottawa. Igor Gouzenko exposed the Soviet network, extending from Chalk River to Los Alamos. Soon thereafter, Alan Nunn May, a British scientist working at Chalk River, confirmed his Soviet connections.

The U.S. House and Senate took action during July 1946, passing a bill known as the McMahon Act. President Truman signed it into law on August 1. With the passage of that act, the FBI took charge of security at all U.S. nuclear facilities.[30] The scope of the espionage problem soon became clear: the biggest leaks out of Chalk River and Los Alamos and into the Soviet system had been via British citizens and British-sponsored émigrés. With these disclosures the U.S.–U.K. nuclear relationship was hopelessly poisoned; with the passage of the McMahon Act, the door slammed shut.

## A FEAR OF AMERICAN WITHDRAWAL

Other postwar political currents within the United States were giving British leaders even more cause for concern. Were the Americans returning to a policy of isolation? Were they once again withdrawing to the safety of the New World, leaving Britain to face the communist menace alone?

The U.S. Government had ended the Allied Lend-Lease program immediately upon the cessation of hostilities with Japan; it did not even await the formality

---

30. During World War II, that security had rested in the hands of the U.S. Army.

of surrender documents. A few younger American troops remained in Germany and moved into Japan to serve as armies of occupation, but for the most part, the Americans in Europe were being recalled and demobilized with frightening speed. At the same time, the Soviet armies were ignoring many an agreement reached at Yalta and Potsdam—they were extending their reach into eastern Europe.

In the winter of 1945 to 1946, Winston Churchill, by then out of office, came to the United States hoping to deliver a wakeup call. He met with President Truman on February 10, and on March 5, he delivered his now-immortal Iron Curtain speech in Fulton, Missouri. He warned of the Soviet threat to come. Some Americans listened, but many more were reflecting the same postwar fatigue that had removed Churchill from power in Britain eight months before. In the autumn of 1946, U.S. voters delivered a massive vote of no confidence in the Truman administration. Republicans gained twelve seats in the U.S. Senate, achieving a majority for the first time since the days of Herbert Hoover. They picked up fifty-five seats in the House of Representatives, again giving the Republicans control for the first time in a decade. Of greater significance to those watching from overseas, many of those elected to the U.S. House and Senate were staunch isolationists. Withdrawal from the quarrels of Europe was in the American air.

Once again standing alone, the British government decided, in 1946, to hedge its bets: to look into nuclear power and to start work on a nuclear reactor with plutonium-production capabilities. In January 1946, Attlee had asked John Cockroft, the professor who had been running the Chalk River facility, to take charge of a nuclear research establishment at Harwell. Attlee assigned the broader job of overseeing all U.K. development of atomic energy to Lord Portal, former chief of the British air staff.

Lord Portal wrote a paper for the prime minister on the matter of weapons; it laid out the options and was reviewed by an inner government circle to make the critical decision. That nuclear-weapon decision group, meeting in January 1947, was known as the Gen 163 Committee. It had but three members: Prime Minister Attlee; Hugh Dalton, chancellor of the Exchequer; and Sir Stafford Cripps, president of the Board of Trade. The makeup of the Gen 163 Committee makes it clear that nuclear policy hung not on science but on the economic conditions within Great Britain, struggling as it was to recover from the disaster of World War II.

The Gen 163 Committee met in early January 1947 to consider the Portal paper. It reached several conclusions: First, to proceed full-bore with the development of nuclear weapons. Second, it called for a bomb test within five years. Third, the committee decided, in a true stroke of genius, to put Sir William Penney in charge. There are indications that the Defence Committee of the British cabinet concurred in these decisions, but the matter was never brought to the attention of the full cabinet.

William Penney had been one of the British scientists working at Los Alamos. He and RAF Group Capt. Leonard Cheshire rode aboard *The Great Artiste*, the photo aircraft accompanying *Bock's Car* on its weapon drop over Nagasaki. Penney and his associates at Los Alamos had excellent insights into the design of Fat Man; upon their return to the United Kingdom in 1946, they prepared extensive memoranda on their recollections and understandings. In the words of a subsequent historian,[31] "[Penney's] modest, unassuming personal manner, with its mixture of heartiness and privacy, enabled him to command respect across a broad range, from the most temperamental cabinet ministers and civil servants to the casual and easygoing servicemen who carved out sites in the Australian desert." But as an indicator of the secrecy of the British decision to proceed into the nuclear arena, even Penney himself did not learn of his assignment until five months later.

The Attlee government decided on a stealth announcement of this program via a planted question in the House of Commons. On May 12, 1948, sixteen months after the decision had been made, the Honorable A. V. Alexander, minister of defence, responded to a question from a fellow Labour Member of Parliament: "Can the minister give any further information on the development of atomic weapons?"

Minister Alexander: "No, I do not think it would be in the public interest to do that." That is all that was said in public for years, although another assurance, that "all types of modern weapons, including atomic weapons, are being developed," was given privately to other MPs.

Relations with the United States warmed in the spring of 1949, as the United States sought overseas sources of uranium, controlled as they were by U.K. interests. Then, in the fall, relations cooled, as the decoded Venona transcripts began to finger Klaus Fuchs, among others, as Soviet spies. In January 1950, Fuchs confessed to his role as a leading Soviet agent inside Los Alamos. With that the U.S.–U.K nuclear door slammed shut a second time.

## A FULL BRITISH PROGRAM

The first U.K. nuclear reactor, built at Windscale,[32] went critical in July 1950. It began to produce useful quantities of plutonium in early 1952, but during that interval, the question arose: "Where to test?" The preferred location was at the U.S. nuclear test site in Nevada. The needed infrastructure was in place, and the British would be happy to pay their fair share of the costs, but those negotiations were

31. Robert Milliken, *No Conceivable Injury* (Victoria: Penguin Australia, 1986), 25.
32. Located on the Irish Sea in northwest England and renamed Sellafield in 1957 after an unfortunate, though nonlethal, fire.

among the casualties of the Klaus Fuchs arrest and confession. The British then turned their attention to the remote provinces of Canada, a nation that had been part of the Allied wartime nuclear triumvirate, but in time the outback of Australia seemed like a better location. The prime minister there was fully supportive. When the Churchill government was returned to power, on October 26, 1951, the British nuclear weapons program was reinforced. Soon thereafter, the decision was made to test off the Monte Bello Islands, fifty miles to the northwest of Western Australia. On February 17, 1952, Churchill announced there would be such a test, "before the end of the year.

The first British nuclear test took place on October 3, 1952, five years and nine months after the decision to proceed and twenty-seven months after the reactor at Windscale first went critical. The device was known as Hurricane, a plutonium-implosion weapon modeled after Fat Man, but with improvements that resulted in a twenty-five–kiloton yield from a device that weighed about three tons (60 percent

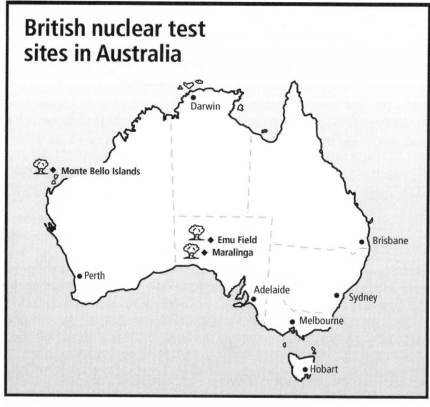

Source: *Graphite Studio*

that of Fat Man). Hurricane was fired in the hold of a retired British frigate, the HMS *Plym*, anchored offshore. Canadian observers were invited to participate.

Over the next four years, there was a series of eight more A-bomb tests. The first two were conducted during October 1953, within the Australian outback at the Emu Field station. Those tests, conducted as Operation Totem, involved instrumentation improved over the rather hurried first shot at the Monte Bello Islands, thus leading to a better understanding of nuclear weapons physics.

## THE THERMONUCLEAR CLOUD AGAIN APPEARS

The early 1950s became years of deep concern within Europe. In the shadow of the Communist conquest of China, the Russian nuclear test, and the seemingly endless war in Korea, the NATO ministers met in Lisbon in February 1952 to discuss the rearmament of Western Europe. They agreed to raise a ninety-division force and thus to return the West to a World War II footing. This was done in the face of an immense Red Army assembling within Eastern Europe. The British were already in the line of fire. Since June 1948, at the time of the Berlin blockade, three American bomb groups of nuclear-capable B-29s had been stationed in East Anglia. They were under the command of the irascible General LeMay. In the event of war, the British Isles would be a prime target, yet the British had no access to U.S. plans, no voice in the decision to use any nukes that might be brought to British soil. In time, successive prime ministers of the United Kingdom and presidents of the United States reached "informal agreements" on consultation and use, but the British Chiefs of Staff continued to worry. During the early 1950s, the United States could have pre-emptively attacked the Soviet Union without much fear of retaliatory strikes hitting the United States. The Soviets had only a handful of nuclear weapons and no intercontinental delivery systems, but the Soviets could have wreaked nuclear havoc on American bases in the United Kingdom

In the midst of this concern, at the end of 1952, the thermonuclear window began to open. That October, the United States fired the ten-megaton Mike device; on August 12, 1953, the Soviets detonated RDS-6s at four hundred kilotons. Sharing of bomb-debris data from "distant nuclear explosions" was allowed under the McMahon Act, so the United States, United Kingdom, and Canada exchanged such data. It implied an unsophisticated, one-stage Soviet design, but even so, William Penney found the results to be "sensational and revolutionary." During the summer and fall of 1953, Churchill opened thermonuclear discussions with his scientific advisor; the conversations continued within the government while British scientists focused on the immediate A-bomb experiments then underway in the Australian outback.

The political calm was shattered in February 1954, when the chairman of the U.S. Joint Committee on Atomic Energy[33] announced the impending test of "a thermonuclear device even more powerful than Mike." Those tests, the Castle series in the Pacific, broke open the door to practical, two-stage thermonuclear weapons. The United States had invited British observers to attend those tests at the Bikini Atoll. British aircraft sampled the resulting radioactive clouds, losing at least one aircraft in the process. Soon thereafter, serious policy discussions started back in the United Kingdom. On April 13, Churchill began to participate. In May, the British military reiterated their uncomfortable conclusions: U.S. nuclear forces could act unilaterally and without fear of retaliation for several years; in such an event the United Kingdom would be a prime target. With an adequate British nuclear capability, however, the Soviets might be deterred from such an attack on bases in the United Kingdom. The British military also reminded their political masters that holding such nuclear cards would strengthen British power and influence on world affairs. On June 16, 1954, the Defence Committee of the British cabinet decided to pursue the thermonuclear option. On June 29, Churchill confided that decision to his Canadian counterpart while seeking Canadian help with raw materials. On July 27, the British cabinet formally authorized the commencement of work on a British H-bomb.

## DEVELOPMENT

The most immediate experiment, of great interest to both U.S. and British scientists, was the detonation of the Soviet RDS-37, a true two-stage, 1.6-megaton thermonuclear, in the Semipalatinsk area on November 22, 1955. By then, the Allies were quite accomplished at sampling other people's bomb debris. Analysis of the American tests in 1954 and the Soviet tests in 1955 provided a roadmap that a British historian[34] later described as "very influential" in the clarification of concepts. Thus it was that the wartime partners once again came to share nuclear secrets.

The United Kingdom resumed testing at the Monte Bello Islands on May 16, 1956; the test series was known as Mosaic. On June 19, the Brits fired a single-stage thermonuclear. It produced ninety-eight kilotons, twice the expected yield, and thus dictated the move of future tests into a more remote Australian outback facility known as Maralinga, or "Field of Thunder" to the local aborigines. The next year, the British moved their test operations to even more remote island sites in the Pacific,[35] testing their first two-stage, radiation-imploded device on May 15, 1957. Short Granite, as

33. A committee composed of House *and* Senate members, known as the JCAE.
34. Lorna Arnold, *Britain and the H-bomb* (New York: Palgrave Press, 2001), 94.
35. Christmas and Malden Islands, near the equator.

the device was known, operated successfully, but the results, at two hundred to three hundred kilotons, were not up to expectations. The British returned to Maralinga that autumn for some follow-up experiments, and then, on November 8, they got it right. A device known as Grapple X, fired at Christmas Island, gave 1.8 megatons. It had operated as planned. Five more tests in the megaton range were conducted in the area of Christmas Island during the year that followed, the objectives being to improve affordability, cut weight, and demonstrate to the Americans that Great Britain was a true thermonuclear power. The latter was essential in reopening the door to nuclear cooperation between the wartime allies. That goal was achieved with the passage of amendments to the McMahon Act, signed into U.S. law on June 30, 1958, which allowed the full exchange of U.S. data and nonnuclear materials with other friendly nuclear powers. Implementing agreements were executed in August.

On November 1, 1958, a tripartite[36] nuclear testing moratorium went into effect, developed in response to worldwide concern about nuclear fallout. It was not a treaty, simply a "gentlemen's agreement" to which the United States and United Kingdom adhered, closing down test facilities and some weapons work. The Soviets used the moratorium to gain a technological lap on the West; they unilaterally broke the argeement, with one day's notice, on September 1, 1961, in a dazzling display of new technology developed during the moratorium. (See chapter 5 for details.)

## THE UNRECOGNIZED GENIUS

Unrecognized by many, digital computing was and remains the *sine qua non* of the thermonuclear age. Calculating the conditions necessary for thermonuclear burn is quite complex. Scientists' hands cannot do those calculations, nor can they be checked by small-scale experiment. Only *gedanken,* or thought-experiments, are possible, and those require extensive computational support. The first American H-bomb would not have been possible without the new Univac digital computers then under development in Philadelphia and accessible to the physicists at Princeton. (In Russia, the Arzamas-16 scientists were supported by acres of women punching desk calculators in Moscow.)

The British H-bomb was made possible by the 1952 arrival of the IBM 704, the world's first commercial digital computer. That machine is now an antique: powered by vacuum tubes, utilizing a magnetic core memory, and utilizing then-dazzling software—floating-point arithmetic. In the mid-1950s, however, as the British grappled with the thermonuclear problem, the 704 sped their deliberations by a factor of twenty and enabled the rapid post-test diagnostics of Short Granite

36. U.S., U.K., and U.S.S.R.

that led to Grapple X. In time, the 704 gave way to the transistor-driven 7040 that your authors used in the design of the American thermonuclear deterrent of the early 1960s. It is this struggle for computational power that lies behind the export-control battles with would-be proliferant states. Any intelligent college student, with enough enriched uranium, high explosives, and truck capacity, can build and deliver an inefficient but deadly A-bomb, but those without large-scale computers will not be admitted to the H-bomb fraternity.

### Some Conclusions

Many have reported on the history of the Soviet nuclear weapons program after Dan Stillman's ground-breaking visit with Yuliy Khariton, and the British have been most forthcoming with their published histories. Through all of these revelations, a few lessons stand out:

- Technology moves fast: Only a year or two is required to go from a chain-reacting nuclear reactor to an exploding bomb.

- Technology is fungible: U.S., Soviet, and British nuclear technology all flowed from the same wellspring: prewar Europe. Junior states "borrowed" from their seniors, but in time all three thermonuclear superpowers came to learn from each other as they recruited each other's scientists and examined each other's nuclear-testing debris.

- The early American and British nuclear programs were carefully conducted. Health records confirm few casualties, although the environmental costs are still being weighed.[37]

- There were no production nuclear reactor accidents in the United States and only a minor (nonnuclear) fire at Windscale in the United Kingdom. The Soviet nuclear program cost thousands of lives, exploited prisoners, and left a generation marked for long-term illness.

---

37. The findings of Dr. Andrew C. McEwan, National Radiation Laboratory, Christchurch, New Zealand, in response to a request from the British Government for an independent survey of the effects of the U.K. nuclear tests on those individuals resident in the Pacific during the tests stated, "There is no evidence that the participants received any significant radiation exposures, and certainly no exposures that would give rise to any observable health effects." NRL Report 1981/9.

- It is the production of plutonium and enriched uranium that separates the nuclear men from the conventionally armed boys. The facilities needed to produce these materials are technically challenging, physically immense, and financially crushing, but it is only the lack of fissionable materials that maintains the exclusivity of the nuclear club today.

- Nuclear weapons are developed and deployed for political, not military, reasons. They are political enablers as much as they are weapons of war. The decisions to develop such weapons, both in the mid-twentieth century and in the decades that followed, have been made by senior politicians, acting virtually alone, with little or no input from—and often over the objections of—their military advisors.

## CHAPTER 5

# FIRST ATTEMPTS
# AT CONTROLS

Never was a ship more inappropriately named. The *Fortunate Dragon,*[1] a fishing boat in search of tuna, left Japanese waters in February 1954. A week later, that vessel and its crew had become the first casualties of the thermonuclear age.

Sixteen months before, the Americans had broken the thermonuclear code; with the dawn of 1954, a half-dozen follow-on weapons were ready for testing in the South Pacific. These trials, to be known as Operation Castle, were once again to be conducted at the Bikini Atoll. They would test two-stage devices, all using lithium deuteride (LiD), a new, solid-state thermonuclear fuel. Each test was to offer a different solution to the H-bomb challenge. Lithium was a new weapon constituent because one isotope of that element, lithium-six (Li6), when bombarded with a neutron, would break into a tritium atom and an alpha particle. The tritium would then fuze with the deuterium in the Li6D compound as part of a fast and highly energetic thermonuclear reaction. The other, naturally occurring, isotope of lithium, Li7, was to be ignored.

The first event in the Castle test series, fired on March 1, 1954, was known as Bravo. The test device weighed 23,500 pounds—large, but still only a quarter the size and weight of Mike. It was to yield five or six megatons. The open ocean area around Bikini had been declared a danger zone in accordance with international protocols; shipping had been warned to stay away. The weather at shot time was as forecast, but within minutes after the 6:45 a.m. detonation, scientific joy turned to concern. Bravo had released three times the energy expected, significantly more than the Mike event sixteen months before, and winds at altitude were blowing differently than at sea level. Huge quantities of coral reef had been vaporized, sucked up into a cloud that soon reached 114,000 feet. Fallout levels were far greater than

1. Full Japanese name: *Diago Fukuryu Maru,* sometimes translated as "Lucky Dragon."

anticipated. Scientific staff and military personnel were instructed to seek cover; the concrete firing bunker on Enyu, twenty miles from ground zero, cracked open; radiation penetrated into the control room. Wooden structures nearby, uninhabited at shot time, were completely destroyed. White ash began to fall onto naval ships 30 miles away; Rongerik Atoll, 120 miles east of Bikini, was rapidly becoming uninhabitable. American service personnel and native Pacific Islanders, temporarily on that island, had to be evacuated. Throughout the Marshall Islands, 28 Americans manning weather stations and 236 resident natives suffered radiation burns, hair loss, and lowered blood counts.

The reason for this unexpectedly large explosion[2] soon became clear. The weapons designers at Los Alamos had focused their attention on the characteristics of Lithium-6; they had neglected to consider the n,2n cross section for Lithium-7, the reaction wherein Lithium-7 will capture one neutron, spit out two, and leave Lithium-6—the prime thermonuclear fuel—in its wake. Bravo was turbocharged with a hidden supply of Lithium-6, delivered unseen.

The *Fortunate Dragon* was operating about eighty miles east of Bikini, well outside the declared danger zone and well away from the predicted fallout pattern, but the ignored n,2n reactions and *Bravo's* triple-the-expected yield rendered those predictions obsolete. The twenty-three men aboard the *Fortunate Dragon* saw the flash; five minutes thereafter they felt the shock wave, but none realized their danger. Two hours later a light rain began to fall, bringing with it flakes of white ash. By the time the *Fortunate Dragon* returned to Japan, the entire crew was ill. All had radiation burns; some were suffering from a dropping white corpuscle count, potentially fatal if not treated. Japanese authorities soon identified the problem as radiation sickness. The ship's tuna catch was recovered from the markets, but panic spread. The next day, headlines erupted and violent anti-American protests swept the streets. Alarm spread to the United States and soon to the rest of the world. None of the *Fortunate Dragon's* crewmembers succumbed in the near term, but for the first time, large numbers of people became aware of and were personally involved with the dangers of the nuclear age. The immediate biological hazards were amplified by press discussions of H-bomb capabilities. Entire cities, even civilizations, could be destroyed with one shot.

With the Bravo test and the five explosions that followed, the thermonuclear bandwagon began to roll. In its wake, lay two tracks of enormous historical significance. The first was the perception by the new U.S. president, Dwight Eisenhower, that with the advent of thermonuclear weapons (and other technologies then beginning to blossom), colossal land armies were a thing of the past. The United States could deter

2. Fifteen megatons, a thousand times the Hiroshima yield.

Soviet expansion with threats of massive retaliation and need not rebuild its armed forces to World War II levels, as the NATO ministers had agreed only two years before.[3] Freed of such a burden, the U.S. economy could prosper and ultimately prevail in its confrontation with the Soviet state. On the other hand, antinuclear activism became a feature of international politics. The possible results of nuclear war came to the fore in many minds; the consequences of even testing nuclear devices became a cause célèbre. India's Prime Minister Nehru espoused a nonaligned philosophy while privately weighing the nuclear option; Pope Pius XII sought to ban the bomb. Nine years after Hiroshima, nuclear weapons moved from scientific and policy-wonk curiosity to the mainstream of political consciousness.

## CONSTRAINT YIELDS TO CONSPIRACY

In the months following World War II, scientists and statesmen sought international control of atomic energy, but none of those proposals worked out. Attention then shifted to national constraints on the transfer of nuclear technology, such as the McMahon Act in the United States and Gulag-enforced security in the U.S.S.R., but with the coming of the second nuclear decade, that technology began to leak.

At first it was via the graduate students. With the end of World War II, war-torn societies sent their brightest and best to the leading universities of the New World. Students from Asia, the Indian subcontinent, and even the ruins of Europe poured into New York, Chicago, and Berkeley. Others settled into Cambridge, Paris, and Zurich. Everyone wanted to build a new and better postwar world. By the early 1950s, these bright youngsters had earned their bachelors degrees in physics, chemistry, and engineering; they had rubbed elbows with the titans of wartime science, the wizards of Los Alamos, Chalk River, and Cambridge, who had returned to their old academic haunts. Many students stayed on to pursue graduate work in nuclear structure, radiochemistry, electronics, and computer science, but as the 1950s drew to a close, they often accepted their degrees and headed home. Amidst this ebb and flow of young talent, leaders of the nuclear superstates began to think about sharing. Some wanted to do so for benign reasons, others were more malevolent.

On December 8, 1953, President Eisenhower proposed to the United Nations a peaceful distribution of nuclear know-how. He laid out an arrangement that came to be known as Atoms for Peace. The American president wished to assist other nations in exploiting nuclear technology for energy production, medical research, and basic science. Atoms for Peace seemed like a good idea at the time, but over the years it tore a gaping hole into the dikes holding back the spread of nuclear weapons. India's

3. Meeting in Lisbon in February 1952.

1974 nuclear test device used plutonium bred in an Atoms for Peace reactor acquired as a gift from Canada.

Soon thereafter, Nikita Khrushchev started working the dark side of the street. Upon gaining full control of the Soviet government in 1956, Khrushchev turned his attention to the nuclear arming of his communist ally, the People's Republic of China. In May 1957, Soviet specialists were dispatched to China with instructions to support Mao in his quest for admission to the nuclear club. They helped organize a nuclear weapons facility outside Beijing while Soviet geologists assisted in the Chinese search for uranium. It was only in 1959 that Khrushchev began to have second thoughts.

## THE CAULDRONS

To build and deploy nuclear weapons, a sovereign state must have a source of fissionable material. Plutonium was the preferred postwar explosive. It was bred in nuclear reactors, but in time many of those reactors became witches' cauldrons. Canada, a wartime member of the nuclear triumvirate, built an early nuclear reactor at Chalk River outside Ottawa. In 1952, it went haywire, melting the core and blowing away a four-ton dome. No one was injured, but the entire reactor had to be disassembled and buried. Four years later, a second-generation reactor caught fire. In neither incident were workers exposed to excessive radiation levels, and medical checkups found no immediate adverse health impacts, but radiation has a long memory.

The United Kingdom started work on its first nuclear reactor in 1946. That facility, at Windscale on the Irish Sea, went critical in October 1950. It ran without incident for half a decade, churning out plutonium for the British nuclear weapons program, but during those years, Windscale was also heating up. On October 10, 1957, the graphite moderator within the reactor caught fire. Attempts to extinguish the blaze only made matters worse; huge clouds of steam transported radioactive materials out of the reactor and across the British countryside. There were no immediate injuries or fatalities, but the local milk supply was badly contaminated. Subsequent investigations suggested perhaps thirty-two deaths and several hundred cases of cancer could be attributed to this radiation release. Since then, the British government has paid the greatest attention to reactor safety; there have been no subsequent incidents involving radioactive release.

As we have seen in chapter 4, the Soviets built their first plutonium producer at Mayak with slave labor and operated it with a hearty disregard for the well-being of the people involved. A prime example: on September 29, 1957, a radioactive-waste storage tank near Mayak blew up, with disastrous consequences for those in the neighborhood. That chemical explosion lifted highly radioactive materials thousands of feet into the air, thereby scattering eighty tons of nuclear debris downwind for hundreds of miles. More than two hundred towns were evacuated; those that were not have suffered a legacy of leukemia. There were, of course, no immediate reports to the outside world, since at that time there was no such thing as satellite reconnaissance. The first published reports of the Mayak disaster came from Soviet dissident geneticist Zhores Medvedev, who escaped to the West and in November 1976, published his allegations of "hundreds of deaths and a thousand square miles contaminated." Unfortunately, there were many more such tragedies. Contamination downstream from the Tomsk-7 and Krasnoyarsk-26 plutonium production reactors was far worse. Reactors aboard Soviet nuclear-powered submarines were equally lethal. Many crewmembers did not live to tell their tales.

Within the United States, plutonium was produced at the Hanford Engineering Works on the Columbia River in southeastern Washington. There were never any serious or life-threatening accidents at Hanford, although wastes have been buried in the surrounding soil, leaving behind a long-lived footprint.

Admiral Hyman Rickover's achievement in moving nuclear power to sea has been a model of safety. As the admiral explained to Congress at the time of his retirement in 1982: "On the high seas, the total amount of gamma radiation in liquids discharged per year for the last ten years from *all* U.S. nuclear-powered ships is less than 0.4 curies—less than the amount of natural radioactivity contained in a cube of seawater 100 meters (about 390 feet) on a side. Within twelve miles of land, the total gamma radioactivity discharged by *all* U.S. ships and facilities in one year is less than 0.002 curies." This safety record stands in stark contrast to the recurrent fires and sinkings of Soviet nuclear-powered craft.[4] American nuclear reactor operations do not enjoy an unblemished record. We speak not of Three Mile Island, a media event where all the containment systems worked and no lives were endangered.[5] The only fatal U.S. reactor "accident" took place in Idaho Falls,

---

4. During the Cold War, Soviet nuclear more than powered submarines suffered over a hundred radiation-producing accidents: reactor meltdowns and explosions, submarine sinkings, nuclear weapon accidents, and undersea collisions. At least fourteen such accidents were so severe that the ship itself was retired or abandoned at sea.

5. Subsequent studies by the U.S. Nuclear Regulatory Commission, EPA, Department of Energy, and Department of Health and Human Services, as well as studies by the State of Pennsylvania, converge on the conclusion that the two million people in the Three Mile Island Area were exposed to an average radiation dose of about one millirem. The maximum dose to an individual at the site boundary would have been less than 100 millirem. By comparison, a full set of chest X-rays constitutes a 6 millirem dose; the natural background radiation in that area (from solar effects, etc.) is 100–125 millirem per year.

at the National Reactor Test Station, on January 3, 1961. The word *accident* lies within quotes here because the triple deaths within that hot cell were not accidental at all—they were a murder-suicide.[6]

During the late 1950s, the U.S. AEC sought to develop a small nuclear power plant for use in remote locations. The first experimental model, known as SL-1 (Stationary Low Power Plant No. 1), went online in August 1958. It produced three megawatts of electrical power while serving as a prototype and test bed. SL-1 had been shut down for maintenance in December 1960; it was due to be restarted on January 4, 1961. The January 3 evening shift, charged with readying the reactor for startup the next day, consisted of two experienced army technicians and one navy electrician's mate. All three men were in their twenties; one had been having an affair with another's wife, a matter that came to light over the Christmas holidays. At 9:00 p.m. on January 3, while all three men were working within the hot cell on the dormant SL-1, the aggrieved husband rapidly withdrew the central control rod from the heart of the sleeping reactor. Within a millisecond, SL-1 delivered twenty thousand megawatts, turning its core into flying shrapnel. The reactor lid was blown nine feet into the air. Two of the men were killed instantly, one being impaled by the flying central control rod. The third was evacuated by heroic crews operating within a lethal one-thousand-rad-per-hour environment, but he died en route to the hospital. His corpse could not be removed from the emergency truck until morning, for even in death he was radiating four hundred rads per hour. Although glossed over in public announcements, the SL-1 affair soon led to stringent mechanical redesigns to preclude the human-accident option, and the personal lives of reactor operators have come under much closer scrutiny. One of your authors reassigned a philandering technician from a reactor facility, years later, for similar marital-conflict reasons.

To put all the above accidents in perspective, we tabulate below the characteristics of a dozen major Soviet nuclear disasters. The worst offenders were the plutonium production reactors at Mayak, Tomsk-7, and Krasnoyarsk-26. The effluent from these facilities, the explosion from Chernobyl, and the results of other Soviet nuclear accidents are then compared to the accident at the U.K.'s Windscale reactor, operations at U.S. nuclear production facilities, and three widely reported (though inconsequential) U.S. nuclear events.

---

6. This bizarre and hitherto unrecognized aspect of the 1961 SL-1 deaths arises from the authors' discussions with one medical doctor who conducted the autopsies, the written records of the other pathologist, the records of the assigned criticality expert, discussions with the SL-1 reactor supervisor, and an internal U.S. AEC memo leaked to the press a decade later.

## Major Nuclear Disasters

| Date | Event | Location | MC* |
|------|-------|----------|-----|
| 1955–present | Waste discharges from Tomsk-7 plutonium production reactor | Central Russia | ~2,000 |
| 1958–present | Waste discharges from Krasnoyarsk-26 plutonium production reactor | Central Russia | 1,000 |
| Aug. 1985 | Soviet SSGN (K-431) submarine reactor explosion during refueling | Chazhma Bay, near Vladivostok | 7.0 |
| Apr. 1986 | Chernobyl power reactor, Unit Four, explosion and fire | Northern Ukraine | 5.9 |
| 1949–1956 | Discharges into Techa River at Mayak plutonium reactor site | Central Russia | 2.8 |
| 1965–1981 | Five loads of submarine debris, including seven spent nuclear reactors, dumped at sea | Northern seas, off Russia, details unknown | 2.3 |
| Sept. 1957 | Explosion in high-level nuclear reactor waste tank | Mayak, central Russia | 2.0 |
| Oct. 1975 | Leningrad I nuclear power reactor core, partial meltdown | Leningrad, Russia | 1.5 |
| Feb. 1965 | Reactor fire in Soviet SSN (K-11) during refueling; two reactors dumped at sea | Abromisov Inlet, north of Russia | 0.8 |
| 1961 | Pump failure aboard Soviet SSN (K-19),** reactors dumped at sea | Off Novaya Zemlya, north of Russia | 0.8 |
| 1965 | Reactor compartment of Soviet SSN 901, two reactors, dumped at sea | Abrisomov Inlet, north of Russia | 0.4 |
| Jan. 1978 | Soviet Cosmos 954 satellite, with nuclear power source aboard, failed at end of mission | Re-entered over Canada's N.W. Territory | 0.046 |
| 1946–90 | Savannah River nuclear facility | Georgia, U.S.A. | 0.9*** |
| 1944–90 | Hanford (Columbia River) facility | Washington, U.S.A. | 0.7*** |
| Oct. 1957 | Windscale plutonium production reactor fire | Northwestern U.K. | 0.0006 |
| Jan. 1961 | SL-1 experimental military reactor explosion | Idaho Falls, U.S.A. | 0.000010 |
| Jan. 1966 | B-52 & tanker collide midair, four nuclear weapons fall to Earth | Palomares, Spain | 0.000003 |
| Mar. 1978 | Three Mile Island, power reactor | Pennsylvania, U.S.A. | 0.000001 |

\* Radioactive nuclides, released to the surrounding environment, in millions of curies (a measure of radioactivity at any given time).

\*\* These events of July 4, 1961, were depicted in the film *The Widowmaker*. Twenty-two crewmembers died.

\*\*\* 1996 residual background after forty years of Cold War operation; no single event. (Source: Don J. Bradley [Pacific Northwest National Laboratory], *Radioactive Waste Management in the Former Soviet Union*. [Columbus, OH: Battelle Press, 1997].)

## THE MORATORIUM MOVEMENT

As noted earlier, the coming of the thermonuclear age unleashed two important historical options. The first was the opportunity to reorient Western defense policies away from expensive conventional armed forces to an affordable nuclear deterrent. The unappreciated corollaries were smaller and more compact nuclear weapons in lieu of multi-megaton city-busters; safer weapons less prone to accident or theft; and cheaper weapons, less profligate in their use of fissionable materials. This latter allowed the United States (but not the Soviet Union) to close down its plutonium production reactors in 1988 as the Cold War drew to a close.

The second thermonuclear consequence was a significant political backlash. Some of this was based on sound thinking, some on junk science, and some on hypocrisy. By the summer of 1954, scientists in the United States and United Kingdom had begun to look into the health effects of nuclear testing and weapons use. "Local fallout," the pulverized coral irradiated by Bravo and deposited hundreds of miles downwind, was the immediate villain. That was the material that had endangered the crew of the *Fortunate Dragon*. Testing well above the Earth's surface and the use of adequate exclusion zones could ameliorate this problem. It was the longer-lived fission products, emerging from within the bombs themselves,[7] which more seriously concerned government and academic scientists. Rational analyses within both the United States and the United Kingdom delineated the problem. The longer-term consequences of properly conducted atmospheric tests were found to be insignificant when compared to the natural or voluntary sources of radiation to which we are all exposed. An American moving his residence from New York City to Denver will increase his dose rate (from solar radiation) far more than from any properly conducted atmospheric nuclear test. X-rays, used to diagnose bone fractures or lung disease, similarly overshadow nuclear testing as a source of radiation. Still, there may be no "safe rate of radiation dosage" in the context of future generations. One bomb explosion will lead to at least one

7. Strontium-90 has a half-life of twenty-eight years; it accumulates in children's bones. Cesium-137 has a similarly long and bothersome half-life.

genetic mutation somewhere. Those were the tradeoffs during the Cold War, but that one casualty was not to be accepted lightly.

During August 1953, the Soviets began to aggravate the fallout problem with the testing of a four hundred-kiloton single-stage, boosted-fission device fired on the surface of the Kazakhstan desert. Joe 4 (RDS-6s to the Soviets) derived 80 to 85 percent of its yield from fission reactions, but it was a start down the Soviet thermonuclear path. Two years later, on November 22, 1955, the Soviets tested a true two-stage thermonuclear. By then, fallout and radioactive contamination had entered even the Soviet consciousness; their scientists demanded the yield of the test device be cut in half (by the replacement of certain uranium parts with less easily fissionable materials) and that the test itself be conducted as an airdrop. Even with these precautions, the contamination and damage to the nearby city of Semipalatinsk was significant. A week after that test, a Moscow radio commentator called for a nuclear testing moratorium. Subsequent discussions at the governmental level confirmed that broadcaster's suggestion to be a propaganda ploy, but it brought the moratorium issue front and center. In 1955, Afro-Asian governments first met in Bandung[8] to organize a formal antinuclear weapon alliance.

The Soviet Union continued nuclear testing throughout 1956, with the United States detecting and announcing most events. During that same summer, the United Kingdom announced its intention to proceed with the development and testing of an H-bomb. The British did so successfully a year later with the Grapple tests of 1957, conducted at Malden and Christmas Islands in the mid-Pacific. Subsequent analyses found "No evidence of any significant radiation exposure," but the public reaction was more strident.

By the end of 1957, the international pressure for a nuclear testing halt, certainly the banning of H-bomb tests in the atmosphere, had become overwhelming. After a final round of nuclear explosions during the summer of 1958, the United States, United Kingdom, and U.S.S.R entered into an unpoliced nuclear testing moratorium. It was to take effect at midnight on October 31; the West complied, while the Soviets fired twice immediately after that deadline.

The United States took the testing cessation seriously, closing down its Pacific test site, mothballing much of the Nevada complex, and relaxing work at the cutting edge of nuclear technology. The British were a little more skeptical, but they played it straight. They had a lot of experimental data to digest from their 1957 and 1958 tests. The U.S. Congress amended the McMahon Act to allow for a full exchange of nuclear weapon calculations between the United States and the United Kingdom in the absence of nuclear testing.

8. In West Java, now Indonesia.

The Soviet government did not share these good intentions; they saw the moratorium as nothing more than a chance to gain another lap on the West.

## TESTS INTENDED TO FAIL

The moratorium of 1958 did not foreclose all nuclear testing, for not all nuclear tests are intended to produce an explosion. Some experiments are intended to "fail"; they are conducted to explore the safety and/or security of a proposed weapon. While the challenge of early nuclear weapons was simply to get them to work, the safety of those weapons soon became an important consideration in the minds of all the nuclear powers. In the event of a fire within a storage facility, an aircraft accident, or an attack while undergoing ground transportation, a nuclear weapon should not go nuclear. Even if the high-explosive components of the device were to detonate, there must be no fission yield. This requirement led to the concept of "one point safety," defined as an assurance that with a detonation at any one point on the high-explosive system, the chance of a nuclear energy release in excess of four pounds of TNT equivalent must be less than one in a million. Such margins of safety were to be achieved, at first, by the geometry of the explosive system and, later, by the use of less-sensitive (but also less-efficient) high-explosive materials. In time such safety considerations led to weapon designs wherein the high-explosive components would not detonate even when exposed to fire or upon ground impact.

A handmaiden to safety was the issue of "security," the assurance that a nuclear device could not be set off without proper authority, even if an unauthorized user had achieved full custody, i.e., theft. Over the years, highly reliable security has been built into U.S., British, and Russian weapons by means of permissive action link systems (PALs), but it is not clear that the more junior members of the nuclear club have achieved such protection.

The testing of safety and security systems is achieved by means of hydronuclear experiments. In these events, a complete weapon-configured high-explosive system surrounds a package of fissile materials of mass far less than that required for a nuclear explosion. During the experiment, the neutron population is measured as it rises and then decays over time. In successive experiments the amount of fissile material is increased and the neutron population decay rate is tracked while staying clear of any nuclear energy release of more than a few pounds of TNT equivalent. If conducted properly, these experiments are not dangerous, and they contribute significantly to the safety of the nuclear stockpile. Even as they "succeed," however, hydronuclear tests can scatter fissionable materials about with great energy unless conducted underground or within containment bunkers.

Both the United States and the U.S.S.R began to plan hydronuclear experiments during early 1958, as the ban on full-scale nuclear testing drew near. In the United

States, these tests were conducted underground, starting in 1960, at Technical Area 49 in Los Alamos County, New Mexico, and at the Area 410 (Dog Pad) at the Nevada Test Site. All were fully contained; there were no adverse effects.

The Soviets initiated a series of hydronuclear tests on March 13, 1958. During the next thirty-two years, they fired eighty-five such devices, mostly on the surface of the Earth, at three test areas,[9] all in northeastern Kazakhstan. These experiments left behind a badly polluted landscape, pockmarked with nuclear hot spots and flooded with radioactive debris. Even worse, the Soviet tests left "unburned" plutonium scattered about the Kazakh landscape, still in place for the collecting. The Soviet hydronuclear tests continued until the empire collapsed in 1989. The environmental price may have been high, but Soviet nuclear weapons now appear to be reasonably safe and secure.

France conducted one-point safety tests on the surface in Algeria. The United Kingdom conducted similar safety and hydronuclear experiments at the Maralinga test site in Australia. Both left unburned plutonium dispersed across their deserts. The French abandoned their sites when that government left Algeria. The British, with U.S. help, have done extensive work in cleaning up the aboriginal lands. The Chinese have conducted similar hydronuclear and safety tests at Lop Nur; it appears they were conducted underground with no surface contamination resulting.

## THE BIG BANG: SEPTEMBER 1961

The nuclear testing moratorium of 1958 to 1961 was, of course, but a Western dream. On July 10, 1961, Soviet Premier Khrushchev gave the final order, in secret, authorizing the resumption of atmospheric nuclear tests two months later. The West only got one day's notice. On September 1, 1961, the Soviet government unilaterally ended the moratorium with a dazzling display of nuclear fireworks. There were fifty-nine Soviet nuclear tests in a little more than two months, almost one a day, conducted at two separate test locations.[10] They included the first-ever Soviet underground test, a complex technical achievement. There were two missile launches, both with live warheads aboard, fired from Kapustin Yar and detonating near the Semipalatinsk nuclear test site. There were two space shots, also launched from Kapustin Yar, timed for the virtually simultaneous detonation of their kiloton-yield warheads. These were intended to test the vulnerability of incoming nuclear warheads to nuclear effects and thus to justify the deployment of a new Soviet

9. Aktanberli, Ploshadka-7, and Degelen Mountain.
10. Near Semipalatinsk, in northeastern Kazakhstan, and on Novaya Zemlya, an Arctic island in Russia, north of the Ural Mountains.

anti-ballistic missile (ABM) system around Moscow. For theatrics, there was a world-record fifty-eight-megaton blast, fittingly conducted in anticipation of Halloween (not a Soviet holiday) on October 30, 1961. Even amidst this typhoon of terror, however, there were environmental concerns among the Soviet nuclear community. This latter bomb, known as Big Ivan, was de-rated[11] from its full one-hundred-megaton potential to accommodate radioactive fallout concerns; only 3 percent of its yield came from fission reactions.[12] The radiochemical analysis of the Soviet test debris, coupled with the detection of quite unusual electromagnetic signals by U.S. collectors, indicated significant breakthroughs in Soviet nuclear weapon technology. It had been a well-planned test series, long in the works. In conversations with Soviet insiders years later, it became clear that no Soviet nuclear scientists had been laid off during the moratorium; no facilities had been shuttered; no radical design options were foreclosed. From the beginning, the Soviet government intended to resume nuclear testing when the time was right.

The American response was an immediate resumption of underground experiments in Nevada. Testing in the atmosphere over the Pacific took place from April to November 1962. In reliance on the moratorium becoming a permanent condition, the United States had abandoned its Bikini and Eniwetok facilities, while the British, equipped with a longer view of history, had maintained her island sites at Christmas and Johnston Islands, making those sites available to the Americans for the 1962 trials. When completed, the American tests explained some of the Soviet achievements, led to a significant modernization of the Polaris and Minuteman missile forces, and improved the safety and security of all U.S. nuclear weapons. But as a reminder of how dangerously complex the world can be, these American nuclear tests continued right through the Cuban Missile Crisis of late October 1962, sending spurious signals into those very tense negotiations at the worst possible times.

## THE LIMITED TEST BAN TREATY OF 1963

As the atmospheric tests of 1962 wore on, and with the resolution of the Cuban Missile Crisis in the autumn of that year, nuclear governments came to appreciate the need for constraint; scientific staffs and political leaders turned their attention to safety. The Hot Line Agreement between the United States and U.S.S.R.[13] was signed on June 20, 1963; a limited test ban treaty was carefully negotiated during

11. By the substitution of tungsten or lead for certain uranium components.
12. According to one of the designers, Yuri Smirnov, at the 1996 Dubna Conference. Confirmed by Prof. Alexei Pevnitiski at Arzamas-16.
13. Formally the "Understanding . . . Regarding the Establishment of a Direct Communications Link."

that same summer. This latter accord would not ban all nuclear tests,[14] nor were there many safeguards built in, but an end to atmospheric contamination seemed to be in the best interests of all concerned. The resulting agreement, known formally as the Treaty Banning Nuclear Weapons Tests in the Atmosphere, in Outer Space, and Under Water, was signed in Moscow on August 5, 1963. It entered into force, after ratification by the appropriate national authorities, on October 10 of that year. The hot line and the Limited Test Ban Treaty (LTBT) were John Kennedy's parting gifts to mankind.

The initial signatories to the Limited Test Ban Treaty were the United States, United Kingdom, and U.S.S.R. During the autumn of that year, more than a hundred other nations, few ever likely to go nuclear, also signed up. Throughout the ensuing decade most other UN member states followed suit, with a few interesting exceptions and several disingenuous participants. Iran, Israel, Pakistan, the Republic of Korea (South Korea), and Taiwan all signed. Since doing so, India and Pakistan have tested underground. Your authors believe the Israelis tested at least once in the atmosphere. Iran and Taiwan remain to be heard from.

Four states never signed the Limited Test Ban Treaty: The Democratic People's Republic of North Korea,[15] Cuba, France, and the People's Republic of China. North Korea has since tested (actually misfired) a nuclear device underground. Cuba is an erratic dictatorship in transition. And, at the time of the treaty's introduction, France and China, two of the postwar Big Five, were certain to test. Both have subsequently done so in the atmosphere, although both nations appear to have long since discontinued that practice.

By the time the LTBT had gone into effect in October 1963, France had already gone nuclear with a February 1960 atmospheric test. Three more tests followed in rapid succession. Toward the end of 1961, however, France shifted to underground testing. It continued in that mode until 1966, when its rights to test in Algeria expired and it began to push the thermonuclear envelope. Those considerations led France to return to atmospheric testing, in French Polynesia, in 1966.

On October 16, 1964, a year after the LTBT took effect, the People's Republic of China joined the nuclear club by firing a twenty-two-kiloton nuclear device atop a tower in the Lop Nur desert. China continued to test in the atmosphere for five years, and then tested both underground and in the atmosphere for another decade.

---

14. Underground nuclear tests would be allowed, and the superpowers continued to do so for the duration of the Cold War. China and France continued to test in the atmosphere for another decade.
15. Formally known as the Democratic People's Republic of Korea.

By the end of the 1970s, the testing of nuclear weapons in the atmosphere appears to have become a practice of the past. The post–Cold War, Third World proliferators seem content to test underground, but that may be because their "nuclear events" may not be physics experiments at all, just political statements—and bluffs. Tunnels and shafts help mask nuclear tests, but they also keep the strontium and cesium away from our children. For whatever reason, the end of atmospheric nuclear tests seems to have been achieved, and that is certainly a step in the right direction.

# FRANCE AND ISRAEL: THE APPRENTICES

F rance was the fourth sovereign state to gain entry to the nuclear weapons club. France's early nuclear leadership warranted greater seniority, but the European wars and the political chaos to follow delayed the admissions process for over a decade.

To open the twentieth century, French scientists Marie and Pierre Curie found radioactivity to be the result of nuclear transitions. In the 1920s, Louis de Broglie discovered the duality of light, being both wave and particle. In the late 1930s, Frédéric Joliot and his wife Irene Curie, daughter of the radioactivity pioneers, were awarded the Nobel Prize in Chemistry for their discovery of artificially induced radioactivity. They adopted the joint name Joliot-Curie in honor of Irene's parents and their desire to carry on the family's pioneering work.

In 1939, Frédéric Joliot-Curie was tracking Otto Hahn's discovery of nuclear fission. He replicated those experiments and saw the possibility of a chain reaction resulting from the multiplication of neutrons. Later that year, Joliot-Curie, along with physicists Lew Kowarsky and Francis Perrin, filed a patent application for a nuclear weapon based on their discoveries. As a man of foresight, Joliot-Curie also ordered six tons of uranium oxide from Belgium and nearly all the heavy water available in Norway. As the winds of war began to blow from the east, he then arranged for both of these reactor-essential commodities to be shipped to Britain and then on to Canada.

As World War II exploded around him, Joliot-Curie stayed in Paris while many of his peers fled to Britain and then Canada to assist the British in their nuclear reactor work at Chalk River. The list of émigrés included Bertrand Goldschmidt, who became a pioneer in the chemistry of plutonium recovery from reactor fuel rods; Hans von Halban and Lew Kowarsky, who physically carried the Norwegian heavy water from Paris to the New World; and fellow physicists Jules Gueron and Pierre Auger.

General Charles de Gaulle also fled Paris, but he settled into London, where, on June 18, 1940, he broadcast a call for all Frenchmen to resist the German occupation;

he declared himself to be the leader of the Free French. De Gaulle organized and led those forces; he then became head of the Provisional Government of France, recognized as such by the Allies as they returned to the continent. During these same years Joliot-Curie, remaining in Paris, avoided any scientific work that would have been of help to the Nazis; in 1942 he joined the Communist Party. In the United States and Canada, nuclear science surged ahead without him.

In July 1944, de Gaulle visited North America, and on July 11, he met with French physicists working at Chalk River. In spite of all security rules, they told him of the Allied nuclear weapon program; he urged their return to France as soon as possible, to pick up where they had left off. Pierre Auger and Jules Gueron promptly did so, resigning their positions at Chalk River and returning to Metropolitan France as the Allies liberated Normandy. Soon after their return, Auger and Gueron undoubtedly met with their patron, Frédéric Joliot-Curie. We must assume they told Joliot-Curie of the U.S. A-bomb program and their vision of nuclear work to be done in postwar France. It is quite likely that Joliot-Curie then passed on that information to his already well-informed Soviet friends.

With the end of the war in Europe in May 1945, de Gaulle assumed governmental authority throughout France. He had his hands full, but the U.S. attacks on Hiroshima and Nagasaki impressed upon him the political importance of nuclear weapons. On October 18, 1945, three months after the end of the war, and in consultation with Joliot-Curie, de Gaulle created the world's first atomic energy commission. It was done with a three-line letter that commenced with, "It is directed that . . . ." By separate letter he installed Frédéric Joliot-Curie as high commissioner of the new agency. The French Atomic Energy Commission (CEA) was to develop nuclear energy to benefit French interests in the fields of science, industry, and national defense. "Industry" referred to the fact that France had no coal or oil; nuclear energy was to power postwar France. "National defense" meant an A-bomb, as soon as possible. After the French loss to, and occupation by, Nazi Germany, France needed to reestablish its credibility as one of the Big Four European victors. Joining the nuclear club would help.

Later, during that same October, France also held its first postwar election. As happened to Churchill in England and Truman's political party in the United States, the mantle of power was stripped from France's wartime hero. The socialists won that October election, and on January 10, 1946, after two months of parliamentary confrontation, Charles de Gaulle retired to his country home in Colombey-les-Deux-Églises, not to be seen for another dozen years.

The postwar socialists in France were closely allied with the communists of the Soviet Union. Many leading members of the French Resistance had been communists, and Joliot-Curie had been a party member for four years. With the elections of October 1945, the French governmental mandate for a nuclear weapon program dissolved. The Soviet Union did not wish to see any more Western states gaining such a capability. At the same time, Joliot-Curie's unabashed communist connections precluded any close nuclear relationships between France and the Anglo-American scientific community. Physics work within France refocused on nuclear power. In July 1946, the CEA moved into Fort de Chatillon, on the outskirts of Paris, where it started work on its first nuclear reactor. The EL-1 utilized uranium oxide and heavy water; it first went critical on December 15, 1948. The French achieved separation of plutonium, from a second-generation reactor at Chatillon, in 1949. For the rest of that postwar decade, Joliot-Curie's philosophy guided all French nuclear work; that vision did not include weapons.

## AUGUST 1949

By the end of the 1940s, the Soviet Union had become a clear and present danger to all of the Western democracies. Coups in the East, the Berlin blockade, and the growing muscle of the Red Army made that clear. In August 1949, the Western allies met to form the North Atlantic Treaty Organization (NATO), and on August 29, 1949, the Soviet Union made it clear why, by testing its first A-bomb in the deserts of Kazakhstan. The shot was detected by excellent scientific work within the United States and announced by President Truman on September 23.

The following April, Joliot-Curie was removed as the CEA high commissioner. The job went to Francis Perrin, the son of a Nobel laureate and an early colleague of Joliot-Curie's in chain-reaction physics. Perrin was a more politically acceptable, non-communist leader, having spent his wartime years in New York and London. At that same time, the Office of Special Weapons was created within the army.

In June 1950, North Korea invaded the South; in October, the Chinese communists "volunteered" to help and nearly drove the Americans off that peninsula. By 1951, the NATO allies were bracing for a follow-up invasion from Eastern Europe, their defense to be organized and led by Gen. Dwight Eisenhower, the conquering hero of World War II. Eisenhower had returned to take command of the once-again-allied forces of Western Europe. The political climate on the continent had undergone a stark change.

On August 21, 1951, Pierre Guillaumat was installed as the new administrator-general of the CEA, operating under the direction of High Commissioner Perrin. Guillaumat promptly drew up a five-year nuclear development plan. It called for the construction of several plutonium-production reactors as well as a reprocessing facility at Marcoule. The implication: when and if France decided to develop an A-bomb, the infrastructure for weapons would be in place. Those facilities were only a hedge. The military was not yet fully supportive of a nuclear weapons program, for while the army had organized a special committee to study weapons' effects, any appropriations for a French nuclear weapon could only come out of the army's budget—not a pleasing prospect. The National Assembly approved the Guillaumat Plan for reactor development in July 1952; the G-1 reactor at Marcoule went critical four years later, on January 7, 1956.

## DIEN BIEN PHU AND SUEZ

The French Army changed its point of view after its May 1954 defeat at Dien Bien Phu, an isolated fort in the northwest jungles of Vietnam. Something more was needed. The French could not depend on others to maintain their colonial reach. Their image as a world power was slipping away. In the discussions that followed, the nuclear option again came to the table. There was no top-down decision to proceed; that result was achieved by consensus-building, formalized by one of France's stronger prime ministers. Pierre Mendes-France had come to power in the wake of Dien Bien Phu and the growing revolt in Algeria. He raised the nuclear alternative at a cabinet meeting on December 26, 1954. By meeting's end the decision had been made to proceed with the development of an A-bomb. The army immediately organized the Bureau of General Studies (i.e., nukes), and in the spring of 1955, it transferred money to the CEA to start serious weapons *research*, not development. Within a year, however, events in Egypt brought French nuclear policy into a much sharper focus.

The Suez Canal, built by the French and Egyptian governments in the mid-nineteenth century, connected the Indian Ocean and Red Sea to the Mediterranean. It opened in 1869, and within a few years, Britain had bought out the Egyptian share. With the coming of the petroleum age, the Suez Canal became the oil artery connecting Middle Eastern wells to European consumers.

In 1952, officers of the Egyptian Army overthrew Egypt's King Farouk. The eventual leader of that group, Gamal Abdel Nasser, was highly antagonistic toward the new state of Israel. He was also an Arab nationalist who supported the anti-colonial rebels in Algeria. On top of all that, Nasser resented French and British control of "his" canal. On July 26, 1956, he announced the nationalization of that canal. The British and French were outraged; the Israelis saw an opportunity to settle some old scores, to buy some protection. From that date, the nuclear ambitions of aging France and newborn Israel became as intertwined as serpents in a tree.

## GENESIS

Israel was born of Jewish terror and British exhaustion, carved out of Palestine on May 16, 1948. It acquired true independence a year later after a bloody war with five of its Arab neighbors. David Ben-Gurion, a native of Poland, was the founding father of Israel. He had served as chairman of the Jewish Agency Executive, the governing body of the Jewish settlement in Palestine, since 1935. After independence, Ben-Gurion held power as the new nation's prime minister and minister of defense. He brought to those offices a grim memory of the Holocaust and a bleak belief that any armistice with the Arabs would be just that: a temporary pause until they could regroup and attack again. Such wars would continue, he believed, until the Arabs accepted their 1949 defeat as final. Pending such realization, survival had to be based on science; brainpower was the only raw material widely available within Israel. When Ben-Gurion left office fifteen years later, he confirmed his earlier views: "Our numbers are small, [but] there is one thing in which we are not inferior to any other people in the world—this is the Jewish brain, and science starts [there]." Within a few years of independence, Israel's "reliance on science" had become code words for the pursuit of nuclear technology and, in time, weapons.

The longest journey begins with one step. The first for Israel, as with most other nuclear proliferators, was to identify her brightest and best youngsters, sending them overseas for study. In 1949, the Ben-Gurion government identified its six top physics students and dispatched them to Europe's centers of learning: two to Zurich, two to England, one to Amsterdam, and one to study with Fermi in Chicago. All six returned two years later to lead Israel into the nuclear age. In time they became the mandarins of Israel's nuclear weapons program.

In June 1952, Ben-Gurion appointed his trusted scientific advisor, Ernst Bergmann, to head up a new and discretely created Israeli Atomic Energy Commission. The existence of the organization was not even publicly acknowledged for two years, but within its first year, the Israeli AEC and its chairman had established a working relationship with their French counterparts in Paris. In 1953, as a result of those relationships, two more Israeli scientists were invited to study reactor physics in France, one at the Institute of Nuclear Science and Techniques, a newly organized weapons-oriented laboratory at Saclay. The other went to the Chatillon Nuclear Establishment, home of the first French nuclear reactor. And during that same year (1953), Ben-Gurion chose a remarkable young thirty-year old, Shimon Peres, to become director-general of the Ministry of Defense. It was Peres who, over the ensuing decade, wove the intricate web of Israel's nuclear cooperation with France that produced the bottom-line results.[1]

At the end of 1953, Israel was in pursuit of nuclear technology, not yet a nuclear weapon, but at age sixty-four, Ben-Gurion felt it was time to retire. Moshe Sharett

1. In 2007, Peres was elected to the presidency of Israel.

took over as prime minister. Pinhas Lavon became minister of defense and gave his name to the Lavon Affair, a hare-brained covert operation within Egypt, targeted at U.S. and U.K. installations. On July 14, 1954, agents of Israeli military intelligence[2] planted firebombs within U.S. Information Agency libraries in Cairo and Alexandria as well as a British-owned theater. The damage was to be blamed on the new post-Farouk leadership of Naguib and Nasser in Egypt; the objective was to stir up anti-Egyptian and thus pro-Israeli sentiment in the Anglo world.

The bombers, all native Egyptian, were incompetent. They used homemade acid and nitroglycerine, placed within packages designed to go off after the libraries' closing hours. Perhaps this was an effort to avoid casualties, but the firebombs did not work very well. They did little damage, caused no casualties, and one blew up in a conspirator's pocket. This gave the Egyptian authorities a suspect, an apartment to search, and pretty soon yielded the names of the conspirators. They were dealt with harshly, but when the Israeli origin of the attacks became known, the political repercussions were disastrous. Within a year, Ben-Gurion had been recalled to reassume the Israeli defense portfolio, replacing Mr. Lavon. By April 1955, Ben-Gurion was back in full charge as prime minister.

During his brief retirement, Ben-Gurion had an epiphany regarding the role of nuclear weapons in protecting the security of Israel. He returned to the leadership endowed with a firm, though seldom expressed, commitment to those weapons. For the next eight years, his goal would be pursued with a single-minded determination, although the campaign would remain hidden behind clouds of secrecy, disinformation, and vagueness. It would be funded off-budget, on a huge scale, by overseas donors[3] to preclude visibility and debate. During those years only a handful of Israeli officials ever understood the true scope or intent of the Israeli nuclear weapons program.

## CONFLUENCE

In the summer of 1955, Ben-Gurion oversaw the dispatch of more scientists to Saclay and Chatillon, but this time they were told exactly why they were going: it was to be "A most secret national project, the building of an Israeli nuclear device." At the same time, an agreement for "peaceful nuclear cooperation" with the United States under the Atoms for Peace plan formalized the extraction of nuclear know-how from that nation. The transaction included the Israeli purchase of a small nuclear research reactor.

---

2. An organization known as Aman. The operation was not run by the more professional national security service, the Mossad.

3. In the United States, an organization known as the Committee of Thirty supported the project.

In the autumn of 1955, the clouds of the next Arab-Israeli war moved into sight. Nasser entered into an agreement with the arms-producing Soviet client state of Czechoslovakia to acquire a substantial shipment of weapons. A week thereafter, he announced the closure of the Straits of Tiran to Israeli shipping, thus cutting off Red Sea access to the Israeli port of Elat. "There can be no peace with Israel," Nasser said at the time, "because we demand vengeance." As 1955 drew to a close, Israel's Shimon Peres and the French government of Guy Mollet came to recognize their common problem. Both French and Israeli citizens had experienced the horrors of Hitler's vengeance first hand; both now faced a new devil. Gamal Abdel Nasser yearned for the destruction of Israel, but he also sought to "free" the French colony of Algeria, thereby turning a million French settlers into refugees.

French pioneers had begun their move into northern Africa, across the Mediterranean from their homeland, in the early nineteenth century. France annexed Algeria as a colony in 1830. For a century, the French tightly controlled the lives of the Muslim natives while seeking to "civilize" Algeria with educational opportunities, business activity, and infrastructure. However, their European arrogance also led their Muslim subjects to revolt. In March 1954, the revolutionaries organized in Nasser's Egypt; on November 1, 1954, they declared war on the French government with a series of simultaneous attacks on police stations and government buildings throughout the colony. The revolt grew, and the million French settlers, known as the *pieds noir,* struck back—brutally. Nasser's actions in 1955 and 1956 lit the torch that welded French and Israeli interests into military partnership and nuclear alliance.

At first it was an armaments, technology, and intelligence-sharing agreement, executed in secret at Vermers, France, on June 22, 1956. That understanding built significant ties between the French and Israeli aerospace and nuclear industries, and it initiated a special relationship between French and Israeli intelligence. The target was Egypt. Then came the detonating spark. Within weeks of the Vermers agreement, Nasser announced his takeover of the Suez Canal.

In response, during the late summer of 1956, representatives of Israel and France, joined by Great Britain, met amidst great secrecy at Sèvres, a southwestern suburb of Paris. They settled on a plan to deal with the problem of Gamal Abdel Nasser: In the autumn, Israel would invade the Sinai and head toward the canal. The British and French would then intervene, instructing the Israeli and Egyptian forces to withdraw ten miles from either side of the canal. The British and French were to install troops within the Canal Zone, reassert control, and resume collection of revenues. The plan was given the code name Operation Musketeer. It was timed to coincide with presidential elections in the United States in hopes that America's pro-Israel politics and the delicacy of its electoral climate would preclude American intervention.

In conjunction with that meeting French and Israeli representatives met separately to start discussions on the matter of nuclear development. In early October, France's Bertrand Goldschmidt and Israel's Shimon Peres and Ernst Bergmann met in Paris to work out the details. The purpose was understood by all: to give Israel a "nuclear capability."

On October 29, 1956, the Israelis invaded Gaza and the Sinai as planned. On October 30, the British and French issued their withdrawal request. Nasser immediately rebuffed it, and the bombardment of Egypt began. With that, President Eisenhower made his decision to oppose the entire operation. On November 5, British paratroopers jumped into Egypt. The invasion went well, but the politics did not. On November 6, the Soviets issued an ultimatum to France, Britain, and Israel to cease and desist; more specifically, they threatened actions that would menace "the very existence of Israel." On that same November 6 (Election Day in the United States),[4] Eisenhower publicly announced his opposition to the Anglo-French incursion, and he announced a cutoff of all aid to the contending parties. On November 8, Israel's foreign minister, Meir, and the director-general of her Ministry of Defense, Peres, were sent to Paris, in great haste and secrecy, to ascertain what help, if any, they could expect from France in the event of a showdown with the Soviets. The answer, from the French defense minister, Bourges-Maunoury, and foreign minister, Pineau, was, "Not much." But it was at these talks that the idea of substantial, longer-term French assistance to an Israeli nuclear weapons program was conceived, perhaps in compensation for Israel's promise to withdraw from the just-conquered Sinai.

As the second week of November 1956 drew to a close, the French, British, and Israelis had been humiliated. There was little they could do in Egypt, but in the face of the American and Soviet threats, there was a lot they could do at home. French and Israelis alike felt they could no longer count on their once-reliable American ally. The week after the Suez confrontation, French Prime Minister Guy Mollet met with his minister of defense, directing him to start work at once on a clearly defined French nuclear weapon program. The Marcoule reactor had already gone critical in January 1956. During the year to follow, it would produce its first twelve kilograms of plutonium. On November 30, 1956, only a month after the Suez fiasco, the French army and CEA executed a nuclear weapon development agreement; the army transferred funds to facilitate the testing and production of nuclear weapons.

At the same time, the French government addressed the details of its nuclear pledge to Israel. It agreed to build a nuclear reactor amidst the Negev Desert, it

4. Eisenhower won reelection with 58 percent of the popular vote and a 531–48 margin in the Electoral College.

contracted to supply the natural uranium to fuel that reactor, and it promised to reprocess the resulting irradiated fuel rods. The French cabinet approved this deal in May 1957. Some agreements were reduced to writing, the first being signed by the appropriate political ministers, reflecting the legal rights and obligations of the nations involved. The second, executed by officials of the French CEA and the Israeli AEC, dealt with the technical aspects of the transaction. It specified the construction of a nuclear reactor, based on the forty-megawatt G-1 reactor at Marcoule; created a financial-front organization to mask the transaction; and authorized direct contracts between Israel's AEC and French industry (Saint-Gobain Nucléaire) to build the plutonium reprocessing facility. These agreements were executed on October 3, 1957. Other aspects of the deal, relating to weapons development, were left as oral understandings between Shimon Peres and France's next revolving-door prime minister, Maurice Bourges-Maunoury.[5]

By the end of 1957, excavation had started at a place once known as Beer Sheeba but now given the new name Dimona, and within a few months thereafter, the ever-inquisitive American U-2s had taken its picture. One of America's great photo-interpreters, Dino Brugioni spotted the excavation, noted its similarity to the French reactor facility at Marcoule, and prepared a briefing for the U.S. National Command Authority (NCA). It went to President Eisenhower in early 1958, at which time the CIA briefers were astonished by the reaction of the usually intelligence-hungry retired general. For reasons unknown, he showed no interest and asked no questions about Dimona. It was as though Eisenhower did not want to hear about it, and/or those on the White House staff, sympathetic to Israel's survival, did not want the subject raised. The U-2s continued to photograph the construction, and agents on the ground noted hundreds of French employees in the area, yet the White House continued to ignore the whole project.

In France, nuclear events moved in lock step with those in the Negev Desert. In early 1957, the prime minister of France signed an official order for the manufacture of a nuclear device, to be tested in the first quarter of 1960. He also laid out a formal structure for France's nuclear weapons program. But at that same time, France had to deal with the growing revolt in Algeria, a rebellion that, by 1956, had turned into a full civil war. Within two years, that war would bring both strong leadership and a sense of nuclear urgency to France.

5. During the 1950s, prior to the second coming of de Gaulle and the Fifth Republic, France suffered through fifteen governments, each lasting for an average of less than eight months. The Peres–Bourges-Mannoury agreements are confirmed in Michael Bar-Zohar, *Shimon Peres: The Biography* (New York: Random House, 2007).

## ALGERIA

By 1958 the *pieds noir* were winning the police actions and military battles within the cities as well as the desert villages of Algeria, but they were losing the political war on the streets of Paris and in the hallways of New York. The French settlers and army resented the vacillation of the weak-willed government in Paris. They joined forces to bring it down, seeking the return of a "real general" and thus a true victory in Algeria. On June 1, 1958, Charles de Gaulle returned to power as prime minister of the Fourth Republic.

The war in Algeria gave de Gaulle his mandate; he used that power to move ahead forcefully on a broad front. One area of immediate interest was nuclear weapons. The influence of Frédéric Joliot-Curie was totally gone; he had died the previous summer. Upon assuming the office of prime minister, de Gaulle first endorsed the nuclear weapon policies of his predecessors. The week after that, he appointed Gen. Charles Ailleret to lead a new Special Weapons Command within the army. A week later, de Gaulle authorized a nuclear test, to be held in the Algerian Sahara within two years. General Ailleret was to command that task force. By the end of 1958, de Gaulle had directed and approved the construction of a uranium enrichment facility, based on gaseous diffusion technology, at Pierrelatte.[6]

When de Gaulle returned to power at age sixty-seven, he was a man in a hurry, but he was also a man concerned about his country's nuclear linkage to Israel. Within weeks of his assumption of power, de Gaulle became aware of the "improper military collaboration established between Tel Aviv and Paris after the Suez expedition, which placed Israelis within all levels of the French services."[7] De Gaulle ordered the Franco-Israeli collaboration stopped, but those orders were given to Jacques Soustelle, his minister of atomic energy, a staunch supporter of Israel and a man with an independent power base within the French Parliament, so nothing of substance happened. Arrangements between French industry and the Israelis remained in place.

In the autumn of 1958, the Fourth Republic dissolved itself, giving birth to the Fifth Republic, an entity with strong executive powers. On January 8, 1959, de Gaulle became its president. He had a broad agenda; in the field of nuclear weapons he wanted immediate results. He sought a full spectrum of strategic nuclear weapon systems in the shortest possible time. In discussions with his nuclear advisors he made

---

6. Pierrelatte began to deliver low-enrichment uranium in 1965; highly enriched, for weapon purposes, in 1967.

7. Charles de Gaulle, *Memoirs of Hope*, trans. Terence Kilmartin (New York: Simon & Schuster, 1971), 266.

his priorities clear: weapon yield was not really important. What counted was an immediate capability. When queried about H-bomb work—in the light of American, Soviet, and by then British accomplishments in that field—de Gaulle responded, "These things take a lot of time." He wanted to see a French A-bomb test as soon as possible, without distractions, and he then wanted those weapons fitted onto Mirage fighter-bombers for operational deployment. During the 1958 to 1963 time period, an H-bomb was not of interest to Charles de Gaulle, and thus it received little attention from the French government.

De Gaulle also continued his efforts to end the Franco-Israeli subterranean nuclear cooperation, but his bureaucracy was controlled by Israeli supporters, and his industry wished to continue with its most profitable work. Throughout 1959, as the French

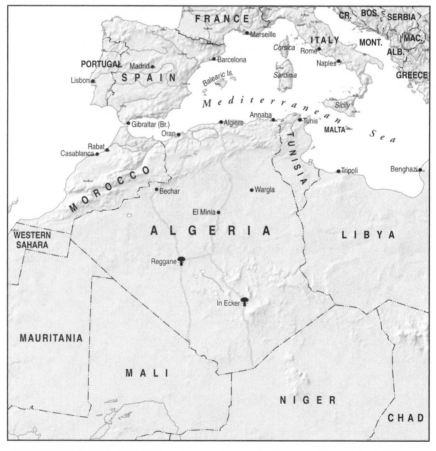

Algeria, showing the location of the French nuclear test sites at Reggane and In Ecker. *Meridian Mapping*

were preparing for their first nuclear test, it is clear that dozens of Israeli scientists then stationed within the Saclay weapons center, the Marcoule reactor facility, and the other CEA institutions were observing and participating in nuclear weapon design work.

During the year of de Gaulle's accession to presidential power, Saclay produced a design, Marcoule cranked out the needed plutonium, and on February 13, 1960, General Ailleret's men detonated France's first A-bomb on a tower at Reggane, an outpost in the Sahara Desert six hundred miles south of Oran. That test occurred forty-nine months after the Marcoule plutonium-production reactor first went critical. Gerboise Bleue, as the device was known, delivered a yield of sixty-five kilotons—large by A-bomb standards. Some wags have noted that on February 13, 1960, two nations went nuclear with one test.

Shortly after the first French nuclear test, Jaques Soustelle vacated the atomic energy ministry. The CEA high commissioner, Francis Perrin, then sought an audience with de Gaulle to explain the extent of the lingering Franco-Israeli nuclear relationship. It was only then that the president of France was able to give clear, unambiguous, and enforceable orders to stop collaboration. On May 13, 1960, the French foreign minister, Maurice Couve de Murville, notified the Israeli ambassador to France, Walter Eitan, that the agreements and understandings of October 1957 were at an end.

As Commissioner Perrin made clear in subsequent interviews, France and Israel worked closely together for two years in the late 1950s to design an atom bomb. Perrin confirmed that this work was based on technology first acquired from the Americans during World War II at Chalk River.[8]

Gerboise Bleue was followed six weeks later by a second, improved design, Gerboise Blanche, and then, in December 1960, by a third test, Gerboise Rouge. The amazing thing is these tests were carried out in a colony torn by civil war. It was as though the Americans had started testing nuclear weapons in Long Binh Province, in Vietnam, in 1971. Those tests within Algeria were also conducted in the atmosphere, contrary to the nuclear testing moratorium adopted by the United States, United Kingdom, and U.S.S.R. two years before.

These events at Reggane came to the attention of the *pieds noir* and the mutinous army generals supporting them. The latter, under Gen. Maurice Challe, had staged a *putsch* within Algeria on April 22, 1961. In the days that followed, the generals moved to take custody of one of the nuclear devices then located in-country. An experimental nuclear device might come in handy in their fight with the rebels or in their confrontations with the authorities in Metropolitan France. General Ailleret had scheduled a fourth shot at Reggane for April 25, 1961, but as the rebels closed in,

8. Pierre Péan, *Les Deux Bombes* (Paris: Fayard, 1982).

79

attempting to seize the weapon, he decided to fire it off prematurely. As a degraded explosion, Gerboise Verte gave less than a kiloton.

After de Gaulle's cease-and-desist orders of May 1960, Ben-Gurion flew to Paris to seek a reprieve, by means of ambiguity. He succeeded, once again breathing life into the lingering Franco-Israeli nuclear relationship. Ben-Gurion and de Gaulle agreed that while the French government would remove itself from further involvement in the Israeli nuclear weapon projects, French industry would be allowed to continue work under existing contracts. Thus it was that throughout the de Gaulle years, those industrial firms responsible for the construction of the Dimona complex never received any definitive orders to stop work. They simply finished their jobs and went home.

After the Algerian *putsch*, and in the face of growing international—especially African—pressure, de Gaulle came to the conclusion that France could not win the war in Algeria. He initiated peace talks with the rebels while, amazingly, continuing nuclear tests in their back yard. After the April 1961 misfire, and in the face of growing opposition to testing in the atmosphere, the French moved their nuclear tests underground, to an oasis at In Ecker, a hundred miles south and east of Reggane. The first underground French nuclear test took place there on November 7, 1961, amidst agonizing peace negotiations in France.

On March 18, 1962, at Evian, the French government and the Algerian FLN[9] signed a peace accord that was not an immediate surrender by either party. The killing stopped the next day; Algeria's independence was recognized, but France maintained her economic interests, access to Algerian oil and gas, and continued use for five years of the In Ecker nuclear test facility. A dozen underground nuclear tests followed, mostly in the twenty-kiloton range, as France modified its designs to accommodate the needs of weaponization and delivery to target. De Gaulle was pleased with his membership in the nuclear club; his wakeup call would not come for another year, from the deserts of Xinjiang Province in northwestern China.

Given French dependence on foreign coal and oil, France continued to pursue an active nuclear power program. Over three-quarters of France's electricity now originates with nuclear reactors, many of which provide both power and plutonium. The French exported that technology aggressively, in some cases to legitimate and properly licensed operators overseas. However, the French also designed, built, and sold plutonium-producing reactors, modeled on their facility at Marcoule, to some interesting proliferators.

9. The Front de Liberation National (National Liberation Front), umbrella organization for the rebels.

## THE COMING OF JOHN KENNEDY

In early 1959, photo interpreter Dino Brugioni again briefed the White House on Dimona. There could be no doubt Israel was going for the bomb with the assistance of French industry. The facilities at Dimona bore too much of a similarity to the plutonium production complex at Marcoule, France. The Eisenhower administration began to take the CIA warnings seriously, but they still did nothing. Then came election day in the United States.[10] John Kennedy was the apparent winner; political transition was in the air, and the nuclear intelligence dam began to leak. First to appear were some excellent British ground-level photographs of Dimona. Then, at the end of November, came the report from a traveling academic, qualified in nuclear science, who had been visiting the technical centers of Israel. Along the way he had made his way into Dimona. Upon returning to the United States, the traveler advised the State Department of his findings in simple, non-bureaucratic English: the Dimona facility was "a Marcoule-type reactor being constructed with French technical assistance." He backed up that observation with his analysis of Israeli scientific priorities. Next, in early December, photographs taken earlier by U.S. Army officers made their way into the intelligence stream. Subsequently, British sources unearthed Israel's covert purchase of twenty tons of heavy water from Norway's Norsk Hydro. (That purchase may have been accomplished through a British conduit.) By year-end 1960, the U.S. and British intelligence communities were converging on a well-documented end-point: Israel was building a large, plutonium-producing nuclear reactor at Dimona.

That was still a tale the White House did not want to hear. Administration inaction outraged Eisenhower's AEC chairman. On December 18, during the Eisenhower-Kennedy transition, John McCone took his case to *Meet the Press* and leaked the story to John Finney of the *New York Times*. The Finney story ran on December 19. It set off a firestorm, both within the United States and abroad. National Security Council members, meeting privately with President Eisenhower, confirmed that Dimona was a plutonium producer. The secretary of state advised it had cost more than a hundred million dollars,[11] perhaps 10 percent of Israel's entire gross domestic product during the 1950s. Secretary of State Christian A. Herter agreed with U.S. intelligence, that the Israeli nuclear program had been funded with private donations and diverted public-aid funds on a scale that would have dominated the entire Israeli economy had the Dimona complex been funded internally.

On December 21, 1960, Ben-Gurion responded to the public outcry with obfuscation. In a prepared speech to the Israeli Knesset (Parliament), he identified

10. November 8, 1960.
11. About a billion in 2008 dollars.

the Dimona reactor as having "a capacity of twenty-four megawatts, which will serve the needs of industry, agriculture, health, and science. . . designed exclusively for peaceful purposes, constructed under the direction of Israeli experts." His ambassador to the United States, in response to a State Department query, followed the same line, advising that Dimona was "a development of scientific knowledge for eventual industrial, agricultural, medical, and other scientific purposes." The Israeli ambassador said the French had assisted in only a minor way.

In its 1961 farewells, the Eisenhower administration advised Congress that, "We have been assured categorically at the highest level of the Israeli Government that Israel has no plans for the production of atomic weapons." Privately, however, Eisenhower's National Security Council (NSC) knew better. At a transition meeting between incoming and outgoing cabinet members, on January 19, 1961, the Eisenhower team advised its successors that the Israelis had a nuclear reactor capable of producing ninety kilograms (two hundred pounds) of weapons-grade plutonium by 1963,[12] and then said goodbye.

The Kennedy administration, to last but a thousand days, constituted the high tide of determined proliferation control. Kennedy made every effort to get American inspectors into Dimona. He hammered at the door but only got annual glimpses, visits by two or three American experts who were not briefed going in, misled during their few hours there, and unable to identify the real story as they left. His Limited Test Ban Treaty was a first. In 1963, he may have given serious thought to a pre-emptive strike[13] on China's embryonic nuclear facilities prior to its first test. In forming his cabinet, Kennedy put party considerations aside in picking a director of central intelligence. He turned to Eisenhower's disgruntled AEC chairman, John McCone, to handle intelligence responsibilities. McCone served with a diligence that sometimes annoyed. McCone's agents found the first indicators of a Soviet missile deployment into Cuba during the summer of 1962, a message the Kennedy White House was not willing to entertain until shown U-2 photos during that fateful October. And in weighing the problem of Israeli nuclear developments, Kennedy recognized the importance of the Jewish vote to his party.[14] Meyer "Mike" Feldman was appointed to serve as deputy general counsel to the president; his job was to provide a White House entrée for that constituency. He did so with great skill throughout Kennedy's term and beyond.

In May 1961, Kennedy met with Ben-Gurion, who continued to lie, claiming desalinization and cheap energy as the ultimate purpose of Dimona. In May 1963,

12. This estimate was a little high. The Dimona reactor only commenced production at the end of 1963.
13. In conjunction with the Soviet Union
14. Eighty percent voted Democratic in 1960.

U.S. intelligence chief McCone waved a red flag, warning of ballistic missiles *and* nuclear weapons in the Mideast. In response, Kennedy sent harsh messages to Ben-Gurion, but to no avail; delay and obfuscation were Ben-Gurion's stock in trade. Perhaps the prime minister knew best. Since the emergence of Israel's nuclear capability, the every-decade Arab-Israeli wars have ceased. Or is it like the shifting of tectonic plates, with energy being stored for a greater convulsion to come?

John Kennedy was the defining antiproliferation president, but those concerns were among the casualties of Dallas. As Lyndon Johnson took over the reins of government, he made his priorities clear to his staff: "Good nonproliferation policies lead to bad politics." Johnson had even closer ties to the pro-Israel fundraisers within the Democratic Party. He wanted nothing to do with a U.S.-Israeli confrontation. By the end of 1963, John Kennedy was gone, David Ben-Gurion had left office, the Israeli nuclear reactor at Dimona was producing plutonium, France was testing underground at In Ecker, and the world's fourth and fifth nuclear states had been born.

## The Big Four Nuclear Club members (and one affiliate), in order of accession

| Country | Decision to go nuclear | Principle triggering event | First prod'n reactor went critical | First A-bomb test, location | Time, reactor to bomb test |
|---------|------------------------|----------------------------|-------------------------------------|------------------------------|-----------------------------|
| U.S.A | Dec. 1941 | War in Europe, 1939–40 | Hanford, Sept. 1944 | July 1945, New Mexico | 10 months |
| U.S.S.R | Aug. 1945 | Hiroshima & Nagasaki, 1945 | Mayak, June 1948 | Aug. 1949, Kazakhstan | 14 months |
| U.K. | Jan. 1947 | U.S. McMahon Act, 1946 | Windscale, July 1950 | Oct. 1952, Australia | 27 months |
| France | Dec. 1954 | Dien Bien Phu, May 1954 | Marcoule, Jan. 1956 | Feb. 1960, Algeria | 49 months |
| Israel | Nov. 1956 | Suez crisis, Nov. 1956 | Dimona, Dec. 1963 | Unknown | ~40 months* |

* Israel had nuclear weapons on hand in June 1967 and could have tested then.

# CHINA BREAKS
# THE EUROPEAN CARTEL

For millennia, while other civilizations remained isolated, the Chinese were the pioneers. They held the high ground of technology; they owned the seas. Every schoolchild, certainly in China, can recite the Four Great Chinese Inventions:

- The Egyptians may have invented papyrus—a marshland reed, flattened and dried to retain records—but it was the Chinese, in the second century of the Christian era, who invented paper. Cai Lun started milling tree bark, hemp, and rags into a flat, absorbing media on which oil-based inks could record the written word. The first paper mill only appeared in Europe a thousand years later.
- Magnetized stones first came into Chinese use during the pre-Christian era as fortune-telling devices; by the eleventh century the Chinese had adapted them to navigational use, supporting the largest navy in the world. The compass did not appear as a European invention for another hundred years.
- Gunpowder was a first-century AD Chinese invention, well integrated into Asian military technology a thousand years later. Fire-arrows (rockets) were used in the battle of Kaifeng in 1232, but gunpowder did not appear in Europe for another hundred years.
- Moveable-type printing was first seen in China in the middle of the eleventh century; the technology made its way to Korea two hundred years after that, but the complexity of the Chinese and Korean alphabets left the industrial honors to Johannes Gutenberg. He developed a truly useful, production-oriented printing machine, with moveable type, in Germany, but only two hundred years after the Chinese had shown the way.

All of this technology and much more supported the world's largest navy. The dawn of the fifteenth century saw armadas of behemoth Chinese ships exploring, trading with, and invading the coasts of Asia, Africa, and perhaps Australia. The Treasure Fleet of Adm. Chen Ho was an exploration machine, with each voyage boasting hundreds of ships and tens of thousands of men. Those multi-masted ships were substantially larger than today's football fields;[1] some carried troops, others only horses or provisions in addition to their sailing crew.

And then, in the middle of the fifteenth century, it all ended. As the Renaissance, Reformation, and Industrial Revolution swept Europe, the imperial court of China decided it had nothing to learn from the barbarians; their ways would merely corrupt the tranquility of the Middle Kingdom. In the mid-1400s, with the birth of Europeans Columbus, da Gama, and Magellan, and as Gutenberg was making possible the spread of European knowledge, a newly enthroned young emperor capitulated to the intrigues within his court; he ordered the burning of the Chinese fleet.

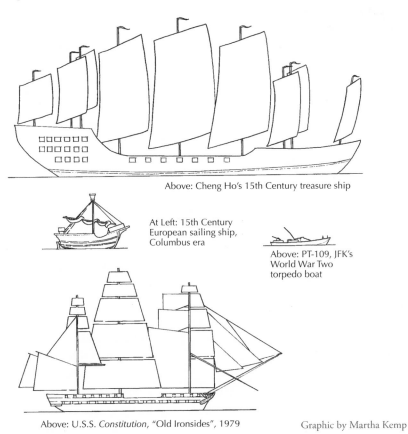

Above: Cheng Ho's 15th Century treasure ship

At Left: 15th Century European sailing ship, Columbus era

Above: PT-109, JFK's World War Two torpedo boat

Above: U.S.S. *Constitution*, "Old Ironsides", 1979

Graphic by Martha Kemp

1. Typically these ships were 350–400 feet long, with a beam of 150–180 feet.

It was no small fire. There were more than four thousand of those huge ships; only the fishing vessels were spared. China turned inward, generating three centuries of good government and great stability, but that stability was a curse, not a blessing, for it left the oceans to the Arabs and the Europeans. The Turks took Constantinople; other empires appeared in Persia and India; and the British, French and Portuguese, among others, took to the high seas. Four hundred years after the Chinese emperors abandoned their global reach, the advance men of the seafaring states were pounding on their doors. The Chinese tried to resist, but it was a losing proposition.

In the 1840s, there was a war with Britain, ending with the first of the "unequal treaties" that opened China's ports and ceded Hong Kong to the British. The 1850s saw more conflict, this time with both Britain and France, another unequal treaty, and more European access. The end of the nineteenth century saw the greatest insult of all: China's defeat at the hands of an industrialized Asian nation, Japan, that had (unwillingly) opened her doors to European ways. Japan had come to accept and exploit the Western technology, turning it against China at the end of the century. The Treaty of Shimonoseki, ending the Chinese-Japanese war of 1895, recognized China's loss, required that nation to pay tribute, required her recognition of Korean independence, and resulted in Japanese sovereignty over the islands of Formosa and the Pescadores.

With that defeat, China's weakness became apparent to all; the land grab was on. France seized Indochina; Britain took Burma; Japan formally annexed Korea; the foreign powers even set up their own enclaves within Shanghai, exempt from any Chinese law. During the turmoil there were attempts at reform; in 1911, the Ming Dynasty was overthrown. A republic took its place, but thirty years of world wars left that embryonic Chinese Republic in chaos. Order was only restored, through the greatest of brutality, with the coming of Mao Zedong's People's Republic of China in 1949. By then it was apparent to many that China's introspective ways had been a disastrous mistake. It was time to rekindle the fires of Chinese technical creativity, and it was time to access the technology of the West.

## OPENING THE DOOR

With the coming of the Chinese Republic in 1911, the leaders of that state began to send their children to schools in the West. Most students went to the United States, but not all the early visitors came for benign purposes. Chinese intelligence agents were inserted into U.S. Army units operating in China during World War II. They continued to serve their Chinese masters well after the revolution of 1949. One such super-spy was Chin "Larry" Wu-Tai, born in Beijing, who helped the U.S. Army monitor Chinese radio broadcasts during World War II. At the time of the Korean War, 1950–52, he was put to work interrogating Chinese prisoners. In 1952, Chin became a naturalized U.S. citizen and joined the ranks of the CIA, with his prewar communist affiliations lost in the shuffle. In time Chin, as a double agent, became the manager of the CIA's Far East network. For thirty years, Chin kept Mao's government posted on the CIA's plans, policies, and networks in Asia. He met with Chinese couriers in Toronto, Hong Kong, London, and the United States to collect over a million dollars in compensation. Chin was arrested in 1985, with two hundred thousand dollars in his Hong Kong bank account alone. He was indicted on seventeen counts, ranging from espionage to income tax evasion. At his trial in February 1986, Chin admitted to most of those activities, but he claimed he was working to achieve a U.S.–Chinese reconciliation. Larry Chin was convicted on all counts; he committed suicide in his jail cell while awaiting sentencing.

China's early collection of nuclear technology may have been less premeditated, but it was just as effective. Joan Hinton was born in Vermont to Progressive parents who were founders of the Putney School. She studied physics at the University of Chicago. As a graduate student she worked with Enrico Fermi in assembling and operating the world's first nuclear reactor. Hinton moved to Los Alamos with Fermi and became a member of the senior scientific staff, holding a white badge with full access to all aspects of the wartime A-bomb program. In 1945, Hinton attended the Trinity test in the New Mexico desert, and then remained at Los Alamos for another three years. She was respected and well liked by the younger scientists at Los Alamos, including those who flew the Hiroshima and Nagasaki missions. Then, in early 1948, Hinton moved to China. Her brother had visited and lived among the communist insurgents there before World War II, and Joan Hinton was a firm believer in the communist cause. She landed in Shanghai, and, as an ardent supporter of Mao's revolution, she made it into Beijing for the city's liberation in 1949. Hinton married a fellow American in China, settled into Xian, and moved back to Beijing in 1966. It seems reasonable to assume that during the early years of the Chinese nuclear effort in the 1950s, Hinton would have met with Qian Sanqiang, father of the Chinese A-bomb. Her insights into the implosion technology of Fat Man could have been a major help in framing the early Chinese nuclear program. To this day, Hinton remains in China, one of the first holders of a Chinese "green card" that formalizes her residency.

With the end of World War II the trickle of Chinese students traveling to U.S. and European universities broke into a flood; the civil war in China did not seem to impede this flow. Students who came to the United States in the 1940s were urged to return to China during the 1950s to help build the new China. Many, including one of our thesis advisors, did so.

This ebb and flow of bright young Chinese talent makes it clear that the Chinese collection of U.S. and European technology did not rely primarily on espionage. The real acquisition of Western knowledge was accomplished one graduate student at a time. It is interesting to look back now at the postwar academic venues of the men and women who later became the top ten scientists in the embryonic Chinese nuclear weapons program. (See chart below.)

| Name of Scientist | Undergraduate Education | Graduate Education | Career Achievement |
|---|---|---|---|
| Chen Nengkuan | Tangshan Jiaotong University, metallurgy, 1946 | Yale University, Ph.D. physics, 1950 | Chair of nuclear weapons diagnostics department at the Ninth Academy |
| Cheng Kaijia | Zhejiang University, B.S., 1941 | University of Edinburgh, Ph.D. physics, 1948 | Academy of Sciences, director of Institute 21 at the Chinese Nuclear Weapons Test Site |
| Deng Jiaxian | Southwest Associated University, physics, 1935 | Purdue University, Ph.D. physics, 1950 | Chair of nuclear weapons theoretical design department at the Ninth Academy |
| Peng Huanwu | Tsinghua University, physics, 1935 | University of Edinburgh, Ph.D. physics, 1945 | Designed first fission and thermonuclear weapons |
| Qian Sanqiang | Tsinghua University, physics, 1936 | University of Paris 1937, Ph.D. physics, 1943 | "Father of China's A-bomb program" |
| Qian Xuesen | Shanghai Jiaotong University, physics, 1934 | MIT, M.S. 1936; Caltech, Ph.D. physics, 1939 | Organized JPL; Head of the Fifth Academy, "Father of China's Space Program" |
| Wang Gangchang | Tsinghua University, physics, 1929 | University of Berlin, Ph.D. 1934; U.C. Berkeley, 1946–49 | Scientific Director, CAEP (Manager of nuclear weapons program) |
| (Madam) Xie Xide | Amoy (now Xiamen) University, B.S., 1946 | Smith College, M.A., 1949; MIT, Ph.D., 1951 | President, Fudan University (feeds talent to CAEP) |
| Zhao Zhongyao | China, details unknown | Caltech, Ph.D. physics, 1950 | Developed China's first charged particle accelerator |
| Zhu Guangya | Southwest Associated University, physics, 1945 | University of Michigan, Ph.D. physics, 1950 | General officer in People's Liberation Army, Chairman of COSTIND (Oversees nuclear weapons programs) |

## THE INTERCESSION OF MAO ZEDONG

During the postwar 1940s, political earthquakes shook the continent of Asia: India achieved independence; the Soviets went nuclear; and the People's Liberation Army (PLA) took control of China. The PLA, in turn, was controlled by Mao Zedong. Mao was fifty-six years old at the time of his takeover. He was a veteran revolutionary, having been in on the founding of the Chinese Communist Party twenty-eight years before. Although Mao has long since departed this vale of tears,[2] historians, biographers, and political successors still tread lightly in dealing with his legacy: a political leader of iron will who resuscitated an ancient civilization while killing off tens of millions of his own people.

Mao was born in the rural village of Shaoshan, important because he returned to those roots to pick his successor. He participated in the revolution of 1911 that ended the Ming Dynasty and gave birth to the Chinese Republic; he then turned to academia, Marxism, and the creation of a Communist Party within China. Upon Mao's death, his personal doctor[3] described him as a man of incredible energy, but a man with no friends—manipulative and thoughtlessly cruel. His inner staff agreed: "The more one knew Mao, the less he could be respected." Yet Mao was certain of his own role in history: destined to return China to its fifteenth-century greatness at whatever the cost.

Within two months of his takeover in Beijing, Mao journeyed to Moscow. He wished to map out the future of world communism, and he needed the support of Josef Stalin and the Soviet Union in establishing his new People's Republic.

In some ways Mao and Stalin were two peas from the same pod: dictators to whom the deaths of a few million "political unreliables" were but one cost of building a new society, but these men were not personally compatible. They had crossed ideological swords a decade before as Mao was organizing insurrection in Jiangxi. Stalin, by then the ruler of the Soviet Union, wanted to focus revolutionary activity in the cities; Mao wanted to win the hearts and minds of the peasants. A grim animosity followed. When Mao arrived in Moscow in December 1949, he found Stalin ensconced as "emperor"; Mao was treated as one more "subject," compelled to cool his heels in Moscow's chilly winter for weeks until Stalin was ready to talk. Mao found it hard to pin Stalin down, to get an answer about the reunification of Korea by armed force, or to get promises of help for Mao's two-month-old People's Republic of China. It was only the threat of a Chinese walkout that produced the Sino-Soviet Treaty of Friendship, Alliance, and Mutual Assistance, signed on December 16, 1949. With that agreement in hand, however, Mao was able to return to China to unleash a ruthless and bloody re-engineering of Chinese society.

2. Died September 9, 1976.
3. Dr. Li Zhisui.

That overhaul was to include an historic change in Chinese foreign policy. China was to end its five centuries of introspection; it would look to the Western barbarians for help. Mao's campaign to retrieve his young graduate students from overseas was meeting with slow but steady success, aided by American paranoia. At the time of the Korean War, with passions inflamed by McCarthy-era accusations, many of the Chinese students studying in America were thought to be security risks. The American government wanted to get rid of them; Mao welcomed their return.

As a result of Mao's conversations in Moscow, Stalin agreed to receive and talk with North Korea's Soviet-installed dictator, Kim Il Sung, about the reunification of the Korean peninsula. Those meetings took place in Moscow in March 1950, and when they were over, North Korea's attack on the South had been set in motion. The Soviet general staff would plan the attack, the North Koreans were to do the fighting, and the Soviets would benefit by a U.S. distraction from the Soviet bottom-line objective: a similar "unification" of Western Europe under Soviet control. In the early 1950s, a Soviet push across Western Europe might be unstoppable if the United States were entangled in the Pacific.[4] The war in Korea started with a well-executed North Korean invasion of the South on June 25, 1950, but soon thereafter, Kim's political troubles began. In response to the northern attack, the president of the United States ordered ten nuclear-configured B-29s to Pacific bases, and he made it clear that nuclear weapons would be "under active consideration" if the Chinese became involved in what was then a North Korean versus UN fight. In September 1950, General MacArthur turned the tide of battle with a brilliant attack on Seoul's Inchon Harbor. He landed his troops in the North Koreans' rear. The northerners were overextended, their supply lines were soon cut, and within weeks, the North Korean army was being destroyed. Kim Il Sung flew to Moscow in panic; Stalin would not help, but together they enticed the Chinese to do so. In October 1950, Chinese "volunteers" appeared within Korea, pushing innocent civilians in front of their forces to clear the defending UN minefields. Chinese and civilian casualties were horrific.[5] The Americans imposed a ten-to-one "kill ratio" on the Chinese, but even so, the American casualties had a debilitating effect on the patience of the American body politic. Mao and

4. As the ensuing war in Korea ground on, Stalin confirmed these objectives when meeting with East European communist leaders, January 9–12, 1951: "Our task is to use the two to three years at our disposal to create a modern and powerful military force. . . . [They] must be combat-ready by the end of the three-year period." (i.e., by the end of 1954.)
5. Well over a half-million Chinese and North Koreans were killed during the first year of the war alone, although this figure includes the lives of the civilians used as human shields and mine-clearers.

Stalin well understood.[6] The battle lines stabilized, Truman refrained from pulling the nuclear trigger, and the war in Korea continued for another two years.

In the American presidential election of 1952, "communism and corruption" were the Republican lines of attack. The Republican candidate, retired Gen. Dwight Eisenhower, promised to "go to Korea" if elected; he further promised to end that war promptly, one way or another, upon his inauguration. Immediately after his landslide election, the president-elect made it clear that, once in office, he would authorize the use of nuclear weapons if there were no immediate armistice in Korea. With those words, another American president flashed the nuclear card in Mao's face.

In March 1953, Stalin died, the North Koreans were no longer a military factor, and the Chinese had developed a changing view of the war. First, it had been a terribly expensive conflict for them, consuming supplies, munitions, and lives in quantities the new nation could ill afford to lose. Second, the new American president, a military hero of World War II, probably meant what he said about the potential use of nukes. Third, the post-Stalin leaders of the Soviet Union were losing interest. They no longer wished to invade Western Europe; they hoped to prevail on the battlefields of technology and industrial development instead. Thus the "distraction of America" factor had lost its value. The Soviets began to withdraw their support; an armistice ending the war in Korea was signed during the summer of 1953. It left the Chinese free to pursue other goals.

During the early Mao years, in April 1950, French Communist Party member Frédéric Joliot-Curie had been fired from his post as high commissioner of the French atomic energy program. Only two years before, his former student, Qian Sanqiang, had returned to China after eleven years of study with Joliot-Curie in Paris. In the autumn of 1950, as Mao began to reflect on the security of his new republic, Qian became Mao's designated liaison with Frédéric and Irène Joliot-Curie. Qian returned to Paris, went shopping for scientific instruments pertinent to nuclear research, received a very helpful piece of radioactive hardware from Irène Joliot-Curie, and brought home a message of passionate support from both Joliot-Curies. As confirmed communists, Frédéric and Irène were dedicated backers of a Chinese nuclear weapons program.

With the end of the war in Korea in 1953, the Chinese-backed insurgency in Vietnam began to heat up. The defining battle, between French and Viet Cong, took place a year later at a remote fort in the northwest corner of Vietnam: Dien Bien Phu. The Chinese were not combatants, but they were active supporters of Ho

6. Stalin to Zhou Enlai, in Moscow, August 20, 1952: " Mao is right. This war is getting on America's nerves. . . . Endurance and patience is needed here. . . . The Koreans have suffered many casualties . . . .They need patience and lots of endurance."

Chi Minh's communist rebels, and they were deeply involved in that war's logistics. The attack on Dien Bien Phu was a long and drawn-out siege, consummated by an artillery bombardment the French did not expect. It should have had a familiar ring. The artillery used to shell Dien Bien Phu into submission was American; it had been abandoned by U.S. forces in Korea four years before as they were pushed south by Chinese "volunteers."

In May 1954, as the battle for Dien Bien Phu raged, U.S. nukes were once again on the table. General Curtis LeMay talked publicly of his support for the use of nuclear weapons if China expanded the Vietnamese fight into a broader Asian war. There were also internal U.S. discussions at the highest level about providing two nuclear weapons to the French to assist in the defense of Dien Bien Phu. The French fort fell on May 7, but once again the nuclear card had been displayed. Mao noted the nuclear threats, but he wanted to talk things over with the new post-Stalin management of the Soviet Union before he took action.

If caution had been in Beijing's air during that summer of 1954, it was totally dispelled in the autumn of that year by the turn of events in the Straits of Taiwan. The island of Taiwan, once known as Formosa, had become a refuge for Gen. Chiang Kaishek's defeated Nationalist army a half-decade before. During the Korean War years, the U.S. Navy had been deployed into the Taiwan Straits to preclude cross-channel invasions or other actions by either side. Upon his inauguration, President Eisenhower withdrew that blocking force. His objective was to pressure Mao, to force an end of his support for insurgencies all over southeast Asia. As part of that pressure, in August 1954, Chiang Kaishek moved some of his troops forward, to smaller islands off the Chinese coast in preparation for an attack on the mainland. Mao's government responded at once with a contrary announcement, "Taiwan must be liberated." In September 1954, mutual bombardments began, and the American Joint Chiefs of Staff again proposed the nuclear option if Mao attempted to invade Taiwan.

During early October 1954, Nikita Khrushchev visited Beijing. While Mao's relationship with Stalin had been fraternal, if not friendly, Khrushchev was not comfortable with Mao. The two did business as needed, entering into agreements for the Soviets to help China with "research into the peaceful uses of atomic energy," but there was no formal promise of Russian help with nuclear weapons at that time.

Crises within the Taiwan Straits continued throughout the fall of 1954, as Mao's forces prepared for their attacks on the Dachen island group north of Taiwan. American concern increased; the president and Congress wished to be firmly on record as supporting Chiang Kaishek, the security of Taiwan, and the eventual dissolution of the communist regime on the mainland. Those sentiments were codified in the U.S.-Taiwan Mutual Defense Treaty, signed on December 2, 1954. That was it for

Mao. If there was a last straw leading to his decision to go nuclear, the U.S.-Taiwan treaty of December 1954 was probably it.

The American threats of nuclear use against communist China are understandable. There was no other feasible military response to an enemy of that size, given its tolerance for massive casualties and the dispersed nature of her economic base. Elsewhere in the world, America's warning of "massive nuclear retaliation" had been the cornerstone of Eisenhower's relationship with the Soviet Union. Stability had ensued, but when nuclear threats are imposed on casualty-tolerant nonnuclear nations, they can have unintended consequences.

## THE RECONSTRUCTION OF CHENG HO'S FLEET

On January 15, 1955, at a meeting of his Central Secretariat, Chairman Mao took formal action. He authorized and directed the development of a Chinese A-bomb. He had been urged to this position by knowledgeable Westerners. He was supported by his peers in the politburo, and he felt confident that in the long run the Soviet Union would help in this endeavor. Mao had been badgered by U.S. nuclear threats since his assumption of power, and he knew that without nuclear weapons, China would remain a Third World backwater. It was an historic moment, fraught with risk, but filled with enormous promise. On that January day in 1955, Mao decreed nothing less than the reassembly of the cinders from Cheng Ho's fleet. The barbarians might seek to destroy his nuclear eggs before they could hatch, but if Mao were successful, he could return China to the central position on the world stage abandoned five centuries before.

Mao and China were starting from scratch. All pre-1949 nuclear technology had sprung from the minds of the European barbarians. Mao would have to unlock the door into that Western world with great care. As a first step, he would temporarily welcome massive help from his ideological partner, the Soviet Union. Beyond that, he would seek to collect technology from overseas with a vacuum cleaner, not a cherry-picker. However, Mao wanted this intellectual traffic to flow one way: inbound, with no leaks back to the outside world. In practice, that would not be simple. And there was the problem of money. China was desperately poor in the aftermath of two world wars, a revolution, and a three-year struggle in Korea, but then the merciless allocation of resources is one of the things dictators do best. Mao's predecessors had achieved superpower status during the previous millennium; why not once again?

## THE SOVIET HELPING HAND, 1955–1960

There was smooth sailing at first. China's leadership understood the scope of the problem: find uranium within China, process that ore into fissionable material, design a weapon, test it, and then produce enough nuclear weapons to return China

93

to the status of a world power. As a foundation, China needed technical talent and industrial infrastructure. Mao wanted the job done within ten years, but he wanted it done the Chinese way—carefully, one step at a time. A slogan articulated by Premier Zhou Enlai during the dark days of 1960 put it well: "When crossing the river, go stone by stone." There was to be no Soviet "storming," no arbitrary deadlines, no accomplishment of some milestone by Mao's birthday. The impressive results we see today are the product of a careful approach, executed by the brightest and best, men and women bound together by years of shared revolutionary experience and totally committed to Mao and his vision of a new China.

The first practical problem was finding uranium ore inside China. Within two weeks of Mao's decision to proceed, the Soviets and Chinese had agreed on a search plan. This was not an altruistic offer on the part of the Russians; they needed an expanded supply of uranium themselves. The Sino-Soviet agreement of January 1955 included a Chinese promise to sell any surplus ore to the Soviet Union.

On a grander scale, the Chinese leadership began to mastermind their "Atomic Energy Cause." In doing so they assumed the "vigorous assistance of the Soviet Union." As a result, in April 1955, the Soviets and Chinese entered into another compact. This one called for "full [Soviet] assistance in the fields of nuclear physics and the peaceful uses of atomic energy." (The word "peaceful" always appears as a qualifier in every proliferant's public statements; that word never seems to preclude the ultimate politico-military option.) As part of the deal, the Soviet Union promised to construct and deliver a nuclear reactor and cyclotron within China, and members of the Chinese Academy of Sciences were welcomed into the Soviet Union to study the theory and operation of such equipment. At the end of 1955, the secretariat's master plan was adopted, and in January 1956, Premier Zhou Enlai announced the follow-up—a specific twelve-year road map for bringing Chinese science and technology up to Soviet standards. A dozen Soviet advisors helped devise this guide; it was completed and accepted by the Chinese politburo at the end of 1956.

It is important to repeat: during these first two years of the Chinese nuclear era, there was no massive, Soviet-style industrial effort, no pouring of concrete, no moving of dirt other than in the search for uranium. The Chinese focused on evaluating the technical approaches, planning the facilities needed, and recruiting the most talented scientists and engineers, one at a time.

One golden apple fell off the tree in 1955, for in that year Qian Xuesen, a twenty-year veteran of work at the cutting edge of American and German rocket science, returned to China. In 1936, Qian had been sent to the United States as a student. He received his Ph.D. from Caltech in 1939. In 1943, he proposed the organization of what became that institute's Jet Propulsion Laboratory. At the end of World War II,

Qian, holding a U.S. Army commission as a full colonel, was debriefing captured Nazi rocket scientists. In conjunction with those interviews he was laying out plans for early American rocket work. But then, with the advent of the war in Korea, Qian was considered a security risk. His clearances were lifted, and he remained under virtual house arrest at Caltech until he was deported in 1955 as part of the Korean postwar prisoner exchange. Qian was welcomed home with open arms. Within a few months he had been installed as the leader of China's Fifth Academy, the organization pulling together China's missile and space program. The Silkworm anti-ship weapon, Dong Feng ballistic missiles, and China's first satellite launch (in 1970) were all of Qian Xuesen's doing. He retired within China, decades later, as a national hero.

The year 1956 brought another important Sino-Soviet agreement, this one aimed at the actual layout and construction of China's nuclear infrastructure. But to the perceptive insider, the year also evidenced the first cracks in the Sino-Soviet wall of solidarity. On February 25, Nikita Khrushchev, speaking in Moscow, attacked and discredited the myth of Josef Stalin. He did so in a secret address to the Twentieth Congress of the Communist Party of the Soviet Union. Mao was shocked; he *believed* in the "cult of personality" and was *revolted* by the thought of "collective leadership." Although he personally disliked Stalin, that man was Mao's kind of dictator: a ruthless killer. Khrushchev was just a consensus-seeking chairman. Khrushchev's speech stirred debate within China; it put Mao on the defensive. The thought of party apparatchiks discrediting the memory of a dictator cast long shadows in Mao's mind. It planted the first seeds of Cultural Revolution.

On the other side of the coin, Khrushchev did not trust Mao. The latter's casualty-tolerant view of nuclear weapons[7] and belief in the inevitability of their use was worrisome to Khrushchev. Even so, the Soviet politburo was determined to work with the Chinese. The year of 1956 had brought uprisings in Poland and Hungary; the men in the Kremlin were paying increasing attention to their communist allies.

In February 1957, Soviet advisors started helping with site selection for the big industrial and research facilities to come. That April, the Soviet leadership gave E. D. Vorobiev, the scientific director of Chelyabinsk-40,[8] the specific job of bringing China into the nuclear age. Vorobiev was a close associate of Soviet nuclear czar Kurchatov. He enjoyed the full confidence of the Soviet security services, and he came from a position of great executive responsibility on the materials side of the Soviet nuclear house. Vorobiev was instructed to give the Chinese the full load: geology and

---

7. In discussing possible Chinese fatalities in a nuclear war, Mao observed that, "We have so many people. We can afford to lose a few. What difference does it make?"
8. Later renamed Chelyabinsk-65

mining, isotope separation and reactor operations, weapons physics, radiochemistry, and the schooling of specialists. He moved to Beijing in May 1957. His first task was training the young technicians, overseeing lectures by returning Chinese graduate students, and expediting the massive flow of more students through Russia. "Chinese youth arrived in the main cities of the Soviet Union by the trainload; they absorbed knowledge at the best universities and institutes of our country."[9] A similar army of experts from the Soviet laboratories, factories, and universities flooded China.

During July of 1957, Anastas Mikoyan[10] secretly visited China to explain recent changes within the Soviet hierarchy and to confirm details of the Sino-Soviet nuclear relationship. Mikoyan returned home an older and wiser man. He was appalled at Mao's nonchalance about the possible loss of life in the event of a nuclear war. Those concerns must have been relayed to Nikita Khrushchev.

October 1957, the time of Sputnik, may have been the high point of the Sino-Soviet relationship. Mao was awed by that Soviet achievement, and on October 15, the two nations codified their plans for Chinese nuclear weapons development with the New Defense Technical Accord. This agreement included a Soviet promise of technical training and data, a supply of ballistic missiles, hands-on construction help, and even a prototype A-bomb. In November of that year, Mao returned to Moscow for the first time in seven years. The occasion was the fortieth birthday of the Soviet Union and a celebration of that Sputnik launch. Mao was in high spirits, feisty and combative. He had a good time, wallowing in the honors accorded him in contrast to his diminution at the hands of Stalin a few years before, but once again the seeds of history were sown. Mao engaged in rhetorical overreach, offending Khrushchev with his irresponsibility. And during this same trip, Mao came to see the production of steel as the fundamental indicator of economic strength. "We produce too little steel," he said ominously to his staff.

## THE GREAT LEAP FORWARD

With the coming of 1958, the Chinese government began to implement its nuclear weapons master plan. The Ninth Bureau, subsequently re-named the Nuclear Weapons Bureau, was organized to oversee operations at:

- The Beijing Nuclear Weapons Research Institute, operating as a headquarters within the nation's capital.
- The Northwest Nuclear Weapons Development Base, in Haiyan within Qinghai Province.

9. Negin & Smirnov, reporting at Dubna Conference, May 1996.
10. At the time the first deputy premier of the Soviet Union.

- An extensive Atomic Energy Complex within Jiuquan Perfection. Initially this complex was to consist of the Nuclear Fuels Processing Plant (to convert enriched uranium hexafluoride, produced at Lanzhou, into metal) and the Nuclear Component Manufacturing Plant (to machine nuclear materials into the needed shapes and to assemble devices). In time this complex would also become home to the Jiuquan plutonium-producing reactor and reprocessing facility.

- A Nuclear Weapons Test Base near Lop Nur in western Xinjiang Province.

Other bureaus were established to manage the geological work, materials production, construction, finance, and so forth, but their existence was a matter of the utmost secrecy, clouded with changing names, ambiguous plant numbers, and devious cover stories. In January 1958, the five men who would oversee the heart of this program started work within a temporary office in Beijing; they and hundreds of others moved to the Northwest Nuclear Weapons Development Base at the end of the year.

That was a fortunate thing, because in January of 1958 Mao Zedong also began to articulate the principles to be embodied in his Great Leap Forward. At the Nanning Party Conference he announced a goal of catching up with British steel production within fifteen years. His politburo concurred, adopting a plan to immediately double steel output by means of backyard furnaces. In May, he accredited the concept of "peoples' communes," huge amalgamations of agricultural cooperatives with centralized dining halls and the abolition of all private farming. During the summer, he initiated a vast water conservation campaign; the resulting construction of dams and canals would draw away much of the rural labor force needed to harvest crops and feed the people.

This ill-conceived plan was intended to vastly increase the production of food and steel, perceived to be the sinews of a modern state, but the result was disastrous. The incentive for efficient farming was gone. Harvest labor disappeared into the black holes of furnace-tending and dam-construction. Peasants burned tables, chairs, and doors to fire the ovens that then melted down scythes, knives, and household utensils into useless iron ingots that were never collected. Much of the grain crop rotted in the fields; that which was harvested was taxed away, sought out by "anti-grain concealment drives" of the greatest cruelty. Come the winter of 1958 to 1959, millions were starving.

Those assigned to the new and remote Northwest Nuclear Weapons Development Base were the last to feel the impact of the Great Leap, but by 1960, even the cadres at the new, government-protected nuclear enclaves were starving to death. During that year, two-thirds of the workforce, afflicted by kwashiokor,[11] were disabled and unable to work. Discipline disappeared in a cloud of Maoist rhetoric. The surviving workers within the nuclear complex felt empowered to "improve upon" the equipment sent by the Soviets, to make it "more Chinese." The result was technological anarchy. The Great Leap Forward did not enter the consciousness of most Americans, but within China it was an unmitigated disaster, dropping agricultural production in half and costing twenty-five to thirty million lives[12] and significantly delaying the start of the Chinese nuclear weapons program.

The Great Leap Forward was only stopped, in 1961, by a courageous leader, Liu Shaoqi, who, as deputy chairman of the Communist Party, was able to seize the chairmanship (i.e., presidency) of the People's Republic. He countermanded Mao's agrarian orders, reversed the process of collectivization, and instituted serious economic reforms. Prior to that time, Liu had been seen as Mao's successor, but no good deed goes unpunished. By mid-decade, Mao had rebuilt his position within the Communist Party. In 1966, he launched the Cultural Revolution, a vehicle designed to destroy those who had usurped his power within that party, starting with Liu Shaoqi. In July 1966, Liu was denounced as a "traitor and capitalist roader" and was displaced as deputy party chairman. By 1967, he and his wife were under house arrest in Beijing. In 1968, he was expelled from the party. In 1969, he disappeared from view, imprisoned in Kaifeng, where he died during November of that year from "medical neglect." But in 1958, all of this sad history lay in the future. During the 1950s, Mao had demanded an atomic bomb; he then starved the people who were supposed to build it.

## THE INFRASTRUCTURE

The Northwest Nuclear Weapons Development Base had been sited by Soviet advisors near the city of Haiyan in Qinghai Province during the winter of 1957 and 1958. This was a remote location in northwest China, separated from Russia by a thousand miles of Mongolian desert. Construction started amidst all the Great Leap chaos in mid-1958. The base enjoyed a variety of names: State Owned Plant 221 to the bureaucrats, the Ninth Academy to the scientists, Koko Nor to U.S. intelligence agencies, and the Qinghai Provincial Mining Zone to passers-by. The facility was laid out by Mao's Russian advisors as a replica of the Soviet nuclear laboratory at Sarov (Arzamas-16).

11. An abdominal swelling arising from malnutrition.
12. Some put the death toll at forty-three million Chinese.

At the same time, Chinese and Russian experts, seeking a site for China's uranium enrichment facility, settled on the nearby city of Lanzhou, 150 miles to the east along the Yellow River in Gansu Province. They picked nearby Jiuquan Perfection for the promised nuclear-reactor and weapon-assembly facilities. Since 1958, Chinese teams had been scouring the western deserts for a test site; in late 1959, they settled on a spot near Lop Nur in the Xinjiang Province of northwest China. The capstone of all this activity was to be the delivery of a prototype Soviet A-bomb in the summer of 1958, to be stored and inspected within a vault at the Beijing Nuclear Weapons Research Institute.

As all of these facilities were taking shape, China's Central Military Commission met to confirm their requirements. Their "Guidelines for Developing Nuclear Weapons" validated priorities for nuclear and, interestingly, thermonuclear weapons, directed a focus on original work (not imitation), and demanded absolute secrecy. China was to accept Soviet aid, but it was not to fall into the Soviet orbit.

The paragon of Soviet aid arrived in Beijing on June 18, 1958, in the form of E. A. Negin, the chief nuclear weapons designer at Arzamas-16, and two of his associates, N. G. Maslov and V. Yu. Gavrilov. The Soviet Ministry of Medium Machine Building[13] had directed this group to "go to our Chinese comrades and tell them how a nuclear weapon is made." Upon their arrival in Beijing, the Negin delegation did just that. Their hosts wanted to know about the organization of Arzamas-16, but soon they got to the heart of the matter: how is an atomic bomb put together, and how is it tested? Gavrilov was the first man up—he covered the physics of nuclear weapon design: blast waves, compression, and critical mass calculations. Negin was next—he described the actual design and operation of RDS-1 (née Fat Man): the explosive charge, the details of the implosion process, and the critical assembly (He covered everything, from the casing down to the neutron fuze). Maslov then took the stage to discuss weaponization: that is, the ballistic case, machinery, and switches needed to make the bomb work. These "chalk talks" took more than a month to complete. The Soviets did not explain to their hosts how they had improved on RDS-1 (to double the yield and halve the weight), but they may have tipped the Chinese on the characteristics of an improved, more compact A-bomb that would be needed as a primary trigger for a two-stage thermonuclear. (The Soviets had tested such a two-stage device three years before.)

---

13. The cover name for the Soviet nuclear weapons ministry.

## THE RUPTURE

It was all too good to be true. Reality encroached when Nikita Khrushchev arrived in Beijing[14] for windup talks with Mao. That meeting was to cap the Negin delegation's work, but the chairman of the Chinese Communist Party was arrogant in the extreme. Mao was unhappy with Soviet demands for military sites in China, displeased at Khrushchev's desire to control Chinese foreign policy, and annoyed that the Soviets had treated him as a pawn on the Cold War chessboard. On the other side of the compound, Khrushchev was irritated by Mao's lack of appreciation for the nuclear help that the Negin team was then delivering downtown.

Mao received Khrushchev poolside, outside Beijing, at his Zhongnanhai fortress. Mao invited the Soviet leader to join him in the pool. Khrushchev did so reluctantly, since he did not know how to swim. It was a disastrous, waterlogged conversation. Mao planned the meeting as a "slap in Khrushchev's face," and he succeeded beyond his wildest dreams.

From Khrushchev's perspective, Mao had gone mad. His continuing disregard for possible nuclear casualties and the prospect of economic chaos as a result of the Great Leap Forward formed the basis of that view. Mao's arrogant bad manners confirmed the findings. Nothing of substance was settled at Zhongnanhai. The visit, scheduled to last for a week, ended after three days.

Inside the Soviet embassy the message was clear: "Khrushchev has left; it is time for [all of us] to pack our suitcases." On August 2, 1958, the Negin delegation joined the exodus. Upon their return to Moscow, they found disquiet in the air. The minister of Medium Machine Building, Efim Slavsky, was distancing himself from those who had approved the Negin trip to China. The ministry had become irrational at the thought of actually shipping a nuclear weapon to China. While that transaction had once been directed and approved at the highest levels, no one would now assume any responsibility for the delivery. Documentation was destroyed, the railcars pulled away, and the weapon was returned to inventory.

There can be no doubt that as the summer of 1958 turned to autumn, the entire Soviet government began having second thoughts. Arming such a heavily populated nation on its southern border was not a great idea. Perhaps Mao meant what he said about the inevitability of nuclear use. The Great Leap Forward, reported by those still within China, confirmed Mao's irrationality. In the West, the Soviets were riding the antinuclear, ban-the-bomb propaganda train, proposing a nuclear testing moratorium to the Americans. What if the West learned of the Soviet's wholesale

14. On July 31, 1958.

export of nuclear technology, even a nuclear weapon, to the East, while propounding a "peace initiative" to the West?

During the autumn of 1958, the Soviets began to withdraw their technical and scientific support. They started to supply outmoded equipment to their Chinese clients. They provided misleading nuclear data: for example, inaccurate nuclear cross-sections, which devastated Chinese efforts to calculate critical-mass assemblies. Comrade Vorobiev, the team leader left behind in Beijing, was instructed to withhold plans for the promised plutonium-production reactor; he was to deliver drawings for an assembly so small it could never go critical. The promised prototype A-bomb, repeatedly scheduled for delivery during the spring, then summer, and then the fall of 1958, never showed up. The charade continued until May 1959, when, according to Nikita Khrushchev's son, Sergei, his father made the decision: "Under no circumstances should the Soviet Union continue to transfer atomic secrets to the Chinese."

The shoe dropped in Beijing on June 20, 1959. In a formal letter from the Soviet Central Committee, Khrushchev advised his Chinese counterparts that the Soviets would not be sending a prototype bomb, nuclear hardware, or any other nuclear weapons–related materials to China. The stated reason was Soviet efforts to achieve a nuclear test ban agreement with the West, but the Chinese leadership saw matters in a more realistic light. They had just gotten the back of the once-helping hand. To Mao, it was a unilateral tearing up of the Sino-Soviet New Defense Technical Accord.

There followed a year of faux-friendship, fourteen months actually, during which time the Soviets and the Chinese attempted to effect a bloodless divorce. The Soviets wanted to get their people out of China safely while covering their nuclear tracks. Having poured the foundation of a nuclear shrine, the Soviets now wished to destroy, disrupt, or hide as much of that monument as possible, while continuing to make nice with their hosts and masking their folly from the West. Khrushchev visited Beijing again in October 1959 to observe the tenth birthday of the People's Republic of China, but it was not a cordial visit. Many key Soviet advisors returned from China soon thereafter, nominally on leave, but they never returned. Moscow was refusing Chinese demands for technical data, raw materials, and parts. Excuses were everywhere, but confrontation was avoided whenever possible.

Even though Mao understood what had happened, the Chinese cadres were not willing to face up to the duplicity of their socialist brothers. At the operating level, the Chinese nuclear empire continued to lurch forward, but it now looked like a disabled and disoriented monster. The labor force, enfeebled by the Great Leap, was starving and insubordinate. The remaining Soviet advisors, secretive and unresponsive, were quietly packing to leave.

## THE THREE HARD YEARS

The fissile materials production plants were to have been the pyramids of this new nuclear kingdom. Soviet experts had chosen locations for both the uranium enrichment plant and the plutonium production reactors. Plans and specifications for these behemoth facilities were under development by experts when the June 20, 1959, mail arrived from Moscow. At Lanzhou, the building to house the mammoth gaseous diffusion plant for the enrichment of uranium was already under construction. By the end of 1959, the shell was complete, but the installation of machinery and equipment sank into chaos. Russian pipes, pumps, and other gear, already in transit, were simply dumped upon arrival. Lanzhou began to look like a warehouse rather than a cutting-edge science center.

The plutonium production reactor at Jiuquan, to be known as Plant 404, was further behind. The Soviets had provided the design; excavation was started in February 1960; by August of that year, the foundations were complete, but by then all pretense of Sino-Soviet cooperation was gone. In the summer of 1960, the construction of China's plutonium production reactor was brought to a halt.

In January 1960, the Chinese government took formal steps to recognize what had happened. The party adopted an emergency decision paper declaring their A-bomb venture to be an indigenous project; there would be no more reliance on foreign industrial assistance. That decision did not preclude the continued mining of overseas information, however. During the previous summer, another golden apple fell into the Chinese net.

Nine years before, in 1950, Los Alamos nuclear spy Klaus Fuchs had been sent to prison for wartime espionage at Los Alamos and later within the British nuclear facility at Harwell. Fuchs was a brilliant German physicist and a communist. He had fled to the United Kingdom before the war, and then relocated to the United States. In both countries he played a leading role in the conception and development of the wartime A-bomb. Fuchs was released from Britain's Wakefield Prison on June 23, 1959. He immediately immigrated to East Germany, where he settled into the teaching of physics at Dresden.

One important "pupil" who paid an early visit was Qian Sanqiang, Frédéric Joliot-Curie's wartime graduate student and, by 1959, the designated mastermind of Mao's A-bomb program. In July of that year, Qian made his way to East Germany, where he met with Fuchs at length.[15] During those long summer days of 1959, Fuchs gave Qian

15. Confirmed by electronic communication from H. Terry Hawkins, a senior fellow at Los Alamos, on March 16, 2006: "I read this report in an unclassified publication, that this meeting took place shortly after Fuchs returned to East Germany. Fuchs gave Qian information that greatly assisted the Chinese program." Also see www.oldatlanticlighthouse.wordpress.com/tag/klaus-fuchs

a full tutorial on the design and operation of Fat Man. He may have added his thoughts on thermonuclears. Thus, it is reasonable to assume that by the time of the Soviet departure from China in 1959 and 1960, three independent sources of information—Klaus Fuchs, the Negin delegation, and Joan Hinton—had given the Chinese a clear picture of how Fat Man worked. Mao had built a first-class cadre of young scientific talent to utilize that insight. China's remaining problem was fissionable materials.

As noted above, in August 1960, the Chinese decided to discontinue work on their reactor and reprocessing facility at Jiuquan. Since the Lanzhou gaseous diffusion shell was complete, and since uranium is a simpler (though less powerful) nuclear explosive, the Chinese decided to place their bets on highly enriched uranium. The cost of the Lanzhou plant would be staggering, requiring a forest of sophisticated pumps, valves, and converters. A similar facility, America's wartime K-25 plant in Oak Ridge, Tennessee, covered over a quarter-million square feet, employed twelve thousand people, and cost $500 million in 1945 dollars to build.[16] The Lanzhou building alone covered

Sketch of shoulder patch worn by Chinese military personnel associated with the nuclear program.

16. Six billion 2008 dollars.

seven acres of floor space. Research on the diffusion barriers between stages would have to start from scratch. That work also began in April 1960, as did construction at the Nuclear Weapons Test Base near Lop Nur. In hindsight, the Chinese feel the twin crises of 1958 and 1959—Mao's Great Leap Forward and the Soviet perfidy—delayed their nuclear weapons program by another two years. On the other hand, they also feel they cut their costs by 40 percent, having avoided time-consuming Soviet-style "storming" mistakes and by using extremely cheap indigenous labor.

The Chinese were so embittered by the Soviet pullout that they turned the June 1959 date, "596," into a symbol of national pride. The Chinese military personnel associated with the nuclear program were soon to proudly wear a 596 shoulder patch on their uniforms (see sketch on page 103). The bomb eventually tested in October 1964 was also given the name 596.

On August 23, 1960, with very little warning and carrying only the residue of their technical papers, the last Soviet advisors left China. It was not a happy departure. "They had to leave their personal belongings behind. They walked to their planes with bowed heads and jeering crowds all around." Those years of famine, stagnation, and unrest came to be known within the Chinese nuclear community as the Three Hard Years.

## THE MOVE TO ZITONG

With the departure of the last Soviet advisor, paranoia blossomed. The Russians knew the exact location of every Chinese nuclear facility. Within the Northwest Nuclear Weapons Development Base they knew the location of every shop, laboratory, and office, since that institute was an exact replica of the corresponding Soviet weapons laboratory at Arzamas-16. As relations between the former partners worsened—for reasons far broader than just nuclear—the Chinese not only despaired of any Soviet assistance, they came to fear a pre-emptive Soviet attack.

Even though construction was not yet complete at Haiyan, the decision was made to move and restructure the activities of the Northwest Nuclear Weapons Development Base to a new site, farther from Russia, with better cloud cover to foil Soviet and American reconnaissance assets while embracing a new layout, well-hidden to frustrate attempted raids. By 1960, a new, interim site had been selected near the city of Zitong, 30 miles northeast of Mianyang in northeastern Sichuan Province. Zitong was 450 miles southeast of Haiyan, equally far away from the Russian border, with cloudy weather much of the year and offering an array of masking valleys. Construction of the new site started in the late 1960s even as the old design base in Haiyan was reaching operational status. The new Research and Design Academy of Nuclear Weapons, as it was to be known, was to be spread out, with facilities strung down narrow valleys. This made for inefficient

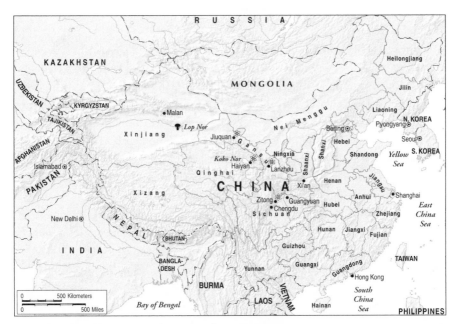

Early nuclear facilities within China. *Meridian Mapping*

travel from one laboratory or test site to another, but it added to the complexity of any targeting scheme. Many buildings were placed underground; no two looked alike. Construction debris was hidden, and vegetation was left in place as much as possible. To spotters overhead these facilities became quite hard to find, but even so, those with eyes in the sky were watching, and those with ears on the ground were listening.

In the summer of 1961, as the costs of the Soviet withdrawal and the ramifications of the Great Leap were sinking in, a major debate began within the Chinese hierarchy: should China continue to shoulder the burden of a strategic nuclear program? Most government officials, led by President Liu Shaoqi, favored a scaling back or even a termination of those grandiose nuclear schemes as well as an end to the Great Leap Forward. Industrial development and/or the purchase of conventional weapons were the cadre's preferred use of state assets, but only one vote counted. Chairman Mao relented on the Great Leap, but he called for further discussion on the matter of strategic weapons. By the end of the year he had achieved a leadership resolution to pursue strategic weapons at all costs, "even if the Chinese had to pawn their trousers" to pay for it.[17] Economic recovery would be slow in coming, but the nuclear ship of state returned to an even keel.

17. An observation by Chen Yi, China's foreign minister at the time: "I do not have adequate backup. If you succeed in producing the atomic bomb and guided missiles, then I can straighten my back."

## EYES IN THE SKY

After the U-2 shoot-down over Sverdlovsk, Russia, in May 1960, President Eisenhower promised the Soviets (and their allies) that he would no longer authorize U-2 flights over Communist territory. In reality he had no choice. The new Soviet SA-2 surface-to-air missiles could reach to seventy thousand feet. The U-2s had become an endangered species. Fortunately, the need for such U.S. overflights had been rendered obsolete by satellite technology. In August 1960, the first photographs from U.S. Corona satellites became available to the American intelligence community. By the end of the Eisenhower years, the Americans were staying abreast of major developments within the Soviet Union without the use of sovereignty-invading aircraft, for with the launch of Sputnik, the Soviets had implicitly approved an "open skies" policy in space.

On January 25, 1961, Eisenhower's successor, John Kennedy, reiterated the "no U-2 overflight" pledge, but in private Kennedy decided it would be acceptable for such aircraft, operated by the Republic of China (Taiwan), to overfly China's mainland, since the Republic of China and People's Republic of China (R.O.C. and P.R.C., respectively) were still belligerents. The Republic of China's Black Cat Squadron began to train in U-2s; on January 13, 1962, the first R.O.C. U-2 overflew mainland China. Such flights continued on a monthly basis, at considerable risk to the R.O.C. pilots. The People's Republic had a few SA-2s, and they were beginning to move them about as they studied the R.O.C. flight paths.

By the summer of 1962, at the time of Sino-Soviet border clashes and multiple U.S.-Soviet nuclear confrontations, U.S., Soviet, and R.O.C. intelligence assets had spotted the original Chinese nuclear weapon institute in northeastern Qinghai Province as well as the uranium enrichment facility at Lanzhou. The toll taken by the Great Leap was also known by the Nationalist government on Taiwan. In their judgment, the summer of 1963 offered the last, best chance to destabilize, if not overthrow, Mao's government on the mainland. In September 1963, the Republic of China's President, Chiang Kaishek, sent his defense minister, son, and heir-apparent, Gen. Chiang Chingkuo, to Washington to explain the opportunities and dangers to the Americans.

General Chiang Chingkuo first met with President Kennedy's director of central intelligence, John McCone, to tell what he knew of the mainland's collapsing economy and its nuclear ambitions. The Chiang government wished to destabilize Mao's regime and attack the nuclear facilities, with American help. McCone was impressed; he arranged for a subsequent meeting with the president's national security advisor, McGeorge Bundy. On September 10, 1963, General Chiang described the Mao-versus-Liu struggles for power to Bundy. He explained how Mao's regime was weaker than it had ever been since the 1949 takeover and urged its overthrow by political means supported by small-scale guerilla military actions. Chiang suggested the first of these latter actions be the destruction of the nuclear facilities at Haiyan and Lanzhou along with missile sites identified by the Black Cat U-2s. At the same meeting, both Bundy and Chiang expressed concern about the possibility of Soviet intercession. Bundy commented on prior R.O.C. operations, noting they had achieved minimal results, but Chiang persisted. He proposed the air-drop and operation of paramilitary teams in China with U.S. air and logistic support. Chiang repeated his argument, that it was "now or never."

General Chiang met with President Kennedy the next day. They discussed the Sino-Soviet split, the nuclear threat, and the greetings sent to Kennedy by the senior Chiang, but the bottom line, after subsequent studies by the U.S. military, was "No." Three months prior, Kennedy had approached the Soviet government on the possibility of joint U.S.-Soviet constraints on Chinese nuclear weapon development, but he had received no encouragement. Without Soviet support, R.O.C. raids on mainland China sounded too much like the Bay of Pigs disaster of the previous year. Two months later, John Kennedy was gone.

The Black Cat Squadron continued to fly a total of 102 missions over and around the Chinese mainland during the ensuing eight years. They lost five aircraft and three pilots to the SA-2s while providing an invaluable insight that kept the peace and perhaps assisted in Nixon's playing of the China card. That president put an end to the R.O.C. U-2 overflights only after his historic trip to China in 1972.

With the end of 1963, China's Three Hard Years were, indeed, over. The feared threat of outside pre-emption had come and gone. With Mao's unequivocal mandate to continue with strategic nuclear weapons, and with the end of the Great Leap Forward, the Chinese scientific community could return its attention to the practical problems of actually building and testing an atomic bomb.

## BUILDING THE BOMB

By the end of 1962, the Northwest Nuclear Weapons Development Base at Haiyan was in full operation. Work was underway on the development of synchronized detonators, needed to initiate the explosive chain of events in exactly the right way. Experimental work on the high-explosive lenses was done south of Beijing at Tuoli, a laboratory that had survived appalling conditions during the Three Hard Years. (Neither food nor heat had been available during the winters.) At Haiyan, experimental work had been completed on the central initiation system that would flood the imploded enriched uranium core with neutrons at exactly the right moment. Materials provided by the Joliot-Curies in Paris had been of great help in this latter effort. During 1963, construction also started at Institute 21, the diagnostics and radiochemistry facility that would provide the technical support and shot assessment for all of China's nuclear weapons tests. Institute 21 was originally located in the Hong Shan (Red Mountain) area ten miles northwest of the planned nuclear test headquarters, and thus, for a while, it was known as the Red Mountain Institute.

On November 20, 1963, the Chinese conducted their first all-up implosion test of detonators, high explosive, uranium (not enriched), and central neutron initiator, all massively instrumented. Everything worked in total synchronization, and the Chinese were sure they could build a working bomb once they had the fissile materials.

By the middle of 1963, in parallel with that work, the Chinese had mastered the technology of uranium isotope separation. In the autumn of that year, the mining and chemical bureaus began to deliver uranium hexaflouride feedstock to the mammoth gaseous diffusion facility at Lanzhou. By year's end, Lanzhou was up and running; it produced its first load of 90 percent enriched uranium on January 14, 1964.

In early 1964, enriched uranium, still in the form of uranium hexafluoride (a most corrosive and deadly gas) was shipped from the Lanzhou facility to the Nuclear Fuel Production Plant in the Jiuquan Atomic Energy Complex. There the gas was reduced to uranium metal, then moved to the Nuclear Component Manufacturing Plant for casting and machining. This entire process was fraught with an unending chain of metallurgical surprises, for the shaping and handling of highly enriched uranium was just one more technology the Soviets had neglected to transfer. During the summer of 1964, however, all weapon parts were brought together for assembly into China's first A-bomb, then shipped by rail to Malan, the new city that had been established 1,200 miles west of Beijing as the support center for the Nuclear Weapons Test Base at Lop Nur.

## CHINA'S NUCLEAR TEST BASE

The administrative offices, laboratories, and infrastructure needed to support the test of China's nuclear weapons were built from scratch, starting in 1960, within a newly constructed town to be known as Malan. That facility, named after a local desert flower, would, in time, become home to two thousand military personnel and eight thousand civilians. At first, the Great Leap Forward had paralyzed construction at Malan. Building crews had subsisted on wild plants and shrubs for over a year, but by 1963, work on town and test facilities had resumed. Lop Nur and Malan were ready to go in 1964. Co-author Stillman had the opportunity to visit there a quarter-century later. The dimensions were overpowering. The Chinese Nuclear Weapons Test Base is seven times the size of the equivalent U.S. facility in Nevada.

Civilian visitors get to Malan by relay. There is a military airfield at the test site, but its use is constrained to weapons matters. International visitors board a rickety Russian transport at Shanghai or Beijing for the flight into the provincial capital of

Urumqi. From there the drive to Malan by "Sure-Rockies" (Jeep Cherokees, imported from the United States) takes six hours. Along the way the history of China is on full display. Stillman passed immense, polluting chemical factories, horsemen herding camels, road crews hand-repairing potholes, and overturned trucks the victims of those potholes. Their drivers were staying warm by campfire as they awaited help.

During this six-hour jolting ordeal, Stillman's traveling companion, Terry Hawkins (also from Los Alamos), lost part of his wristwatch. A spring-loaded pin had flown from the watchband assembly; the watch had fallen from his wrist to the vehicle floor. Hawkins collected such pieces as he could find, put them in his pocket, and thought no more of the matter.

Welcoming the travelers to Malan when they arrived in the middle of the night was a meal of a lamb barbeque and fresh fruit galore. The wait staff at the banquet, all female PLA army privates, spoke some English; the interpreters were fluent, including in the colloquialisms of the language. Their "day jobs" were the translation of a flood of U.S. publications into Mandarin for use by scientists at the test base. The senior staff reeked of U.S. training; the engineer responsible for drilling vertical test shafts at Lop Nur had worked in the United States during World War II. By 1990, all of his children were enrolled in America's top engineering schools.

In the morning, the Jeep convoy re-formed for the two-hour ride, over somewhat better roads, into the test site itself. Once there, the visitors passed an unending array of newly constructed infrastructure that made clear the sophistication of the blossoming Chinese nuclear test program.

Every nation should consider its nuclear tests to be giant physics experiments. The Chinese understood that very well; other proliferants do not. The latter often consider their early nuclear shots to be demonstrations and/or simple proof tests. In contrast, the instrumentation of even the first Chinese nuclear test was sophisticated in the extreme.

Data from a nuclear test is collected in several ways. Prompt diagnostics involve pipes or tunnels that allow the collection of real-time data and its conversion to electrical signals before the entire "laboratory" is blown away. A hundred optical, coax, and multi-conductor cables confirm the operation of the detonation process to trailers, nearby but out of fireball or shock range. Optical and electromagnetic instrumentation, located still farther away, can give a quick estimate of internal device performance. Radiochemistry (the collection of post-explosion bomb debris by aircraft and/or excavation) can provide good insight to a foreign observer, but it is indispensable to the host organization. Nuclear device designers usually position trace elements at key locations within their experiments so as to later ascertain temperatures, neutron flux, burn efficiencies, and so forth, as the explosion proceeds—an event that unfolds fully in less than an instant. From the very beginning, Chinese nuclear tests employed all of these diagnostic technologies.

After Stillman and Hawkins had completed their historic visit, and before their return to the guesthouse at Malan, Hawkins asked his guide (a female PLA captain) if there was a watch-repair facility in town. Could he buy a replacement pin for his broken watch? The captain walked over to her Jeep, returning with closed hand and smiling face. "Is this what you need?"

Chinese counterintelligence, scouring the Hawkins jeep after the inbound trip in search of "bugs," had found all of the tiny but suspicious leftover watch parts on the vehicle floor. The security people had collected them and delivered same to Captain Bi. This episode at Malan was not unique. It only served to remind Stillman and Hawkins of the meticulous surveillance within China.

At an earlier time, on the morning after their arrival in Shanghai, the two men took an after-breakfast stroll around their hotel. They went into a bookstore that offered many items of interest, including Chinese-language flash cards. The cards obviously had been there for some time, since they were covered with dust. Hawkins was interested in learning Chinese, so he opened the box, riffled through the cards, but decided against a purchase and replaced cards and box on the display table. During this time Stillman browsed through some English-language paperbacks on a rotating display. After a brief interlude, both men decided to proceed, unencumbered, with their morning constitutional. Twenty minutes later, en route back to their hotel, the travelers decided to buy those flash cards and books. They returned to the bookstore, but the boxes of flashcards were gone; every book that Stillman had touched was also gone. With some agitation the clerk explained that they had just been sold. Clearly, the counterintelligence service of the Ministry of State Security had followed the men into the store. They had picked up anything touched by the foreigners, looking for intelligence-related drops to "contacts" in China. Hawkins and Stillman are intelligence professionals, but they never knew they were being followed. So it was throughout every visit: bugged hotel rooms, attentive companions, and a well-orchestrated symphony of nominally-academic questions, day after day.

Stillman and Hawkins were among the first Caucasians ever to visit Malan;[18] they were the target of stares and gawks by the long-time residents of that enclave. Yet, American technology was on display everywhere.

## "596"

At the beginning, on January 15, 1955, Chairman Mao articulated his hopes for an A-bomb within ten years. On October 16, 1964, the People's Republic of China joined the nuclear club with a twenty-two-kiloton test of a U-235, imploded core-fission device named "596" fired atop a 330-foot steel tower in the Lop Nur desert.

18. Preceded only by a formal visit by Los Alamos Director Harold Agnew in 1982.

596 weighed in at 3,410 pounds, about one-third the weight of America's enriched-uranium weapon dropped on Hiroshima at the end of World War II; it gave almost 50 percent more yield. Mao got his wish with three months to spare.

The chart below makes clear the sophistication of that first Chinese nuclear device—four times better than the comparable U.S. Little Boy; almost as good as the Soviet's second generation, plutonium-fueled RDS-2.

## Initial Nuclear Tests by the United States, U.S.S.R, United Kingdom, France, and China

| Name of device | Owning country | Date Fired | Place fired | Fuel | Yield, kilotons | Weight, pounds | Yield/* Weight |
|---|---|---|---|---|---|---|---|
| Fat Man | U.S.A. | July 16, 1945 | New Mexico | Pu | 21 | 10,300 | 2.0 |
| Little Boy | U.S.A. | Aug. 6, 1945 | Hiroshima | HEU | 15 | 8,900 | 1.7 |
| RDS-1** | U.S.S.R. | Aug. 29, 1949 | Kazakhstan | Pu | 22 | 10,300 | 2.0 |
| Green-house Dog | USA | April 7, 1951 | Eniwetok | Pu | 81 | 3,175 | 25.5 |
| RDS-2 | U.S.S.R. | Sept. 24, 1951 | Kazakhstan | Pu | ~40 | ~5,000 | ~8 |
| Hurricane | U.K. | Oct. 3, 1952 | W. Australia | Pu | 25 | 6,000 | 4.2 |
| *Gerboise Bleue* | France | Feb. 13, 1960 | Algeria | Pu | 60-70 | ~3,250 | ~20 |
| *Gerboise Blanche* | France | April 1, 1960 | Algeria | Pu | 20*** | 2,840 | 7.0 |
| 596 | China | Oct. 16, 1964 | Lop Nur | HEU | 22 | 3,410 | 6.5 |

* Device yield, in tons of TNT equivalent, divided by device weight, in pounds: a reasonable measure of weapon sophistication.

** RDS-1, the first Soviet A-bomb, was internally an exact copy of Fat Man.

*** Since succeeding French tests gave ~20 kilotons (if successful), we believe this first French device was over-filled with plutonium to assure success. The second French test, Gerboise Blanche, fired six weeks later, gave 20 kilotons in 2,840 pounds. This latter seems like a better figure of merit for initial French tests.

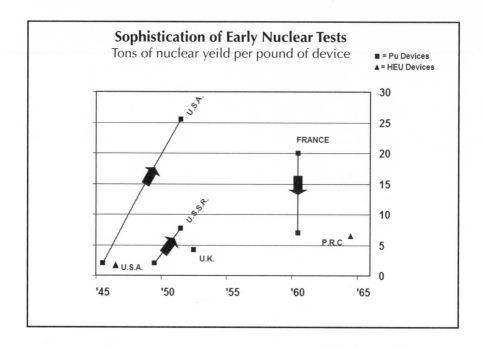

The Chinese approach to the development of nuclear weapons had been quite different from both the bumpy path taken by their one-time Soviet sponsors and the well-engineered thoroughfare driven by the Europeans. The Chinese nuclear program received the highest priority, but it was conducted with the greatest care amidst conditions of hardship unimaginable in the West. Hundreds of experiments, months of hand-calculations, and years of thought went into every decision. Thus, the choices the Chinese made were usually correct. China entered the nuclear club on a par with her European predecessors. In the process she built a technical foundation, poured by American-educated students and reinforced with scoured U.S. technology, that would produce impressive nuclear and thermonuclear breakthroughs in the decades to come.

# NUCLEAR MATURITY COMES TO THE LITTLE THREE

The nuclear detonation of October 1964 illuminated more than the desert sands of western China. It was a giant flare, lighting up the ridgelines of a cultural divide within the United States, a time that has come to be known as "the Sixties."

The first of those years held golden promise. A vigorous young former lieutenant replaced a stolid wartime general as president of the United States. John Kennedy wanted to "get the country moving again." He articulated his willingness to, "pay any price, bear any burden, meet any hardship, support any friend, oppose any foe to assure the survival and success of liberty." He was determined to preclude the use of nuclear weapons by the superpowers and to stop their proliferation into the Third World. John Kennedy's oft-repeated fear was, "Fifteen to twenty nuclear states within twenty years."

Unfortunately, Fate had other plans. Even before his inauguration, Kennedy was entangled in the weavings of the nuclear black widow. In 1960, the French marked the kickoff of his presidential campaign with an impressive sixty-five-kiloton nuclear test over the Algerian desert. They fired twice more before his inauguration, and they blew up a fourth device in 1961 to keep it out of their rebel generals' hands. From the outgoing Eisenhower administration, Kennedy learned of Chinese nuclear developments, Soviet rocket ambitions, and an Israeli nuclear reactor. In talks with Eisenhower on the day before inauguration, Kennedy was told the Israeli reactor would be producing weapons-grade plutonium by 1963. The prime minister of Israel had denied such allegations, assuring his parliament and the American president that the Dimona reactor was small, intended only for peaceful scientific and agriculture-supporting research, but that was hardly the case.

Kennedy was to spend much of his time in office seeking a clarification of the

Israeli nuclear program. He wanted technically qualified Americans[1] to visit the Dimona facility, but Israeli obfuscation and delay built a stone wall around that desert enclave. When a handful of U.S. nuclear experts finally made it into that country, late in the Kennedy administration, the U.S. ambassador to Israel considered their visit to be a bad Israeli joke. The visiting engineers were given extended tours of every historic and academic site within the State of Israel, yet their visit to Dimona lasted only forty-five minutes.

Kennedy began his presidency with a failed summit in Vienna, a confrontation over Berlin, a call-up of the military reserves, and a unilateral Soviet abrogation of the U.S.-U.K.-U.S.S.R nuclear testing moratorium. He responded courageously, with the resumption of American nuclear tests, but when those tests ended, Kennedy sought and achieved an enforceable treaty among the three thermonuclear powers to end such tests for all time.[2] As part of those treaty negotiations,[3] Kennedy asked his ambassador to discuss with his Soviet counterparts possible "joint efforts to limit or prevent" Chinese development of a nuclear capability, presumably including the use of force. There was no meeting of the minds.[4] Thus, when a delegation of generals from Taiwan came to Washington in the autumn of 1963 seeking U.S. support for an attack on the Chinese nuclear facilities (as described in chapter 7), Kennedy declined any participation; he lacked Soviet support.

The young president was slow to recognize intelligence indicators out of Cuba, but when photographic evidence of a Soviet nuclear weapons buildup on that island came forcefully to his attention, he handled and settled that crisis without resorting to nuclear arms. In the aftermath he executed a Hot Line Agreement with his Soviet counterparts in an effort to head off future nuclear misunderstandings. President de Gaulle was fully supportive of U.S. actions at that time, but as the decade wore on, de Gaulle grew restive with the scope of the American military presence within France. There were more than 190 U.S. military installations within the country, Paris was NATO headquarters, and the Americans were not gracious guests. American nuclear weapons were being deployed throughout the NATO countries with little oversight or control by the host governments. When faced with the need to entrust

1. Independent-minded officials from the U.S. AEC's Reactor Development Division and employees of the contractor operating the U.S. AEC's Savannah River reactors.
2. "A Treaty Banning Nuclear Weapons Tests in the Atmosphere, in Outer Space, and Under Water," signed in Moscow on August 5, 1963.
3. Instructions to Ambassador Harriman, en route to Moscow, July 1963.
4. It is ironic that when the Soviets queried the United States on such an attack six years later, in the summer of 1969, the Nixon White House declined. Source: Henry Kissinger, *The White House Years* (New York: Little Brown, 1979), 56.

U.S. nuclear weapons into NATO hands, Kennedy directed the installation of locks to preclude their use without his personal approval.

President de Gaulle had little confidence the United States would use those weapons to defend his homeland if only Europe came under Soviet attack. He ordered a speed-up in the French fission-weapon program, requesting American assistance in the process. None was forthcoming. On the contrary, U.S. surveillance of the French nuclear weapons complex was increased, and every effort was made to block the transfer of U.S. nuclear weapon technology to France. In 1963, the American secretary of defense[5] ordered a massive cutback in the scope of U.S. operations within France while providing no advance notice to the thousands of French employees to be laid off. De Gaulle was outraged; his complaints to the U.S. ambassador were ignored. That anger mellowed into disdain as Lyndon Johnson, a new and less Eurocentric American president, accompanied by the same annoying secretary of defense, took center stage only a few months later.

## CONVERGENCE OF THE SHOCK WAVES

John Kennedy took his fear of nuclear proliferation with him to his grave. Lee Harvey Oswald, a communist sympathizer, effected the transition. Lyndon B. Johnson brought different priorities home from Dallas.

In the beginning, Johnson talked a good antinuclear game. In seeking election to the presidency in his own right, Johnson characterized his opponent as a nuclear madman. A 1964 campaign highlight was the "nuclear daisy" ad, a sixty-second TV spot that depicted a small girl being blown away by a sudden nuclear burst—an event attributed to his opponent's potential carelessness. After the first Chinese nuclear test, in the fall of that election year, Johnson said, "Nuclear spread is dangerous to all mankind. . . . We must continue to work against it, and we will."

But once the campaign of 1964 was over, things changed. The sun had passed over the ridgeline and was setting on the western side of the cultural divide. One Westerner, a Texan, had taken over the White House. Another, from Arizona,[6] had wrested control of the opposition party from the hands of the eastern establishment. A third, from California,[7] had appeared as a shooting star, a portent of the future, amidst that miasmic election.

John Kennedy had been mindful of the importance of the Jewish vote to the Democratic Party, but he also understood the dangers of nuclear proliferation.

5. Robert McNamara.
6. Barry Goldwater.
7. Ronald Reagan.

Lyndon Johnson was cut from different cloth. In the words of Kennedy's CIA director,[8] Johnson's top priority was simply "his standing in the polls." Little else mattered. Israeli-linked financiers enjoyed unfettered access to the Johnson White House; Kennedy's concerns about nuclear proliferation went out the door. "Good nonproliferation policies make for bad politics," Johnson told his staff. After the 1964 elections, Johnson's National Security Council confirmed their president's disinterest in proliferation control. As they weighed withdrawal of active support for such controls, the national security advisor counseled subterfuge: "Don't talk about it." As the shock waves from Dallas and Lop Nur converged on Washington, they blew away all semblances of nuclear constraint.

## ISRAEL'S PIVOTAL DECADE

The mid-1960s were the critical years for the Israeli nuclear program. A plutonium-producing nuclear reactor had been built in the Negev desert under the nose, but out of the sight, of a proliferation-adverse American president. With a wink and a nod, the president of France had pretended to withdraw his personal support of that program, while allowing his industries to continue work. It had taken the industrial superstates (United States and Soviets) only ten months and fourteen months, respectively, to go from reactor criticality to first bomb. While it might take Israel twice as long, the demagogues ruling Israel's neighbors knew that time was running out. By the end of the 1960s, Israel would have the bomb unless the Arabs did something.

Immediately upon taking office, and even before election in his own right, LBJ had to deal with the legacy of Kennedy's confrontation with the Ben-Gurion government over Dimona inspections. At the end of the Eisenhower years, U.S. intelligence assets had exposed Dimona as a nuclear reactor in gestation. Early in the Kennedy years, in preparation for a Kennedy–Ben-Gurion meeting, two foreign-born, U.S. citizen-scientists, men of enormous prestige and a clear conflict of interest, were invited to visit Dimona. Eugene Wigner and I. I. Rabi, born in Hungary and Austria respectively, visited that facility in April 1961 as a prelude to a Kennedy–Ben-Gurion meeting set for May of that year. At the time of this visit, Professor Rabi was already a member of the board of governors (and presumably on the payroll) of Israel's Weizman Institute of Science, the incubator of most nuclear weapons work in Israel. After their visit, Wigner and Rabi gave Dimona a clean bill of health, finding "no evidence of weapon-related activity."

As construction progressed, more dispassionate U.S. technical experts were allowed only brief glimpses of the project. As noted earlier, the U.S. Ambassador to Israel found

8. John McCone.

117

their tours "laughable." Meanwhile, Nasser and the Egyptian government were growing concerned about the evidence of a nuclear weapons capability next door.

Israel's solution to this quandary was another inspection charade. On January 18, 1964, the Israelis hosted a visit by three qualified American nuclear reactor engineers. Prior to that, in the privacy of their government offices, the Israelis also decided to build a nuclear Potemkin Village, a parallel control room full of dials and buttons, computer-controlled to simulate the operation of a small-scale nuclear research facility. The Israelis bricked off the entrance to areas that would have disclosed the size and true scope of their operation, and they disallowed any American inspection of the reactor core, "for safety reasons." The ruse worked. The operations the Americans did see were consistent with the harmless scientific work advertised by the Israelis. The visitors neither spoke nor read Hebrew, and thus they were at the mercy of their tour guides and interpreters. Upon their departure from Israel, the American visitors reported to U.S. and Egyptian authorities that the Israeli reactor "has no immediate weapons-making capability." In fact, the production of Israeli plutonium had started one month prior.[9]

Bomb building and plutonium production require uranium. The Israelis hoped to produce enough from phosphate deposits in the Negev, but in the late 1950s, the French agreed to provide the uranium needed for the reactor under construction. As time went by, the Israelis began to import yellowcake ore from Argentina and South Africa, but some feel that a windfall of enriched uranium, more than two hundred pounds, came from an Israeli sympathizer in Ohio. In 1965, Zalman Shapiro's NUMEC Corporation, a reprocessor of reactor components, seems to have misplaced 206 pounds of enriched uranium. Mr. Shapiro had many business and personal connections with Israel; key CIA officers were convinced the missing material was the basis for Israel's initial, 1967 A-bomb assemblies. Those charges against Mr. Shapiro were never proven; the disappearances were claimed to be standard industrial losses.

Another, better documented disappearance took place in 1968, when several hundred tons of uranium ore, stored in Brussels and available for sale to Euratom users, was purchased by a Mossad front, nominally on behalf of a Milanese customer. The ore left Antwerp on a renamed Turkish freighter. Once at sea, the ore was transferred to an Israeli ship and delivered to Israel. The disappearance was blamed on a hijacking. No one seemed to care, and that transaction gave Israel enough uranium to make it through the 1960s. After the Yom Kippur War of 1973, Israel and South Africa established closer nuclear ties, and Israel was assured of a uranium supply well into the future.

9. Seymour M. Hersh, *The Samson Option* (New York: Random House, 1991), 111 et seq.

During the 1960s, there were ongoing pressures on President Johnson to control such proliferation, but his ambassador to Israel understood the real agenda. In later years, Walworth Barbour recited his instructions from LBJ: "Your job is to keep the [Israelis] off my back. Keep them happy." In 1967, just prior to the Yom Kippur War, AEC intelligence expert Arnold Kramish wangled a back-channel invitation from the Israeli security service to visit the Dimona complex. Before going, he wanted to check with the American ambassador in Tel Aviv. "Oh, no," Ambassador Barbour shouted in horror. "If you learn anything about Dimona, I'd have to tell the president, and then he would have to do something, and he doesn't want to. Stay in Brussels." Kramish stayed put; the American president remained detached.

In the autumn of 1966,[10] Israeli scientists conducted an important experiment 2,600 feet below the Negev desert. We believe that event was a hydronuclear or near-zero-yield test of a supercritical prototype bomb. Such a test would have confirmed the validity of detonation, implosion, and initiation calculations, and with that proof, the Israeli government knew it had the technology to build an A-bomb. All that remained was the production of a few pounds of plutonium from the Dimona facility.

By 1967, Egypt's Nasser was organizing an alliance of the Arab states surrounding Israel. The objective was to avenge earlier damage to Arab sovereignty and ego and to act before Israel went nuclear. Nasser closed the Straits of Tiran to Israeli shipping, thus precluding Israel's access to the Red Sea. He overflew Dimona with pre-strike reconnaissance aircraft, and he massed his troops in the Sinai while kicking out the UN peacekeepers who had been installed there in the wake of the 1956 Suez confrontation. In the face of what the government of Israel saw as imminent attack, Israel struck first.

The Six-Day War began on June 5, 1967. It was a rout. On day one, the Israelis destroyed the Egyptian Air Force on the ground and blew away their tank corps. By day three, Israeli troops were on the eastern bank of the Suez Canal, holding thousands of Egyptian prisoners and having suffered minimal casualties of their own. The Israeli army could have rolled on into Cairo, but instead they stopped, leaving but a holding force at the canal. The Israelis withdrew their main forces into the homeland, then redeployed to the north and east, to attack Syria and Jordan. Syria had joined Egypt in prewar denunciations of Israel, but there were implicit statements from the Israelis that the June 5 attack in the Sinai was solely an Israeli-Egyptian fight. In fact it was not, a secret the Israelis did not wish exposed until they had finished off the Egyptians. On June 8, the Israelis reoriented their forces; by June 11, they had taken Syria's Golan Heights, Jordan's West Bank, and custody of the entire city of Jerusalem.

10. One source puts the date as November 2; another gives a window of September 26 to October 3.

It is now clear that nuclear weapons played a major role in the initiation of the Six-Day War. In the eyes of the Egyptian leaders, the Israeli capability posed a clear and present danger, while to the Israelis, nukes meant downside insurance. Prior to that conflict, Israel cobbled together two A-bombs from prototype components; if things went awry, the Israelis would still have the weapons needed to deliver war-ending devastation and decapitation onto Cairo and Damascus.

On June 8, 1967, the United States was drawn into this war, and LBJ was forced to show his hand. It was a crisis that cost dozens of American lives. On that day, the USS *Liberty*, an American electronic intelligence-collection ship, was loitering off the Egyptian coast, in international waters, collecting signals intelligence. During the previous day, the Israelis had warned the United States to get the *Liberty* out of there. The skipper never got the word, and on June 8, the *Liberty* came under deliberate and murderous attack by Israeli aircraft and torpedo boats. The reasons for that attack remain unclear, and the Israelis continue to claim "mistaken identity," but the *Liberty* was too well marked, the attack too well planned, and the continuing assaults over several hours too lethal to allow for any ambiguity.

At the time of the attack, the *Liberty* was assigned to the U.S. Sixth Fleet, patrolling the Mediterranean. As it came under attack, the spy-ship called for help. The aircraft carrier USS *America* immediately launched A-4 aircraft in response. An American ship was under attack; the skipper of the *America* did not wait for approval; he would seek permission once his aircraft were off the deck. Today, the pilot of the lead aircraft confirms the heartbreak that followed. Once in the air and en route to the *Liberty*, that pilot was told to abort his flight's mission. They were to return to the *America*. The A-4s were not to proceed to protect the *Liberty*, an American ship in distress. The order came from Secretary of Defense Robert McNamara, calling from the National Military Command Center. Upon his return to the *America*, that lead pilot[11] asked his skipper for the details. Admiral Geist, commander of the Sixth Fleet, had gotten the call from McNamara. The admiral had refused to issue the abort order unless he heard those instructions directly from the commander in chief. LBJ came on the line and confirmed that directive, to abort the A-4 flights, in his usual abrupt and unmistakable way.

The reasons for the Israeli attack remain clouded. Israelis and Arabs alike respected American signals-interception and decoding skills. One motive for the Israeli attack might have been a fear that U.S. intelligence would learn of the Israeli intent to turn on Syria once it had reached the Suez Canal, and that the Americans would then protest, or worse, warn Syria. The Americans had done that sort of independent thinking at the

11. William Knutson.

120

time of Suez, eleven years before. Others think the Americans would have learned of atrocities being visited on captured Egyptian troops, thereby energizing human-rights activists. Conspiracy theorists hold that it was an LBJ-Israeli plot to blame the sinking and death of all hands aboard the *Liberty* on the Egyptians, thus ensuring U.S. support for the Israelis in their ongoing battles with the Arabs. This was exactly the purpose of Operation Suzannah, an Israeli plot to destroy Anglo-American libraries in Egypt three years before and subsequently exposed as the Lavon Affair.

Whatever the reasons, the attack on the *Liberty* and the U.S. response makes clear the link between LBJ and Israel. Even though 34 Americans were killed and 172 were seriously wounded during this attack, the ensuing naval inquiry was terminated abruptly. The admiral in charge of that inquiry[12] subsequently confided to co-author Reed that his gag orders to all concerned had been a mistake. The Israelis apologized for the attack and offered compensation to the victims' families, but there has never been a proper inquiry by U.S. naval authorities into the incident. Admiral Thomas Moorer, chief of naval operations in the 1960s and chairman of the Joint Chiefs of Staff in the 1970s, in a last appearance before the U.S. Congress in 2004, pleaded for a full examination of the *Liberty*'s fate. "We owed the sailors and marines aboard the *Liberty* our best defense. We gave them none. Why would our government put Israel's interests above our own?" No navy secretary, no secretary of defense, no president has responded.

Lyndon Johnson was driven from office by other conflicts far from the Mediterranean, but his successors were as unconcerned as he on the matter of nuclear proliferation. In 1968, candidate Nixon spoke against ratification of the Nonproliferation Treaty, although once in office, he sent it forward to the U.S. Senate for confirmation. At that same time, however, he executed an internal national security decision memorandum instructing the bureaucracy to refrain from any active support of the treaty. They should neither lobby the Senate nor urge American allies to sign. As the 1960s ended, that president's national security advisor, Henry Kissinger, was expressing the view that, in time, most regional powers would develop nuclear weapons; that it was futile to try to stop such proliferation; and that America's best interests would be served by such developments, since those nations, once armed with nuclear weapons, would no longer need to rely on the U.S. nuclear umbrella for their security. Israel had become one such regional power; France was another.

## WHAT GOES AROUND COMES AROUND

Richard Nixon barely lost his race for the presidency in 1960, but in 1962, his political career appeared to end with another unsuccessful campaign, this one for the

12. Admiral Isaac "Ike" Kidd.

governorship of California. Nixon confirmed the evident end of that road with his oft-quoted remark to the press, "You won't have Nixon to kick around any more." But soon thereafter another recovering has-been, Charles de Gaulle, started to pay attention to the former vice president. In 1959, de Gaulle had returned from political exile himself, recalled to power by a France desperate to end the war in Algeria. He had met the American vice president while the latter was still in office, but after Nixon's two defeats, de Gaulle continued to stay in touch—one of the few world leaders to do so. De Gaulle was hoping for an American restoration.

In June 1963, Richard Nixon and his wife Pat took a trip to Europe before settling down to the practice of law in New York City. In Spain, dictator Francisco Franco warmly welcomed him at his summer residence outside Barcelona, but in Paris, the reception was overwhelming. The Nixons were hosted at a luncheon on the patio outside the Élysée Palace, and he was treated as though he were still a high government official. In what Nixon called a "warm and friendly toast," de Gaulle noted Nixon's recent difficult times, but he also predicted, "at some time in the future [Nixon] would be serving [his] nation in a very high capacity." With the death of John Kennedy in the autumn of that year, and with the onset of perceived Johnsonian insults, de Gaulle nurtured his relationship with the former vice president.

Four years later,[13] upon his assumption of the American presidency, Nixon returned to Paris. President de Gaulle was on hand at Orly to greet him—in English no less—as Air Force One touched down. The now-reunited friends returned to the Élysée Palace for extensive private meetings, where we must assume nuclear weapons were on the agenda. Following those discussions was an impressive state dinner. The American Embassy returned the hospitality. De Gaulle's toasts were euphoric; he made it diplomatically clear that he was glad to be rid of Lyndon Johnson and delighted to have a true friend in the White House. De Gaulle retired from office a year later, but his loyalty to Nixon paid off with a major sharing of Franco-American nuclear secrets early in Nixon's second term.

## THE WINDING FRENCH ROAD

Throughout the year that followed Kennedy's death, France conducted three more underground nuclear tests within Algeria, their enriched-uranium facility at Pierrelatte went into operation,[14] and the Chinese entered the nuclear club with a bang. It was the

---

13. In February 1969.
14. A gaseous diffusion plant near the Marcoule reactor, eighty miles northeast of Marseille. Serious construction started there in 1958; in 1964, the plant was producing 2 percent enriched U-235. Pierrelatte commenced full HEU production in April 1967.

Chinese event that got de Gaulle's attention, for until then he had attached a low priority to advanced nuclear technology; he just wanted a deployed and operational A-bomb, deliverable by aircraft or missiles, as soon as possible. As late as July 1962, following the end of the hostilities in Algeria and the commencement of underground nuclear testing in that country, de Gaulle remained fully focused on the creation of his A-bomb–oriented Force de Frappe. In conversations with his scientific staff, de Gaulle made it clear that H-bomb work would interfere with the more immediate tasks at hand, and he did not want the distraction. But then, two years later, with the October 1964 entry of China into the nuclear club, de Gaulle changed his tune. He feared those Third World upstarts might beat France into the inner club of thermonuclear powers. "Are we going to let the Chinese get ahead of us?" he asked of his minister of research. "Go figure out [what to do]!"[15]

French underground nuclear tests continued within Algeria through February 1966, although French rights to conduct such tests within that now-independent country were about to expire. In June 1966, at the height of the Johnson administration's rule, de Gaulle decided to terminate his military participation in the North Atlantic Treaty Organization. He demanded all U.S. forces be withdrawn from France by April 1, 1967. "Does that include the men buried there as well?" the displeased American president asked.[16]

In the summer of 1966, France implemented the relocation of her nuclear test site. Ignoring the Limited Test Ban Treaty (to which she was not a signatory) and with disdain for the genetic and environmental dangers involved, France returned to the testing of nuclear weapons in the atmosphere, doing so at her colonial atolls in idyllic French Polynesia.[17]

The initial explosions at Mururoa Atoll, starting in July 1966, focused on the weaponization of a tactical nuclear weapon, but back at the French nuclear weapons laboratory at Limeil, nothing thermonuclear was happening. There were a lot of blackboard discussions, there were constant reorganizations, but there were no H-bomb designs in the offing, until the spring of 1967. In April of that year, one Michael Carayol published an internal paper on a strange new phenomenon: radiative compression. Most of the scientists at Lemeil were "hesitant and perplexed."[18] The Carayol idea "remained locked up within Limeil."

15. Alain Peyrefitte, *Le Mal Francais* (Paris: Fayard, 2006).
16. Dean Rusk, *As I Saw It* (Norton, 1990), 271; confirmed in private conversation with an LBJ-era White House aide, 2006.
17. The Defence Council first made this decision, in the face of Algerian independence, on July 4, 1962.
18. Primary source: Pierre Billaud (former director of the nuclear weapons laboratory at Limeil), "The Incredible Story of the French H-Bomb," trans. D. C. Amsden, *La Recherche* no. 293 (December 1996), 74–78.

During the summer of 1967, there were further management changes at the laboratory. The H-Committee was formed to broaden the search for solutions, but none were evident, while Carayol sat on a back bench. The H-Committee conducted a "summer study" at Valduc, which ended during the first week of September amidst a terrible funk.

During that summer of 1967, French nuclear tests continued at Mururoa,[19] with three small experiments involving the newly available highly enriched uranium, but on June 17, to the despair of the French scientific community, the Chinese fulfilled de Gaulle's darkest fears; they crashed into the thermonuclear club with a 3.3-megaton burst. It came from a weapon dropped by a Hong 6 bomber over the Lop Nur desert. That explosion occurred only thirty-two months after the first Chinese A-bomb test. The French were left to puzzle in the dark.

Amidst this gloom, while reviewing the Valduc proceedings, the laboratory at Lemeil received an "informed visitor" from London. (Thomas Cochran, NRDC, identifies this individual as William Cook, then deputy director of the Atomic Weapons Research Establishment at Aldermaston and director of Britain's H-bomb program. Cochran suggests Cook's September 1967 trip to France was an attempt by the British to end de Gaulle's continuing veto of British membership in the European Union. It did not work. De Gaulle vetoed again on November 27, 1967.) On September 27, this gentleman, clearly sent by the highest officials in the British government, joined the H-bomb discussions. (Britain had gone thermonuclear a decade before, in 1957.) When Michel Carayol's turn came at the blackboard, the visitor, with a nod of his head, quietly labeled the Carayol solution as correct. At a follow-up meeting, on September 29, the senior staff at Lemeil was told that "information had been received [about H-bomb design] from abroad; it should remain confidential." French scientists now understood how to make such a weapon.

From that moment on, things moved quickly. As Pierre Billaud, director of the nuclear weapons laboratory at Lemeil in the summer of 1967, later put it, "the Department of Military Applications' admirable machine started working towards its new objectives with great determination." It designed, assembled, and tested a thermonuclear device in less than a year.

Canopus, France's first two-stage thermonuclear device, was fired over Fangataufa Atoll on August 24, 1968. The six-thousand-pound experiment, using an enriched-uranium primary and an Li6D secondary, gave a yield of 2.6 megatons. It also rendered the atoll useless for years, inaccessible to humans for reasons of radioactive contamination. As a result, the second H-bomb experiment, Procyon, was fired

19. Co-author Stillman monitored these tests aboard U.S. aircraft based in American Samoa.

elsewhere, at Mururoa. It delivered 1.2 megatons. With that, France had undeniably joined the thermonuclear club. As 1968 drew to a close, de Gaulle had his H-bomb. He was still president of France, and Lyndon Johnson was still president of the United States, but within six months both would be gone from the world stage.

## CHINA MOVES AHEAD OF THE PACK

In 1959, as France, Israel, and China all prepared for their first nuclear test, the Chinese were already thinking, "What next?" In the immediate wake of Qian Sanqiang's meeting with Klaus Fuchs, the Central Military Commission established new guidelines for the Chinese nuclear weapons program. These guidelines included a decision to pursue thermonuclear weapons. In 1960, China's Second Ministry instructed her Institute of Atomic Energy to form a separate group with a charter to investigate such materials and reactions. Huang Zuqia, Qian Sanqiang, and a bright young graduate of Beijing University, Yu Min, were to lead that effort.

By 1964, Lanzhou was beginning to deliver highly enriched uranium, and throughout the Jiuquan Atomic Energy Complex, machinists and electronics technicians were practicing for the moment when those precious bomb materials and components would be entrusted to their care. But with the end of the Three Hard Years, work had also resumed on the plutonium-production reactor, known as Plant 404, in Jiuquan. Plant 404 would go critical in October 1966, although at a very low power level. There were recurring mechanical breakdowns and political interruptions, the latter arising from the Cultural Revolution. Even so, Plant 404 would begin to produce irradiated fuel rods in 1967. By September 1968, the nearby reprocessing facility would be turning out weapons-grade plutonium. Within weeks thereafter, at the nearby Nuclear Component Manufacturing Plant, that gray metal would be cast, machined, and assembled into a weapon core for use in a multistage thermonuclear experiment. By the end of 1968, China had two routes to fissionable materials.

The Chinese had fired the bomb dubbed 596 on October 16, 1964. American intelligence analysts were astonished by the lack of plutonium in the fallout debris and by the speed with which China had broken into the nuclear club, but that was only the beginning. In the spring of 1966, the Chinese entered the thermonuclear world with the detonation of a boosted-fission, airdropped device that utilized Li6. That test, only the third in China's march to nuclear parity, achieved a yield of 200 to 300 kilotons in an important display of new fusion technology. At the end of that year, the Chinese made the leap to multistage know-how with an experiment that yielded 122 kilotons. The principles of staging and radiation implosion had been tested. The Chinese closed the circle on June 17, 1967, with an unambiguous 3.3-megaton burst from an aircraft-delivered weapon that again utilized Li6 and displayed multiple uranium isotopes in the fallout debris. China had joined the H-bomb club. She had done so with no plutonium in that first H-bomb design,[20] since the nuclear reactor at Jiuquan was only then coming online. And she had achieved the leap from first test, in October 1964, to a 3.3-megaton thermonuclear blast in a record-breaking thirty-two months. It had taken the United States seven years to accomplish this feat. (See chart below)

### Months elapsed between a nation's first fission bomb test and it's first test of a true thermonuclear

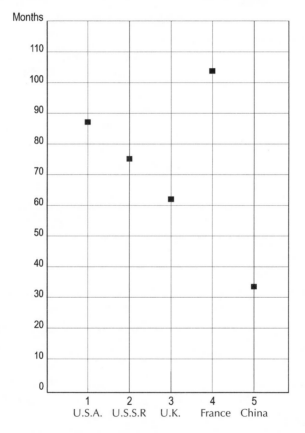

UN Security Council members, in order of first nuclear test.

Source: *Bulletin of Atomic Scientists*, Sept/Oct 2003, pp71–72

20. The use of an inefficient enriched-uranium primary made China the first of the H-bomb entrant states to do so.

Just as the Chinese had achieved their first A-bomb in the face of the Great Leap Forward (1958–60) and the withdrawal of Soviet support (in June 1959), so it was that China achieved full thermonuclear status in 1968 despite the Cultural Revolution.

That 1966 outbreak of anti-intellectual hostility took millions of lives, destroyed centuries of historical artifacts, paralyzed the Chinese economy, and decimated the Chinese nuclear weapons laboratories. The Red Guards were everywhere, turning workers against each other in a frantic search for revisionists and counterrevolutionaries. During one of his visits to China, co-author Stillman met a scientist who had earned his Ph.D. in physics from Brown University during the early 1960s. Upon his return to China in 1966, the man was assigned not to nuclear weapons work but to rice farming, where he stayed for two years.

How were the Chinese able to pull off an H-bomb test in thirty-two months amidst this chaos? There were several contributors, perhaps starting with the already-mentioned Klaus Fuchs. By 1959, when Fuchs was released from his British prison and fled to East Germany, both the United States and Soviet Union had fired H-bombs. Russian historians credit their 1954 H-bomb epiphany to a re-examination of Fuch's 1948 disclosures about staging and radiation implosion. Ten years later, after reading only the open literature while in prison, Fuchs should have developed his own understanding of how the U.S. and Soviet thermonuclears worked. When he met with Qian Sanqiang in Dresden, Fuchs could well have given that Chinese scientist not only the details of Fat Man—he could have furnished priceless insight into H-bomb design as well. Only a few months passed between those Qian-Fuchs discussions and the approval of a Chinese H-bomb program by the Central Military Commission.

Another interesting aspect of Chinese nuclear sophistication lies in that country's analytic and computational skills. Chinese scientists conducted many experiments on paper and in machines, not at Lop Nur. After China's first nuclear test, in 1964, the nation needed only two other detonations suitable for the development of an H-bomb primary before testing an H-bomb prototype. Other nations have required many more.

A third source of Chinese insight was surely technical intelligence: that is, the collection of radiochemical data from U.S. and Soviet nuclear tests within the atmosphere. The collection of samples from the U.S. tests in the Pacific during the early 1950s might have posed a challenge, but the detonations of 1958 and 1962 would have provided most helpful insights. The Chinese also collected against the Soviet tests in Kazakhstan and probably Novaya Zemlya.

One must not discount the extensive network of Chinese technical intelligence agents within the United States, tied to an army of graduate students and supported by Soviet "research." All of these sources were feeding information to an incredibly good native scientific community back home. At every stop within China, Stillman found

English-speakers translating U.S. documents night and day, alumni of prestigious and lesser-known U.S. schools working the problems, and a suffocating attention to every scrap of information dropped by visitors.

In 1990, Stillman met Yu Min, the generally accepted "father of the Chinese H-bomb." He was an incredibly talented man. And there can be no doubt Yu Min did, in fact, design the first Chinese thermonuclear. However, we believe he did so with the assistance of key ideas from Fuchs, an incredible domestic computational capability, indicators from other nations' tests, access to an enormous library of Western publications, and the support of a vast array of intellectual talent, much of it trained in the West.

## GOING UNDERGROUND

For the first five years of China's nuclear program, all tests were conducted in the atmosphere: six by airdrop or missile delivery and two atop 330-foot-high steel towers. While China had not (and never did) sign the Limited Test Ban Treaty of 1963, from the very beginning, its scientists were attempting to minimize fallout. Until China began to study weapon effects in the 1970s, there were no surface bursts at Lop Nur sucking up great clouds of radioactive debris.

In 1969, with two years of preparatory study, the Chinese conducted their first underground nuclear test. They did so within an excavated tunnel, not a borehole. There was more than one reason for this Chinese move away from atmospheric testing. As the Nixon administration entered office, as the Third World gained traction in its campaign to preclude atmospheric nuclear testing, and as the Nuclear Nonproliferation Treaty was headed toward ratification, environmental benefits and proliferation control were the oft-stated reasons for those transitions. But there is another advantage to an atmospheric test ban: the privacy it gives the testing nation. Without tests in the atmosphere, competing and inquisitive neighbors cannot collect fallout debris. They will have a harder time understanding the devices tested by their rivals; it becomes easier for the testing nation to bluff.

The first Chinese underground test, of September 23, 1969, was as much a rock-dynamics experiment as it was a device test. After that detonation, the Northwest Institute of Nuclear Technology (NINT) undertook a thorough—and by now typically Chinese—examination of subterranean nuclear testing phenomena. They did not test underground again for another six years, until they had gained a full understanding of rock mechanics, sampling, and environmental hazards.

The Chinese bid farewell to atmospheric nuclear testing with a seven-hundred-kiloton airburst on October 16, 1980—the last such test by any nuclear power. Over a period of fifteen years, China had achieved parity with the West (and preeminence over her Asian peers) in her understanding of underground nuclear testing. Yet one startling aspect of co-author Stillman's visits to the Chinese test base stands out. Every aspect of every Chinese nuclear test was conducted exactly as we do it in the United States.

## ADVANCES IN BOMB TECHNOLOGY

On December 27, 1968, the Chinese bid farewell to the LBJ years with the detonation of an improved three-megaton thermonuclear device that, for the first time, utilized plutonium within the primary. The interesting thing is that the Chinese did not feel the need to test that new primary separately. They simply included it within a second-generation H-bomb design that went off as planned.

It is interesting to now review an earlier chart of initial plutonium-production reactor criticality and first nuclear tests, augmented with this Chinese data:

| Country | First plutonium production reactor goes critical | First test of a Pu-based A-bomb or primary | Time, reactor to bomb |
|---|---|---|---|
| U.S.A. | September 1944 | July 1945 | 10 months |
| U.S.S.R. | June 1948 | August 1949 | 14 months |
| U.K. | July 1950 | October 1952 | 27 months |
| France | January 1956 | February 1960 | 49 months |
| Israel | December 1963 | ~ June 1967* | ~40 months |
| China | October 1966 | December 1968** | 26 months |

  * It is clear that Israel had one or two nuclear weapons on hand at the time of the Six-Day War in June 1967 and could have tested them had it desired to do so.

** China's first nuclear detonation was October 16, 1964, an all–highly enriched uranium weapon; plutonium was first used in a nuclear test on December 27, 1968.

It is clear from the reactor-to-bomb times that, by 1968, China had unequivocally entered the European nuclear cartel, on a par with Great Britain. Her rapid ascent to thermonuclear status, far faster than her predecessors, confirms that parity.

## WHO HAS BEEN DANCING WITH WHOM?

Since the birth of the nuclear age, no nation has developed a nuclear weapon on its own, although many claim otherwise. Los Alamos was a multicultural community. The Soviets extracted knowledge via spies. The British helped with the design of Fat Man; their scientists returned to the United Kingdom to replicate it. We believe the Chinese drew heavily on U.S. and Soviet technology while doing brilliant scientific work on their own. So who else was dancing at the Nuclear Masked Ball?

It is quite clear that France and Israel undertook a joint nuclear weapons program in the aftermath of Suez. That relationship, on a commercial basis, continued for decades.

After the Chinese went thermonuclear in 1967, it appears the British made a deliberate decision to help the French join that club. Once the French succeeded in August 1968, and once Richard Nixon had succeeded to the American presidency, the United States joined the discussions.

Charles de Gaulle was still president of France at the time of Nixon's election in 1968. As noted earlier, those two gentlemen held lengthy discussions in private at the Élysée Palace in February 1969. While Nixon's predecessors had been opposed to any nuclear cooperation with France, Nixon and Kissinger saw a nuclear-armed France as adding uncertainty to Soviet calculations. They wanted to make the French Force de Frappe more stable, survivable, and cost effective. In the summer of 1969, the United States began providing France with the data it had collected from the 1967 and 1968 French atmospheric tests in the Pacific. In exchange, the French furnished information on the design of those devices to the United States.

The United States and France would consummate a more intimate connection after de Gaulle left office, but in July 1973 (a year prior to Nixon's forced departure from the presidency), National Security Advisor Henry Kissinger and French Foreign Minister Michel Jobert met at the "Western White House"[21] to put those pieces in place. On September 24 and 25, the French minister of armed services, Robert Galley, visited the Pentagon to consummate the deal. He met with Secretary of Defense James R. Schlesinger on the 24th and with Schlesinger's assistant for atomic energy, Don Cotter, on the following day. Schlesinger's general counsel urged caution in these discussions, but Minister Galley had his nuclear experts in tow, Kissinger wanted the technology transferred, and thus the connections, based on "negative guidance,"[22] were made. Two decades later, as the Cold War ended, historians made

21. San Clemente, California.
22. Advising the French when they were headed in the wrong direction.

clear that "For a decade and a half, the United States has provided substantial covert assistance to the nuclear forces of France."[23]

This assistance went beyond concepts. It included French participation in the U.S. underground nuclear tests in Nevada, exposing French weapon components to bursts of radiation to confirm French vulnerability calculations. After 1991, when world opinion forced the French to end atmospheric testing in French Polynesia, and when Richard Nixon and Charles de Gaulle were long gone from the world stage, it was the Chinese who secretly extended the hospitality of their Lop Nur nuclear test site to the French.

In 1982, once Deng Xiaoping had consolidated power within China, his government apparently decided not only to tolerate, but also to actively support the proliferation of nuclear weapons within the Third World. China welcomed Pakistani nuclear scientists to Beijing and passed along information on the CHIC-4 A-bomb design to those visitors. Unfortunately, Pakistan's A. Q. Khan then resold that information to his customers. Drawings and specifications for CHIC-4 turned up in a white plastic tailor's bag[24] in Libya. There is also evidence the Chinese conducted an underground nuclear test for the Pakistanis at Lop Nur on May 26, 1990, well before Pakistan's announced 1998 shots in south Asia.[25]

Nuclear technology has spread in strange and wondrous ways. Its constraint was of little interest to U.S. presidents in the late 1960s and early 1970s, but during those years, other, more reflective, minds were at work. The watershed moment may have come in 1973 with the publication of John McPhee's *The Curve of Binding Energy*. That book, detailing the concerns of Los Alamos weaponeer Ted Taylor, crystallized the thinking of American nuclear policymakers. Perhaps it was time to close the barn door before it was too late.

23. Richard H. Ullman, "The Covert French Connection," *Foreign Policy*, no. 75 (Summer 1989), 3–33.
24. Bearing the logo of the "Good Looks Tailor Shop."
25. See chapter 15 for details.

CHAPTER 9

# STRUGGLING WITH
# THE BARN DOOR

No one asked Colonel Tibbets if he had authority to release an A-bomb over Hiroshima, and everyone knew that Little Boy and Fat Man were unsafe. As World War II drew to a close, and with a prospective bloodbath on the southern shores of Japan less than ninety days away, the Allied scientists had but two objectives: get their gadgets delivered to the skies over Japan and, once there, release hitherto-unseen amounts of energy. Those 1945-era bombs were not "weapons"; they were glorified physics experiments. Safety was on everyone's minds, but it was hardly built in. Fat Man, rolling down the runway aboard the *Bock's Car* B-29, was an accident waiting to happen. No one worried about the possible theft or unauthorized use of those bombs. The exigencies of war set the calendar; military discipline was in control. But once the war was over, a different challenge arose. How were the custodians of that awesome wartime power to preclude the release of even the smallest amount of nuclear energy except at the time and place of their choosing? Even an "Act of God" would not be an acceptable excuse for the accidental detonation of a nuclear weapon.

## SAFING, ARMING, FUZING, AND FIRING (SAFF)
As a nuclear weapon is being designed, thought must be given to the various environments it may encounter during storage, handling, and delivery to target. These may be the anticipated circumstances (heat and cold, vibration and shock), or they may arise from unintended events: crashes, fires, lightning strikes, or terrorist actions. Weapon reliability is important, but safety must come first. In the design, production, and handling of U.S. nuclear weapons, positive steps are taken repeatedly to preclude the accidental detonation of high-explosive components, but beyond that, in the event of accident or malevolent act, there must be no chance of significant nuclear yield from the weapon under any circumstances.

For the first few years of the nuclear age, when timely use of a weapon was not an issue, and when the Atomic Energy Commission nominally retained ownership of all nuclear materials, the solution was simple: redesign Fat Man such that the plutonium core could be physically separated from the weapon itself. That was the solution employed during the 1940s. The fissile core, known as the capsule, would be held and carried apart from the weapon. Only upon presidential release would that capsule be turned over to the military; only en route to the target would it be inserted into the weapon.

The Atomic Energy Act of 1946 envisioned such a civilian-military separation of custody continuing indefinitely, but that was when the United States thought it held a nuclear monopoly; the world was at peace. As the Iron Curtain came down and as the Cold War began to unfold, President Truman decided to deploy nuclear-capable[1] bombers to forward locations as a clear warning to others of what might follow. While nuclear-capable B-29s were sent to the United Kingdom at the time of the Berlin blockade, they carried no nuclear weapons. Within North America the new, long-range B-36 propeller-driven, nuclear-capable aircraft began to fly training missions, again with no actual nuclear weapons aboard. Then came the first Soviet nuclear test and Mao's takeover in China, both in the latter half of 1949. The general officer assigned to military applications at the Atomic Energy Commission requested the transfer of some nonnuclear weapon components—that is, the bomb minus the fissionable core—to combat units. The president agreed. In the summer of 1950, upon North Korea's invasion of the South, the president sent additional nuclear-capable aircraft to the western Pacific, and in April 1951, the Joint Chiefs requested the transfer of a few fissionable cores themselves to air force units on Guam. The president soon approved. With that, the civilian-military firewall had been breached, and since aircraft do not invariably remain in the sky, the crashes and accidents soon began. During 1950 alone there were five events involving an aircraft with an unarmed nuclear weapon aboard. (See appendix C, table I.) None of these accidents produced any nuclear yield, and there was no contamination of the crash site, but the separation of weapon from capsule was becoming operationally cumbersome.

The in-flight insertion of a plutonium ball and the rearrangement of the surrounding high explosive, all within the bomb bay of an operating aircraft, were not easy. The need to do so was beginning to hinder the design of more sophisticated nuclear weapons; alternatives were soon adopted. These included mechanical blocks to

1. Aircraft fitted with the racks and electronics needed to carry and deliver a nuclear weapon. Such aircraft might, or might not, have a weapon aboard. In the 1940s and early 1950s, these aircraft seldom flew with a capsule of fissionable material anywhere on board.

the delivery of energy to arming switches and detonators, the insertion of retractable mechanical devices within the fissile core, and the development of high-explosive designs that were "one-point safe." This latter expression refers to the requirement that, in the event of a detonation occurring at any one point within a weapon's high-explosive system, no matter the cause, the nuclear explosive will have no more than one chance in a million of producing more than four pounds of fission yield. The need was identified in the late 1950s and solved by Livermore's Johnny Foster in the early 1960s.

When the decision to use a nuclear weapon has been irrevocably made, it must be armed. That means safety catches must be released, capacitors charged, and valves opened. As the weapon approaches its target, it must be fuzed; it must be told that it is at the correct detonation point. Lastly, it must be fired, meaning that detonators, neutron sources, and other electronics must be triggered so as to achieve the design yield. To understand these concepts, consider the sketch below.

## CONCEPTUAL IMPLOSION A-BOMB

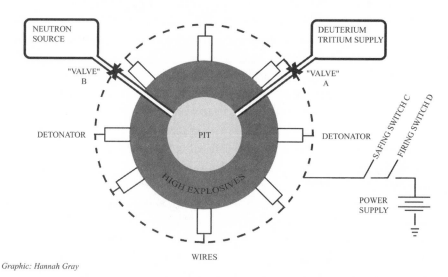

Graphic: Hannah Gray

To arm this weapon, one must open the deuterium-tritium valve, "A" (thus admitting boosting gas into the weapon's core), and close the safing switch, "C," thereby connecting the weapon's electronics to its fuze-protected power supply. In modern U.S. weapons, these steps are dependent on sensors known as environmental sensing devices (ESDs), which block electrical power until the weapon senses the environment expected en route to the intended target. For instance, missile warheads must sense the intense G-loading associated with missile launch or warhead re-entry before they will arm. In later years, computers and inertial sensors were built into other munitions to confirm their location outside the United States before arming. Some nations' weapons now include permissive action links or PALs. These electronic locks require release authority from the National Command Authority, not just the officer on duty or the individual having custody (more on this subject later).

To actually fire the weapon, one must energize detonators and other devices, then trigger a flood of neutrons into the assembled core at exactly the right moment. The fuze, be it radar, altimeter, or ground-sensor, tells the weapon when and where to detonate; the firing circuits effect that detonation. In the sketch above, these circuits are suggested by a firing switch, "D." Neutrons do not come in bottles: things are more complicated than this sketch implies, but we have suggested the start of neutron flooding with a neutron valve, "B." Initially, neutrons were provided to the imploding core by a polonium-beryllium ball at the center of the fissile material, compressed by the implosion shock wave. This released the needed neutrons at the moment of maximum density. In modern weapons, neutrons are provided externally by electronic devices known as zippers. Their timing is critical; thus, the reference to an electronic valve that must be fired at exactly the right moment to provide those initiating neutrons.

Fortunately, many of these safety measures had been designed into U.S. weapons as the nuclear age entered its second decade. By the mid-1950s, U.S. and Soviet nukes were becoming quite portable; both nations were testing thermonuclears; the Soviets were displaying Bison bombers in May Day parades; and the first all-jet U.S. bomber, the B-47, was entering service with the U.S. Air Force.

The newly inaugurated American president, Eisenhower, was deeply concerned about the possibility of "another Pearl Harbor," an attack out of the blue on U.S. forces and cities. He sought advice from a panel of experts. Active reconnaissance (overflights of the Soviet Union by aircraft and then satellites) was one response. Increasing the alert status of the U.S. bomber force was another. By the mid-1950s, the new B-47s and other aircraft were flying practice alerts with the separate-capsule A-bombs aboard, and thus the accidents began again. (See appendix C, table II.)

In 1954 and 1955, the United States and U.S.S.R first tested compact H-bombs. These weapons were far more complex and more lethal than their World War II predecessor A-bombs. Air warriors could no longer tinker with their weapons en route to the target; both superpowers began to deploy new, fully assembled nuclear weapons onto their alert aircraft. While the potential for disaster was always present, the engineers had done their part. Safety (assurance against accidental nuclear yield), if not security (assurance against unauthorized detonation), had been built in. The engineers' innovations were put to the test in 1958; in that year alone, five fully armed B-47s crashed on takeoff, collided with other aircraft, or caught fire on the ground. In no case was there any nuclear yield or contamination beyond the aircraft wreckage. (See appendix C, table III.)

In the late 1950s, nuclear weapons were deployed in tactical circumstance as well; the inevitable accidents followed there, too, but in the five nuclear-weapon episodes of those years, there was neither a hint of nuclear yield nor of contamination beyond the weapon facility involved.

## TRIAL BY FIRE

In 1962, the U.S. Atomic Energy Commission demonstrated (unintentionally) the absolute safety that had been built into most U.S. nuclear weapons. The occasion was the Dominic nuclear test series conducted in the summer of that year.

Before that summer, the Soviet Union had abruptly broken the nuclear testing moratorium that had been in effect since October 1958. In a dazzling display of technology and logistics, the Soviets fired daily: underground, in the atmosphere, and in space. The space tests were intended to ascertain the vulnerability of space assets (satellites and re-entering warheads) and the ground environment (communications and electronics) to nuclear detonations taking place well above the Earth's atmosphere. The resulting data was later used to harden Soviet space systems against such nuclear effects, to assist in the development of the Soviet Galosh ABM system then being built around Moscow, and in planning a possible Soviet nuclear laydown on the United States. The Americans wished to replicate these experiments, to see what the Soviets had learned, and to exploit the resulting technology.

The United States planned high-altitude nuclear tests for the summer of 1962. Nuclear devices were to be lofted from Johnston Island in the Pacific to detonation points well above the atmosphere and away from that island. Instrumentation would be space-borne and surface-deployed all across the Pacific. The devices to be used would contain the safety features developed and installed within U.S. weapons during the 1950s; they turned out to be foolproof under the most trying of circumstances.

The first test, known as the Bluegill event, took place on June 3. A Thor intermediate-range ballistic missile was to lift a kiloton-class thermonuclear device to an altitude of 160,000 feet, well away from Johnston Island. Prior to launch there had been problems with the downrange tracking radar; five minutes after launch that tracking system failed. Unable to monitor the missile's flight path, and with only five minutes to go until detonation, the range safety officer destroyed the missile in flight. The explosives within the nuclear device on board the missile detonated at only one point, as designed; there was no nuclear yield. The debris fell into 12,000 feet of Pacific Ocean. There was no detectable contamination.

The next test, known as Starfish, utilized another Thor and a different megaton-class thermonuclear device. The missile was launched on June 20. Sixty seconds after liftoff there was a malfunction due to the instrumentation pods attached to the sides of the missile. This was followed by an explosion of rocket fuel, oxidizer, and warhead at around 30,000 to 35,000 feet. Again the nuclear device disappeared harmlessly in a ball of fire. There was no nuclear yield, although there was some plutonium contamination of an adjacent island that required a few weeks to clean up.

On July 8, Thor finally performed as planned. The Starfish Prime event was a repeat of the attempted June 20 launch, minus instrumentation pods. A 1.4-megaton device detonated at an altitude of 248 miles above the Earth, nineteen miles downrange from Johnston Island. The electromagnetic pulse affected satellites on orbit and disrupted power-distribution systems in Hawaii, eight hundred miles away. Important data was collected from around the world.

Thor was entrusted with two more launches during the summer and fall of 1962; unfortunately, neither worked as planned. In the first case, on July 25, the Bluegill Prime rocket engine malfunctioned immediately after ignition and before liftoff. The range safety officer fired the destruct mechanism while Thor and its warhead were still on the pad. The explosion destroyed both missile and the Johnston Island launch complex,[2] although there were neither casualties nor nuclear yield.

The next shot, Bluegill Double Prime, was attempted on October 15. It suffered an in-flight failure 88 seconds after liftoff, and the range safety officer destroyed the rocket 156 seconds after launch. There was no nuclear yield, but there was some plutonium contamination of the Johnston Island facilities.

Thor and Bluegill finally got their act together on October 26, in the Bluegill Triple Prime event. The warhead within the Mk 4 reentry vehicle detonated at an altitude of 160,000 feet, 19 miles downrange from Johnston Island. The burst was low enough, within the fringes of the atmosphere, to produce a fireball seen in Hawaii.

After these six missile firings—four Bluegills and two Starfish—four warheads of two different designs had suffered the most violent accidental destruction, but throughout there had been no nuclear yield.[3] The absolute safety of the weapons involved was, and remains, a great testimonial to the hard work of the American nuclear scientists and engineers.

---

2. Requiring three months to repair, rebuild, and resume testing.
3. The results of Operation Dominic missile-launch events may be found in the AEC's *Dominic Test Bulletins*, nos. 23, 29, 31, 36, 39, 40, 42, 47, 51, 54, and 55 (May–Oct. 1962).

## NUKES ON AIRBORNE ALERT, AND MORE
## UNINTENDED SAFETY DEMONSTRATIONS

Analysis of the Soviet nuclear test debris from 1961 revealed a shocking improvement in their nuclear weapon sophistication. An improved Soviet ICBM force would soon be able to threaten U.S. missile bases and aircraft sitting on the ground. The then-operational fifteen-minute ground alert for Strategic Air Command (SAC) bomber crews was no longer good enough; SAC rapidly went to airborne alerts. B-52s, fully loaded and armed, would take off from the United States, fly to the edge of the Soviet Union (with two dangerous refuelings en route), and then return—unless they had received the command to execute a war plan. In January 1966, a classic display of the dangers involved played itself out over the Spanish fishing village of Palomares.

An armed B-52, returning from its aborted dash down the Mediterranean Sea, collided with the KC-135 refueling tanker that had risen from Morón, Spain, only moments before. The tanker and all of its crew disappeared in a ball of fire. Four of the B-52 officers bailed out successfully, and four other "passengers" made it safely to Earth: the four Mk 28 megaton-class H-bombs carried in the bomb bay of the B-52. Two parachutes deployed as designed; those nukes fell to the ground and awaited recovery by the U.S. military. (The casing of one, recovered from under the Mediterranean Sea, is on display at the National Atomic Museum in Albuquerque.) Two others fell without the benefit of parachutes. They picked up speed and detonated on impact, but with no nuclear yield. Cleanup crews scooped up 1,400 tons of Spanish soil, contaminated with plutonium, and reburied it in the United States.

Your authors take great pride in the fortuitous outcome of that sad crash. A long line of physicists, military personnel, chemists, technicians, and engineers devoted much of their professional careers to working in the unrecognized field of weapon safety. They maintained a low profile while reaching for the brass ring—perfection—and it paid off. The nuclear weapon that landed by parachute on the beach at Palomares simply sat there, innocent and impervious to local tampering, until the Americans came to take it away.

The incident over Palomares was a landmark because it gave the Johnson administration pause. By the mid-1960s, long-range missiles were entering the U.S. inventory, rendering obsolete the need for bombers on airborne alert. In 1966, subsequent to the Palomares event, those missions were curtailed, but two years later a similar accident served as a forceful reminder of the dangers still involved. In January 1968, a fully-armed B-52, coming in for a landing at Thule, Greenland, crashed and burned seven miles short of the runway. Six of the seven crewmembers survived, but all four nuclear weapons aboard were destroyed in the fire. There was no nuclear yield, nor did any contamination remain after cleanup, but the lesson finally sank in. Armed airborne alerts were discontinued, and the nuclear weapons laboratories were inspired to turn their attention to high explosives that would be truly resistant to high-impact crashes and explosions. A new type of insensitive high explosive, known as TATB,[4] was developed at Los Alamos and first tested in 1974. Five years later, nuclear weapons so equipped entered the U.S. stockpile. They could withstand bullet impact, crashes, and fires without detonating.

At the same time, new, highly reliable electronic and mechanical switches were introduced to the interior of U.S. nukes. The resulting weapons could be welded shut; they would melt down if an "unauthorized mechanic" attempted access.

There has never been an accident involving a U.S. nuclear weapon wherein any nuclear energy was released. Other countries are notoriously closed-mouthed about their weapon status, be it custody, procedures, or safety, but there is little evidence of a nuclear weapon mishap within any other nation, anywhere, ever. If there had been, we would probably know about it by now; such events are hard to hide. Fissile material may have been lost or stolen, but once assembled into a nuclear weapon, the resulting assets seem to have been treated with the greatest care. Whether Third World proliferant states will continue to display this caution is another matter.

## WEAPON SECURITY AND POLITICAL CONTROLS

It is one thing to assure the stability of a nuclear weapon in the event of fire, lightning strike, or other accident. It is a different matter to assure the stability of those with their fingers on the firing sets. Since the 1960s, the United States (and we believe other nations) have enforced a strict "two-man rule" when it comes to nukes: No nuclear materials, weapons, or launch controls may be left in the custody of a single human being; there must be two people present at all times. Within U.S. production facilities, any worker who is to have physical contact with any nuclear weapon component must undergo regular medical and psychiatric evaluation. But beyond these precautions lies conflict.

Military authorities in every nuclear-weapon state have resisted the installation of locks or barriers to the use of nuclear weapons. Sometimes the arguments are technical: security controls will interfere with the reliability of the weapon. Sometimes the objections are procedural: In time of war it is hard enough to get the word out to all the troops. What if those on the nuclear front lines were told to fire but never got the password? An alternative approach to nuclear security has been a reliance on strict military and political discipline. The Soviets relied on people (KGB officers) watching other people (special army troops), who watched the weapons.

4. Triaminotrinitrobenzene.

In the United States, it was the senior scientists at the nuclear weapons laboratories, backed up by thoughtful political leaders, who secured the U.S. nuclear arsenal. In the mid-1950s, Livermore's Johnny Foster watched in horror as a young GI tested the circuits of live A-bombs with conventional, battery-powered continuity testers. Foster felt safety should be built in. Arming signals should be locked out unless a key or signal had been received from far higher authorities. Foster first broached this idea to the Armed Forces Special Weapons Project, the military agency responsible for nuclear custody. There was no interest; military discipline was seen as working just fine. Foster thought of some solutions that could be built into the physics package of any new weapon. The laboratory directors saw this as a distraction from the challenging-enough physics problems they faced—"That's Sandia's job." The Sandia National Laboratories are responsible for the arming and firing systems external to the physics package. Foster took his thoughts there, but he ran up against the reliability wall. The engineers he talked to were appalled at the idea of putting more switches, intended to work without fail for decades, inside metal cans that were to be welded shut. Foster then attempted to convince the military officers managing the air force and navy's ballistic missile programs of the need for locks. Both were more concerned about the possibility of the passwords not reaching the launch officers than they were about the danger of an unauthorized nuclear explosion.

The secretary of the air force at that time[5] had once served as president of the Sandia Corporation. In early 1957, Secretary Quarles visited Sandia to hear about recent weapon developments and to discuss their safety. As a result of that trip, he empanelled a committee of officers to investigate some obvious problems. By the end of the year, that group was warning of weapons that were mechanically safe in the event of an explosion or crash, but highly vulnerable to a knowledgeable saboteur or lunatic. Recommendations for remedial action led to the development and installation of the environmental sensing devices (ESDs) described earlier. The first of these, then known as a trajectory sensor, was added to the W-49 warhead being deployed atop the early Atlas, Thor, and Jupiter ballistic missiles in the late 1950s, but that was only a start.

Harold Agnew of Los Alamos had been one of the scientific aircrew members flying over Hiroshima. He had *seen* an early A-bomb explode, and he understood how easy it would be to short-circuit any of the safety devices on those weapons. By the end of the 1950s, he had become head of the Los Alamos Weapons Division, and in that capacity he was the beneficiary of a Sandia briefing on the new ESDs being installed in the Los Alamos W-49. The problem with those trajectory sensors was that they would be useless within the atomic demolition munitions[6] (ADMs)

5. Donald Quarles.
6. Sometimes known as backpack bombs.

under development for deployment into potential combat zones overseas. There was no unique environment for an ADM to sense. To deal with this problem, Sandia's engineers had developed an electromechanical switch, to be located within the ADM but operable only by a coded signal inserted from the outside.

With that as background, in 1960, Agnew was invited to travel with a subcommittee of the Joint Committee on Atomic Energy (JCAE) as they toured NATO installations in Europe. The United States had begun to deploy significant numbers of nuclear weapons into the hands of its NATO allies while retaining nominal custody. The strength of that custody was of concern to the committee; the reasons became clear to Agnew when the group arrived at a German air base during the tour. Four F-84F aircraft, bearing the markings of the German Luftwaffe, were on five-minute alert. Their most capable German pilots were ready to go; fully armed Mk 7 A-bombs hung under the belly of each aircraft. The only evidence of U.S. "custody" was a nineteen-year-old American GI with a rifle. He had neither radio nor instructions as to what to do if the aircraft started to move without apparent orders. Any one of those four pilots could have started World War III had they chosen to do so.

Agnew put two and two together: the ADM technology he had seen at Los Alamos and the NATO custodial arrangements that only nominally complied with U.S. law made it clear to him that disaffected allies or a few disgruntled locals could easily seize and use the nuclear weapons we had deployed overseas. Agnew returned to the United States, discussed this convergence of ideas with the Sandia engineers already concerned about the safety of the Mk 7, and came up with a plan: design internal locks into overseas-deployed weapons, and switches that would preclude the arming and firing of a U.S. nuke without the insertion of a code held only by the American commander in chief.

The Director of the Los Alamos Scientific Laboratory[7] did not want to hear about this problem, since it did not involve his core mission: physics. "Not our business," he said, but when Agnew wrote up a plan of action, the director was willing to forward it on to AEC officials for consideration. During this period, Agnew and his Sandia engineers designed a prototype internal-lock system they could display to President-elect Kennedy's science advisor.[8] Another prototype, developed independently at Livermore, was displayed to incoming Secretary of Defense McNamara. During this campaign for acceptance, Agnew was heartily supported by the staff of the JCAE,[9] and in early 1961, Sandia and Los Alamos were directed to proceed with the development

---

7. Norris Bradbury at that time.
8. Jerome Wiesner.
9. Specifically, James Ramey, executive director of the committee.

of the first permissive action link (PAL), for installation in NATO weapons. By the end of 1961, seven months after funding authorization, the first MC-1541 coded switch was embedded within the W-49 warheads accompanying the Jupiter missiles headed for NATO. These were the deployments that led Nikita Khrushchev to send equivalent Soviet rockets to Cuba in 1962, although none of his nuclear warheads had locks of any sort.

Further deployment of the coded locks was not easy; the campaign to gain military acceptance required the personal transfer of Agnew to NATO headquarters for a year of service as science advisor to the supreme Allied commander in Europe. The commanding general did not want these devices on his weapons. He felt PALs reflected a lack of confidence in the military, and he feared they would constitute a serious problem in time of war, but his operations deputy felt differently. The new PALs would allow subordinate military commanders to disperse their nuclear-armed troops while still maintaining control.

On February 15, 1962, the JCAE warned the president, in writing, about "the fictional nuclear weapons custody system now in use" overseas. On March 23, 1962, in a conference at Berkeley, the nuclear weapons laboratory directors met with President Kennedy and his defense advisors to discuss the new PALs. At that time they demonstrated their prototypes, and they made a convincing case. On June 6, 1962, the president signed National Security Action Memorandum 160, "Permissive Action Links for Nuclear Weapons in NATO", which mandated PALs within all NATO-deployed weapons and directed continued development efforts on a full national system.

At first these PALs were simply five-digit combination padlocks on all weapon containers overseas. Over time the early MC-1541 locks evolved into sophisticated electromechanical devices built into every weapon. Current PALs, now deployed on virtually all U.S. nukes, require the insertion of a twelve-digit code into nuclear weapon control panels. There is a "limited try" feature, which permits only a few attempts to enter the correct code. These twelve-digit PINs are carried by, and known only to, the president, his designated successors, and those in the cryptologic chain of custody. With the coming of PALs, the mere custody of a nuclear weapon no longer includes the ability to detonate.

All UN Security Council nuclear weapon states now employ some sort of PAL systems to secure their nuclear weapons; we do not believe that Indian and Pakistani weapons are similarly protected, but the details are not clear. All nuclear state governments consider such matters to be highly confidential. The availability of low-cost, highly reliable microprocessors does imply that any nuclear state or proliferant can secure its nuclear weapons if it decides to do so.

## TRYING TO CLOSE THE BARN DOOR:
## THE NUCLEAR NONPROLIFERATION TREATY OF 1970

By the summer of 1968, the five victors of World War II, ensconced as the permanent members of the UN Security Council[10], had not only joined the nuclear club, they had tested (or were about to test) two-stage thermonuclear weapons. They well understood that Israel constituted a de-facto sixth nuclear weapon state, since many had aided and abetted that condition, and they all recognized that the losers and neutral bystanders of World War II were perfectly capable of going nuclear on short order if they decided to do so. In addition, regional industrial states with grudges and fears were considering the nuclear option, and the two principal nations of south Asia[11] were enjoying covert nuclear benefits from one or more of the Big Five. It became the collective wisdom of American, British, and Soviet academics that something had to be done to cap the flow of nuclear weapon technology or the actual transfer of such weapons before matters ran out of control. On parallel tracks, the nonaligned movement had long advocated the total abolition of nuclear weapons.

The government of Ireland proposed concrete action. On July 1, 1968, the resulting Treaty on the Nonproliferation of Nuclear Weapons (NPT) was executed by the United States, United Kingdom, and Soviet Union, along with 59 other countries. The People's Republic of China and France did not sign, implying they would do so when their nuclear weapons programs had matured, when they had caught up with the Big Three, and when they had satisfied their nuclear technology transfer obligations to allies and customers.

The NPT entered into force on March 5, 1970, with the deposit of ratification documents at the UN. In the years that followed, virtually every nation has joined the NPT regime. The People's Republic of China acceded to the treaty on March 9, 1992, and France joined on August 3 of that year. The disassembly of the Soviet Union in 1991 created four nuclear weapon states where there had been but one, but soon thereafter Belarus, Kazakhstan, and Ukraine transferred all the Soviet nukes once in their territories back to the Russian Federation and then acceded to the treaty. At present, 187 states are parties to the NPT. Cuba was the last to sign, in 2002, while only Israel, India, and Pakistan have failed to join. North Korea withdrew on January 10, 2003 (although it appeared to be in the process of resubscribing as of this writing). Taiwan, although no longer a UN member, has pledged its continuing observance of the treaty provisions.

10. The UN did not recognize the People's Republic of China's Beijing government as the government of China until October 1979. At that time, Beijing took Taiwan's seat on the Security Council.
11. India and Pakistan.

The Nonproliferation Treaty obligates the five acknowledged nuclear weapon states (China, France, Russia, United Kingdom, and the United States) not to transfer nuclear weapons, other nuclear explosive devices, or the associated technology to any nonnuclear weapon state. For their part, the nonnuclear weapon states agree to eschew the acquisition or production of nuclear weapons or nuclear explosive devices and to accept safeguards to detect the diversion of nuclear materials from peaceful activities, such as power generation. The International Atomic Energy Agency (IAEA), with headquarters in Vienna, was established to supervise these safeguards and to conduct inspections, but only with the concurrence of the host country. Implicit in this agreement was the intent of the major powers to provide a nuclear umbrella over their allies, removing the incentive for them to go nuclear, and for those Big Five to refrain from the use, or threat of use, of nuclear weapons on nonnuclear states unless such states were acting in alliance with a nuclear weapon state. In recent years, however, the United States, United Kingdom, and France have all noted the possibility of using nuclear weapons in response to "nonconventional attack" by "rogue states" or their terrorist agents.

Over the years the NPT has come to be seen by Third World states as a conspiracy of the nuclear "haves" to keep the nuclear "have-nots" in their place. Abdul Qadeer Khan, mastermind of the Pakistani nuclear franchising industry, referred to the NPT in 1990 (before his proliferation efforts had been exposed) as "highly discriminatory in nature; it allows the nuclear weapon powers to accumulate and enhance their stockpiles of nuclear weapons while putting severe restrictions on even the peaceful utilization of nuclear power by the have-nots." This argument has its root in Article IV of the treaty, which obligates the nuclear weapon states to liquidate their nuclear stockpiles and pursue complete disarmament. The nonnuclear weapon states see no sign of this happening. They also take offense at the nuclear arming of NATO, which they consider to be a violation of the treaty. Nominal U.S. "custody," as described above, is the political fig leaf used to fend off this argument, and it is one reason why the installation of PALs within the NATO-based weapons was so important.

Unfortunately, the NPT has one giant loophole. Article III gives each nonnuclear weapon state the "inalienable right" to pursue nuclear energy for the generation of power. This entitles such states to enrich natural uranium (0.7 percent U-235) to fuel grade (~3 percent U-235). From there it is a short step to weapons-grade highly enriched uranium (HEU: over 90 percent U-235). Similarly, a power reactor produces neutrons that are indifferent to their ultimate use. They can breed plutonium, generate power, or both.

The NPT was to expire after twenty-five years (in 1995), but in that year the parties to the NPT met in New York and agreed to extend the treaty indefinitely, with review conferences every five years. By then, however, the challenge of nuclear proliferation had taken on a new dimension: the recently discovered covert programs in North Korea and Iraq. The latter country, a signatory to the NPT, had successfully circumvented IAEA safeguards by exploiting the rigidity of that agency's charter: the IAEA could only examine "declared" nuclear facilities. Since 1993, UN personnel have been working on amendments to the NPT intended to constrain illicit nuclear programs. The tools to do so would include better disclosure of nuclear-related activities, broad environmental sampling systems, no-notice inspections, remote monitoring equipment, and streamlined administrative procedures.[12]

Given the difficulty of amending an existing treaty, the UN member states, in May 1997, adopted a model Additional Protocol to the NPT in hopes that the treaty signatories would voluntarily subscribe to this agreement. The Big Five signed at once. The United States led the way, in June 1998, with France and the United Kingdom following in September of that year. China signed in December 1998. Russia completed the list in May 2000, just as the next NPT review conference was getting under way.

That conference, again held in New York, produced an "unequivocal commitment by the nuclear weapon states to the ultimate goal of complete disarmament under strict and effective international controls." They also endorsed the Comprehensive Test Ban Treaty, preservation of the ABM Treaty, and the timely conclusion of safeguards agreements with the IAEA: that is, the Additional Protocol.

There followed a change of government within the United States, the sad events of 9/11, and a reconsideration of U.S. policy on all of these topics. The review conference of 2005, again held at the UN, produced stark disagreement between the nuclear and the nonnuclear states. The U.S. secretary of state did not attend, it took three weeks to agree on an agenda, and at conference's end, there was no final statement. The conference chairman described the event as "a failure." Most of the four-week session was spent in confrontation. The nonnuclear weapon states demanded action by the nuclear weapon states on disarmament and ratification of the Comprehensive Test Ban Treaty. Across the table, the United States and the European powers focused on the proliferation activities of North Korea and Iran, seeking sanctions and penalties for their destabilizing behavior. The treaty loopholes went unaddressed; the IAEA was left to do the best it could, constrained by its limited inspection and negligible enforcement powers. By then perhaps half the member states had signed and put into effect the Additional Protocol, but that list of signatories did not, and does not now, include the most worrisome Middle Eastern and south Asian states. As

12. Faster visas and better communication systems.

noted earlier, India, Israel, and Pakistan are the only states that have failed to sign the Nonproliferation Treaty. Israel's refusal to do so has become the touchstone of Arab recalcitrance. Egypt, Algeria, and Saudi Arabia have rejected the Additional Protocol. Iran signed in December 2003, but has since withdrawn. Pakistan and India remain outside the entire nuclear-control regime. A reformed Libya is the only major Arab petro-state to sign both NPT and the Additional Protocol.

## THE POSSIBLE RESUMPTION OF NUCLEAR TESTING

Sooner or later one or more of the nuclear weapon states may feel it necessary to resume nuclear testing, to preserve confidence in a stockpile of intricate devices made of unstable materials that were assembled using industrial processes and components no longer available. The U.S., Russian, and U.K. nuclear weapons are all reaching the end of their certified life. Think of keeping a 1980 Ferrari in the garage, never driven, the ignition key never turned, until it was needed to drive an expectant mother to the hospital. The machinery might work, but that is not the way to bet when the lives of mothers—or countries—are at stake.

Any such nuclear testing, and certainly any advanced nuclear weapon work[13] by any of the nuclear weapon states, will surely provide grist for political leaders in the Third World. They will use such events as concrete evidence that the nuclear haves want to relegate Third World have-nots to permanent second-class status with no ability to deter the legacy (long-standing) nuclear powers from encroachments on their Muslim-world or other local interests.

The immediate issues of nuclear proliferation and the terrorist tendencies of the rogue states may be settled in the skies over Natanz as they were over Osirak[14] a quarter-century ago, but the destruction of fissile-material-production facilities by acts of war is not a cure; it is only a treatment, like dialysis or chemotherapy. Such attacks would have to be repeated every decade, as the victim's bitterness grows.

Even though the Israelis had destroyed Iraq's Osirak reactor in 1981, the United States had to destroy another Iraqi approach to nuclear weapons at Tuwaitha in 1991 during the war to free Kuwait. Addressing the insecurities and nuclear ambitions of the not-yet-nuclear states and/or finding the politico-technical means to deter such activities is preferable to repeated bombings, but it will not be simple. Finding a cure for this nuclear ambition disease is one of the defining challenges of our new millennium.

13. Such as small nuclear weapons carried within "bunker-busting" earth-penetrating warheads or a "robust replacement warhead" capable of long-term storage without testing.
14. Iran's underground uranium-enrichment facility and Iraq's weapons-oriented reactor, respectively.

# CHANGES OF STATE IN THE MIDEAST AND SOUTH ASIA

As the 1960s drew to a close, kings and emirs friendly to the West ruled most of the Middle East. India was thought to be a peaceful and non-aligned (although Soviet-friendly) backwater. Cheap oil was a glut on the market. Producing states and independent drillers had to rely on the major oil companies to refine and market their product using price wars, advertising, glassware, and customer service as enticements. Nuclear weapons were solely the province of the Big Five, the victors of World War II, enshrined as the permanent members of the UN Security Council. But then the cradles of early civilization began to rock. By the end of the 1970s, the landscape from Tripoli to Trombay was unrecognizably different.

## SEPTEMBER 1969: LIBYA GOES RADICAL

For the quarter-century after the end of World War II, Idris al-Senousi had been in charge of the United Kingdom of Libya. A wartime hero who had fought the Italians, Idris was installed by the British at the end of the war and legitimized by a plebiscite soon thereafter. Idris ruled his utterly impoverished kingdom with a kindly hand until the discovery of oil in 1955. Then the corruption set in. Oil production rose from nothing in 1958 to three million barrels per day a decade later. In 1968, the world price of oil was only $3.50 per barrel, but even that gave the Kingdom of Libya a *daily* cash flow of over $10 million—a multibillion dollar annual kitty[1] for the ruler of that desert kingdom.

King Idris had no children, and he had done little about planning for his succession. In 1964, at age seventy-four, he had tried to abdicate for reasons of health. His subjects would hear none of it. There was a nephew, Hassan al-Reda, known as "the Black Prince," but his reputation for graft and his lack of gravitas ruled him out

---

1. Over $20 billion per annum in 2008 dollars.

as a serious contender for the throne. The family tree stood without solid roots, yet it had produced the low-hanging fruit of newly discovered oil deposits.

In the summer of 1969, at age seventy-nine, King Idris headed off to the Turkish spa at Bursa for treatment of a leg ailment. Most other high government officials were also vacationing outside the country. On September 1, with the decks clear, Capt. Muammar al-Qaddafi mounted a coup.

Muammar al-Qaddafi was born in the desert south of Sirte during World War II (in 1942) as Montgomery and Rommel battled for the coast. Qaddafi grew up in Seha, a small village in the southern desert of the Fezzan. As a poor Bedouin boy from the interior, he joined the army at age seventeen because there were no other opportunities. He brought with him a resentment of material wealth, foreigners, and infidels.

In 1952, as the British turned over their postwar authority to the newly independent Libyan government, they also started to train a constabulary and an officer corps for the infant kingdom. In time, Muammar al-Qaddafi was identified as one of the army's brightest and best. He was sent to the Royal Libyan Military Academy in Benghazi for officers' training. Upon graduation in 1965, he was invited to attend Sandhurst, the United Kingdom's military academy, for further training as a military engineer. En route home, in 1968, Qadaffi visited post-Farouk Egypt, picking up a healthy dose of Nasserite Arab nationalism along the way. Upon his return to Libya, Qaddafi and a few of his fellow junior officers began to organize. They called themselves the Free Officers' Association, and they gave their intended revolution a name: Operation Jerusalem.

On September 1, 1969, the twenty-seven-year-old Captain Qaddafi and a handful of his fellow officers made their move. Armed with only a few revolvers and a mere forty-eight rounds of ammunition, they closed in on two targets. One was the military headquarters in Tripoli, whose officers already were predisposed to the radical views of the Free Officers' Association. The other target was Tripoli's radio station. Qaddafi and his men stormed and took over both. That's all there was to it. No rolling tanks, no action in the streets of Benghazi or Tobruk. Just a gang of young rebels at the radio station in Tripoli and a sympathetic group of duty officers at headquarters, but that was enough. Once on the air, the rebels announced the end of the United Kingdom of Libya, the abolition of all existing government structure, and the birth of the new Libyan Arab Republic.

At first it was not clear who was behind this coup. Qaddafi was the most senior of the plotters, but he was only a captain. The other insurgent officers were junior captains and lieutenants, all in their twenties. To give the coup some credibility (and to protect the key players), one Colonel Bushwerib was first announced as the coup leader. Then, a week later, a government was announced, with Mahamoud al-Maghreby as its prime minister. Lurking in the background, however, as the ultimate source of authority, was the Revolutionary Council. Qaddafi was its chairman; the captains and lieutenants constituted the membership.

Due east of the city of Tripoli lay a U.S. Air Force facility known as Wheelus Air Base. It was a NATO training site, a place where the pilots based on the foggy and crowded European continent could come unfold their wings. Wheelus was a gorgeous place, the site of a Mussolini-era racetrack right on the Mediterranean Sea. The beach and the scuba diving were spectacular. But Wheelus was also secure—it could be reinforced from that same sea. Ten thousand U.S. troops and civilian personnel were stationed at Wheelus, one of the best-defended American air bases in the Near East.

The wing commander at Wheelus during the late summer of 1969 was Col. Daniel "Chappie" James, an outstanding fighter pilot just returned from seventy-eight combat missions over Vietnam. In later years, when both co-author Reed and by-then-General James worked at the Pentagon, James came to tell Reed of the events that took place during that historic night in September 1969.

Colonel James had arrived in Libya only a month before, but he was a quick-witted and sharp officer. On that fateful night of September 1, his operations center at Wheelus picked up the Qaddafi-organized broadcast. A few phone calls around the country revealed the very narrow base of this coup-in-progress. Colonel James knew that Qaddafi's accession and Idris' departure would not be beneficial to Western interests, and he so advised his superiors in Washington. He had a well-armed, well-trained, and highly mobile security force on base. It was there to protect that NATO facility from insurrections, terrorists, or Soviet-inspired attack, since Wheelus was home to some very valuable assets. The colonel formulated a plan: send an armed detachment downtown, break into the radio station, arrest the ringleaders, and secure the government facilities as needed. But before acting, Colonel James sought the approval of the National Military Command Center in the Pentagon. The officers on duty there referred the matter to the Situation Room in the White House.

Richard Nixon's memoirs make no specific reference to this event, and Kissinger writes in generalities about the precarious military balance in the Middle East during those years, but neither official seems to have given the Qaddafi coup much attention. When queried, Kissinger said that he and Nixon wanted to overthrow Qaddafi, but the foreign service specialists at State saw Qaddafi as a "reformer." In all probability the new Nixon administration simply did not have the self-confidence needed to deal swiftly with Qaddafi. Taking any action would be "interference in the internal affairs of a sovereign state," Kissinger said later.

Colonel James' troops stayed in their barracks at Wheelus. Qaddafi consolidated his power. By the morning of September 2, he was extending his control throughout all of

Libya. The Black Prince renounced his claim to the throne, calling on Libyans to support the new government. Within a week, the United States recognized the junta as the de facto government of Libya, and during that same week, King Idris was told to stay in Turkey. His cabinet fled their homeland, and a campaign of assassination and kidnapping of former officials began. Only the noisy disturbance created by a former prime minister, locked into the trunk of a kidnapper's car, alerted a London policeman to his plight. On December 2, 1969, the Revolutionary Council arrested the Libyan Army's chief of staff and the chief of security. A counter-coup was attempted on December 11. It failed. Qaddafi promoted himself to colonel. Then, on January 16, 1970, Qaddafi took off the wraps. He assumed the roles of prime minister and minister of defense.

Within five years of his takeover, during Israel's Yom Kippur War in 1973, Qaddafi organized the OPEC[2] embargo of oil shipments to the United States and its Western allies. He also pioneered the first "oil shock," raising the price from $3.50 to $13 per barrel and making those increases stick. Within ten years, Qaddafi was enjoying oil revenues of over $50 million *per day*.[3] Some of those petrodollars made their way into the schools and hospitals of his citizens, but much of Qaddafi's cash went to finance an impressive chemical warfare complex, a plague of terrorist attacks on Americans abroad, and at least two forays into the development of nuclear weapons. The first was undertaken in the early 1980s, a time when China was transferring nuclear weapons technology to Pakistan and when China had contracted, in secret, to build the El Salam nuclear reactor in Algeria.[4] Qaddafi's scientific advisers hoped to travel a similar plutonium route; contractors from Japan and Belgium were to supply the technology, but the project proved indigestible to the limited Libyan scientific infrastructure.

During the decade following the oil shocks, Qaddafi's terrorist activities drew a response from the Reagan administration. On April 15, 1986, the American president ordered an air attack on Tripoli and Benghazi in response to an earlier Libyan-sponsored assault on La Belle Discotheque, a West Berlin hangout of American GIs. While the April 15 attacks were aimed at Qaddafi, they only succeeded in killing his infant daughter

---

2. The Organization of Petroleum Exporting Countries was founded in Baghdad in 1960 to coordinate the producers' oil policies. It remained an innocuous trade association until the 1973 war inspired the Islamic radicals to use its pricing and allocation power to dictate economic policy to the industrialized West. At the present time (2008), OPEC accounts for about 40 percent of the world's oil production and about 66 percent of its proven reserves. Neither Russia nor any of the former Soviet republics are members of OPEC.

3. A quarter-billion dollars per day in 2008 dollars.

4. El Salam was to be a fifteen-megawatt reactor, to be built at Ain Oussera, 170 miles south of Algiers and 600 miles east of Tripoli. Western intelligence failed to discover El Salam until 1991; it went critical in 1992. See chapter 17 for details.

and wounding several others in his family. Some claim Qaddafi "calmed down" after that, but in fact he just became more discreet—and more determined. From disclosures arising after the seizure of the BBC *China* in 2003, it is clear that Qaddafi's second nuclear weapons effort, with roots in Pakistan, was born after the 1986 attacks on Libya.

Qaddafi became an important force for evil in the Cold War and in the power vacuum that followed, a role made possible by visionary oil men, a negligent king, and a timorous White House unwilling to intercede when Western interests were clearly at stake.

## JUNE 1972: A. Q. KHAN TAKES A JOB IN HOLLAND

In 1936, Abdul Qadeer Khan was born in Bhopal, India, to a Pakistani family. When the British granted independence to the Indian sub-continent in 1947, they used the partition of Hindus in India from Muslims in the split territories of East and West Pakistan as the fig leaf for their withdrawal. As with any partition, minorities were left behind on both sides. Life was grim for the Muslim Khan family in Bhopal; at the age of eighteen, the young Khan migrated to Karachi, in West Pakistan, on foot.

Once in Karachi, Khan attended the D. J. Sindh College of Science, graduating in 1960 with a degree in metallurgy. After a brief stint in local government, Khan decided to pursue graduate studies in western Europe. He met and married a Dutch girl, spent four years at the university in Delft, Holland, and emerged with a master's degree in metallurgical engineering. In the process, he became fluent in the Dutch and German languages. In 1968, the young Khan family moved to Leuven, Belgium; Khan entered Catholic University to continue his studies in metallurgy, in French.

Through all of those years, Khan's life had been that of the innocuous student and family man, but in 1971, events at home brought a sense of urgency to his life. In the spring of that year, the political leaders of East Pakistan rebelled, declaring independence from West Pakistan and adopting the name Bangladesh for their side of the subcontinent. A bloody civil war ensued, with India intervening on the side of the rebels. The Indian government wished to dismember, if not destroy, what it considered to be the rebellious remnants of old India. The war was a disaster for West Pakistan. In December 1971, her army surrendered, with the Indians having taken ninety three thousand troops prisoner. The military regime in the West fell, Zulficar Ali Bhutto came to power, and all loyal Pakistanis (including the thirty-five-year-old Khan) decided they had to "do something" about India.

At home, unbeknownst to Khan, the new government of Ali Bhutto already had decided what to do: go nuclear. There had been rumors of Indian nuclear ambitions for some time. In January 1972, President Bhutto called together seventy of his leading scientists for a discussion of this option. The meeting took place in Punjab.

His audience was enthusiastic; they promised results within five years.[5]

Meanwhile, in Belgium, A. Q. Khan was about to receive his Ph.D. in metallurgy from Catholic University. In June he did so, and then he moved to Holland to take a job with a subcontractor working for the Uranium Enrichment Corporation. URENCO was organized by the British, Dutch, and German nuclear power industries to develop the technology needed to separate U-235 fuel from natural uranium compounds. Ultra-centrifuges, rotating at very high speeds, were the preferred route. The resulting URENCO technology was the best in the world. In 1972, Dr. A. Q. Khan began collecting—i.e., stealing—that know-how with meticulous care.

On May 18, 1974, the hated Indians tested a nuclear device under the Rajasthani Desert. That was the final and defining moment for Khan. During the month that followed, he wrote a letter to President Bhutto (whom he did not know) explaining the role of the centrifuge in producing fissionable material. Khan offered to help with any Pakistani nuclear weapons program. (He did not know one was already under way.) Bhutto responded with interest through his embassy in The Hague.

During the fall of 1974, Khan spent sixteen days at the URENCO facility. His day job was to translate documents, but during his spare time he toured the plant, taking notes on the design and operation of the equipment. His observations were written in his native Urdu to disguise them from prying eyes. In December 1974, President Bhutto and engineer Khan met in Karachi while Khan and his family were home for the holidays. The covert Pakistan Atomic Energy Commission had already embarked on a plutonium-based nuclear weapon plan, but it was in trouble. At their meeting Bhutto decided to put Khan in charge of a parallel enriched-uranium effort.

In the spring of 1975, Khan returned to his post in Amsterdam, now fully committed to collecting information and parts while Pakistani authorities began to purchase components for a uranium-enrichment program.[6] A co-worker became suspicious; Khan was moved to a less sensitive job. In December 1975, he again returned to Pakistan for the holidays, but this time he never returned to URENCO. In the spring of 1976, Khan started work at the Pakistan Atomic Energy Commission, headed by Munir Ahmad Khan.[7] Friction quickly developed. With the full support of the Bhutto government, Khan was authorized to organize the Engineering Research Laboratory in the town of Kahuta, fifteen miles due east of the Islamabad airport.

5. In reality, it took more than two decades for Pakistan to achieve nuclear weapon status, and then only with Chinese help. See chapter 15.

6. These purchases began in August 1975. See Shahid-ur-Rehman, *The Long Road to Chagai* (Islamabad: Printwise Publications, 1999).

7. No relation. Khan is a common name in Pakistan, like Jones or Smith in the United States.

That facility was to develop a uranium-enrichment capability for Pakistan. It opened for business on July 31, 1976. Khan stayed in touch with his friends and informants in Holland, and his work may have received additional funding from Libya and Saudi Arabia. During the years that followed, China began the transfer of nuclear weapons technology to Pakistan—presumably to A. Q. Khan—in part as a consequence of the Chinese-Indian border clashes of the previous decade.

In the late 1970s, the American intelligence services learned of all this activity, and CIA surveillance of A. Q. Khan apparently began in earnest. However, in December 1979, the Soviets invaded Afghanistan, and the Americans needed all the help they could get from neighboring Pakistan, so hard questions about covert nuclear programs were off the table. By the end of that decade, Khan had an operational enrichment centrifuge line up and running at Kahuta as the Americans busied themselves elsewhere.

## OCTOBER 1973: ANOTHER ARAB-ISRAELI WAR

The State of Israel has been around as a concept for all of the twentieth century. Jewish settlers and refugees began a return to the holy lands of Palestine while it was still part of the Ottoman Empire; World War I accelerated the process. In 1917, the British Foreign Office began making promises to the inhabitants of the Middle Eastern deserts then under the control of the Turks. The objective was to build support for the rebellions growing in that wilderness. *Lawrence of Arabia* is the popular tale of the Arab uprising. Arthur Balfour, Britain's Foreign Secretary, played the Jewish card. On November 2, he advised Lord Rothschild, a leader of Britain's Jewish community, "His Majesty's Government views with favor the establishment in Palestine of a national home for the Jewish people."

A year later, World War I was at an end. In Versailles, Great Britain was granted a thirty-year mandate to administer the southern and eastern part of the fallen Ottoman Empire. (France was given the northern part.) Palestine was one piece of the British package; it was left to the local British commander to make good on the Balfour Declaration. At that time over 90 percent of the residents of Palestine were Arabic.

During the following interwar years (the 1920s and 1930s) the Jewish population within Palestine grew to half a million, an immigration spurred by the fascist persecution of Jews within central Europe. By 1939, 30 percent of Palestine's inhabitants were Jews. The native Arabs were not welcoming these new residents; civil strife had broken out all over. Thus, in that last pre–World War II year, the British government was looking forward to the end of its mandate; it declared its commitment to a "national home for the Jewish people" had been met. In a white paper issued on May 17, 1939, the British government denied the existence of any policy "that

Palestine should become a Jewish State," implying that what the Balfour Declaration meant was that the Jewish people should be welcomed into an independent Palestine governed jointly by Arabs and Jews. The May 17 white paper also imposed a limit on immigration (seventy-five thousand new Jewish settlers during the next five years, none after that without Arab consent), and it imposed limits on the transfer of native lands to the Jewish settlers. These edicts led to heart-rending scenes as refugees from the pending Holocaust in Europe were turned away from Palestinian shores.

Then came World War II. As the war ended, a flood of Jewish refugees headed for Palestine. Immigration limits were unenforceable, physically and morally. Civil war broke out between Arabs and Jews; hundreds of thousands of Palestinian Arabs were driven from their homes and farms by terrorism, house demolitions, and eventually outright massacres, with the British authorities included on the target list. One Jewish terrorist organization, known as the Irgun, blew up the King David Hotel, killing ninety. The Haganah blew up the Semiramis Hotel. The Stern Gang invaded Arab villages to wreak havoc. While the embryonic UN tried to broker a partition, the British tired of the fight. When their thirty-year mandate expired, at midnight on May 14, 1948, they left.

At exactly midnight on that date David Ben-Gurion, chairman of the Jewish Agency Executive, proclaimed the independence of the new State of Israel. The Jewish National Council had adopted the resolution earlier in the day. Within eleven minutes of that proclamation, the American president, Harry Truman, recognized the provisional government of Israel as the de facto authority of that state. The American ambassador to the UN and much of his delegation were outraged and attempted to resign en masse, understanding full well the bloodshed that would follow, but the American recognition stuck. Others in the West soon followed suit, but Israel's Arab neighbors did not join in the celebration. On May 15, 1948, the armies of five[8] neighboring countries attacked that newly proclaimed State of Israel, joining an internal battle that was already raging between Palestinians and Jews in the streets of Jerusalem. The Israelis won the ensuing war, although it dragged on well into 1949.[9] By the time the armistice agreements had been signed, Israel had expanded its controlled territory by one-quarter, and most of the Arab people once living within the new Israel had fled or had been expelled.

Since that time, every decade has seen another Arab-Israeli war or guerilla action. In 1956, it was a joint effort with France and Britain to reclaim the Suez Canal, nationalized

8. Egypt, Syria, Jordan, Lebanon, and Iraq.
9. Fighting ended with five separate armistice agreements, starting with Egypt on February 24 and ending with Syria on July 20, 1949.

by the Nasser government in Cairo. As we have seen earlier, Israel's displeasure at American interference and lack of support in that war led the government of Israel, in late 1956, to initiate work, hand-in-hand with France, on nuclear weapons.

A decade later, in June 1967, when Nasser mobilized to invade Israel, the Israeli government detected those activities and preempted. In what became known as the Six-Day War, Israel held the trump cards—A-bombs and the aircraft with which to deliver them—but those weapons were not necessary. Israel overwhelmed the Sinai, West Bank, Golan Heights, and the City of Jerusalem with minimum casualties in less than a week—victories accomplished without apparent U.S. help. To the contrary, with the attack on the *Liberty*, some in the Arab world saw the United States as a fellow victim.

After that 1967 war, the UN passed Resolution 242, which called for the return of captured lands. Israel did not comply, and Resolution 242 became the rallying cry for those in the Arab world seeking a redress of their grievances. On October 6, 1973, the third Arab-Israeli war began. On the Yom Kippur holy day, the Egyptian and Syrian governments staged an unexpected attack on the Israeli state. (Jordan had learned to stay out of these fights, and Lebanon had ceased to exist as a functioning country.) The reasons for this attack seem strange, but most scholars agree that Egypt's President Sadat simply wanted to get U.S. attention, to seek U.S. assistance in enforcing UN Resolution 242. He was not out to destroy Israel, but he did enlist the support of Syria's President Assad, who had much more malevolent territorial goals, and of Saudi Arabia's King Faisal, who promised to use the "oil weapon" to enforce Arab demands.

The Israelis were taken by surprise; only their regular forces were on duty. Within a day, the Israeli front lines crumbled; the Syrians had retaken the Golan Heights; Egyptian troops had poured across the Suez Canal. Attempted Israeli counterattacks failed. By October 9, the Israelis had lost four hundred tanks to Egyptian gunners and one hundred to Syria. President Meir of Israel ordered her Jericho missiles armed with nuclear weapons.[10]

The U.S. and Soviet superpowers took an immediate interest in this conflict; by October 10, both sides had begun to resupply their clients. In light of this initial American support for Israel, several Arab states (Kuwait, Saudi Arabia, and Libya) proposed an oil embargo and price increase to discourage further American intervention. Despite that warning, on October 15, the American resupply of Israel began in earnest: F-4 aircraft, Sidewinder missiles, antitank weapons, and a host of other items were airlifted from U.S. inventories in Germany and the United States. By October 18, the tide of battle had turned. Israeli forces had crossed the Suez; in the north they were within striking distance of Damascus. The world economic tide had turned as well. In

10. At that time, Israel held more than a dozen such weapons.

mid-October, the Arab members of OPEC initiated the oil boycott, posting the associated price increases that were to become the cutting edge of that weapon.

The superpowers (United States and U.S.S.R.) brokered a cease-fire on October 22, but subsequent misunderstandings led to a continuation of the fighting. That, in turn, led to a U.S. fear of Soviet intervention and an elevation of the U.S. military alert status to DEFCON III.[11] By the end of the month, aggressive diplomacy had effected a truce, but the damage was done. The autumn and winter that followed brought gas lines and skyrocketing energy prices, a major recession to the U.S. economy, an awareness of the need to conserve energy, and a renewal of U.S. domestic oil exploration in previously marginal fields. For the first time the oil-producing Arab states had made common cause with their OPEC brethren, constrained the economies of the industrialized world, and set in motion the financial independence of radical Islam.

Of far broader import, those Arab nations had watched the United States clearly and unambiguously protect Israel from defeat at the hands of advancing Arab armies. While America's historic support for Israel was well understood, the Americans had also protected Egypt in 1956 and had remained quasi-neutral in 1967. It was the massive resupply of Israel in October 1973 that indelibly marked the United States as a primary enemy of the Arab world, thus triggering the oil embargoes and price-fixing that would become Arabia's prime weapons in the decades to come.

## MAY 1974: INDIA CONDUCTS ITS FIRST NUCLEAR TEST

In the years before World War II, many bright Indian students were making their mark in the world of quantum physics. In the 1920s, S. N. Bose of Dacca University developed what has come to be known as Bose-Einstein statistics through correspondence with Albert Einstein. Others trained in England and then stayed in the West to unravel the mysteries of the universe. Subramanyan Chandrasekhar graduated from the Presidency College of Madras in 1930, and the government of India then sent him to Cambridge to study under R. H. Fowler. After receipt of his Ph.D. and completion of his postdoctoral work, Chandrasekhar moved to the University of Chicago. In 1983, he was awarded the Nobel Prize for Physics (along with Fowler) for his work in explaining the evolution of stars—which are, after all, giant thermonuclear reactors. Others of the Chandrasekhar generation returned home to lead their peers in the world of physics and to build great universities on the Indian subcontinent.

Other aspects of life in postwar India were not so easy. Partition at the time of independence in 1947 had taken its toll on every family. Disputes with the neighbor

11. Defense Condition III, an intermediate alert status between full war (DEFCON I) and peacetime readiness (DEFCON V).

to the north, China, nagged at India's consciousness, as the Chinese-Indian border had not been properly defined when the British left. On October 20, 1962, after a month of skirmishes, the Chinese took matters into their own hands, launching an assault along two thousand miles of their border with India. The contested land was vital to China, as it provided a major road link between Xinjiang Province and Tibet. The Indian army was ill equipped to fight in the Himalayas,[12] and they were no match for the battle-hardened troops of the People's Liberation Army. The war ended a month later, on November 21, 1962. The Chinese won, if success is to be measured by real estate taken, but that loss lit a resentment within India that still burns. It also generated a determination within China to support India's enemies, whoever they may be. The principal beneficiary turned out to be Pakistan. Two years later, on October 16, 1964, China completed its application for membership in the nuclear club, firing a twenty-two-kiloton A-bomb atop a tower in Xinjiang Province.

These events, plus India's ongoing desire for great-power status on a par with China, led the Indian government to expand its nuclear weapons program from the foundation laid at the time of independence. In 1947, India's first prime minister, Jawaharlal Nehru, was already holding nuclear weapon discussions with his close associates. Upon opening the Indian Atomic Energy Commission, in April 1948, Nehru said, "We must develop atomic energy quite apart from war, [but] if we are compelled to use it for other purposes, no pious sentiments will stop the nation from using it that way." In public, Nehru had been a vocal proponent of nonaligned policies for the emerging nations of south Asia and Africa. He urged the leaders of those new nations to steer a middle course between the Soviet and Western superpowers, a territory that would become known as the Third World. Nuclear abstention was an underlying theme of the first Bandung Conference, hosted by Indonesia in April 1955. Yet, in the very year of that conference, the Indians started down the nuclear weapons path. They made a mockery of Eisenhower's Atoms for Peace vision as they negotiated the gift of a "safeguarded" forty-megawatt CIRUS (Canada–India Research United States) nuclear reactor from Canada and twenty-one tons of heavy water ($D_2O$) from the United States. Both acquisitions were accompanied by assurances of "peaceful intent," but in those days there were no arrangements for inspection or verification. The reactor utilized uranium feedstock mined within India.[13]

In July 1958, in anticipation of the need to extract plutonium from the resulting irradiated cores, Nehru authorized construction of the Phoenix reprocessing facility at

12. The fight took place at an elevation of fourteen thousand feet.
13. The CIRUS reactor went critical in 1960.

Trombay. The technology was developed within India, using components purchased on the commercial market from European suppliers. That plutonium separation facility went online in 1964.

Nehru died in 1964, and during the brief reign of his successor, Lal Shastri, a second Indo-Pakistani War broke out in Kashmir.[14] Shastri then succumbed to a heart attack in January 1966. At that time, Nehru's daughter and only child, Indira Gandhi, took control of the government.

Nehru had been a widower throughout his years as prime minister; when Ms. Gandhi was herself widowed, in 1960, she took over management of the presidential residence and her father's personal life. There can be no doubt that they discussed the need for nuclear weapons during the early 1960s, although there is little evidence of an actual weapon program until Ms. Gandhi came to power in 1966.

In early 1967, Ms. Gandhi was elected prime minister. In June of that year, the Chinese conducted their first thermonuclear test, only thirty-two months after first going nuclear. By year end, perhaps triggered by the Chinese H-bomb development, Ms. Gandhi made the very secret decision to proceed with a nuclear weapons program of her own, a closely held action with no government ministers involved. To implement that decision, in September 1972, Ms. Gandhi gave the go-ahead for the fabrication and test of an actual nuclear device. Only Ms. Gandhi's immediate staff, along with the scientists assigned to do the work, knew of her plans.

Ms. Gandhi continued to espouse her father's nonaligned philosophies, but when the Nuclear Nonproliferation Treaty was opened for signature in July 1968, India declined to sign. That nation has never done so.

On May 18, 1974, India became an announced nuclear state with a single underground shot labeled "a peaceful uses experiment." The Indian national-security cabinet members (defense and foreign affairs) apparently learned of India's nuclear weapon program only a week before that test. India's nuclear weapon technology appears to have been homegrown, developed without significant overt or covert outside help, other than from the students trained overseas and the reactor acquired from Canada. Certainly the test facilities were native. The May 1974 test was conducted under the Rajasthani Desert in a shot hole dug manually, perhaps to escape detection by orbiting satellites, or perhaps just because that's the way they did things in India a quarter-century ago. That Indian nuclear test served its intended purpose—the Chinese were put on notice that India was now a nuclear power. But that explosion also served some unintended purposes—A. Q. Khan was inspired to begin the theft of nuclear technology from Holland, and within a few years, the Chinese began to

14. Known, logically, as the Second Kashmir War, April–September 1965.

share their nuclear technology with Pakistan on the theory that "My enemy's enemy is my friend."

## SEPTEMBER 1976: MAO DIES AND THE RULES CHANGE

Mao Zedong was born to middle-class parents in Hunan Province in 1893. He joined the army, then the Communist Party of China, gaining control during the 1930s. Mao subsequently contested with Chiang Kaishek's Kuomintang for national power. When Japan invaded, that struggle turned into a three-way battle, with Mao's communists appearing to challenge the Japanese while also forming local alliances at the expense of the Kuomintang. By the end of World War II, Mao and Chiang were locked in a fight to the death; Mao's forces prevailed. On October 1, 1949, Mao proclaimed the birth of the People's Republic of China. Chiang Kaishek's troops, escorting many of China's cultural treasures, had long since fled to the island of Formosa.

Life on the mainland turned bloody, with mass executions of intellectuals, rural landowners, and small businessmen. Mao's killings appear to have taken a million lives every year. It was his policy that at least one "landlord" be executed within every village, every year, to confirm his control.

Once in power, Mao turned his attention to rebuilding the Chinese nation, to making trouble for the West,[15] and to nuclear weapons. In January 1958, he initiated the Great Leap Forward, an ill-conceived attempt to collectivize farming, increase the production of steel, and expand the construction of infrastructure. The Great Leap was a disaster; tens of millions starved to death. It only ended when Liu Shaoqi took control.

Disaster struck again in 1966, as Mao reclaimed power, initiated the Cultural Revolution,[16] and again plunged his country into chaos. He called on the youth of China to rise up, disregard established authority, and to then seek out and purge the old guard: people whom Mao felt had regressed from revolutionaries into bureaucrats. Mao's revolutionary zeal once again decimated the economy and slaughtered millions. It destroyed families, friendships, and the entire fabric of Chinese society. As part of the process, Mao allowed his wife, Jiang Qing, to move from the role of "housewife" to "political queen," giving her control of the Cultural Revolution[17] in exchange for her tolerance of Mao's undisguised womanizing. Jiang began to oversee a murderous reign of terror.

---

15. In Korea and then Indochina.
16. Via the May 16, 1966, circular of the Central Committee of the Chinese Communist Party.
17. Via her chairmanship of the Central Cultural Revolution Small Group.

Mao turned eighty in December, 1973, and time was taking its toll. He had trouble speaking, and the slightest physical activity left him exhausted.[18] He was a dying man. All had assumed that Zhou Enlai, China's premier and Mao's oldest ally, was to be his successor. Mao had so identified Zhou amidst an earlier medical sinking spell: "I cannot make it," Mao told his assembled staff on January 21, 1972: "You [Zhou] take care of everything after my death. Let's say this is my will." During his spring 1972 recovery, Mao attempted to erase this pre-delegation of authority, but it did not matter. Zhou was a dying man himself. During the summer of 1972, Zhou's urine first showed cancerous cells. Succession was in the air.

Mao decided to rehabilitate Deng Xiaoping, an energetic former member of the politburo, to manage the economy while others were positioned for succession. Deng had been purged during the Cultural Revolution. In December 1973, he was returned to the politburo and added to the Military Affairs Commission, the seat of real power, while others were positioned for succession.

Illness continued to incapacitate the leadership of China. With the coming of 1975, Mao was immobile, blind, and on oxygen; Zhou lay dying of bladder, colon, and lung cancer in Beijing's 305 Hospital. The Chairman's compound at Zhongnanhai, outside Beijing, was electric with intrigue. The fate of a billion Chinese, leadership of the Third World, and control of China's nuclear genie hung in the balance—but no one dared move. Then, on January 8, 1976, Zhou Enlai died. Jiang Qing's faction held the upper hand, but as Zhou's biographer[19] puts it, Jiang "combined high ambition with minimal talent." Other successors had been named,[20] but all had fallen by the wayside. Deng Xiaoping was under attack for empiricism.[21] An immediate decision on succession was required. Much to the astonishment of all, a feeble Mao turned to a fifty-five-year-old party chief from his home prefecture to lead the New China. Hua Guofeng, first party secretary of Hunan province, had seldom been seen in court. Few people knew who he was, but shortly after Zhou's death, in January, 1976, Mao proposed the appointment of Hua as premier and first vice-chairman of the party. On January 28, 1976, the politburo gave its approval. In April, Mao confirmed this succession plan in writing.

---

18. Mao was diagnosed as suffering from amytropic lateral sclerosis (Lou Gehrig's Disease) in July 1974.

19. Gao Wenqian, *Zhou Enlai* (Public Affairs, 2007), 253.

20. Lin Biao and Wang Hongwen, among others.

21. Deng's legendary 1961 quote: "I don't care if it's a white cat or a black cat. It's a good cat as long as it catches mice."

During the weeks that followed, Hua was solicitous of Mao's health, but the heart attacks soon began. Shortly after midnight, on September 9, 1976, "the line on Mao's electrocardiograph turned flat."[22] A fierce power struggle ensued; it was triangular warfare.

Mao's widow Jiang Qing and her allies, known as the Shanghai Faction, wished to continue Mao's policies of revolutionary mass mobilizations, purges, and killings. The more pragmatic members of the leadership, while holding differing views on future policies, saw Jiang Qing's faction as a clear and present danger. Within a month of Mao's death, Hua arranged for her arrest and imprisonment[23] along with her key associates. Together they would come to be known as the Gang of Four. The politburo was not consulted in advance of these arrests—they approved after the fact. Thus, the Cultural Revolution was brought to an end and the political realignment of China began.

Premier Hua favored a civilized return to central planning in pursuit of the Soviet model; the empiricists, led by Deng Xiaoping, advocated a turn to the free market, so long as the communist party maintained ironclad control. A new constitution was adopted in 1978. By 1979, Deng's arguments and organizational skills had gained the upper hand. In 1980, Hua was replaced as premier by reformer Zhao Ziyang, although Hua retained the title of chairman of the Communist Party of China.

In 1981, the transition was complete. Hu Yaobang replaced Hua as party chairman, Deng Xiaoping took real control by assuming the chairmanship of the Central Military Commission, and Hua moved on to a safe and comfortable retirement. When the transitions of 1976–1981 were over, China had opted for a somewhat free economy, with political power and perks remaining in the hands of the elites. Those shifts would give rise to a booming economy, but they also brought to power a man who had decided to proliferate nuclear weapons into the Third World.

## FEBRUARY 1979: KHOMEINI TAKES POWER IN IRAN

Persia, now known as the Islamic Republic of Iran, is not an Arab nation. Its residents speak Farsi, although Islam is the predominant religion. For much of the twentieth century, Iran has been caught in the jaws of history. The Caucasus Mountains and the Soviet Union lie to the north; the old British Empire of India and Transjordan spread to the east and west; the Persian Gulf bounds Iran on the south. Within Iran lay the oilfields that were the prize in "The Great Game" of the early part of the twentieth century.

Iran entered that century as an independent monarchy, the ruler known as the shah. There was one revolution in 1906 that limited the power of the shah and established a National Assembly. In 1925 there was another transition wherein Reza

---

22. Mao's lead physician, Dr. Li Zhisui.
23. Jiang Qing took her own life, while still under house arrest, fifteen years later.

Pahlavi seized power (with the concurrence of the National Assembly) and declared himself shah. In September 1941, three months after Hitler's surprise invasion of Russia, both Britain and the Soviet Union, now allied in the fight against the Nazis, invaded Iran. They deposed the sitting shah (a Hitler sycophant) and installed his twenty-two-year-old son, Mohammed Reza Pahlavi, as the new shah.

When the war was over, getting the Russians back out again was not easy; only a firm stand by President Truman staved off a partition of Iran. Then there was the difficulty with Mohammad Mossadeq, the prime minister who, in 1951, decided to nationalize Iran's oil industry. At that time Iran was dependent on foreign markets for the sale of a surplus commodity. In 1953, military officers sympathetic to the shah (and supported by the United States and Britain) removed Mossadeq from power. That move reopened the foreign markets for Iranian crude, and that, in turn, brought prosperity to Iran and its leader, but that coup also brought a resentment of Anglo intrusion that persists to this day. For twenty-five years after the Mossadeq removal, Shah Mohammed Reza Pahlavi ruled as a staunch Western ally.

But Iran is a Muslim country. In 1963, the shah introduced a package of social and economic reforms, widely hailed in the West, but highly offensive to the religious leaders within Iran. The forced Westernization of Iran had begun; those opposed to the shah's plans would have to go. The shah imprisoned, and soon thereafter exiled, one of Iran's leading religious activists of that time, the sixty-year-old Ayatollah Khomeini: thus, the latter's arrival in Iraq.

The Pahlavi-Khomeini relationship had a long history. The ayatollah's father had been killed by agents of the elder shah; Khomeini lost one of his sons, Mustafa, under mysterious circumstances that implicated the younger shah's regime. Thus, once exiled to Iraq, Khomeini began to plot his revenge. In 1965, his agents assassinated the shah's prime minister, Hassan Ali Mansur. In the years that followed, the ayatollah began to articulate his vision of an Islamic Iranian republic.

In 1971, the British government decided it could no longer support an empire, or even military bases, in the Middle East. As the British moved out, the Nixon administration took over as the shah's patron. Nixon and Kissinger wanted the shah and Iran to take over the job of policing the Persian Gulf. After the first oil shock in 1973, the United States started selling lots of sophisticated aircraft, missiles, electronics, and other equipment to the shah's oil-rich regime. The Soviets were not pleased; they began to expand their support of the Tudeh (Communist) Party in Iran. The Tudeh never enjoyed a broad base of support, but in 1971, it made common cause with the Islamic radicals, organizing the first armed uprisings against the shah.

In 1977, Jimmy Carter took office as President of the United States. With him came a new approach to human rights. Those policies may have been morally just, but they proved fatal to the shah and a blessing to the Ayatollah Khomeini. In response to pressures from Washington, the shah made concessions to his internal critics, which only emboldened them to ask for more. Riots broke out in the holy city of Qom. The shah had tried to westernize a very old culture; many of its custodians did not approve, and his enlightened post-war leadership had degenerated into a despotic egomania. The shah had antagonized the ayatollahs *and* much of the Iranian middle class, and he was dying of cancer.

In 1978, the Carter administration, probably unintentionally, undertook a two-track approach to the future of Iran. William Sullivan, a career foreign service officer and by then the U.S. ambassador to Iran, was the voice of the State Department. He and his backers saw Iran's future in the hands of the clerics. He wished to meet and negotiate with Khomeini, whom he envisioned as a Ghandi-like figure whose accession to power would reflect the values and would serve the best interests of the United States. At the same time, Carter's national security advisor[24] and the Carter Pentagon wanted to rely on the shah's well-trained military to maintain order. The Brzezinski components of the Carter administration hoped the Iranian armed forces would hold together, to run the country when and if the shah left. They saw radical Islam as a serious threat to the West. As 1979 dawned, U.S. Ambassador Sullivan was already in Iran, conversing with the clerics, while President Carter still thought the shah could be saved and/or that the shah's generals could succeed him. To facilitate that transition, the White House dispatched a four-star air force general, Robert "Dutch" Huyser, to Iran. His instructions were to "convey the president's concern and assurances to the military leaders at this most critical time."

The choice of an air force emissary was unfortunate. General Huyser was the most talented of men, but within Iran, the shah's air force was bitterly resented. It was soaking up national treasure in the purchase of exotic aircraft, radars, and control systems that were of little help to the Iranian army. The survival of the shah's rule would depend on that army taking control of the streets. An air force general from the United States, the vendor of all those airplanes and other gadgets, would not be able to solidify that army's support.

For an entire month, from his covert arrival in Tehran on January 2, 1979, to his helicoptered evacuation at dusk on February 3, Huyser was, as *Pravda* put it, "The American Viceroy in Iran." Upon his arrival, Huyser found a reasonably honest government and a well-trained military ready to carry out its leaders' orders. He encountered an ill shah suffering from cancer, dreaming of progress that many of his citizens did not want, and unwilling to order the Imperial Guard to fire on his own people to enforce his visions of a better life.

24. Zbigniew Brzezinski.

General Huyser also found an economy paralyzed by work stoppages, organized by the clerics and the Tudeh. Striking customs officials had closed the borders to foodstuffs while admitting a flood of arms for the rebels. Huyser found a banking system operating sporadically, and then only to effect domestic transactions: no settlement of international accounts. He found an oil industry with production cut back to a few hundred thousand barrels a day, with no refined products delivered to the military. And he found streets filled with demonstrators. In Huyser's view, the total support for the clerics and Tudeh never stood at more than 15 to 20 percent of the people; the remaining opposition was held together by their personal dislike of the shah, his egomania, and his campaign to westernize their culture. Adding to the chaos, the schools were closed during this crisis. The median age of Iran's citizenry was only sixteen; there were too many kids on the street with nothing to do.

Huyser inherited a military leadership utterly devoted to and dependent upon the shah yet riven by interservice rivalries. Thus, they were incapable of acting on their own. The army chief, resentful of an American air force officer usurping the throne, would not use his troops to take over customs; the navy chief would not use his experienced technicians to operate the oilfields and refineries. The air force and the procurement minister were under constant pressure from Washington to execute sales agreements for weapon systems en route, even though the regime was mortally stricken, with only days to live. The chief of the supreme commander's staff (army General Gharabaghi) was probably reaching an accommodation with the ayatollah. This is now apparent from that general's freedom of movement in post-revolutionary Tehran and his subsequent comfortable retirement to Paris. The incoherence of the Iranian military chiefs and their inability to organize a coup undoubtedly led to their downfall and eventually to their exile or death.

On Tuesday, January 16, 1979, the shah left Tehran aboard his 707, headed to Cairo "on vacation." The rejoicing was tremendous, but the pressure seemed to be off. The National Assembly had confirmed a successor government, led by Shaphur Bakhtiar, but that regime would not use its military to break the strikes, which it could have done. Thus, the economic paralysis continued; the military chiefs did not know what to do. For a week after the shah left, Ayatollah Khomeini held court in Paris, issuing statements and pulling the strings on the demonstrations, now turning to fire bombings back in Iran.

On Thursday, February 1, the ayatollah returned to Iran on an Air France jet. Upon landing in Tehran, he declared the Bakhtiar government illegal and announced his intention of replacing it with a true Islamic government. Army troops escorted Khomeini safely from the Mehrabad Airport to downtown Tehran, where they turned him over to his followers. By then the military was on full alert, ready for a fight. Neither the troops nor their leaders showed any signs of folding, but the safety of any

American in Tehran was in question. Most had been evacuated; on Saturday, February 3, the White House ordered General Huyser to do the same. In the late afternoon of February 3, as dusk was settling in, the American Viceroy in Iran took off from the Iranian equivalent of the Pentagon. He traveled by helicopter to Mehrebad, wearing his bulletproof vest, and from there flew home to Stuttgart, Germany.

During the week that followed, the Bakhtiar-Khomeini standoffs hardened, yet the military kept their hands off the power centers of the economy. Then, on Friday evening, February 9, order collapsed. At the Doshan Tappeh Air Force Base, the enlisted troops began to riot. The next day, weapons were stolen from the Imperial Armory, and fires began to break out throughout the city. By Sunday, February 11, it was all over: the army chief, General Badraie, was assassinated outside his own headquarters, perhaps by his own troops. The supreme commander's staff headquarters came under gunfire, with the officers retiring to the command post deep underground. The surviving senior officers were arrested and imprisoned. Deprived of its leadership, the military collapsed, and with it, the Bakhtiar government.

In time, the air chief, General Rabii, was tried then executed by firing squad. The navy chief, Admiral Habiballahi, escaped from prison, migrated to the Turkish border, and later reached the United States. The vice minister of war, also the procurement chief, was imprisoned, but he escaped and also walked to the Turkish border. As 1979 ended, brutal executions ordered by revolutionary councils were widespread, and a new Islamic constitution had been ratified by referendum. The shah died of cancer in Cairo on July 27, 1980.

In General Huyser's view, the mistakes started with an arrogant shah trying to impose twentieth-century industrialization on a medieval society. Then there was the indecisive administration in Washington, sending an ambassador to "work with the opposition, to compel a hundred senior Iranian officials to leave the country," while at the same time telling General Huyser to hold the military together, to support a successor government to the shah. At the end, it was Mr. Bakhtiar's refusal to use the army, the only effective lever he had, that ended all American hopes. How differently history might have been if the prime minister had made full use of those forces during the closing weeks of January 1979.[25]

As it was, a grimly anti-American radical Islamic government came to power, again with the assistance of an inattentive American president. And once again, the chaos in the wake of that transition triggered another three-fold increase in the price of oil.

---

25. Upon his retirement from the U.S. Air Force in the 1980s, Huyser dictated his memoirs of those incredible thirty days at a desk in Reed's office. Robert E. Huyser, *Mission to Tehran* (Andre Deutsch Ltd, 1986).

## JULY 1979: SADDAM HUSSEIN TAKES FULL POWER IN IRAQ

Saddam Hussein al-Tikriti, as his name implies, was born in 1937 in Tikrit, the site of his final and inglorious spider hole. From the beginning of his adult life, Saddam was drawn to terrorism and power, joining the Ba'ath Party in 1957 at age twenty. During the years that immediately followed, Saddam failed in his attempts to gain admission to the Baghdad Military Academy, and he failed in his first big terrorist assignment, the assassination of Iraq's prime minister.[26] In 1959, Saddam fled to Egypt, where he hid out for four years as a "student."

Saddam returned to Iraq in 1963, when the Ba'athists finally came to power. He organized the Jihaz Haneen, which in time became the core of Saddam's personal security apparatus. Internal political convulsions tore at Iraq during the 1960s, but by the end of July 1968, a relative of Saddam's, one Ahmed Hassan al-Bakr, had taken over as president of Iraq and as chairman of the Revolutionary Command Council. Thirty-year-old Saddam was the power behind the old man. He became the clean-up hitter, killing off some competitors for power while sending other, more visible officials[27] into exile. Within a year, by the autumn of 1969, Saddam had become deputy chairman of the Revolutionary Command Council and vice president of the country, with full control of the security and intelligence organs of the state. He ran those shops with an iron hand; on July 8, 1973, Saddam executed his own internal security chief[28] and thirty-five others suspected of conspiracy. To clean up other old business, on October 6, 1978, the Sunni-led government of Iraq kicked out a troublemaking Shiite named Ayatollah Sayeed Ruhollah Khomeini.

Saddam and that ayatollah were cut from different cloth. Not only were they Sunni and Shiite, respectively, but the former was a newly minted Muslim fascist, awash with a fresh supply of petrodollars, yearning to be the nuclear-armed jefe of the Arab world. Power was Saddam's goal; terror was his way of achieving it. Ayatollah Khomeini also sought power, but for a different reason. He wanted to repeal the twentieth century, to return his flock to the dark ages, because it would be good for them. A dozen years before, the shah had kicked Khomeini out of Iran, and as Saddam rose to full power in Iraq, he wanted no competitors, no Shiite insurgent leaders, on his turf. Khomeini was again given the boot; the French, hedging their bets, took him in. They welcomed Khomeini to the Parisian suburb of Neauphle-le-Chateau, whence the ayatollah could better mount his campaign to overthrow the shah of Iran.

---

26. Abdul Karim Qasim, elevated to power after the 1958 revolution that removed King Faisal II of Iraq.
27. Defense Minister Dawood was sent to Jordan; Prime Minister Nayif was sent to Morocco.
28. Nadhim Kzar.

As described above, the autumn of 1973 brought a three-fold increase in the price of oil, thus delivering new riches to the Iraqi government. By the summer of 1979, it was time for Saddam to take full control of his country. On July 16, he forced al-Bakr to resign, assuming the posts of president of the republic, chairman of the Revolutionary Command Council, secretary-general of the Ba'ath Party, prime minister, commander in chief of the armed forces, and field marshal in the Iraqi army. He then marked twenty of his peers, possible competitors for power, for execution in a most bizarre public meeting.

Earlier in that same year, Ayatollah Khomeini had seized power in Iran. With absolute power, newfound wealth, and a sizeable army at his disposal, Saddam started a border fight with Khomeini's Iran; it ran on for eight years. As the 1970s ended, Saddam also initiated a nuclear weapons program, based on French-supplied technology and hardware, that twice teetered on the verge of success.

## NOVEMBER 1979: SAUDI RADICALS TAKE OVER THE GRAND MOSQUE OF ISLAM

On November 20, 1979, more than a thousand organized and well-armed men seized control of the Grand Mosque at Mecca, Islam's most holy place. The insurrection was led by Juhayman al-Utaibi, a former captain in the Saudi National Guard who, in November 1979, had come to see himself as the Messiah of Islam. His followers included Islamic holy warriors from Egypt, Kuwait, Sudan, Iraq, and Yemen, many with training received in Iran. Sympathizers in the National Guard had smuggled automatic weapons and supplies into the mosque. Once in place, the militants called for the overthrow of the Saudi royal family and a return to strict Islamist practices, an echo of the revolution in Iran ten months before.

The Saudi royal family was more functional than the one in Tehran; the insurrection was put down with more than two hundred coup-plotters killed, but the Saudis were also on notice that radical Islam was on the move locally. Having dealt with the attempted coup, the royals then moved to co-opt the radicals. Madrassa schools that teach a hate-filled and murderous Wahhabi doctrine were allowed to propagate, and Saudi Arabia's newfound petrodollars were used to finance those schools. It is not surprising that most of the 9/11 terrorists who attacked the United States twelve years later were from that realm. In 2004, the Saudi government turned over their Ministry of Education to a hardcore Wahhabist, one Abdullah al-Obaid. That ministry controls over a quarter of the Saudi national budget; it will surely shape the thinking of the generations to come.

According to former CIA Director James Woolsey, the Saudi government and wealthy Saudi individuals now spend about three billion dollars per year to promote

Wahhabi ideology in the international marketplace. This is done, in part, by the operation of madrassas in other countries such as Pakistan, by the distribution of textbooks to Turkish children in Germany, and by the operation of mosques throughout Europe and the United States. In comparison, during the 1970 to 1980 depths of the Cold War, the Soviet Union only spent about one billion dollars per year on propaganda and political activism beyond its borders.

Observers at the time of the attack on Mecca thought nothing had happened, since the attempted coup was put down so well, but the seeds of accommodation were planted in royal minds. They have germinated well and may soon produce a harvest of nuclear terror well beyond the kingdom's walls.

## TEN YEARS LATER

The decade of the 1970s had come and gone. In its wake were strewn the crowns of departed monarchs, glassware from long-closed gas stations, and abandoned trinkets from the cradles of civilization. A river of petrodollars was now flooding those early empires, supporting the whims and ideologies of the new dictators. Many of them would come to earn the sobriquet "Islamofascist."

The United States had been marked as "the enemy" in Arab eyes. The once-moribund Chinese giant had revived. Nuclear weapons had been introduced into the Third World. Thus, the stage was set for the nuclear pandemic to come.

# SOUTH AFRICA

The autumn of 1973 was not a good time for Golda Meir and John Vorster.[1] On October 6 of that year, an Egyptian-Syrian coalition attacked Israel out of the blue, in what came to be known as the Yom Kippur War. Prompt logistical intervention by the United Statess saved the day, but for a week Israel's survival hung in the balance. Postwar inquiries within that country faulted Prime Minister Meir and Minister of Defense Moshe Dayan for their inattention to prewar indicators. In year-end elections their party lost parliamentary seats, but they did not lose control of the government. As the Meir-Dayan security team took a hard postwar look at its defense posture, a renewed interest in nuclear weapons emerged. While Israel had gone nuclear during the 1960s, and although it owned a modest inventory of A-bombs at the time of the Yom Kippur War, that capability had not been enough to deter her Arab neighbors.

During that same autumn, anti-Afrikan political tides were swirling around the Cape of Good Hope. Pretoria's apartheid policies and Lisbon's changing leadership were converging to create the political tsunami that would impel John Vorster to seek the nuclear haven.

Apartheid, a colonial system of racial segregation, was enacted into South African law by the Afrikaner Party, winners of the 1948 elections and custodians of power until the advent of black rule four decades later. The unacceptability of that policy in Great Britain led South Africa to withdraw from the British Commonwealth in 1961. In 1966, Nazi-sympathizer John Vorster, a champion of apartheid, became the prime minister of South Africa.[2] By 1973, the situation within the country had turned violent, with industrial unrest in Durban, lethal riots in the goldfields, and the formation of the African National Congress[3] as an armed political force. On

---

1. The prime ministers of Israel and South Africa, respectively
2. Upon the assassination of his predecessor, Hendrik Verwoerd.
3. At the time a militant guerilla group, now the governing party within South Africa.

November 30, 1973, the UN General Assembly took note of these developments, chastising the government of South Africa with Resolution 3068, which identified apartheid as a "crime against humanity." This declaration did not enjoy the support of the G-7 countries;[4] Resolution 3068 was a creation of the Third World and the Soviet Empire, but it was a clear harbinger of political storms to come.

During these same years, change was coming to the capital of the Portuguese empire, a seafaring state that had once colonized Brazil, the Cape Verde Islands, and an assortment of provinces within Africa, including Angola and Mozambique. From the chaotic days of 1933, the year Hitler came to power, Portugal had been ruled by a reasonably peaceful dictator, Antonio Salazar, a lawyer of conservative Catholic views who kept his country out of World War II. In the summer of 1968, President Salazar fell ill and was replaced by Marcello Caetano, an ultraconservative politician whose lot it was to cope with the wars of independence then flaring within the African colonies. (Brazil had achieved independence from Portugal a century before.) At the time of Caetano's accession, the African wars were consuming 40 percent of the Portuguese budget. By the end of 1973, liberal factions within the Portuguese army were plotting a coup. They pulled off the Carnation Revolution[5] on April 25, 1974, setting off a two-year transition to a liberal democracy in Portugal—and anarchy within the colonies. The insurgents gaining control of the former Portuguese colonies of Mozambique (South Africa's neighbor to the northeast) and Angola (to the northwest) were sympathetic to, and supportive of, the disenfranchised black majority in South Africa. Those former colonies would, in time, provide safe havens for the guerillas of the African National Congress.

Directly to the north, Ian Smith's Rhodesia had also broken its ties with Great Britain in an attempt to perpetuate white rule. By 1973, the native insurgency within Rhodesia, known as the Bush Wars, was gaining momentum. By the end of the decade, that former British colony would gain independence, under black rule, as the Republic of Zimbabwe.

## EARLY 1974: DEVELOPING A COMMUNITY OF INTEREST

In response to the rude awakenings of 1973 to 1974, the South African government of John Vorster reoriented its nuclear activities from scientific research to a formal nuclear weapons program. During the 1950s, South Africa had acquired its first nuclear research reactor (Safari-1: a twenty-megawatt research reactor that went critical in

---

4. Canada, France, Germany, Italy, Japan, the United Kingdom, and the United States abstained from supporting the resolution.
5. So called because it was an essentially peaceful revolution that met with little resistance.

1965) under the terms of the Atoms for Peace Program. In the years thereafter, work on uranium enrichment to fuel that reactor was started at Valindaba.[6] By 1970, the nation's Atomic Energy Corporation was reflecting on the use of nuclear explosives for mining, as advocated by the Plowshare program in the United States and similar experiments within the Soviet Union. That work was started at the Somchem plant, part of the Somerset West military manufacturing facility[7] near Capetown. In 1971, the minister of mines approved research into "peaceful" nuclear explosives, but it was the UN resolutions and the neighboring political transitions of 1973 that moved the Vorster government to action. Those threats led it to refocus its thinking from nuclear explosives onto weapons.

In late 1973, South African scientists received instructions to look into the full spectrum of nuclear weapon possibilities: a gun-type enriched-uranium weapon, an implosion-type bomb, and theoretical work on thermonuclear processes. Materials investigations expanded from uranium to plutonium and on to the separation of lithium isotopes needed for the production of tritium and ultimately thermonuclear weapons. During the year, some of the nuclear weapons work underway at Somchem was moved from Capetown to a facility within the Valindaba uranium complex.

During similar reviews at the same year's end, Israel identified uranium availability as her primary external concern. The initial feedstock for Israel's Dimona nuclear reactor had come from France in the early 1960s, and Israeli engineers had hoped to refuel that reactor with material from the Negev Desert. Potash deposits containing uranium oxide were to be the source, but those ores turned out to be low-grade and difficult to process. After the Six-Day War of 1967, Israel turned its attention elsewhere. The first acquisition was the 1968 covert purchase of several tons of uranium ore on the Brussels Euratom market,[8] but that was only an interim measure. During that same year, Israel's AEC chairman, Prof. Ernst Bergmann, paid his first visit to South Africa, a country rich in uranium ore.

In the aftermath of the 1973 Yom Kippur War, Benjamin Blumberg, a member of the Israel Council for Scientific Liaison, made a specific request to the South African government for fifty tonnes[9] of uranium oxide, a sale approved by Prime Minister Vorster in early 1974. Israel's outgoing minister of defense, Moshe Dayan, also visited South Africa at that time, a guest of the South Africa Foundation.

6. Interestingly enough, *Valindaba* is a Zulu word meaning, "We do not talk about this at all."
7. Developers and producers of gun, rocket, and propellant technology.
8. Ore originating in the Belgian Congo, now the Democratic Republic of the Congo. See chapter 18 for details.
9. Metric tons, or 1,000 kilograms, equal to 2,200 pounds.

In addition to raw materials, Israel needed a nuclear testing ground. That country had confidence in the reliability of her first-generation, French-tested A-bomb, but in the wake of the Yom Kippur attack, the Israeli government felt the need for a truly tactical nuclear weapon. Specifically, Israel wanted a neutron bomb.

Such weapons involve very sophisticated technology; their development requires at least one confirming test.[10] The United States and the Soviets pioneered the development of these "enhanced radiation weapons" in the early 1960s, since they are of interest to those who may have to fight in close quarters or on their own soil. Neutron bombs deliver more radiation and less blast than a "standard" nuclear device of the same yield, although there is still a fireball and enormous casualties whenever a nuclear weapon is involved. But the objective of an enhanced radiation weapon is the decimation of concentrated enemy forces, such as mobile troops and those driving tanks, while sparing *some* homeland infrastructure from complete destruction. In the wake of the massive and nearly disastrous 1973 tank battles in Suez and the Golan Heights, Israel wanted a neutron bomb. In time she would need some place to test it.

By the spring of 1974, it was clear to both Israeli and South African political leaders that their nations were pariah states, surrounded by racial/ethnic enemies driven by suicidal hatreds. Both states had problems in common; nuclear weapons were one apparent solution. And while Israel had spent much time and treasure during the 1960s courting the newly independent governments of formerly colonial Africa, the Yom Kippur War had shattered those relationships. Almost every African government (twenty-two in all) had severed diplomatic relationships with Israel after the 1973 war. There remained no reason for Israel to hide its developing affiliation with the South African regime.

## 1974: TAKING ACTION

In the summer of 1974, Golda Meir resigned the leadership of Israel. She and her minister of defense were succeeded by Yitzhak Rabin and Shimon Peres, respectively. The latter, as the young director general of the Ministry of Defense twenty years before, had woven the web of nuclear cooperation with the French in the aftermath of Suez. In 1974, the newly empowered Peres met secretly in Geneva with Prime Minister John Vorster of South Africa. The result was an agreement on strategic cooperation and mutual defense. The details have never been published, but we believe Peres agreed to supply nuclear technology to the beleaguered South African state: that is, elementary nuclear weapon design and materials production advice. In exchange, South Africa would supply the Israelis with uranium ore and access to the

---

10. It took the Chinese five tests to achieve a successful neutron bomb.

wide-open spaces of the Kalahari Desert and/or the South Atlantic for the purpose of nuclear testing. The products of this partnership would be a standard uranium-based, gun-type A-bomb for South Africa and a family of boosted primaries, generic H-bombs, and a specific neutron bomb for Israel.

During the summer of 1974, Israel extended formal diplomatic relations to South Africa, credentialing its first ambassador to Pretoria. The South Africans responded with an ambassador to Israel a few months later. And during that same year, the South Africans started construction at their uranium-enrichment facility at Valindaba. This facility, home to the Y and Z Plants, was to use a unique jet-nozzle process for separating uranium isotopes. Time was of the essence, for in April of that year, the Caetano regime in Portugal had come crashing down,[11] and Portugal's former colonies were becoming sanctuaries for the guerrilla forces of the African National Congress. By the end of 1974, John Vorster had approved funding for work on a gun-type uranium weapon as well as for excavations and infrastructure at a nuclear test site in the Kalahari Desert.

## THE LATE 1970s

By mid-decade, nuclear matters were impacting much of southern Africa. On one hand, a South African scientific delegation visited Israel and was welcomed warmly by the prime minister, minister of defense, and cabinet. Within South Africa, construction of the Valindaba uranium-enrichment plant was completed, and the installation of equipment began. In New York, the UN, via Resolution 3379, came to recognize the Israeli-South African relationship as an "unholy alliance between South African racism and Zionism."

In March 1976, Israel's defense minister (and nuclear webmaster) Shimon Peres visited South Africa. While there, he undoubtedly extended his network of nuclear relationships. As a deal closer, he invited South Africa's prime minister to visit Israel. John Vorster made that trip during the following month, cementing several pieces of the Israeli-South African defense relationship. At the core of the Vorster discussions was the trade of Israeli weapons and defense technologies for South African capital and raw materials. The ministers agreed on the sale of Israeli mortars, electronic surveillance equipment, anti-guerilla alarm systems, night-vision devices, radar, patrol boats, helicopters, and armored cars to the South Africans. For their part, the South Africans agreed to sell more uranium oxide ore (yellowcake) to the Israelis, and they apparently confirmed Israeli use of the Kalahari Desert or ocean areas adjacent

11. Mozambique achieved independence on June 25, 1975, and Angola on November 11 of that same year.

to South Africa for nuclear testing. Israel planned to expand its Dimona facility to produce tritium, deuterium, and lithium isotopes for the benefit of both states.

Back in South Africa, the Soweto riots rocked Johannesburg, while the South Africans contracted with the French for a nuclear power reactor at Koeberg. The South Africans also began excavation of the nuclear explosion test shafts at the Vastrap military test range, and they moved forward with the modernization of their uranium mining facilities throughout the country. The latter could be done without much fanfare, as uranium is a byproduct of the vast South African gold mining industry, but the Soviets took notice anyway. During 1976, the Soviets asked for U.S. cooperation in halting South Africa's nuclear weapons program; one option was a pre-emptive assault on the Valindaba uranium-enrichment plant. The United States declined.

By the beginning of 1977, the engineering of a South African gun-type weapon was well along. The South African procurement arm made arrangements to acquire thirty grams of tritium from Israel[12] in exchange for another fifty tonnes of yellowcake ore. It may be that a South African promise of some enriched uranium was part of the deal, as Israel had no facilities for producing HEU, a material needed to fulfill Israel's thermonuclear ambitions. Test preparations were going forward at the Kalahari test hole, but it is quite clear that even by the summer of 1977, the South Africans would have no weapon of their own to test. Their Valindaba uranium-enrichment facility would not be producing highly enriched uranium until late 1978.

Most observers now believe the 1977 preparations at the Kalahari hole were simply for a dry run, a test of cables, diagnostics, signal processing, firing circuits, as well as all the logistics involved in an underground nuclear test. No nuclear detonation was planned; no dynamic simulation was needed since the South African device did not utilize an implosion design. It was to be a practice run, conducted down hole in preparation for a full-up nuclear test the following year. At the time, some Washington intelligence officials believed Israel was the intended user of the Vastrap excavation (planning on a full-up nuclear test), but after the fact, there is little evidence to confirm that belief.

In time South Africa planned to test its own nuclear device. India had conducted a "peaceful nuclear test" in 1974 without adverse political consequences. The South Africans expected a similarly mild global response to their planned 1978 shot in the Kalahari.

Unfortunately for the South Africans, on July 30, a Soviet reconnaissance satellite noticed these test preparations at the Kalahari Desert site. A second look seven days later, and then a U.S. satellite pass, confirmed these findings. It looked

12. Delivered in 2.5-gram capsules under the code name Project Teeblare (Tea Leaves).

like an impending nuclear test to the Cold Warriors overhead. Britain, France, and West Germany joined the United States and the Soviets in strong protests to the South African government; the planned August 1977 event was cancelled. The South African engineers on site report that there was a call from Pretoria with instructions to pack up and return to Valindaba as soon as possible. They did so overnight. By dawn, all activity at the wellhead was gone, but even so, the South Africans took the rap. On November 4, 1977, the UN Security Council imposed a complete arms embargo on South Africa.[13] That action only served to remind the South Africans how reliant they were on their Israeli partners, how unfocused their scientific community was, and how South Africa needed to achieve a nuclear weapon capability as soon as possible.

In response to the events of 1977, management of the nuclear weapons program within South Africa changed. Scientific exploration of nuclear explosives, physics work, and advanced technology was to continue at Valindaba,[14] but responsibility for the covert development of a practical and viable nuclear deterrent, to include the production of a safe and secure nuclear weapon, was moved into a more business-oriented organization. Production engineering was entrusted to the new South African Armaments Corporation (ARMSCOR), with a planned home a dozen miles west of Pretoria.

As the 1977 clamor died down, the Y Plant at Valindaba came online. In January 1978, it produced its first enriched uranium; by the end of the year, it had produced a "significant quantity" of HEU, enriched to 80 percent U-235. The South Africans could not get their Helikon jet-nozzle process to produce weapons-grade HEU as defined in the United States (93 percent U-235), but their product was good enough for a first-generation gun-type weapon. By the end of 1978, Valindaba was producing enough HEU for the assembly of one gun-type uranium A-bomb every year.

During 1978, South Africa's neighborhood continued to deteriorate with the introduction of Cuban troops into Angola, the formerly Portuguese but now-independent nation to the north of South-West Africa. The latter, a former German colony, had been mandated to South African control after World War I. In 1966, the UN revoked that mandate, the South Africans refused to leave, and local insurgents adopted the name Namibia for the disputed territory. For the balance of the Cold War years, Namibia was a battleground; Soviet-supported Cubans and well-trained South African special forces contested for control.

---

13. Security Council Resolution No. 418, prohibiting trade with South Africa in conventional *or* nuclear weapons. Enforcement was spelled out in Resolution 421, dated December 9, 1977.
14. Lithium isotope separation, improving tamper densities, and developing external neutron sources for advanced initiation schemes.

During that same 1978, John Vorster retired as South Africa's prime minister. Defense Minister P. W. Botha took his place, and as part of the transition, the South African government crystallized its thinking regarding a nuclear strategy. The prior views of the Atomic Energy Board had been that a simple underground nuclear test, of either a South African or Israeli device, would send an adequate message to neighbors and friends. It would deter the newly independent states on South Africa's borders, and it would compel U.S. policymakers to "include us within your security arrangements, or we will go nuclear."

The new South African government of P. W. Botha did not wish to accept mere symbolism; it wanted useable nuclear weapons. The assistance of Israeli scientists would be critical in achieving that goal, and they were there, in significant numbers. Disgruntled chefs at the nuclear facilities, annoyed by the kosher culinary requirements of their guests, confirm that fact. We believe one product of the Israeli-Afrikan alliance went on display over the South Atlantic in the late summer of 1979.

## THE SUMMER OF 1979

The events of September 1979 remain controversial to this day, but we, and many members of the nuclear and defense scientific communities,[15] feel that two years after the confusing events of 1977 in the Kalahari desert, Israel and South Africa were ready to try a different approach.

Although a nuclear event had been planned for 1978 as a political demonstration, a full-up test of South Africa's gun-type A-bomb was not necessary.[16] Instead, we believe that by 1979, Israel wished to test a small, enhanced-radiation weapon—a neutron bomb. The device would be fired on a barge, located near a ship-borne command post, operating in the vicinity of South Africa's Prince Edward and Marion Islands, 1,500 miles southeast of Capetown.

The device may have been detonated inside a large steel container (perhaps a commercial bank vault) to garble the signal, although such an arrangement would have complicated the diagnostics. The operation would await a major South Atlantic typhoon, to wash any radioactive evidence back into the sea. The only problem might be the U.S. Vela satellites that orbited Earth looking for atmospheric nuclear detonations.

15. The director of central intelligence's Nuclear Intelligence Panel, scientists and analysts at the Los Alamos National Laboratory, Lawrence Livermore National Laboratory, SRI International, Sandia National Laboratories, the Defense Intelligence Agency, Mission Research Corporation, and the Aerospace Corporation all conclude that the event of September 22, 1979, was most probably a nuclear test.
16. Like America's Little Boy, fired over Hiroshima, gun-type weapons will surely work. The only question is the magnitude of the yield.

But the Velas did not focus on the Southern Hemisphere, and the U.S. government openly published the Velas' ephemeris data. During the summer of 1979, South Africa's military attaché in Washington, D.C., made his first inquiry of Vela ephemeris data. Armed with that information, those planning the test chose a window in time when no U.S. Vela would be anywhere near Prince Edward and Marion Islands. We believe this test was conducted on the night of September 22, 1979, amidst a terrible storm, and that it went off as planned, yielding one or two kilotons—but with one problem. The U.S. government publishes ephemeris data on active satellites. The Vela passing over the South Atlantic on the night of September 22 had been launched more than a decade earlier and, on the books of the satellite-tracking agency, had been "retired," its ephemeris no longer actively reported. But it was there.

The Vela carries two optical sensors, known as bhangmeters. These are very sensitive instruments that look for the double-peaked signal typical of nuclear events; their space-borne and ground systems are designed to ignore all the other distracting events, such as sun glint and lightning. Both bhangmeters aboard the Vela over the Prince Edward and Marion Islands saw the shot on September 22.

Three of the U.S. Navy's acoustic sensors on Ascension Island detected the September 22 event.[17] Not only did the signal time match the suspected nuclear event recorded by Vela, the use of three hydrophones allowed the navy to identify a bearing to the signal source. Upon subsequent examination of the signal structure, the director of the Naval Research Laboratory confirmed that it matched those detected during the French nuclear tests in the Pacific during the 1970s and thereafter. As confirmation, the explosion's signal was reflected off the Antarctic Shelf; the bounced signal was again detected by navy sensors. Time-difference-of-arrival calculations allowed the navy to pinpoint the event's location: the vicinity of Prince Edward and Marion Islands. On the other hand, no other navy acoustic sensors detected any signal at all.

The world's largest radio telescope at Arecibo, in Puerto Rico, detected an anomaly: an electromagnetic ripple in the lower surface of the ionosphere coming from the direction of the lower Atlantic/Indian Oceans. Mail home from South African seamen, operations by the South African navy, infrared sensor data, and subsequent statements by officials of the post-1994 government of South Africa all lend credence to these findings. The U.S. nuclear weapons labs, senior officials at the U.S. Defense Intelligence Agency, and many members of the U.S. scientific community agreed: there had been a small-scale nuclear test in the south Atlantic on September 22, 1979.

17. In the opinion of U.S. Navy specialists, the indicators were unmistakable, with a signal-to-noise ratio of 25 db: i.e., the signal was an order of magnitude larger than the background noise level. An observer could not miss it.

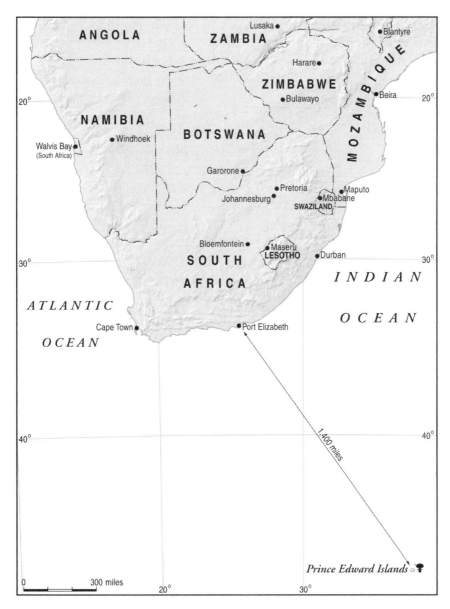

The South Atlantic Ocean, showing the alleged Prince Edward and Marion Islands test site. *Meridian Mapping*

But in 1979, there were other political considerations in the air. The Camp David Accords were fresh in everyone's mind, peace prizes were at stake, and Israeli nuclear tests were not an acceptable part of the landscape. Others claim the White

179

House wished to castigate the South Africans as soon as possible, to strengthen President Carter's anti-apartheid credentials. The first intelligence indicators were treated as "close hold" by the White House until reported by John Scali of ABC News on October 25. To deal with this controversy, in October 1979, the White House science advisor, Frank Press, empanelled a group of highly competent scientists[18] to look into the September 22 event. The committee was led by MIT professor Jack Ruina, and after ten months, in the summer of 1980, the Ruina Panel submitted its report:

"The panel concludes that the Vela signal was probably not from a nuclear explosion. Although we cannot rule out the possibility that this signal was of nuclear origin, the panel considers it more likely that the signal was one of the zoo events, possibly a consequence of the impact of a small meteoroid on the satellite." Elections were underway in the United States, and the topic disappeared from view.

As these experts were starting their work, and before many insiders knew about the event, co-author Dan Stillman was visiting CIA headquarters. He was there to meet with Dr. Jack Ingley, chief of the agency's nuclear energy division, on other matters. In the course of those discussions, and without disclosing the source, Dr. Ingley asked Stillman his opinion of an interesting piece of data. It was a chart of an optical signal, intensity versus time. "What caused this curve?" Ingley asked. Stillman took a look at the time-and-magnitude scales and immediately responded, "Bhangmeter trace of an atmospheric nuclear burst. Unmistakable." It was an easy call for a scientist who had spent his career diagnosing signals from other people's nuclear detonations.

"Unacceptable," Ingley said. "That's not an acceptable answer. Think of something else that could have caused this signal." Stillman could not do so.

In recent interviews, Chairman Ruina and the surviving members of his committee stand by their findings. These are highly competent individuals, supported by fellow MIT professor John Deutch (in 1979, the director of research at the Department of Energy and in later years, the director of Central Intelligence), Hans Mark (then director of National Reconnaissance), and Harold Brown (at the time, secretary of defense). The latter two gentlemen are both alumni of the Lawrence Livermore National Laboratory, with years of experience in nuclear weapon design. They know what they are talking about.

All the other nuclear experts with whom we have talked, however, and all the nuclear weapons laboratory directors then on duty, felt then and feel now that the event

18. Jack Ruina, MIT (chairman); Luis Alvarez, UC Berkeley; William Donn, Columbia; Richard Garwin, IBM; Riccardo Giacconi, Harvard; Richard Muller, UC Berkeley; Wolfgang Panofsky, Stanford; Allen Peterson, Stanford; and F. Williams Sarles, Lincoln Lab.

of September 1979 *was* a nuclear test and that U.S. intelligence was deliberately suborned then (and often since) to deliver the desired answer. As John Adams said long ago, "Facts are troublesome things." In any event, according to Mordecai Vanunu's 1986 revelations,[19] Israel's neutron bomb was in full production by 1984, five years after the 1979 event.

## THE 1980s

After the 1979 event—or nonevent—the South Africans moved out on their own, continuing to furnish yellowcake to the Israelis while purchasing a stream of antiguerilla weapons. On the A-bomb front, the South Africans focused on the development of a low-tech (but extremely safe, secure, and reliable) replica of America's Little Boy HEU weapon. By 1981, they had completed construction of a nuclear weapons engineering facility within the Girotek vehicle test facility west of Pretoria. This new complex was known as the Circle Facility, an attempt to confuse its identity with an electronics company named Kentron Circle, a recruiting and procurement front for the nuclear weapons program, also located in the Pretoria area. (To this day, many writers erroneously refer to the nuclear weapons complex as Kentron Circle.) In time the Circle added a business entity known as Advena.

In April 1982, the first prototype South African U-235 A-bomb, given the code name Melba, was delivered to the weapon storage vaults at the Circle. Melba was not a weapon, nor was it particularly safe. Subsequent attempts at production were delayed as the newly enfranchised South African engineers at the Circle focused on safety and security as well as nuclear yield. After extensive delays, needed to incorporate separable components, locks, and sophisticated propellants within the weapon system, A-bomb production began. It continued during the late 1980s at a rate that came to average almost one nuclear weapon per year.

The production models of the South African A-bomb were about two feet in diameter, six feet long, and weighed about 2,200 pounds. They were suitable for delivery by Buccaneer bomber or by the thousand-mile-range ballistic missile being developed jointly with Israel, a spin-off of the Jericho-2 IRBM. Each weapon was capable of delivering yields in the Little Boy range, up to about fifteen kilotons.[20] At around seven tons per pound of total weapon weight, this design was comparable to the first Chinese device, the all-uranium implosion weapon named 596, fired twenty years before.

---

19. *The Sunday Times* (London), October 5, 1986.
20. As reported by David Albright, president of ISIS, and by Roy Horton, USAF Institute for Security Studies, August, 1999 (INSS no. 27).

By 1985, the Cuban presence in Angola had grown to an alarming size: thirty-one thousand troops, supported by three thousand East German and Russian advisors. The South African government feared a "total onslaught by communist forces." It decided to send troops through Namibia into Angola in an attempt to defuse that threat. The invasion was tactically successful, but the Soviets responded by upping the ante. By 1987, there were fifty thousand Cubans and seven thousand East German and Soviet helpers in-country. The Botha government felt the need to send an immediate nuclear message to the Soviets *and* to the Americans. The president of South Africa directed ARMSCOR to ready the Kalahari test site for a short-notice nuclear test. Visible work soon began. In the late 1980s, contractors poured a large concrete pad around one of the Kalahari shafts and then built a hanger over the excavation, nominally to shield activities from satellite detection. As intended, construction only called attention to that work. To a satellite observer, it would appear that a nuclear device was soon to be lowered down the hole.

It could be that that the march of technology within South Africa dictated that renewed interest in nuclear testing. Engineers had been working on a new, spherical implosion bomb as well as the neutron initiator needed to make it work. Those improvements would have increased weapon yield significantly, but such changes also would have dictated a nuclear test to confirm their viability. More likely the Cuban troop deployments in Angola were the decisive factor in South Africa's nuclear reactivation. Interviews a decade later confirmed the targeting of Luanda, capital of Angola, for a nuclear strike if peace talks failed. By preparing for a test, the South Africans signaled the U.S. and Soviet governments that South Africa was ready to go nuclear, in both testing and use, if the Soviet reinforcement of Angola continued. As expected, American and Soviet satellites detected the hangar over the test shaft. An agreement ending the Namibian hostilities was signed in December 1988, as the Soviet empire was in its final stages of collapse.

By 1989 the South African nuclear weapons program had produced about nine hundred pounds of HEU, and South Africa's Jericho-2 IRBM had flown successfully, but change was blowing in the wind. South Africa had six gun-type U-235 nuclear weapons in storage at the Circle, but that was not enough to maintain an apartheid society. On September 14, 1989, the South African voters turned to F. W. de Klerk for leadership. He was elected to the presidency[21] of South Africa as the Cubans were leaving Angola and as the Berlin Wall entered its final month of service. De Klerk did not show his cards during the election campaign, but once in office,

21. Following constitutional reforms within South Africa in 1984, the office of president became an executive post; the office of prime minister was abolished.

he announced his intent to end apartheid and to close down South Africa's nuclear weapons program. As later confirmed by South Africa's AEC chief, Waldo Stumpf, these two policies were joined at the hip. The de Klerk government did not wish the impending black African government of South Africa to enjoy custody of nuclear weapons. In November 1989, the orders were given to shutter the South African nuclear weapon complex.

Nelson Mandela was released from prison in February 1990. In July, the actual dismantlement of nuclear weapons began, and on July 10 of that year, South Africa acceded to the Nuclear Nonproliferation Treaty. By September 1991, South Africa's six nuclear weapons had been disassembled and the components scattered, with the nuclear materials headed for recycling into South Africa's nuclear power and medical isotope industries. Most documentation had been shredded.

That was the easy part. Retiring the thousands of South African nuclear technicians and erasing their memories was not so simple. As the plans to de-nuclearize the country were announced, sixteen technicians working at ARMSCOR demanded a million dollars in unemployment benefits, threatening to sell information to the highest bidder unless they were paid off. They were dissuaded from those threats, but the brain drain picked up steam as the agents of A. Q. Khan began to recruit. Some technicians opened sophisticated machine shops in Johannesburg, some migrated to other countries, and some went directly to work for the Khan network. The South Africans' specialty became the fabrication of intricate plumbing and uranium hexafluoride feed stations, made to order for the Khan centrifuge systems. Throughout the country, nuclear engineering hardware began to disappear in droves. Adding to this disarray was the 1992 arrival of more than five hundred Soviet nuclear experts, refugees from the collapsing Soviet weapons complex. A corps of underemployed nuclear mercenaries was forming within South Africa.

On March 24, 1993, President de Klerk disclosed many aspects of the South African nuclear weapons program to his parliament. He revealed the number of weapons produced and by then disassembled, the extent of the facilities and staff involved, and the program cost: around 800 million rand ($400 million U.S. dollars at that time, $600 million in 2008 dollars). At the same time, however, de Klerk implicitly denied any nuclear collaboration with foreign governments—clearly untrue—and he rebuffed any claim of a nuclear test in the South Atlantic. His language was accurate: "We never benefited from any nuclear tests by others in our developments," but that statement would have been consistent with an Israeli test of an Israeli design with South African participation limited to logistical support. In June 1993, the first teams of inspectors from the International Atomic Energy Agency arrived in South Africa to document this historic rollback of a once-nuclear state.

On May 10, 1994, Nelson Mandela and his African National Congress took over the government of a nuclear-free state. In earlier times, South Africa had been pushed to the nuclear precipice by external and internal threats to its security; it stepped back as cease-fires and treaties dealt with the former, and moderate black leadership precluded the latter. Even so, several thousand nuclear scientists and engineers, concerned about their security within an ANC-ruled democracy, had begun to look elsewhere. Revelations by the Libyans a decade later identified at least two South African firms as villains in the intended nuclear weaponization of Libya. The Krisch Engineering Company, managed by Gerhard Wisser,[22] and Trade Fin, owned by Johan Andreis Meyer,[23] were two prime suppliers of centrifuge feed stations for Qaddafi's nuclear program. Their involvement was confirmed in German courtrooms a decade later.

The southern tip of Africa is not a good neighborhood. The availability of uranium and the presence of underemployed nuclear mercenaries, both eagerly sought by radical Muslim states awash with petrodollars, has drawn a swarm of bad actors to the back streets of Johannesburg. As the old saying goes, "Idle hands do the Devil's work."

22. A German, resident in South Africa, under arrest by the South African government.
23. A native South African who became a star witness for the government in the Libyan case.

# THE SOVIET UNION

The Soviet Union that emerged from the World War II was a starving fascist state; at least, that is how leading Soviet nuclear weapons physicist Lev Landau saw it.[1] The Soviet government had built an incredible war machine on the backs of its peasants; some had constructed new tank factories from scratch in open fields east of the Urals. Others stood their ground, ill fed and inadequately armed, in the face of Nazi terror amidst the snows of Mother Russia. The war had been won by brutally brilliant generals, willing to execute thousands of their own troops to enforce discipline. But the "leaders" in that war were not leaders at all—they were political commissars. Stalin came unhinged when the Nazis invaded; his apparatchiks could only award each other military rank, jockey for power, and enjoy the perks as bloodshed and famine swirled around them. By 1945, starvation was gripping the land. Even so, the Soviet government retained its monopoly on information. The Soviet people believed in the alleged evils of the West. The state retained its bizarre agricultural theories, continuing to starve its people while turning to the construction of civil works as the route to recovery. Some of those edifices were beneficial: dams and canals well photographed for the enlightenment of the masses. Others, the citadels of the nuclear empire, were hidden from view, for their products would be lethal to all.

The Stalin era ended with a Last Supper, an unheralded event held on February 28, 1953, at Stalin's dacha outside Moscow. The dictator's then-favorites, Georgi Malenkov, Nikolai Bulganin, Nikita Khrushchev, and Lavrenti Beria, had gathered for an evening of movies and drinking. We believe Stalin's wine glass was regularly refilled[2] with overdoses of warfarin, a blood-thinning drug that led to the dictator's

---

1. In 1957 Landau said, "Our regime, as I knew it from 1937 on, is definitely a fascist regime; it could not change by itself in any simple way." (Source: Gennady Gorelik [Boston University], *Scientific American*, vol. 277, no.2 [August 1997], 57.)
2. By Lavrenti Beria.

death by internal hemorrhaging after a grim four-day deathwatch.[3] On March 2, as Stalin lay comatose on his deathbed, the four survivors met to divvy up the dictator's authority. In such an illegitimate system there was bound to be but one true survivor, so it is interesting to reflect on how the Soviet Union might have evolved differently if others beside the Khrushchev-Brezhnev line had succeeded to power.

The most ambitious and ruthless contender was Lavrenti Beria, a modestly educated, long-serving head of the Soviet security services.[4] After World War II, Stalin added nuclear weapons to Beria's portfolio. Beria's scientific staff came to respect his managerial and intellectual talents while fearing the punishments meted out for "sabotage." During his final year in power, Beria defended the theory of relativity and other cutting-edge scientific concepts against the junk science advocated by Marxist ideologues. Many historians believe Beria was not even a dedicated communist; he was a competent manager, an ambitious autocrat, and an evil man. Some suppose Beria would have used the Soviet Communist Party as the Chinese leaders use theirs today: to run an oligarchy focused on commercial and military strength; he would have pursued perestroika decades before Gorbachev gave that word visibility; he might have scrapped the collectivization then starving the Soviet people; he might have aimed for true economic growth. But none of that was to be. Beria's competitors were intoxicated with decades of revolutionary rhetoric; they all understood their fate if Beria seized power. With only the Red Army still outside Beria's control, Khrushchev, Malenkov, and Bulganin used that tool to arrest, incarcerate, and execute Lavrenti Beria before 1953's year end.

Georgi Malenkov was the next in line, the deputy head of the Soviet government. As Stalin's designated heir apparent, he was given the title of premier. Malenkov was the most educated man within Stalin's inner circle, which is not saying much, but Malenkov *had* graduated from a Moscow engineering school. He respected science. At the end of World War II, Malenkov was entrusted with the roundup of German rocket and nuclear scientists for "transfer" to the Soviet Union. After the 1954 U.S. thermonuclear tests in the Pacific, Malenkov met with his nuclear experts to learn of the new weapons' implications for science and civilization. He became the first Soviet leader to understand that a new world war, fought with nuclear weapons, would undoubtedly end civilization. Malenkov bragged publicly about his country's newfound nuclear muscle, but in private, he wanted to negotiate a relaxation of

---

3. Others believe the official Soviet party line, that Stalin died slowly of a stroke that struck on March 1. Whatever the cause, historians agree that, once disabled, Stalin was "neglected to death" by Beria et al.

4. Each of Beria's predecessors held their jobs for only a few years before Stalin ordered their execution.

tensions with the United States and United Kingdom. His ascendancy to full power might have defused the Cold War before it became the age of nuclear confrontation, but Malenkov was inept. He was good at neither management nor conspiracy. Forced out as premier in 1955, he tried to organize a coup in 1957, but in that he failed as well. Malenkov left town at the direction of his peers, retiring to Kazakhstan to manage a power station instead of the affairs of the Soviet Union.

Nikolai Bulganin was the most durable of the four acolytes. He was an old-timer, having served as mayor of Moscow before the war and a military planner during that deluge. At the time of the Last Supper he was Stalin's defense minister, a portfolio he retained during the 1953 transition, and he used that power to arrest and confine Beria three months later. With Khrushchev's support, Bulganin replaced Malenkov as premier in 1955, but Bulganin had no overarching vision for the future of the Soviet Union. He was simply an apparatchik. Bulganin survived for three years as Khrushchev's traveling companion before being put out to pasture.

It was Nikita Khrushchev and his protégés who were left standing at the end of the 1950s. Khrushchev had been Stalin's viceroy in Ukraine. As the Germans swept through that republic, Khrushchev had been recalled to Moscow and then reassigned to Stalingrad, where he served as a political officer during that pivotal battle. In later years, hagiographers have painted Khrushchev as a kindly grandfather, but at the end of the 1940s, Khrushchev was better known as the Butcher of Ukraine. In an end-of-life interview, Khrushchev was asked what he regretted most about his career. His response: "The blood. My arms are up to the elbows in blood."[5]

Among Khrushchev's lieutenants on the Ukrainian Front was the ten-years-younger Leonid Brezhnev. Both men wore the uniform of the Red Army, and both enjoyed general-officer rank without ever commanding any troops in battle. They formed the core of what became "the Brezhnev Generation," party bureaucrats who reflected the lessons learned during the Great Patriotic War: ironclad discipline and massive industrial production are what count; costs are to be ignored. After Stalin's death, Khrushchev took the title of general secretary of the Communist Party; his assistant, Leonid Brezhnev, became the political overseer of the armed forces. Within three years, Nikita Khrushchev had taken full control of the Soviet Union.

Khrushchev wished to compete with the West on industrial and technological grounds; he did not wish to contest on the military battlefield, but as the years rolled by, Khrushchev's moves became erratic. His rash judgments made his peers in the politburo nervous; his quirky conduct was endangering the nomenklatura;

---

5. William Taubman, *Khrushchev, The Man and His Era* (New York: W.W. Norton & Co., 2004), 639.

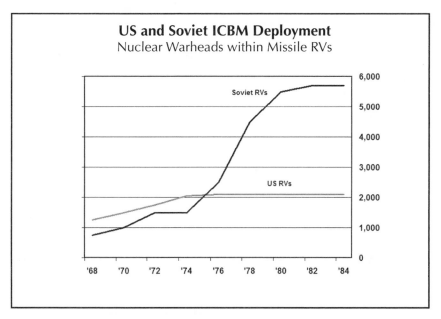

**US and Soviet ICBM Deployment**
Nuclear Warheads within Missile RVs

Deployment of nuclear warheads within missile reentry vehicles (RVs) during the Brezhnev years. *Source:* U.S. Department of Defense, *Soviet Military Power, 1983*

his parsimonious ways made the generals unhappy. On October 14, 1964, while the seventy-year-old Khrushchev was on holiday, he was removed from power by a coup organized by Anastas Mikoyan. Mikoyan became head of state; Aleksei Kosygin became prime minister, Leonid Brezhnev became party first secretary, and Khrushchev was consigned, bloodlessly, to supervised retirement.

Brezhnev had been brought to Moscow in 1956 to oversee and expand the defense, space, and capital-equipment industries. Production, power, and perks soon became the Brezhnev trademarks; controls and cost analyses went unheeded. Thus, when Brezhnev took power in 1964, the Red Army and the design bureaus were overjoyed. They had gained full access to the public purse. The military spending authorized in the early Brezhnev years led to a massive deployment of submarines, aircraft, tanks, and troops, made possible by an uncontrolled proliferation of shipyards, missile ranges, and nuclear materials production plants. By 1970, the Soviet Union had achieved nuclear parity with the United States; by 1980, the Soviet nuclear war machine was running amok.

## THE BEHEMOTH ROCKETS
## THAT COULD NOT SHOOT STRAIGHT

Khrushchev's successors abandoned his dreams of space exploration; Brezhnev's military supporters preferred a massive buildup of the Soviet strategic rocket forces.

In 1960, at the height of the Khrushchev years, and at the time of the alleged "missile gap" in U.S. politics, the Soviet Union had only three SS-6 intercontinental rockets on operational alert.[6] A decade later, as the Brezhnev priorities took hold, hundreds of far more effective Soviet ICBMs had been deployed. By 1980, thousands of Soviet nuclear warheads sat atop over three hundred SS-9 and SS-18 monster rockets, each capable of delivering more than seven tons of payload to the far side of the Earth. At that time, U.S. intelligence believed the SS-18 could, on average, deliver those megaton-scale warheads to within a thousand feet of their intended target.[7] Based on this analysis, the U.S. Minuteman missile force was considered to be at risk; a Soviet first strike could destroy well over 80 percent of it. Complicated basing schemes were devised to hide or constantly move the Minuteman force to deal with this threat.

The facts now turn out otherwise. Recent analyses of SS-18 flight tests suggest that, "the Soviet ICBM force never had the capability to destroy most of the U.S. Minuteman force in a counterforce [first] strike."[8] In 1980, the SS-18's average miss distance was more like a third of a mile, a big difference when targeting hardened, underground silos. Half the Minutemen would have survived. (U.S. technology, embodied in the Peacekeeper ICBM, was capable of accuracies of three hundred feet.) If the Soviets were to attack U.S. missile bases successfully, guidance improvements or some other targeting scheme would be needed.

## BALLISTIC MISSILE DEFENSE

Nikita Khrushchev was the godfather of Sputnik; he well understood the potential impact of a Soviet ballistic missile force on the global correlation of forces, but he also recognized the inevitability of an American response. As he rose to positions of full authority, Khrushchev authorized an energetic antiballistic missile (ABM) program. The payoff came on March 4, 1961, when a Soviet V-1000 rocket, fired from the Sary Shagan test site, intercepted an incoming R-12 (SS-4) target missile at an altitude of eighty thousand feet over the Kazakh desert. Based on that success, and in light of other political considerations, Khrushchev soon[9] authorized the resumption of nuclear testing by the Soviet Union. One major objective of those tests was to be the high-altitude detonation of nuclear weapons to examine the vulnerability of incoming warheads to the planned Soviet ABM system. The results were incorporated into the

6. At that time, the United States had six Atlas ICBMs on alert in Wyoming and one missile-firing submarine on patrol.
7. On average: i.e., a circular error probable (CEP) of one thousand feet.
8. Pavel Podvig, *International Security*, vol. 33, no. 1 (Summer 2008), 118–138.
9. In meetings with his scientific staff on July 10, 1961.

design of an interceptor known in the West as Galosh. By the late 1960s, Brezhnev had authorized the massive deployment of that ABM around Moscow. Eight sites would host sixteen missiles each, all armed with multi-megaton warheads to be detonated, hopefully at high altitudes, over Moscow in defense of that city.

The United States dealt with the Galosh defenses by the introduction of multiple reentry vehicles, decoys, chaff, and, if necessary, an overwhelming attack on the ABM launchers and supporting radars themselves. By the mid-1970s, hundreds of U.S. nuclear warheads were targeted on Moscow alone as part of the U.S. contingent attack plan.

The Soviets poured more resources into a major ABM upgrade in the late 1070s: an improved Galosh missile; an added, lower-altitude, second-tier defensive missile known as Gazelle; and better ABM radars, at least one of which, at Krasnoyarsk, was in technical violation of the now-abandoned 1972 ABM treaty. By the end of the Brezhnev era, the Soviets had spent over a decade and no small portion of their gross domestic product on an ABM system that was massive, that would have blanketed Moscow with hundreds of H-bomb detonations, and that was ineffective. It was then that the United States announced its plans for a space-based defense against missile attack.[10] Documentation and interviews now available confirm a mid-1980s Soviet realization: they could no longer compete on the ABM playing field; some new approach was necessary.

## THE SPECTRE OF BIOLOGICAL WARFARE

Ever since the World War I, the spectre of chemical and biological warfare had hung over the civilized world. A Geneva Convention in 1925 outlawed such weapons, but many nations, including the United States, did not ratify that treaty. After World War II, the concepts of chemical and biological warfare were separated, since "chemical warfare" was an ambiguous term. Are herbicides and tear gas chemical weapons? On the matter of bacteriological warfare (BW), however, a groundswell of opinion in the West led the Nixon administration in 1972 to agree to a ban on the development, production, and stockpiling of bacteriological weapons. A convention to this effect, an agreement between the superpowers, was signed in Washington, London, and Moscow in April 1972 and duly ratified by the U.S. Senate two years later.

We now know, from documentation delivered by some very courageous Soviet scientific defectors, the politburo had no intention of abiding by this biological warfare agreement. In 1973, immediately after the agreement's effective date, responsibility for development of the most virulent BW agents was assigned to an undercover Soviet organization known as Biopreparat. The work was spread among civil agencies

10. Reagan's Strategic Defense Initiative, also known as SDI and eventually as Star Wars.

nominally in the business of developing vaccines, pharmaceuticals, drugs, and defenses against BW attack, but in fact they were developing biowar weapons of the most ghastly scope. The pathogens included strains of anthrax, diphtheria, and smallpox, with quirky responses to conventional antidotes. The resulting Soviet weapons were designed to kill not only people but crops and livestock as well.

These diseased chickens, as it were, came home to roost in 1979. An officer at one of the biowar laboratories in Sverdlovsk (Compound 19) failed to properly cap a filtration machine. Anthrax spores escaped from the laboratory and wafted downhill into the ventilation system of a nearby ceramics factory. Within days employees were dying. Courageous local pathologists did their best to understand the strange lung afflictions of the deceased, but as with all Soviet misdeeds, no information was forthcoming from the perpetrators. A hundred civilians died; "contaminated meat" was the named villain. The local party boss (at the time Boris Yeltsin) ordered an uninformed and thus ineffective cleanup, while the Soviet hierarchy placed a top-secret classification on the whole episode. To this day, the Soviet and its successor governments have refused to discuss any aspects of the Sverdlovsk Compound 19 event, with the exception of an offhand statement by Yeltsin in May 1992. At that time he confirmed military responsibility, but no action was taken, no hearings held, and the government said no more.

The scope and virulence of the Biopreparat activities were only revealed to the West in October 1989, as the Soviet Union was collapsing. At that time a key manager within the Soviet BW complex packed up his files and headed for the door. He appeared a few days later within the Paris offices of Britain's MI-6.

Vladimir Paschenik had been managing a plague research facility known as the Ultrapure Institute in Leningrad. His files made clear the extent and duration of that Soviet BW work. The Institute's task had been not only to develop virulent pathogens, immune to common antidotes—Paschenik's staff was also developing the means to deliver those pathogens, via long-range rockets, across the entire U.S. and British landscape. The trick was to encapsulate those bugs within plastic life-support pellets, to keep them alive during their journey through space and the subsequent rigors of reentry. Before the Paschenik disclosures, biological warfare had been viewed as a tactical threat, a technology for use in battlefield weapons. The 1989 disclosures made it clear the Soviet Union was planning to target every human, animal, and food source within the Western Alliance for contamination with the most ghastly of plagues.

A few months later, U.S. Secretary of State James Baker, meeting with Soviet Foreign Minister Eduard Shevardnadze in Moscow, and without showing his hand, asked for a confirmation or denial of the ongoing Soviet BW work. In August 1990, at a follow-up meeting between the two foreign ministers in Irkutsk, Shevardnadze delivered a bald-faced denial. That response was a total lie, and Baker knew it, but he, his president, and the national security staff all decided to drop the matter. History was moving too fast. The Soviet empire was crumbling. Strategic Arms Reduction Treaty (START) negotiations were on the table. If Jesse Helms, chairman of the Senate Foreign Relations Committee, got wind of the Soviet perfidy, he would have (perhaps justifiably) upset the entire U.S.–Soviet applecart. Rather than calling the Soviet hand, the Bush Sr. administration decided to settle for mutual inspections. Those assessments of the U.S. and Soviet BW facilities took place in early 1991. The United States passed with flying colors; the Soviets failed. They tried to cover up, but the evidence was incontrovertible. Then came the attempted coup of August 1991, the collapse of the Soviet Union, and the end of the Soviet government. The Bush Sr. administration left office; inquiries into the Soviet BW program left with it.

In 1992, another Soviet scientist with a broad overview and a sense of responsibility stepped forward to confirm the Paschenik disclosures. Ken Alibek was a Soviet medical doctor who had served as the deputy director of Biopreparat. He re-told the whole story to a U.S. intelligence agency.[11] When queried as to why Russian scientists would undertake such terrible work, he responded, "Because the U.S. had similar programs; that's what the KGB told us." In fact, the United States had complied with the Biological and Toxin Weapons Convention since its ratification by the U.S. Senate in 1974.

## NUCLEAR MATERIALS

Soviet nuclear weapons had been conceived in the 1930s and brought to fruition in the 1940s, but it was only during the Khrushchev years that the sorcerer's apprentices began to run wild. In the 1950s, serious production of enriched uranium and plutonium started, and the environmental due bills soon followed. A decade later, on Brezhnev's watch, the Soviet appetite for nuclear weapons became insatiable. The demand for fissile materials led to the continuing construction of supporting infrastructure. As a result, two sets of nuclear facilities came into being. The first generation of laboratories, reactors, and separation facilities was built within European Russia, accessible to Moscow. Then, to guard against a preemptive Western attack, a second network was constructed east of the Urals; many were dug into mountains and hidden underground.[12] As the Brezhnev years ended, the legacy of the Great Patriotic War—labor-intensive production pushed to the breaking point—had come

---

11. Later published in the United States: Ken Alibek and Stephen Handelman, *Biohazard: The Chilling True Story of the Largest Covert Biological Weapons Program in the World* (Delta, 2000).
12. See appendix D for a tabulation of the principal Soviet nuclear production facilities.

full circle. The Soviet Union was enriching uranium, producing plutonium, building reactors, and assembling weapons throughout a vast nuclear archipelago, spread across the entire Russian Federation.[13] It was running out of control.

From 1946 until the present time, we believe the Soviet Union produced about 140 to 162 metric tonnes of weapons-grade plutonium,[14] but this is only an estimate; even the Russian government does not know for sure. This plutonium came from nuclear reactors at Chelyabinsk-40 (Mayak), Krasnoyarsk-26, and Tomsk-7. The Russian Federation continues to operate three of these reactors; it dare not turn them off. To do so would leave the cities of Seversk and Zheleznogorsk freezing in the dark, for the reactors at those facilities not only produce plutonium, they are the principal source of power and heat to their host cities. The Russians agreed to discontinue plutonium production as of the end of 2006, but those reactors themselves will continue to operate for several more years.

During the Cold War years, the Soviets also produced more than 1,200 metric tonnes of highly enriched uranium. Some was destined for use in weapons, but much was also headed for the Soviet submarine fleet. (Nuclear reactors within ships require weapon-grade uranium to fuel their very compact reactors.) The Soviet Union ceased the production of HEU in 1988.[15]

During the Brezhnev years the Soviet military sought and achieved nuclear parity with the West. Huge numbers of nuclear weapons of every size and shape were assembled within the facilities noted in appendix D; the Soviets then entrusted the custody of those weapons to the Twelfth Main Directorate of the Ministry of Defense. The officers of the Twelfth Main Directorate were a tough, dedicated, and competent bunch of people. In later years, as we came to discuss Cold War history with them, their commitment to nuclear responsibility came through loud and clear. We believe the Twelfth Main Directorate took nuclear safety and weapons accountability quite seriously; we doubt there are significant numbers of nuclear weapons unaccounted for within Russia, and none elsewhere within the outlying republics.

---

13. The Soviets were meticulous about siting their nuclear weapons complex within Russia itself. Only the nuclear test site (near Semipalatinsk), the Ulba metallurgical plant, and the Zhelty Vody uranium mine were located outside Russia but within the other Soviet republics, for reasons unavoidably dictated by geography.

14. During the Cold War, the United States produced 111.4 metric tons of plutonium, mostly from government reactors built for that purpose; nine light water reactors at Hanford, Washington; and five heavy water reactors at Savannah River, Georgia. By 1989, the United States had discontinued all plutonium production.

15. The United States produced 994 metric tons of HEU during the Cold War. Production ended in 1992.

No inventory scheme can work perfectly, of course. It is possible that a nuclear weapon could be stolen or purchased from the Russian inventory, but every such weapon requires continued care and feeding if it is to remain operational.[16] A nuclear device, produced at Avangard in the 1980s and untended since, is not likely to work twenty years later. For these reasons we do not feel that "loose nukes" (assembled but unaccounted for nuclear weapons within Russia) are an immediate challenge to Western safety.

The same cannot be said for the ocean of fissionable materials floating through the former Soviet Union. MINATOM,[17] the Soviet Ministry of Atomic Energy, was run by a bunch of cowboys. While the nuclear designers we have come to know are cautious in the extreme, the bureaucrats in Moscow imposed few safeguards on the production or custody of raw nuclear materials. Plutonium and enriched uranium emerging from the Soviet facilities were treated like so much coal. In the aftermath of the Cold War, our U.S. associates visiting Russian nuclear facilities often found fissionable materials within barns, secured only by one padlock and a disintegrating barbed wire fence. The guards, long unpaid, were gone. For example, Project Sapphire's removal of highly enriched uranium fuel discs from Kazakhstan in 1994 recovered six hundred kilograms (more than 1,300 pounds) of that deadly material from an abandoned warehouse in Ust-Kamenogorsk.[18]

Prior to that American airlift, when the Russians were asked how much U-235 they thought might be stored at that site, they could only make a guess, and they missed, big time. The landscape of the former Soviet Union is now littered with such unaccounted-for nuclear materials; we have been in a decade-long race with the terrorists and the proliferant states to find it.

The post–Cold War Russian governments of Messrs. Yeltsin and Putin have worked, with U.S. assistance, to secure this material. The U.S. Department of Energy has funded a Materials Protection, Control, and Accounting program within the Former Soviet Union to achieve this result. Once designed and installed, these systems are to be run by Russians, but the problem has turned out to be much larger than expected, and corruption continues to corrode the integrity of whatever safeguards are put in place. The U.S. nuclear weapons laboratories are assisting their Russian counterparts in dismantling unneeded weapons and safely disposing of the fissionable materials therein, but that is not a simple job either. The U.S. Enrichment Corporation[19] has been purchasing Russian uranium once the weapons-grade material (93-percent

16. See the discussion of nuclear weapon storage in chapter 13.
17. Known during the Cold War by its opaque title: the Ministry of Medium Machine Building.
18. See chapter 13 for details.
19. The U.S. fabricator of commercial reactor fuel rods.

U-235) has been blended down to reactor grade (3-percent U-235). Over the next few decades that will get rid of several hundred tons of Soviet HEU, but such collection and blending takes time.

There are other U.S.-Russian cooperative ventures aimed at the detection of radioactive materials and the control of smuggling, but no human endeavor operates at 100 percent. American certified public accountants consider manufacturing inventories to be "accurate" if they account for 99 percent of the materials in question. Within the retail trade, inaccuracies of 5 percent are acceptable. In very high-value industries with computerized control systems, inventory errors can sometimes be limited to 0.1 percent of the goods in question. It is unlikely any Soviet inventory system could operate to such standards, but let us assume they do, when plutonium is involved. If the Russian government and its Western partners succeed in locating, locking up, or moving into the commercial market 99.9 percent of the fissionable material produced within the Soviet Union during the past half-century, that still leaves 0.1 percent of the Soviet plutonium and HEU unaccounted for. How many primitive A-bombs could that make? Dozens:

| | Highly Enriched Uranium | Weapons Grade Plutonium |
|---|---|---|
| Estimated production within the Soviet Union, 1945 to the present | 1,200 metric tonnes | 140–162 metric tonnes |
| Possible missing material, @ 0.1% of production | 2,640 pounds | 310–360 pounds |
| Fissile material needed for a weapon | 164 pounds in a steel-encased cylinder[20] | 13.4 pounds of Pu in Fat Man |
| Possible number of weapons to be made from missing Soviet material | 16 gun-type weapons | 23–27 Fat Men |

## THE COLD WAR ENDED, BUT THE MYSTERIES LINGER ON

In the 1980s, the Brezhnev years ended, but that generation left its mark: forty-five thousand assembled nuclear weapons, hundreds of tons of fissile materials, and a military-industrial complex consuming more than half of the Soviet gross domestic product. As the Cold War drew to a close, the Soviet state continued to rely on the West for food, it continued to create nuclear materials and environmental disasters

20. See LANL 2203, July 16, 1958, table II. The critical mass of an HEU cylinder surrounded by iron is given as 91 lbs. A physicist might assume the rapid assembly of two nearly-critical masses of 0.9 crits each. Thus, the HEU needed for a gun-assembly weapon might be 2 x 0.9 x 91 lbs = 164 lbs.

at a prodigious rate, and it continued to cloak its military programs in secrecy and obfuscation. To what end?

**First, consider the matter of missile accuracy.** In response to the antiballistic missile programs undertaken by their opponents, both the United States and U.S.S.R adopted schemes to fractionate their missile payloads into multiple warhead-carrying reentry vehicles (RVs). In time, the technology to independently target each RV was adapted to Trident, Minuteman, and Peacekeeper missiles in the United States and was similarly deployed on the Soviet rocket systems introduced during the 1980s. In parallel with that splitting-up of payload, the search was on for a high degree of accuracy. Both sides wanted to be able to hit within a few hundred feet of the intended target. The U.S. Peacekeeper was able to do so; the Soviet behemoths were not.

One path to super-accuracy *and* ABM avoidance would be to internally steer and maneuver each RV as it approached its target. Such a solution was politically unacceptable to the U.S. Congress, enamored as it was with mutual assured destruction (MAD), but within the unconstrained Soviet Union there was a need for (and in time there came verification of) maneuvering reentry vehicle development. In the mid-1970s, U.S. intelligence picked up evidence of KY-9 test flights. (The letters *KY* refer to the Soviet Kapustin Yar missile launch facility.) These RVs showed "an impact-point correction capability of up to thirty nautical miles through the use of a restartable second stage [and] an inertial guidance system aided by an onboard passive ELINT[21] target sensor. . . . Against a 'cooperative target' it is capable of a CEP of a few hundred feet."[22]

Why would a target "cooperate"? Consider the abandoned and thus no-longer-secret Titan missile launch silos. In the 1970s, fifty-four of these weapons stood on alert within the United States. They lay buried within sturdy concrete bunkers, but a covered system cannot afford to ignore what is going on above. What if an intruder, more likely a team of saboteurs in time of crisis, attempted to disable the silo from outside? The launch crews would need to know, in order to summon outside military help. To provide that situational awareness, each Titan silo was surrounded by an intrusion detection system consisting of two radar transmitters and two receivers. They were known as the "Tipsie Thirty-Nines" (TPS-39). Each transmitter radiated a watt of power at 1.7 gigahertz: a rather weak signal, but an interesting beacon.

We believe the U.S. Minuteman silos were, or could be made to be, similarly "co-operative targets." Almost every military target gives away its location in some way or another. We believe that by the end of the Cold War, the Soviets were able to home,

21. Electronic intelligence, "listening" for electromagnetic signals from the target.
22. *Handbook of Selected Soviet Weapon and Space Systems*, U.S. Air Force, June 1976.

onto Minuteman launch silos. With that information, a hundred kilotons of energy delivered "within a few hundred feet" of a silo would simply excavate that launcher, no matter how much concrete and steel had been put in place to protect it.

**Second, consider the evidence of Russian efforts to develop enhanced radiation weapons.**[23] The last nuclear warhead designed during the Soviet era was tailored to augment the production of high-energy X-rays. Total device yield was to be only three hundred tons.[24] Since then, Russian writings have confirmed the need for these very low-yield nuclear weapons, with powerful advocates within the Russian military urging their development.

In part the leaders of the Russian Federation fear they may have to fight on their own soil, in contention with China in the East, the Muslim states on its southern border, or with the West. Given the collapse of the Red Army, Moscow considers nuclear forces the only route to the prevention of large-scale conventional attacks on Russia. It also appears they wish to blur the distinction between conventional and nuclear war. The Soviet pledge of "no first use" seems to be gone; Russian nukes might well be used first in the event of a local conflict or as a "warning shot," in an attempt to preclude further escalation.

Faced with the overwhelming dominance of U.S. smart weapons on the electronic battlefield, the Russians may be introducing their own New Look into weapons procurement, opting for electromagnetic pulse (EMP) weapons to shut down those networks and sensors. In space, the Russians may seek to disable all U.S. satellite systems not hardened to withstand electromagnetic attack.[25]

It is important to consider the activity of Russian scientists at their Novaya Zemlya nuclear test facility. Dozens of instrumentation trailers and miles of cabling show up every summer. Obviously, they have been testing something. Why have we not detected and denounced those tests? It may be because the Russians well understand the geophysics of "decoupling," i.e., firing nuclear experiments within large caverns to mask the signal. Or their experiments may be of very low yield: hydronuclears or focused-energy tests. Or the U.S. intelligence community may not wish to disclose these politically inconvenient developments—that has happened before. In any event, in 1999 the Russian defense minister, Igor Sergeyev, advocated "the continued development of advanced military technologies, including weapons

23. In this context, weapons emitting enhanced numbers of neutrons *or* amounts of electromagnetic radiation.
24. As set forth in CIA intelligence memorandum dated August 30, 2000, and declassified October 2005.
25. Satellites belonging to any state would be equally vulnerable in such an attack unless hardened against EMP effects.

based on new physical principles." Marshall Sergeyev was well known and respected by your authors. We believe him. Our readers should do likewise.

In November, 2004, Vladimir Putin pointed with pride to new Soviet missile advances. His country "would soon deploy new nuclear missile systems that would surpass those of any other nuclear power." At the time most observers believed that was just talk, giving comfort to his rocket forces in times of economic hardship, but two years later, in May 2007, President Putin's defense minister announced the successful testing of "a new ICBM with multiple and independently targetable warheads." Putin claimed it "could penetrate any defense system." Did this signal the deployment of the KY-9 MARVs? At the same time, Defense Minister Ivanov announced the testing of a new, stealthy, survivable, and long-range tactical cruise missile.

Is American electronic dominance of the battlefield soon to be a thing of the past? Has KY-9 technology been married to the new Russian Topol road-mobile missile, with all hard targets now at risk? Russian insiders confirm this is now the case: according to Alexei Arbatov, a respected former member of the Russian Duma, and Gen. Vladimir Dvorkin, the former director of the Fourth Central Research Institute, "Russia has accelerated development of a new strategic offensive weapon system fitted with a gliding and maneuvering reentry vehicle designed to penetrate any BMD [ballistic missile defense] system."[26]

Does that matter any more? Do we care?

**Third, consider the Soviet and now Russian ballistic missile defense quandary.** Construction of the Brezhnev-era Galosh/Gazelle ABM systems around Moscow were contributing to the bankruptcy of the state, their use would have blanketed Moscow with radiation and fallout, and they were not likely to work. On top of that, the United States had announced a space-based defense plan with which the Soviet military could not cope. What was to be done?

We believe the answer can be found, strangely enough, in the INF[27] Treaty of 1987. At that time the Gorbachev and Reagan governments agreed to dispose of *all* intermediate-range missiles. One approved means of destruction would be to launch those expendable rockets downrange on practice or experimental flights. Missile destruction started in January 1988, a year in which co-author Stillman first saw evidence of an interesting light show above the atmosphere off Scandinavia. These

26. Alexei Arbatov and Vladimir Dvorkin, *Beyond Nuclear Deterrence* (Carnegie Endowment, 2006), 2.
27. Intermediate-Range Nuclear Forces Treaty, a bilateral U.S.-U.S.S.R. agreement that required the elimination of all missiles held by the parties, with ranges between 625 and 3,500 miles, by June 1, 1991.

events came to be known as the domes of light. They expanded very rapidly, at around ten thousand feet per second, with the centers of the expanding iridescent spheres remaining quite transparent. One could see the stars in back of them. Astronomical observatories located in Sweden and Finland recorded dozens of these events.

These observations led Stillman to look for other, similar events. It turns out the Swedish Institute of Space Physics had been operating an all-sky camera for some time. An examination of their nighttime photographs from a decade before revealed a number of similar light shows. In 1985, geophysicists at the University of Hawaii had published a report of a "round, ball-shaped cloud; looking like a nuclear explosion," seen by a Japan Airlines flight crew en route from Tokyo to Anchorage. The pilot of that 747, Capt. Charles McDade, turned his aircraft away from the "brilliantly luminous and rapidly expanding bubble," fearing a shock wave from a nuclear explosion, but the airshock never arrived. "The bubble-shaped cloud just grew larger and dimmer until it filled the entire sky and was no longer discernible," McDade said. Geophysicists at the University of Hawaii concluded the mystery cloud originated at an altitude of about two hundred miles, that it had grown to hundreds of miles in diameter, and that it must have been associated with Soviet rocketry.

In 1990, Stillman's hosts within China told of their concern about similar mysterious light sources on their northeastern border. At that time the Chinese also went to the trouble of describing these events in an English-language magazine clearly intended for U.S. consumption.[28] Via both channels, the Chinese were asking for our help. Informants in China attributed these bursts of light to Soviet missile events. The domes of light over Scandinavia probably came from INF missile-disposal launches from Plesetsk; those over China were thought to originate at the Chita and Kansk missile sites.

These tests continued across the Soviet Union for the duration of the INF treaty-dictated missile destruction window. Their cause has never been explained. Highly placed Russian sources confirmed to us that the origins of these domes of light are classified "top secret" within the Russian security system.

We believe the domes of light were tests of a missile-defense system employing a nonnuclear mechanism for disabling the arming and fuzing systems of any incoming warhead well above the atmosphere and well away from the asset being protected. INF missile-disposal launches were used as the test beds. On the other hand, those who designed the firing systems aboard U.S. warheads dispute that explanation. They claim their circuits are too smart to be so easily spoofed. Still other experts think

28. "Strange Optical Phenomenon Observed in Northeast China," *China Pictorial* (fourth quarter 1989), 4.

the domes of light were tests of a self-destruct mechanism built into the SS-20s. Whatever the explanation, everyone agrees the domes of light happened; no one in the West really knows why.

**Finally, consider the aftermath of the Biopreparat discoveries.** It is clear that with the end of the Cold War, most "civilian" biowar facilities within the former Soviet Union were abandoned and essentially closed, but the military had other plans. They ignored the weak Yeltsin government—who knows what orders they are getting from the Putin regime. Marina Litvinenko, the widow of former Russian security man Alexander Litvinenko,[29] has no doubt that the orders to kill her husband came from Putin. British attempts to extradite a key suspect from Russia have met with nothing but obstruction.

While the Soviet civilian researchers were developing ever-more malevolent strains of pathogens, the separate and distinct military laboratories were in the business of weaponizing those viruses and bacteria, arranging for their delivery to target. Their job was to plan production: to breed enough anthrax spores on twenty-eight days' notice to annihilate the West and then to plan their delivery to target. The Russian Ministry of Defense still operates three of these biowar facilities, presumably with Putin's approval. One is the infamous Compound 19; another is the virology institute at Sergiev Posad, north of Moscow; and a third works on bacteriological weapons at Vyatka, another name for Kirov. Are these facilities secured against terrorist infiltration?

Biological warfare is not some leftover from a dark age; biotechnology appears to be the new frontier of science, the subject that every ambitious graduate student wishes to pursue. As the *Economist* put it in June 2007, "What physics was to the twentieth century, biology will be to the twenty-first." Are the formerly-Soviet facilities of Biopreparat pushing the envelope on those frontiers? Why?

All of the above is not to argue that the present Russian state is malevolent to U.S. interests; in the matter of nuclear materials we clearly enjoy a good working relationship, but the raw materials for dozens of A-bombs still lay within Russia, unaccounted for. The viruses and bacteria of Biopreparat vegetate in the dark. Weapon technologies continue to mature. Governments change. Vladimir Putin waxes nostalgic about lost Soviet glory. Many scientists within the former Soviet Union remain underemployed, and consulting with al Qaeda or the governments of radical Muslim states can be financially rewarding. There are too many mysteries, too much technology spilling over into this twenty-first century to allow for complacency.

29. Litvinenko died in London on November 23, 2006, killed by the ingestion of polonium-210. This is a highly radioactive substance bred from bismuth in a nuclear reactor and not readily available to other than nuclear-sophisticate states, clearly biological warfare at the retail level.

## THE WORLD THAT MIGHT HAVE BEEN

World War I ended with an armistice, not a surrender. The victors repaired to the outskirts of Paris to dismember the German and Ottoman Empires, to perpetuate the *status quo ante*, and to return to a life of frolic. The losers had been defeated, but not occupied; recovery was their problem. America brought the boys home, let the good times roll, and sank into a moral swamp. There was nary a care for the rest of the world. The Roaring Twenties lasted for over a decade and ended with a crash. Hitler rose from the ashes, fifteen years after the Treaty of Versailles.

World War II ended differently, with an abject surrender by the Axis powers. They had been reduced to rubble. Their neighboring "victors" in Europe and Asia had been reduced to financial if not physical ruin. But this time around the Americans were smarter. Two visionary American presidents demanded the creation of a world dispute-resolution body, the United Nations, and a thoughtful secretary of state, George Marshall, laid out a route to recovery via self-defined national paths. The losers of World War II reorganized, elected new governments, joined the family of nations, and soon returned to peaceful positions of economic power. Only Asia harbored dictators. One, in Moscow, had been there for over two decades. Another seized power in Beijing amidst the postwar chaos. They became the protagonists of World War III.

That war, known more accurately as the Cold War because massive hostilities were avoided, again ended with an armistice, not a surrender. During the closing years of that conflict, the American president made clear his intent to respect only a legitimate Soviet government. He identified the land of the pretenders as an "evil empire." On February 16, 1989, the last Soviet officer left Afghanistan. On October 9 of that year, the Berlin Wall was breached. On Christmas Day, 1991, Josef Stalin's heirs dissolved that empire, turning over the nuclear keys to an elected Russian president. Mao had given up the ghost, literally, a decade before.

Unfortunately, when the armistice of 1991 came, the earlier Roosevelt-Truman vision of a postwar world was nowhere to be found. George Marshall was *not* secretary of state.[30] A succession of U.S. presidents once again ignored the fallen foe, welcomed the good times (the dot-com boom), and set a Hardingesque moral tone until, once again, the good times ended with a crash. Eight years after the 1991 armistice, Vladimir Putin took power in Russia, and the Taliban ruled Afghanistan.

Suppose, for a moment, that the ghosts of postwar reconstructionists Harry Truman and Dwight Eisenhower had been at the American helm from 1991 to 1999.

30. James Baker III was.

Might they have responded to Gorbachev's Christmas 1991 call with an invitation to the general officers of the Red Army to participate in a New Year's Day parade down Broadway, a celebration of "peace with honor"? Might they have asked Gen. Colin Powell to fill General Marshall's shoes, to proceed to Moscow, Leningrad, and Kiev to map out a recovery plan that would stabilize the families of officers and men, of scientists and secretaries, of pensioners and the disabled without economic chaos?

Might they have asked Ross Perot to assist President Yeltsin in privatizing the immense state-owned assets of the former Soviet Union before the oligarchs could steal them?

Might the U.S. president have gone to Moscow himself during the first week of May 1992, to celebrate Victory Day, to lay a wreath on the tomb of the Unknown Soldier, to rekindle the wartime bonds between the Russian and the American people, to express his hopes for the future?

It would have been a tough mission. Russia was in a state of shock, but in any event, no one tried. Instead, America partied, and, in time, a new dictator took power in Russia. Vladimir Putin is not a man of Hitlerian evil, but he does describe the dissolution of the Soviet Union as "the greatest geopolitical catastrophe of the twentieth century." Many Russians now agree with him. His critics in the East and West seem to be dying violent deaths with some frequency. We should not think we know everything about the threats to our safety incubating within the remains of our former foe, the potential friend we spurned when the Cold War was over. We do not.

CHAPTER 13

# THE ONCE-NUCLEAR
# SOVIET REPUBLICS

In May of 1982, the U.S. government formally adopted a plan for ending and winning the Cold War. "Victory" was defined as "convincing the leadership of the Soviet Union to turn their attention inward, to seek the legitimacy that only comes from the consent of the governed, and thus to address the hopes and dreams of their own people."[1] Five years and three general secretaries later, Mikhail Gorbachev advised the Communist Party of the Soviet Union of his intention to do just that: to allow free elections, openly contested with a secret ballot. The Supreme Soviet adopted new election laws on December 1, 1988; three months later, republics throughout the empire were electing legitimate legislative bodies for the first time in seventy years.

Within a year thereafter, the Baltic States, forcibly annexed into the Soviet Union in 1940, began adopting resolutions of sovereignty. Within another year, the east European nations that had been added to the Soviet Empire by invasion, coup, or armed force were deposing and/or executing their dictators. By the summer of 1990, the Soviet Republics themselves were declaring sovereignty: Russia on June 8, Ukraine on July 16, Belarus on July 27, and Kazakhstan on October 25. At first, "sovereignty" was not the same as "independence"; it was a more ambiguous marker, laid down to help the individual republics negotiate a better deal with the central Soviet government. Within a year, however, the Baltic States were holding referenda on true independence. All passed by huge margins, at least three-to-one in favor. By early March 1991, Estonia, Latvia, and Lithuania had declared a total break from the Soviet Union.

A draft treaty attempting to federate the remaining pieces into a new Soviet Union was the trigger for the coup attempt of August 1991. When that coup failed,

---

1. National Security Advisor William P. Clark, Jr., on May 21, 1982, at CSIS (Center for Strategic and International Studies), articulating the policies set forth within National Security Decision Directive 32, signed by President Reagan earlier in the month.

most of the Soviet republics started passing true declarations of independence. By December 1991, many had elected and installed legitimate presidents. On December 7, three of those leaders, representing the three European republics (Russia, Belarus,[2] and Ukraine) met in a hunting lodge known as the Bison Forest (outside Brest in southwestern Belarus) to abolish the remaining husk of Marxist history. A handful of advisors to these embryonic states had done some preparatory homework, but it took Boris Yeltsin, Leonid Kravchuk, and Stanislav Shushkevich only two days to dissolve their ties to the Soviet Union, create an ill-defined Commonwealth of Independent States as a covering fig leaf, and go home. Little attention was paid to some very real-world problems, such as who owned the nukes left scattered about the broken empire. Nominal management of the confederation's armed forces was to be entrusted to a conceptual commonwealth commander, Marshal Shaposhnikov, but he had little real authority.

The Bison Forest conference was not a meeting of nascent nuclear states. It was an assembly of Slavic peoples who wanted to abolish the Soviet Union. Together those three republics held enough seats in the U.S.S.R.'s Congress of People's Deputies to close it down simply by failing to show up for a quorum call.

The Ukrainian and Belarusian governing bodies immediately ratified the Brest agreement on December 10—Russia's Congress followed suit on December 11. Upon the announcement of the birth of the Confederation, almost all the other Soviet Republics expressed their desire to join, thereby rendering the concept of a Soviet Union moot. Nursultan Nazarbayev, the president of Kazakhstan, had been a Gorbachev supporter through much of the autumn's turmoil, but he could read the writing on the wall. He called for a Kazakh parliamentary vote on independence immediately after Bison Forest. He got overwhelming approval on December 16, and thus Kazakhstan was in on the ground floor of the independence movement, enabling Nazarbayev to host the union-ending meeting of the Soviet republics during the following week. On December 22, 1991, the leaders of eleven republics (all but Georgia) met at Alma Ata, then the capital of Kazakhstan, to sign the new Commonwealth Declaration. On December 25, Mikhail Gorbachev resigned the presidency of a nonexistent U.S.S.R., turning over the electronic keys to some nuclear weapons, wherever they might be, to Russia's President Boris Yeltsin.

## THE NUCLEAR DETRITUS

Upon the dissolution of the Soviet Union, twenty-seven thousand nuclear weapons remained scattered about the formerly Soviet republics. That number was down

2. Belorussia until changing its name on September 18, 1991.

by 40 percent from the Cold War, Brezhnev-era peak, but those weapons still represented a serious threat to Western security. About eleven thousand of them were thermonuclear strategic weapons, sitting atop ICBMs and submarine-launched missiles or loaded aboard long-range bombers. All were poised to strike the United States and its allies on a moment's notice. Most of those strategic weapons were affixed to their launchers; we knew where they were, and most were equipped with security and release procedures running to the president of Russia, his minister of defense, and the chief of their general staff. For a while after the breakup of the Soviet Union, the Ukrainians clamored for "administrative" control of the nuclear weapons on their soil, but none of the former Soviet republics ever achieved true unilateral nuclear release authority. That remained in Moscow.

The other sixteen thousand nuclear weapons in the Soviet arsenal posed less of an immediate threat to the United States, but they were far more unsettling, because they were the portable (and hence more easily stolen) tactical nuclear weapons: artillery shells, interceptor-missile warheads, nuclear torpedoes, sea-launched cruise missiles, and portable atomic demolition munitions. Many of these lacked even the most rudimentary locks or safety devices. During the Cold War, a large number of these tactical weapons had been stationed outside Russia; they had been placed within other states closer to prospective theaters of operation. Many lay within the strife-torn Transcaucasus mini-republics adjacent to Chechnya.

This requirement for basing nuclear weapons outside Russia changed drastically in the summer of 1991. In June, Boris Yeltsin was elected president of Russia, one of the twelve Soviet republics. In July, the presidents of the United States and the U.S.S.R. (Bush Sr. and Gorbachev) signed the long-negotiated START I treaty.[3] In August, the attempted Soviet coup collapsed, discrediting the power of the Communist Party and casting an aura of disintegration over the entire Soviet Union. On September 29, President Bush Sr. seized the moment with a radio and TV address, offering a unilateral withdrawal of all U.S. tactical nuclear weapons from overseas and from the surface ships of the U.S. Navy, in hopes that President Gorbachev would follow suit.[4] The Soviet president did so, in full, during the week that followed. By the end of 1991, the Soviets and Americans had withdrawn almost all of their tactical nuclear

---

3. The Strategic Arms Reduction Treaty, initially negotiated by presidents Reagan and Gorbachev at Reykjavik and Geneva in 1986 and 1987, clarified at various Bush-Gorbachev summit and ministerial meetings in 1989 and 1990, and executed in Moscow on July 31, 1991, just before the attempted coup.

4. Bush also announced plans to take U.S. bombers off alert, reduce the number of strategic nuclear weapons, de-MIRV (multiple independently targetable reentry vehicle) much of the U.S. force, and to terminate development of a new, small, road-mobile ICBM.

weapons from their forward operating bases. The Soviet nuclear weapons within eastern Europe, the Baltics, Armenia, and Azerbaijan, and aboard its surface fleet all came home, although some tactical nuclear weapons remained within Ukraine, Belarus, Georgia, Kazakhstan, and the Central Asian Republics (the "Stans"). Those republics were still part of the Union of Soviet Socialist Republics.

So it was that most of the inventory of Soviet nuclear weapons, at least three-quarters of them, came to be relocated within Russia itself at the end of 1991. Unfortunately, that still left thousands deployed elsewhere. There were five thousand nuclear weapons within Ukraine alone. With the coming of independence, that inventory made Ukraine the third largest nuclear power in the world, taking a back seat to only the United States and Russia. On January 1, 1992, Ukraine held far more nuclear weapons than Britain, France, and China combined: 1,240 strategic warheads sat atop long-range missiles; six hundred cruise missiles were assigned to Tu-95 Bear and Tu-160 Blackjack bombers at Uzin and Priluki, respectively; another hundred or so gravity bombs were assigned to those same aircraft; and three thousand highly portable tactical nuclear weapons were still scattered about the Ukrainian countryside and seaports.

The problem of Kazakhstan was not as bad, it was just different. Nearly two thousand nuclear weapons remained in Kazakhstan on December 31, 1991: perhaps a thousand multi-megaton warheads sat atop the monstrous SS-18 missiles buried in the Kazak desert, another 320 cruise missiles were assigned to the forty Tu-95 bombers located in-country, and hundreds of tactical weapons remained hidden in bunkers and tunnels throughout the land. Beside the warhead legacy, however, Kazakhstan held rooms full of weapons-grade uranium fuel disks, refined for a Soviet submarine fleet no longer operational, and it had been home to the principal Soviet nuclear test site,[5] an activity that left behind a vast warren of tunnels, shops, and machinery as well as a legacy of pollution and accidents that made all things nuclear most unwelcome in the Kazakh Republic.

In 1991, Belarus, the third major nuclear heir, held only eighty-one strategic warheads. They were associated with the road-mobile SS-25 Topol missiles located in-country. By virtue of its frontier with Poland and the West, however, Belarus also continued to host a large number of tactical weapons.

## THE PROBLEMS OF NUCLEAR WEAPON STORAGE

As we have seen, the end of the Soviet empire came with such speed that there was neither time nor authority for the Russian government to recall its nuclear weapons to central storage. We do believe that all tactical nuclear weapons within Georgia

---

5. Semipalatinsk-21 in eastern Kazakhstan.

and the Stans were recovered and returned to Russia within a few months after the creation of the comonwealth of Independent States, but within Ukraine, Belarus, and Kazakhstan, strategic nuclear status became a heady issue. The problem was that the care and feeding of such nuclear weapons would not be simple; nukes are not pieces of stone one can leave in the garage, untended for decades.

The central material in most nuclear weapons is plutonium, specifically plutonium-239. Once bred in a reactor, this metal has a half-life of 24,100 years, but as in any family, there are some black sheep. The breeding process also produces plutonium-240, counterproductive to reliable bomb ignition, and plutonium-241, a real disturber as the plutonium family settles down for a long winter's sleep.

Plutonium-241 decays fairly rapidly[6] and in steps[7] to become neptunium-237. In so doing it gives off an alpha particle and a bit of energy. The alpha becomes a helium atom; the resulting gas collects in bubbles, while the energy release within the plutonium core continually transfers heat to outer shells of the primary assembly. This differential heating and simultaneous helium generation weakens the carefully machined plutonium parts; the resulting surface irregularities will lead to an asymmetrical implosion of the fissile material, thus degrading or precluding an effective nuclear yield.

After fifty years of storage, 0.1 percent of the plutonium atoms will have given birth to a helium daughter; in a thirteen-pound capsule (the size of Fat Man) that amounts to almost a liter of helium gas at standard conditions, which poses a real problem. After those same fifty years, another 0.5 percent of the plutonium atoms will have transmuted into some other heavy element, lazy offspring not helpful in the ensuing fission process. In the design of nuclear weapons, these small disturbances can make a big difference. After fifty years, the owners of uncared-for nuclear weapons cannot place much confidence in the operation of those weapons; after a hundred years, probably none at all.[8]

External to the plutonium capsule, modern nukes also rely on a supply of tritium to assist in the boosting of the chain reactions. Tritium is an isotope of hydrogen with a half-life of only 12.3 years (it decays to helium-3). Tritium is stored within the bomb case, under pressure, in a metal container. It must be replenished, and the helium

6. With transition half-lives measured in dozens and hundreds of years.
7. 94Pu241 ‡ (-1)beta + 95Am241 ‡ 2He4 + 93Np237.
8. Independent advisors to the U.S. Department of Energy have suggested an eighty-five year life-time for "a majority of pits" within properly maintained U.S. nuclear weapons. NNSA to Senate Armed Services Committee, November 29, 2006. Weapons without maintenance become unreli-able within a few years.

decay products cleaned out of the storage bottles every few years. Doing so is a difficult task, but even more challenging, the weapon owner must have a supply of replacement tritium on hand. That material must be bred in a nuclear reactor, just like plutonium—no small job. The United States and Russia change out their tritium bottles every few years. Failure to do so will assure a malfunction.

Nuclear weapons contain a lot of uranium and steel (iron), both of which occur in nature as an oxide. Those metals would prefer to return to their natural state; they will rust if not protected. Many nuclear weapons also utilize lithium hydride, a very active member of the alkali metal family. Sodium is lithium's down-chart neighbor in the periodic table; both are highly active reducing agents, neither is to be treated lightly. Exposure of lithium hydride to moisture will produce an immediate explosion.

Within a nuclear weapon, lithium is often alloyed with deuterium and tritium in the form of LiDT. As noted above, the radioactive decay of the tritium releases helium, which will not stay bonded to its lithium host. That causes the LiDT to degenerate from a cream-colored solid into a swelling and crumbling black paste.

The A-bomb detonation process is started by a high-explosive charge, and those materials can be temperamental. Nuclear weapons cannot be left exposed to direct sunlight for an extended period of time, nor can they survive widely varying environmental conditions. If thermally cycled, the high explosive will crack; with enough cracks, the primary implosion will become asymmetric, thus failing to drive the core to super criticality.

Beyond these internal materials problems, nuclear weapons in storage must have fully charged batteries if the safety features are to remain in place and if the arming and fuzing circuits are to work properly. Cables and detonators must be regularly checked and replaced. In the case of Soviet tactical weapons, it is necessary to track the device's whereabouts carefully, since most of those 1991-era Soviet nuclear weapons were neither inherently safe nor totally secure.

With all these complications, however, and despite blandishments and warnings from the senior nuclear club members, there were still fears in 1992 that Ukraine, Kazakhstan, and Belarus might wish to keep their nuclear weapons as national assets. All three of these fledgling states enjoyed the first flush of nuclear club membership.

## THE TRANSITION AGREEMENTS OF 1992

In early 1992, this multiple custody of nuclear weapons was high on the agendas of Presidents Bush Sr. and Yeltsin as well as those of the leaders of the newly enfranchised nuclear states. In organizing the commonwealth of Independent States, all had agreed that the highly portable tactical nuclear weapons should be returned to Russian custody as rapidly as possible. We believe that was done by May 7, 1992, but not without difficulty. The contributing states wanted assurances that the Russians were destroying those weapons, not returning them to inventory for ultimate use against disrespectful neighbors—the donors. Deliveries stopped during March and April while the four larger commonwealth states[9] developed a dismantlement monitoring protocol. By early May, however, all of the tactical nuclear weapons once housed in the outer republics had been relocated back into Russia. It was the strategic nuclear weapons that remained out there under marginal control.

In May 1992, the five nations concerned with this proliferation of strategic nuclear weapons (Russia, Ukraine, Kazakhstan, Belarus, and the United States) agreed to meet in Lisbon to deal with the problem. They were to execute a protocol to the START I agreement that would recognize Russia as the successor state to the Soviet Union's nuclear rights and obligations. In Lisbon all five states became parties to the START agreement, the three non-Russian former Soviet republics agreed to join the Nuclear Nonproliferation Treaty (NPT) "in the shortest possible time." Those three states also pledged the elimination of all strategic nuclear weapons on their territories within the seven-year START horizon. With that agreement in hand, postwar euphoria was truly in the air. Presidents Bush Sr. and Yeltsin met in Washington on June 19, 1992, to reconfirm the SALT understanding and to reach a number of other accommodations. The Kazakh Parliament ratified START I on July 2; the U.S. Senate ratified on October 1; the Russian Duma on November 4. The year 1992 ended on a high note.

## 1993: THE INTRUSION OF THE REAL WORLD

The Belarusian parliament ratified both START I and the NPT on February 4, 1993, but by then clouds of uncertainty were beginning to obscure the nuclear horizon. The United States had a new president with a talented national security team, all fully committed to accelerating the START process, but the old relationships were gone. The outgoing American president, Bush Sr., had served as a director of Central Intelligence; the new president, Bill Clinton, came from a small-state gubernatorial background. He was new to Washington, had a lot on his plate, and was not focused on the disintegration of the Soviet empire. His secretary of defense, Les Aspin, had been drawn from the Congress (as had his predecessor, Dick Cheney), with a broad agenda tied to that constituency. The diamond in the rough was William Perry, the man who would ultimately bring about the grandest deproliferation of nuclear weapons in the history of the postwar world. Perry joined the Clinton team almost unnoticed as the new deputy secretary of defense. Perry would be aided and abetted in his work by the chairman of the Joint Chiefs of Staff, Gen. Colin Powell.

9. Ukraine, Kazakhstan, and Belarus as donors, Russia as recipient.

As the new administration in Washington was settling in, politicians within the Ukrainian Rada (parliament) were raising objections to the ratification of START I. Some wanted compensation for the valuable materials within the weapons being exported: the enriched uranium that could fuel Ukraine's nuclear power grid. Others simply wanted to retain Ukraine's nuclear capability. They did not trust the Russians; they did not trust the West. Nuclear club membership had already brought status, prestige, and protection to the new republic. Other, more provincial, parliamentarians pointed out that the SS-24 missiles had been produced within Ukrainian factories. They *were* Ukrainian—they should stay in Ukraine. As the debates continued in April 1993, the Ukrainian minister of defense demanded that all troops within his nuclear-weapon control centers, many of them Russian, take an oath of loyalty to Ukraine.

Elsewhere, confederation representatives were trying to define the meaning of "multinational nuclear control," but those discussions never converged. How could they? At the time of the Lisbon Protocols, all the parties had agreed that Russia was to be the successor to the Soviet Union's nuclear responsibilities. In June 1993, Marshal Shaposhnikov's joint confederation command was dissolved. He turned over his launch authorization codes to the Russian minister of defense and closed up shop.

In September 1993, after half a year of debate, the Russians and Ukrainians, with U.S. help, agreed on a formula[10] for Ukrainian participation in the profits of uranium sales from the weapons being returned to Russia. That agreement was repudiated a few weeks later after a confrontational vote in the Ukrainian Rada.[11] Nominally the issue was the ownership of the forty-six SS-24 missiles and their five hundred nuclear warheads, but in fact, Ukraine's problems were broader than that.

The first problem was food: the people were starving. At the beginning of the twentieth century, Ukraine had been known as the "breadbasket of Europe." It was a massive producer and exporter of grains. Then came the revolution, the collectivization of the farms, the eviction of the talented farmers, and World War II's immense tank battles across the Ukrainian farmlands. By the mid-1990s, during co-author Reed's residency in Kharkov, Ukraine had become a net importer of food. Store shelves were empty; there was not a single piece of machinery to be seen on any farm. An immediate supply of food was essential.

Ukraine was also starving for energy. It had a large industrial base but had no oil or gas supplies within its own territory. A number of hopelessly inefficient coal mines provided jobs, but not much coal. At the end of empire, about one-third of

10. Known as the Massandra Agreement.
11. On November 18, by a 254–9 vote against ratification.

211

Ukraine's electrical power was coming from nuclear reactors. That dependence grew as conventional power plants closed for lack of maintenance and as the other former Soviet republics began to shut off Ukraine's gas supply for lack of payment.[12] As the Ukrainian minister of energy put it on November 22, 1993, "If nothing is done, Ukraine could expect an Armenian winter," in reference to Armenia's winter of 1992 and 1993 without heat. By the autumn of 1993, the new Ukrainian government desperately needed fuel rods for the remaining Ukrainian nuclear power reactors.

Ukraine's third problem was the large number of Soviet military facilities within Ukraine. Getting those Russian troops to "go home" was easier said than done, because, as became a recurring theme in other Soviet outposts, there was no place for those soldiers to go home to. Throughout the Soviet satellite states, from East Germany to Ukraine, the inducement for Russian departure became the construction of housing for its troops once back in Russia.

All of these considerations played a role in the very tense Slavic negotiations overseen by Deputy Secretary Perry during the autumn of 1993, just as other developments were shaking the Pentagon to its foundation. At that time, the U.S.

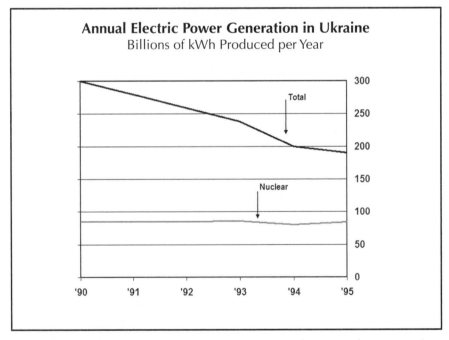

Source: Nuclear Energy Safety Challenges in the FSU. *Center for Strategic & International Studies. 1995*

12. Turkmenistan was, and remains, the principal supplier of natural gas to Ukraine.

military had been ordered into Mogadishu, a port city in Somalia, to "do something" about a local warlord named Mohamed Farah Aideed. On June 5 of that year, Aideed's militia had slaughtered twenty-four UN peacekeeping troops[13] as they searched for contraband arms within Somalia. A raid on Aideed's Mogadishu stronghold was set for early October; Secretary of Defense Les Aspin declined to provide armor in support of that operation. On October 3 and 4, eighteen Americans were killed and eighty-four were wounded in a fiasco that became the basis of the *Black Hawk Down* book and movie. Congress was outraged; Aspin resigned as secretary of defense on December 15, 1993.

After a confusing interval, the president named Bill Perry as his new secretary of defense. Perry was sworn in on February 3, 1994. During that tumultuous autumn, winter transition, and distracting holiday (all prior to his confirmation), Deputy Secretary Perry was overseeing the most intricate negotiations between Ukrainians, Russians, and Americans. The challenge was to create a new and definitive agreement on nuclear deproliferation: one that would stay in place and would be observed until all nuclear weapons were out of Ukraine. He got the job done in early January 1994.

## UKRAINE: 1994–1996

On January 14, 1994, presidents Kravchuk of Ukraine, Yeltsin of Russia, and Clinton of the United States met in Moscow to sign the resulting Trilateral Agreement. The United States would provide foreign aid ($60 million via the Nunn-Lugar Cooperative Threat Reduction program) to support the fabrication and shipment of reactor fuel rods to Ukraine and the return of nuclear weapons to Russia. A mini–housing boom was organized within Russia for the benefit of the returning Russian troops. The Russian Federation agreed to send one hundred tons of uranium to fuel Ukraine's nuclear power plants. Ukraine agreed to return all of its strategic nuclear weapons to Russia and would commence the disassembly of the strategic missiles and launch facilities located on Ukrainian soil. This latter was no small job, as the 130 SS-19s deployed in Ukraine utilized a highly toxic liquid fuel (heptyl) that could not be easily burned off. The parties added mutual security guarantees to protect Ukrainian independence, although those guarantees were not in the form of a treaty as the Ukrainians had hoped.

The trilateral agreement was approved by the Ukrainian Rada three weeks after its signing, on February 4, 1994, although Ukraine delayed accession to the NPT until after its 1994 national elections. Perry used that time wisely, understanding that the tripartite agreement involved both carrots and sticks, and that it would stay in place only if both were always on the table. He invited the Ukrainian chief of

13. All Pakistanis.

the general staff, Gen. Anatoliy Lopata, to visit Omaha, home of the U.S. Strategic Command,[14] for an "orientation tour."

This tour, held on April 19 and 20, 1994, was the cultural shock of the century for the old SAC hands still on duty. A three-star general from the heart of the Evil Empire was welcomed into the inner sanctum of the U.S. nuclear Goliath. General Lopata toured the National Emergency Airborne Command Post, a 747 jet aircraft from which World War II would have been fought. He visited the commander in chief's office, where Admiral Chiles gave him an overview of how STRATCOM worked. General Lopata then moved to the command center. His transit down those very secure halls and stairwells, past the countless guard posts and reinforced concrete doors, left the SAC officers and enlisted men aghast. The briefers could hardly get their words out as they explained to General Lopata how wave after wave of Trident-launched missiles, launched from the North Atlantic; NATO fighter-bombers attacking from Germany; Minuteman warheads; and finally waves of B-52 and B-1 bombers would utterly decimate his homeland within thirty minutes. Secretary Perry wanted General Lopata to understand that the U.S. nuclear target list is not a good place to be, and we think the general got the message. He left as an older and wiser man, saying to the press, "We are on the road to nonnuclear status—to get rid of all the nuclear arms that Ukraine has inherited from the former Soviet Union. [We are not planning to turn back.]"

During the following summer there was a change of government in Kiev. Leonid Kravchuk, a fierce advocate of independence, was replaced as Ukraine's president by Leonid Kuchma, a more Russia-friendly industrialist from Dnipropetrovsk. The earlier agreements reached with Russia and the United States were quite acceptable to the Kuchma government, and thus the Lisbon and Moscow agreements survived the transition. The Rada approved START I on November 16; it entered into force on December 5, 1994. Shipments of nuclear weapons to Russia, and reciprocal shipments of fuel rods to Ukraine started on schedule. A year and a half later, on June 1, 1996, the Russian and Ukrainian presidents jointly announced that all nuclear weapons once located within Ukraine had been accounted for and returned to Russia. STRATCOM took Ukraine off its target list, and the Ukrainian nuclear reactors (including the survivors at Chernobyl) continued to operate, for better or worse, for years to come.

14. STRATCOM, successor to the U.S. Strategic Air Command, which added a navy (SSBN) element in 1992 and changed its name. A navy admiral, Hank Chiles, was the STRATCOM commander in chief (CINC) at the time of the Lopata visit.

## BELARUS

The participation of Belarus in the Bison Forest conference was a true accident of history. The presence of Stanislav Shushkevich, an unlikely president of Belarus, was indispensable to its success. Belorussia (as it was known until September 1991) is a landlocked state of no natural borders, about the size of Kansas, whose population of ten million might best be described as "apathetic," worn down by history. Belarus is surrounded by Latvia, Lithuania, Poland, Russia, and Ukraine. It is essentially flat; the highest mountain reaches only 1,100 feet above sea level. Fittingly, that landmark is known as Mt. Dzerzhinsky, named after the first Soviet security chief.

In 1917, as World War I ground to its grisly end, Belorussia tried to declare its independence from the Russian empire. Within weeks, after the Bolshevik takeover in St. Petersburg, Red Guards also closed down the attempted Belorussian National Congress in Minsk. For seventy years, Belorussians farmed while serving as hosts for wars between East and West.

History's wakeup call came in April 1986 with the explosion of one of the Chernobyl nuclear power reactors north of Kiev. Chernobyl lies within Ukraine, but it sits one hundred miles north of Kiev on the Belorussian border. The winds were blowing from the south that fateful day; 70 percent of the emerging radioactive contamination fell onto neighboring Belorusia. Twenty percent of the republic's cropland was affected; a hundred thousand people had to be resettled. Chernobyl's devastation and the apparent unconcern of both Soviet and Belorussian government officials horrified many young Belorussian intellectuals. Fifty-five-year-old Stanislav Shushkevich, a young physicist at the state university, was one of those energized to action. With the coming of the first Gorbachev-era free elections, in 1989, Shushkevich ran for, and was elected to, the U.S.S.R.'s Congress of People's Deputies. In 1990, when sovereignty was on the ballot, Shushkevich was elected to the Belorussian parliament. Once there, he served as a pro-independence deputy chairman to a Moscow loyalist, Mikalay Dzyemyantsyey. After the coup attempt of August 1991 failed, Shushkevich took over the Belorusian government, the head of a small band of liberal activists eager to achieve total independence from Moscow.

These men were not riding a popular wave. In the elections of 1990, 4 percent of the parliamentary seats went unfilled for lack of candidates; 83 percent of the population voted to preserve their ties with the U.S.S.R. It was only when Russia's parliament voted for sovereignty, in June of 1990, that Shushkevich's parliament followed suit.

No one in Belarus really knew what "sovereignty" meant, but in the chaotic aftermath of the attempted coup of August 1991, Shushkevich and his allies parlayed that parliamentary resolution into a full declaration of independence on August 25 and a renaming of the country. He also began to communicate with Boris Yeltsin. By November, those emerging national leaders were talking confederation; on December 1, neighboring Ukraine voted overwhelmingly for independence, instructing Leonid Kravchuk to bring it about. During the week that followed, Shushkevich floated the idea of a Slavic summit for the purpose of terminating the old order. He wanted that meeting held within Belarus, at the Bison Forest Lodge. The Russians knew it well; it was a Khrushchev favorite, and it lay only a few dozen miles from the Ukrainian border. To confuse their opponents, when leaving their national capitals in early December 1991, the participants announced a meeting in Minsk, but they actually met at Bison Forest to change history.

In the aftermath of independence and the breakup of the U.S.S.R., the Shushkevich government favored a reduction of strategic arms and the turnover of nuclear responsibilities to Yeltsin's Russia. The legacy of Chernobyl made most Belarusians supportive of that posture. Shushkevich signed the Lisbon Protocols, worked to remove the tactical nuclear weapons from Belarus as fast as possible, and caused his parliament to ratify START I and the NPT in February 1993, without crippling amendments. He sought removal of the eighty-one road-mobile SS-25 missiles as quickly as possible, agreeing to do so by 1995, although that would not be so simple. The problem was economics; as the heady days of 1992 gave way to the reality of 1993, the Belarusian economy began to implode.

Like Ukraine, Belarus has no oil or gas. It could not pay for the imports from Russia. In August 1993, the Russians began to cut back on gas deliveries to Belarus. Price controls were removed from Belarusian foodstuffs to encourage production and delivery; by the end of 1993, the annual rate of inflation had reached 1,000 percent. The Belarusian people grew tired of independence—it cost too much. In early 1994, the parliament removed Shushchevich as chairman; in June, the people elected a dark horse, Alexander Lukashenko, to the presidency. His principal claim to fame: three years before he had been the only deputy to vote against independence from Russia.

The good news was that Lukashenko continued to support the withdrawal of the SS-25 missiles from Belarus, although with fits and starts, as he sought compensation for the uranium within the warheads, help with the cost of the missile removals, and political leverage in his attempts to slow the expansion of NATO against his western border. By November 1996, however, Russian and Belarusian officials confirmed that all eighty-one of the SS-25 warheads had been returned to Russia. The missiles themselves were removed shortly thereafter. Since they were on wheels, it should have been an easy chore, but it was not.

The bad news for Belarusians is that Mr. Lukashenko seeks to be president for life. He "won" re-election in October 2004, and he will probably continue to "win" successive elections as he presides over a criminal yet apathetic society for years to come. Lukashenko is doing what he can to reaffiliate Belarus with Russia, but at least the nukes are gone, the roads are paved, the shops are full, and the streets are quiet.

## KAZAKHSTAN

Conceptually, Soviet Kazakhstan was a combination of Nevada and the Dakotas, although much larger in size. It is a land of fifteen million people and home to a nuclear test site (456 nuclear explosions over 41 years) and the heavy artillery of the Strategic Rocket Forces (104 SS-18 rockets). For twenty years, Kazakhstan has been run by Nursultan Nazarbayev, an adaptable dictator who first rose to power as the chairman of the Kazakh Council of Ministers, became first secretary of the Communist Party of Kazakhstan in 1989, and then, after the tumultuous events of 1990, was elected to the presidency of that republic. There is every indication President Nazarbayev intends to keep that job for life, which may be just as well.

The Kazakh drive for independence was less a matter of ideology and more a matter of Kazakh aversion to Russian domination, a desire to control its own economic destiny (i.e., wealth), and its weariness with the disastrous nuclear and military activities within its borders. For more than forty-two years Kazakhstan had been the home of the principal Soviet nuclear test site, known as Semipalatinsk-21. Given the Soviet disregard for environmental matters, nuclear testing there had taken a terrible toll on the lives and safety of the Kazakh people. At the time of the first Soviet H-bomb test in 1953, conducted only one hundred miles west of the city of Semipalatinsk, splinters of window glass flew into the ground beef at the local meat-packing plant and was then duly passed on to the customers. In August 1991, when President Nazarbayev ordered the Semipalatinsk-21 complex closed (one of his first post-coup acts of independence), 181 nuclear weapon test tunnels remained within Degelen Mountain alone. The landscape was pockmarked with the debris from seventy Soviet hydronuclear tests that had been conducted on the surface of the Kazakh desert.[15]

Like the Dakotas in the United States, Kazakhstan became the preferred site for the Soviet Union's large-payload, long-range ballistic missiles as well as its strategic bomber force: dozens of Tupolev-95 Bear bombers loaded with nuclear-tipped cruise missiles were based there. As independence came peacefully to Kazakhstan, two thousand strategic nuclear weapons and a similar number of tactical bombs remained within the country. President Nazarbayev did not seek unilateral control of those weapons, but he did want a voice in their use. At the beginning of 1992, he envisioned the new republic as a "temporary nuclear state," home to a substantial ICBM force under his partial

---

15. The United States conducts such tests within contained facilities underground.

control, but as that first year of independence unfolded, reality began to set in. How were those weapons to be maintained? Industrial intercourse with Russia, the source of most replacement parts, had collapsed. Did he really want to be targeted by the other major nuclear powers? Nazarbayev decided not. In May 1992, he signed the Lisbon Protocols to START I, confirmed that all tactical nuclear weapons had been sent home to Russia, and pledged to remove the strategic weapons by the end of the decade.

Like his Ukrainian neighbors, Nazarbayev began to have second thoughts in early 1993. In February, he sought an ironclad guarantee of Kazakh security from the United States, and he wanted U.S. financial assistance in removing the Soviet rockets, launch silos, and control centers. The very busy Deputy Secretary Perry negotiated these deals during the autumn of that year. On December 13, 1993, the Kazakh parliament ratified the Nonproliferation Treaty, thereby agreeing to become a nonnuclear state.

The actual removal of weapons began in 1994, but shipments stopped when it occurred to Nazarbayev to ask for compensation for the valuable enriched uranium within those warheads. He also wanted to get paid for the aircraft being returned to Russia. Nazarbayev and Yeltsin apparently reached agreement on these matters in March 1994 and shipments resumed; perhaps half the nuclear warheads and all the Tu-95 bombers had left Kazakhstan by year end. The work continued into 1995; by May, Russian officials confirmed they had recovered and accounted for all the nuclear weapons once in Kazakhstan. In September 1996, Russian and Kazak officials confirmed that all SS-18 silos had been destroyed in accordance with the SALT I agreement. Bill Perry visited to assist in one such explosive destruction event.

It turns out, however, that weapons were not the only nuclear assets secreted within Kazakhstan. As President Nazarbayev was ordering the removal of nuclear weapons, he learned about another stash of highly enriched uranium on his territory. Nuclear-powered submarines run on weapons-grade (93-percent U-235) uranium in order to achieve a compact power source. Fuel discs for a long-abandoned Soviet submarine project known as the Alpha had been found within drums in a poorly secured warehouse near Semipalatinsk. President Nazarbayev called the president of the United States, asking for help. The obvious solution was for the United States to buy this material for dilution and then use in its commercial power industry, but the matter was soon entangled within the American bureaucracy. Who would pay for this material? Who was to process it? Finally, on the night of November 23, 1994, a U.S. Air Force C-5 aircraft arrived and departed from the Kazakh town of Ust-Kamenogorsk in the greatest of secrecy.[16] The aircraft was departing with over *half a ton* of weapons-grade uranium on board, only a step ahead of the Iranian buyers who

16. A project code-named Project Sapphire.

had been casing the Ulba Metallurgy Plant two months earlier. Secrecy was essential because President Nazarbayev did not want his own government or citizens to know of this deal; he just wanted that material gone. And gone it was, en route to Oak Ridge for dilution and reprocessing into fuel rods for sale to commercial U.S. power reactor operators.

Kazakhstan has not faced the economic collapse that afflicted other interim-nuclear states. Its military and space facilities appear to be deteriorating, victims of age, pilfering, and lack of spare parts, but its economy is booming. Gross domestic product growth has exceeded 9 percent per annum since independence. Energy is the key ingredient. Once pipelines are built across many a political fault line, Kazakhstan expects to produce more than three million barrels of oil per day. That will make Kazakhstan one of the top ten oil producers in the world. The Sunni Muslim population of Kazakhstan is returning to majority status as the Russian immigrants, dispatched to the provinces during the Soviet years, return home. President Nazarbayev now presides over a nuclear-free nation of growing prosperity; would that other Muslim petro-states sought similar goals.

## THE RESIDUE

The formerly nuclear states of the former Soviet Union all turned in their nuclear weapons, as they agreed to do. That was a historic achievement, led by a talented and determined American secretary of defense. It made the world a far safer place—at least for a while. But as in South Africa, erasing the memories and retiring the intellectual talent was a little more complicated. The lower Dnieper basin, in southeast Ukraine, was the heartland of the Soviet Union's military-industrial complex. Weapons factories remain. In the post–Cold War years, they became major suppliers of conventional arms to Iraq, via Syria, and they continue to produce. . . for whom? Given the size of Ukraine's aerospace industry, it is not surprising that the nation has a huge residual air fleet. Ukrainian "independent operators" are now active in the air transport business; they will fly anything anywhere. That includes regular deliveries to and from Africa.

Kazakhstan, although hosting a smaller industrial base than Ukraine, is the domicile of a far greater stable of nuclear technicians. Ust-Kamenogorsk, the industrial city near the former Kazakh nuclear test site, is a beehive of scientists and engineers knowledgeable in the arcane arts of nuclear weapon design, the processing of uranium hexafluoride, and the long-term maintenance of nuclear weapons.

The Kazakh government may be firmly committed to de-nuclearization, but the individuals with the knowledge and training to produce and care for those weapons could be having second thoughts. Representatives of the Iranian government seem to think so; their recruiters appear regularly throughout the Stans.

# CHINA'S DECADE OF NUCLEAR TRANSPARENCY

The visitors seemed innocuous enough. The five of them had flown from China to Albuquerque to attend an American Physical Society meeting, to hear and talk about shock compression of condensed matter. Stillman met their plane, took care of their transportation and nutritional needs, and escorted them through the very public National Atomic Museum in Albuquerque. All five seemed to be academic tourists, jolly visitors. But when dealing with China, nothing is what it seems. In later years, all five revealed themselves to be top scientists within the China Academy of Engineering Physics, the equivalent of the U.S. nuclear weapons laboratories at Los Alamos, Livermore, and Sandia put together. Those visitors from China were scouting the American turf.

Another guest at another time was Prof. Yang Fujia,[1] a multitasking Chinese technocrat. Besides serving as the director of the Shanghai Institute of Nuclear Research, he held positions at Fudan University and within several international scientific bodies. He came to visit Los Alamos in June of 1988 with an ill-defined agenda. At the time, Stillman was in his tenth year as leader of the Los Alamos Technical Intelligence Division. While Stillman had great respect for satellite photography (known as PHOTINT), electronic intercepts (ELINT), and human intelligence arising from defectors or agents in place (HUMINT), he had learned through years of experience that the best, but often overlooked, source of intelligence was ASKINT: simply ask an informed person what you want to know; often he will tell you the answer. Stillman welcomed the Yang visit to Los Alamos; he wanted to ask a few questions.

During a break in the scientific discussions, Stillman queried the professor:

1. In China, family names come first, and we will observe this custom in the material that follows. The professor's family name is Yang; Fujia is the equivalent of "Tom" or "Dan".

"Does the Chinese nuclear weapons program have a prompt burst reactor?"[2] The answer: "Of course."

Never one to be shy, Stillman pulled out a map of Sichuan Province. "Can you show me where it is?" Stillman thought he already knew the answer, but much to his surprise, Professor Yang pointed to a location off in the mountains, a considerable distance west of the known Chinese nuclear weapons facilities. Stillman fired a third fastball, right over the plate: "Can you arrange an invitation for me to visit that facility?"

"Certainly," the professor responded. "Just send me a copy of your résumé and tell me what other nuclear weapon facilities in China you would like to visit." Thus began a most remarkable unveiling of the Chinese nuclear weapons program, a deliberate disclosure of its nuclear crown jewels, to a central player in the American nuclear intelligence community. The Chinese knew exactly who Stillman was. It is clear they had chosen to show him, firsthand, the achievements of their nuclear world. In time, they wanted him to take the information home, to tell the American government, scientific community, and citizenry all about China's technical capabilities. Why would they do that? Nuclear weapon design information is supposed to be a deep, dark secret.

First of all, the Chinese probably sought deterrence. An American awareness of Chinese nuclear capabilities should lead to a more cautious American military posture around Taiwan and in the Pacific. Or perhaps it was an intelligence gimmick. The Chinese often displayed the inner workings of their technical devices to American visitors just to see how they would react. A raised eyebrow or a sudden scowl could confirm or discount a year's work.

Maybe Chinese nuclear technology was no longer top secret. With the coming of the Deng regime earlier in that decade, the proliferation of nuclear technology into the Third World had become state policy. Perhaps it was time to let the Americans have a look. But the most likely reason for the Chinese hospitality was probably a simple yearning for scientific respect. Your authors found this same phenomenon within the Soviet nuclear weapons laboratories: excellent scientists doing incredibly good work but publishing nothing. In their lives behind the iron or the bamboo curtains, those scientists had received no recognition from their countrymen or from the international scientific community.

It would take another half-decade for the windows to open into the Soviet nuclear world—the opportunities came faster in China. Mao Zedong had died in 1976; within four years, Deng Xiaoping had consolidated power and was leading China in new, more pragmatic directions. By the end of the 1980s, perestroika was

2. An experimental reactor, located in remote areas, which can operate in the supercritical state for a fraction of a second to simulate the efflux of radiation and particles from a nuclear detonation.

sweeping the entire continent. The Chinese leaders were seeking respect from the Western world, and by the time the Stillman tours were over, they had earned it.

As an experienced intelligence officer, Stillman made it a point to travel with, and always be in the company of, another American. After a diplomatic delay caused by the difficulties at Tiananmen Square, Stillman and his intelligence deputy from Los Alamos[3] landed in Shanghai on April 3, 1990. It seemed like Alice's trip down the rabbit hole: quite conventional upon departure from the United States, an eye-opening respite in still-colonial Hong Kong, and a descent into chaos as they approached Shanghai. "First come, first served" seemed to be the protocol within the Shanghai landing pattern; guidance from a ground controller was an afterthought. Upon touchdown, and while still taxiing, the experienced Chinese travelers leapt to their feet, extracted baggage from the overhead, and crowded the exit door so as to gain priority in the customs and quarantine line to come. "Tray tables locked, seats in an upright position" was an invocation seldom heard, never observed.

Upon arrival in Shanghai, Stillman and Hawkins were met by their host, Prof. Yang Fujia, who outlined the itinerary planned for the coming weeks. The professor repeatedly emphasized that Stillman and his assistant were the first Americans (he did not say "foreigners") to visit these Chinese nuclear weapon facilities. He also made clear that an enormous amount of political *guanxi* had been expended in making the arrangements.

## MEETING THE SCIENTISTS

The first stop, next day, was Fudan University, an enormous, fenced, and guarded complex in the northeast quarter of Shanghai. It is home to dozens of research institutes, research centers, and state-level laboratories. A tour of one, Yang Fujia's Institute of Modern Physics, revealed bright and motivated students doing cutting-edge research with antique equipment acquired in the flea markets of China. They worked in unheated laboratories, drafty because of the broken windows. It was Stillman's first exposure to the contrasting cultures of old and new that he would encounter often throughout China.

Fudan University is a prime instrument of the Chinese nuclear weapons complex, pursuing research as directed and feeding its best graduates into that system. There are other equally large and prestigious universities within China, such as Tsinghua and Beijing, but Fudan is the intellectual fount of its nuclear world. While at Fudan, Stillman dined with its recently retired president, Madame Xie Xide, a prime example of the interconnected Chinese system. At that time Madame Xie also served as

---

3. H. Terry Hawkins.

chairman of the Shanghai Communist Party Central Committee, making her the de facto mayor of Shanghai. In an earlier time she had graduated from Smith College and the Massachusetts Institute of Technology; in the immediate future she would assume control of the Center for American Studies at Fudan, part of the vast vacuum cleaner "studying" the West. Madame Xie was charming, fluent in colloquial English, and supportive of the Stillman visit, an imprimatur that opened many a door during the weeks that followed.

The next day's stop was the Shanghai Institute of Nuclear Research (SINR), also directed by the ubiquitous Professor Yang. That institute employed more than a thousand people, half of them scientists. It had been in existence since 1960. One topic of discussion at the SINR was the mysterious domes of light emanating from the Soviet Union during the previous year (and discussed in chapter 12). Those discussions produced a gift of thirty-five-millimeter photos[4] but no explanations. The Chinese were puzzled by the domes of light and were interested in American thoughts.

The third day of Stillman's visit started with another drop down the rabbit hole of air travel within China: the thousand-mile flight from Shanghai to Chengdu, capital of Sichuan Province and the heart of the inland nuclear empire. The flight was accomplished on a very elderly Boeing 707. Stillman's guide and interpreter, while assuming the head-between-the-knees position during the harrowing takeoff, assured his guest, "This is a good American airplane; do not worry."

Upon arrival in Chengdu, Stillman was met by one of the affable Chinese scouts he had first met and hosted in New Mexico the year before. It was only within China that those individuals would reveal their seniority within the Chinese nuclear establishment. Throughout the days that followed, the Stillman party traveled by treacherous road from Chengdu to Mianyang, Zitong, and Science City. In talks with his hosts along the way, Stillman came to understand the extent of the 1989 Tiananmen confrontations between generations. Massive riots had extended throughout China; in Chengdu, crowds of students had burned buildings while their elders looked on, accepting the system as it was. It is within this generational gap, actually a canyon, that we in the West must place our hopes for the future of China.

During the days that followed, Stillman visited a relativistic electron beam accelerator, located within an industrialized bay capable of accommodating large targets. Stillman's hosts admitted the machinery was used to generate bursts of electromagnetic energy, capable of simulating a nuclear detonation at a distance. His hosts later inquired about U.S. work on X-ray lasers while disclosing their own achievements with prompt-burst reactors.

4. From Prof. Yang Fujia, at a later meeting.

The tour next brought Stillman face-to-face with another of the earlier visitors to New Mexico, this one the director of the Southwest Institute of Fluid Physics, a euphemism for the Chinese high-explosives test facilities. That institute has access to nine test pads: three outdoors in the hills well beyond Science City, four large containment vessels[5] located within Science City, and two smaller containment vessels housed indoors at the Institute of Applied Physics in Chengdu. All of these test facilities were carefully instrumented to collect reams of data. The Chinese scientists involved were not simply conducting proof tests; they wanted to *understand* the dynamics of nuclear-pit implosions.

Then came the highlight of the tour: Science City, the immense central laboratory and office complex that manages the Chinese nuclear weapons program. It was undergoing final completion as Stillman arrived, having been constructed over the previous decades to replace the Soviet-planned (and targeted) complex at Haiyan and its successor, the intermediate facility at Zitong. There was a high-rise administration building, dormitories and guesthouses, a high-explosive test facility, a computation center housing one of China's then-few supercomputers, and a vast array of experimental laboratories and machine shops. Stillman was warmly greeted; he was a celebrity. Because he was the first American visitor to Science City, his hosts and all of their associates were curious, welcoming, and as forthcoming as the security guidelines would allow.

But then, days later on the road back to the Chengdu airport, old China reappeared. Stillman thought the carwash station along that route reflected an attempt to isolate a radiological danger left behind in Science City. Not so. That shed was a de facto toll booth, operated by a local clan within the mountains of China. His driver could preclude delay by simply paying the "car wash" fee and driving on, but the credentials of foreign dignitaries visiting the heart of the Chinese nuclear weapons complex could not effect a waiver.

The next stop was Xian, home to the terra cotta soldiers, but also the city nearest the Northwest Institute of Nuclear Technology. The NINT's expertise lies in the diagnostics of nuclear detonations. It serves as home to almost a thousand scientists working in fields of earth sciences, radiochemistry, instrumentation, microcomputers, and nuclear hardening. As was becoming the custom, Stillman's escort was fluent in English and was a recent graduate of a U.S. center of technical excellence. This one had earned a Ph.D. in physics from Caltech. Xian and the NINT all bore the unmistakable Soviet imprint: Stalinist architecture and workmanship; buildings that

5. Large steel spheres designed to contain the energy released by a few pounds of high explosive. They are sealed so as to recover the valuable and sometimes toxic metals involved in the experiment.

looked and felt old immediately upon completion; broken windows, secured against the cold with cardboard; elevators that delivered their passengers within a foot or so of the desired floor level. But all of these inconveniences were forgotten upon the visitors' arrival at the most sophisticated flash X-ray equipment they had ever seen: instrumentation to support implosion diagnostics and/or radiation-hardening tests. The scientific staff at NINT asked all the right questions; they indicated an uncanny familiarity with U.S. nuclear test procedures.

During discussions within China, and again later in the United States, it became clear that neither safety nor weapon security were at the top of the Chinese nuclear priority list. As in the Soviet Union, the Chinese relied on "politically reliable" guards to protect their weapons from unauthorized use. Terrorism was not considered to be a threat. Since then, we believe weapon safety and security have become more important in the Chinese scheme of things.

An exhausting night in Xian was the prelude to an initial ascent back up the rabbit hole of Chinese air travel: a flight to the metropolis of Beijing aboard a rickety, but adequately powered, Russian aircraft. Beijing is not only China's capital, it is the administrative core of the nuclear weapons program. That includes the weapons design center known as the Institute of Applied Physics and Computational Mathematics (IAPCM). One of the managers of the IAPCM turned out to be another of the anonymous visitors to New Mexico the year before.

Nuclear weapon design has grown to be highly dependent on computational support, but in 1990, the Chinese had only one operational supercomputer, known as the Galaxy-2, and it was located at its producing factory in Changsha, eight hundred miles south of Beijing. Galaxy-2 was the first machine capable of performing two-dimensional hydrodynamic calculations, but because the location of that machine was in Hunan Province, coupled with the complexity of the designs planned for test, the designers in Beijing had to commute back and forth to Changsha. Within a year thereafter, a second Galaxy-2 was up and running near the IAPCM and the commuting was over.

The IAPCM not only designs nuclear weapons, it is home to those who think about arms control. At the time of Stillman's visit, conversations turned to the Limited Test Ban Treaty of 1963. The Chinese advised they did not plan to sign that agreement, but as of 1990, they were in compliance and intended to remain so. They also wanted to talk about the U.S.-Soviet-British Threshold Test Ban Treaty (TTBT), negotiated in 1974, but at the time of Stillman's visit, not yet entered into force. The TTBT was to limit the nuclear Big Three to 150 kilotons of maximum yield per underground test, but ratification was hung up on verification protocols. The Chinese wanted to know if that threshold was going to be lowered. How could the United States develop new missile warheads within that limit? And from those discussions re-emerged the

Chinese mantra: "We oppose nuclear weapons, they should be abolished, but until they are, we will remain competitive, and we oppose proliferation." Unfortunately, the Chinese actions before and since have spoken much louder than those misleading words. They *do* believe in proliferation.

Upon the completion of his conversations in Beijing, Stillman began his return to daylight: the trip to Hong Kong, San Francisco, and thence home for a six-month breather until his return to Shanghai in the autumn of 1990. He had been invited to return to China, but that trip would require the intercession of China's newly invested boss, Jiang Zemin,[6] since Stillman and his traveling party were unwilling to return unless they were assured of a visit to the nuclear crown jewels: the Chinese nuclear test site, nuclear test diagnostics facility, and prompt-burst reactor. When all those pieces were in place, and by the time the invitation came through, Stillman's fame had spread. As often happens within a bureaucracy, Stillman's bosses within Los Alamos and the Department of Energy wanted to come along—which they did.

Upon their return to Shanghai, the expanded American delegation was greeted by senior Chinese leaders. The visitors were installed in the Jin Jiang Hotel, then told they were "on their own" for the afternoon. Stillman knew better; the delegation was under constant and most professional surveillance, indoors and out. At the airport they had been separated from their luggage for a suspiciously long time: long enough to facilitate a thorough inspection of the contents. But every cloud has its silver lining. Since the delegation's rooms were wired for sound, every wall constituted an excellent "back channel" route for communication with the delegation's hosts. Stillman has come to call this process "wall talking." Whether to complain about tonight's warm beer or tomorrow's agenda, an articulate complaint to the acoustic-friendly partitions always produced an immediate and favorable result. On that particular evening, Stillman spoke to the walls about casual comments made to him at the time of his arrival. They had concerned "washed out roads" at the nuclear test site. That sounded like a prelude to canceling the promised visit. By speaking to the walls, Stillman made it clear: no test site tour, no remaining in China. The excursion, as originally planned, began the next day.

The initiation was once again the flight to Chengdu, an overnight at the Jin Jiang Hotel in that city, followed by an all-morning motorcade to a hitherto-unknown facility, identified by the hosts once there as the Southwest Institute of Nuclear Physics and Chemistry. The location was mountainous and remote, the facilities

6. Deng Xiaoping had been removed from substantive power in December 1989, in the wake of the Tiananmen Square demonstrations. At that time he was replaced as chairman of the Central Military Commission by Jiang Zemin. The latter also became president, replacing figurehead Yang Shangkun, in March 1993.

were hidden within canyons, the guesthouse was comfortable and modern, but the main attraction was the long-discussed, but never-seen, fast-burst reactor. This was the machine, known as a prompt-burst reactor in the United States, that first drew Stillman and Yang into discussions a year before.

On that historic afternoon, the Stillman delegation passed through heavy security, guards all armed with Kalishnikovs. Site badges bore the emblem "596," commemorating the date of the Soviet abandonment of their Chinese comrades. The delegation was thoroughly briefed and then donned the protective clothing needed to visit the reactor itself.

That reactor, FBR-2, was capable of delivering an intense flux of neutrons and gamma rays within microseconds, thereby simulating the radiation emitted during an actual nuclear device detonation. (The trick was to shut the reactor down before it blew the laboratory away.) Stillman had known there must be such a device somewhere within China; that is why he asked Yang about it. But upon their arrival, the American delegation learned that a first-generation machine, FBR-1, had gone into operation fourteen years before. It had long since been abandoned in favor of this new machine, the FBR-2. The Americans were given a complete tour; at the end of the day, older and wiser, they moved on, over the same nearly impassable roads, to their accommodations at Science City.

This was Stillman's second visit to that epicenter of Chinese nuclear weapons technology, and it was far more informative than the first. He was taken to see the high-explosive test facilities, chambers capable of containing the debris from the detonation of a dozen pounds of high explosives wrapped around heavy metals simulating uranium. Adjacent to these test chambers were most impressive flash X-ray machines, designed to illuminate implosions as they took place. Framing cameras nearby could operate at *millions* of frames per second. Pin dome diagnostics within the imploding spheres delivered more data on implosion symmetry. The technology was above and beyond first rate.

At seminars that followed, the Chinese launched a bewilderingly well-planned barrage of questions. Some were about diagnostics, some related to nuclear weapons design, others centered on free electron lasers, and the broader discussions involved laboratory relations with industry. The Americans dodged where appropriate, and their Chinese hosts did not press. Those sessions were pleasant, but planned.

When it was time to leave Science City, the Americans were treated to a convivial farewell banquet, receiving gifts of lovely tea sets commemorating the Asian Games then underway in Beijing. The assistant secretary of the Department of Energy (DOE) in attendance, being the senior member of the U.S. delegation, delivered a DOE pen and pencil set to his counterpart. During his visit he had been dispensing DOE pens at every turn.

The Americans returned to Chengdu and, with a blatant use of wall talking, made known their thoughts on the day and their wishes for the morrow. Within minutes one of their Chinese hosts appeared at Stillman's door to clear up misconceptions. Later that evening, obviously in further response to that afternoon's wall talk, two hitherto-unseen Chinese engineers appeared at dinner, seated beside Stillman and his intelligence deputy. The Americans had earlier expressed an interest in release procedures for Chinese nuclear weapons. The new dinner companions were senior engineers from the Institute of Electronic Engineering, the organization responsible for weapon controls. An enlightening discussion of permissive action links ensued. The Chinese were well aware of U.S. PAL systems, but they were, unfortunately, more concerned about the reliability of their own weapons than their security.

From Chengdu the group flew to Urumqi, the capital of Xinjiang Province and the city nearest the nuclear test base headquarters at Malan. The usual suspiciously long delay to recover baggage was followed by a gruesome six-hour drive through mountains and desert to the new town of Malan. The guesthouse was luxurious, the rooms obviously just redecorated for this historic visit. The lamb barbeque that ensued was attended by everyone who counted in the Chinese nuclear test community. Many had flown in from Beijing, most spoke excellent English, and all wanted to talk about the achievements of their children in the United States.

The next morning and during the two days that followed, Stillman and his scientific traveling companions received the long-promised tour of the Chinese nuclear test base at Lop Nur (described more fully earlier, in chapter 7). Their hosts were forthcoming and the facilities vast: seven times larger than the U.S. Nuclear Test Site in Nevada.

The return by Jeep Cherokee to Urumqi and by Russian airborne relic to Xian was punctual due to the accompanying Chinese brass. There ensued a revisit to the diagnostics center at the Northwest Institute of Nuclear Technology. The most surprising revelation this time around was that of a unique pinhole imaging neutron experiment, a dual-axis analytic tool known as PINEX. This disclosure was a stark reminder that, even in 1990, the Chinese nuclear weapons program was pulling ahead of the United States in many areas. Other indicators included high-energy gamma ray spectrum analyzers and the presence of gigahertz-compatible oscilloscopes.

A peaceful night in Xian was followed by a flight onward to Beijing and a check-in procedure that confirmed the omnipresence of electronic surveillance. At the Beijing International Hotel, Stillman's deputy requested a room change; his assigned room reeked of cigar smoke. Even though the vicinity appeared to be devoid of hotel guests, the floor lady advised that no other rooms were available. By wink and nod the interpreter explained, "No *wired* rooms available." Open windows had to suffice to clear out the smoke.

While Stillman and his deputy were in Beijing, the Chinese made efforts to separate them from one of their American traveling companions.[7] It was a blatant attempt to discuss weapon design in private with a knowledgeable American. It is not likely those efforts succeeded.

Farewell ceremonies took place in the conference room of the Institute of Applied Physics and Computational Mathematics in Beijing. Representatives of all the visited facilities were present. Each had received a DOE pen from the assistant secretary. Every scientist arrived with the DOE pen in his or her shirt pocket, displaying a large, black blotch where that pen had been leaking: a silent but most telling comment on comparative U.S. and Chinese technologies.

The Americans flew home, to be invited for further tours and conferences during the decade that followed. Formal handshakes at the airport had long given way to hugs, laughter, and family photographs. As the Soviet empire collapsed and the Cold War ended, symposia were organized in Beijing, Shanghai, and the western United States to discuss arms control, nuclear weapons history, and business opportunities. It was during these trips that Stillman's Chinese hosts let slip the details of their international connections.

During the 1994 exchanges, a reliable source advised that the president of the Chinese Institute of Atomic Energy "had been spending a lot of time with scientists from Iran, Iraq, and Pakistan trying to sell them scientific equipment." In the late 1990s,[8] two of Stillman's Chinese hosts admitted, "The French are very cooperative; their visits have been a good thing for the Chinese." Or another: "China has learned some very clever nuclear weapons designs from the French nuclear weapons scientists." The chefs at various Chinese installations, having to accommodate the French palate, confirmed the French presence. It is clear that China extended nuclear hospitality to the French during the time period from 1994 to 1996 as both nations wound up their nuclear testing programs. Such trials apparently involved hydronuclear experiments and effects tests, not full-scale device detonations.

## CLOSING THE DOOR

For reasons not clear, in 1999, the American door into China's nuclear world slammed shut. In a carefully planned dinner speech to his Beijing guests, on May 17, Hu Side, by then the director of the China Academy of Engineering Physics (overseer of the Chinese nuclear weapons program), announced that closure and articulated some reasons.

---

7. Los Alamos Associate Director John C. Hopkins.
8. During conversations within China as well as at academic venues within the United States, 1997–2005.

First of all, in January of that year, the U.S. Congress had released the Cox Committee Report, prepared by the House Select Committee on Intelligence.[9] That paper covered the Chinese collection of intelligence within the United States. Its starkest conclusion: "The People's Republic of China has stolen design information on the United States' most advanced thermonuclear weapons." It was a heavy-handed report; much of the U.S. academic community took issue, but none more so than Stillman's host within China. "You have accused us of espionage," Hu Side proclaimed. "We did not need you."

Adding fuel to the fire was the May 8 accidental bombing of the Chinese embassy in Belgrade by U.S. aircraft supporting the war in Serbia. Hu found that attack to be inexcusable. "We find it hard to believe this [attack] was a mistake."

As a capper, the arrest and detention of Wen Ho Lee, a Los Alamos scientist, during 1999 confirmed to some Chinese eyes the anti-Chinese attitude in America.[10]

The reasoning behind these remarks seems convoluted at best. In subsequent discussions within the United States, Chinese visitors reconfirmed their earlier disclosures on nuclear testing. They further tipped the Chinese hand on their relationships with other nuclear-aspirant states. But the earlier hospitality was gone.

## HIGHLIGHTS FROM THE TWENTIETH CENTURY

During Stillman's visits to China, his hosts went out of their way to earn the respect of their American peers. In a series of meetings spanning that decade, they spelled out the complete history of their nuclear weapons test program. What stands out is the Chinese forethought and attention to detail in conducting these tests. They were not demonstrations or political statements; they were serious scientific experiments that moved the Chinese understanding of nuclear weapons forward at a steady, determined pace. There were a few fizzles, as there should be in any experimental program, but there were no theatrics.

At the time of the first Chinese test in 1964, American analysts were astonished to find no evidence of plutonium in the bomb debris. Only a quarter-century later would Stillman learn that the Chinese had abandoned their plutonium reactor in the aftermath of the Great Leap Forward and the Soviet perfidy, placing their bets instead on enriched uranium for the first four years of their test and production program. When plutonium became available in 1968, the Chinese had no hesitancy in using that material within a larger thermonuclear experiment, apparently without any preliminary testing of the primary alone. Most other designers would hesitate to make such a technology-spanning leap.

9. Chris Cox (R-CA), chairman.
10. Wen Ho Lee was probably collecting information for Taiwan, not the People's Republic of China.

Stillman's hosts were willing to admit that their fourth nuclear test was of a super-simple unboosted, enriched-uranium weapon "that anybody could build." It was the export design eventually passed on to Pakistan and then by A. Q. Khan to his customers throughout the Arab and Asian world.

The Chinese movement from first A-bomb to thermonuclear in only thirty-two months was the subject of enormous pride. It had taken the United States more than seven years to make that leap.

During the 1980s, the Chinese developed a neutron bomb after four failed attempts. They were unabashedly concerned about their "northern neighbor," Russia, and they were quite open about the studies done to confirm the ability of enhanced radiation weapons to destroy mobile tank forces without obliterating their own countryside.

On September 25, 1992, the Chinese tested a new and quite sophisticated primary. The test employed diagnostics beyond any U.S. capability at the time.

On July 29, 1996, the Chinese fired their last shot, a ten-kiloton explosion that probably confirmed some last-minute engineering or safety detail. That was it, the forty-sixth test in a thirty-two-year series of nuclear experiments. The U.S. nuclear community had counted only forty-five such tests because during one drop, on September 13, 1979, the bomb's parachute did not deploy. The device went into a ballistic trajectory, crashing into the desert far from the intended ground zero. There was no appreciable yield, but the Chinese wanted the United States to have an accurate count.

## THE ROLE OF INTELLIGENCE COLLECTION

Stillman found the Chinese to be paranoid about *any* accusations of espionage. Over and over his hosts would repeat: "We *never* found it necessary to steal *any* U.S. nuclear weapon secrets."

And yet every American scientific visitor to China knows he is under constant and stifling surveillance. An army of linguists is translating every scientific journal and paper, Chinese students flood American universities, and every so often unambiguous evidence of Chinese espionage appears within the American counterintelligence community.

By interesting coincidence, just as Stillman and his associates were being invited to visit the Chinese nuclear facilities, the Chinese Ministry of State Security was publishing *Sources and Techniques of Obtaining National Defense Science and Technology Intelligence*. This 250-page primer[11] written by two Chinese government intelligence professionals was completed in the autumn of 1990, and was intended for use at the China Defense Science and Technology Information Center (CDSTIC, the

11. Huo Zhongwen and Wang Zohgxiao (Beijing: Kexue Jishu Wenxuan Publishing Company, 1991); available online at http://intellnet.org/documents/800/000/806.htm.

"spy school" in Beijing). Perhaps Stillman and his associates were to be the first lab rats; they felt like it.

The CDSTIC offers everything from tradecraft courses to an academic study of "information collection theory, research, and applications." To those successfully completing their theses, the Information Center is prepared to award a master's degree in intelligence collection.

The *Sources and Techniques* book provides an interesting insight into the CDSTIC curriculum. It starts with a history of intelligence collection, stretching back through centuries of Chinese culture. It discusses the nature and functions of intelligence, such as ascertaining consumer needs, channels for collection and transmission, sources, and the recruitment of those sources. The book points out the different roles played by human and machine-oriented collection, noting that 80 percent of useful intelligence comes from openly available sources and human interactions. In this regard, the Chinese concept of intelligence collection is far different from the heavy-handed Soviet "recruit the spies and steal the drawings" approach.

*Sources and Techniques* identifies the characteristics to look for in prospective agents. These include superior social instincts, good personal interaction skills, strong research capabilities, and specialized knowledge. It then provides guidelines for novice intelligence collectors, who are to "learn the names of foreign authors and specialists in your field; learn their sexual preferences; biographical background; work and home addresses; phone numbers; occupations, achievements, writings and primary interests. Have they ever visited China? Do they have friends or relatives here?" There follow ninety pages on the identification of sources and another twenty on surveillance and collection techniques: signals intelligence, eavesdropping, and other means of collection-at-a-distance. But the book's emphasis is not on the cloak-and-dagger stuff of spy movies. It is on the need for a comprehensive theory of information collection and practice, "based on more than thirty years of experience in science and technology work."

This Chinese approach to the massive dispatch of students, the careful collection of every scrap of information, the well-rehearsed casual questions, the suffocating surveillance and the meticulous attention to detail contrasts markedly with Hu Side's claim of "*never* [finding] it necessary to steal *any* U.S. nuclear weapon secrets." We doubt this claim, just as we doubt China's proliferation disclaimers.

## CHINA'S FUTURE

The Chinese say they are antinuclear, they want to rid the world of nuclear weapons, and they are opposed to nuclear proliferation. As one PLA general said to Stillman, "China will never proliferate nuclear weapons technology to other countries," but

A partially assembled nuclear implosion device, showing multiple high-explosive lenses. Note the many irregular and non-similar shapes. *Los Alamos National Laboratory*

A postwar meeting of prewar colleagues: Prof. Yoshio Nishina, director of the wartime Japanese nuclear weapon program, and Prof. I. I. Rabi, a Nobel laureate and American A-bomb developer. These men had co-authored a physics paper in 1927. They met again, in the United States, in 1948. Physics Today, *August 2006*

The Little Boy enriched uranium A-bomb, being loaded into the B-29 *Enola Gay*, August 1945, prior to its drop on Hiroshima. Little Boy used up most of the HEU in the American stockpile. It was a one-of-a-kind weapon. *Los Alamos National Laboratory*

Fat Man, the first U.S. plutonium bomb, upon completion of assembly on Tinian Island, August 1945. Another Fat Man would be available mid-August, with weapons available thereafter at the rate of one a week. *Los Alamos National Laboratory*

Yuliy Khariton, director of the Soviet A-bomb project from its inception in 1945 through 1992, shown here with RDS-1, the first Soviet A-bomb. Internally it was an exact copy of the U.S. Fat Man. Strategic Nuclear Forces, *Russia's Arms & Technologies, Moscow*

**Mysterious light sources, the "domes of light," appearing above
Soviet missile test ranges, 1985–1992:**

First appearance, upon launch.

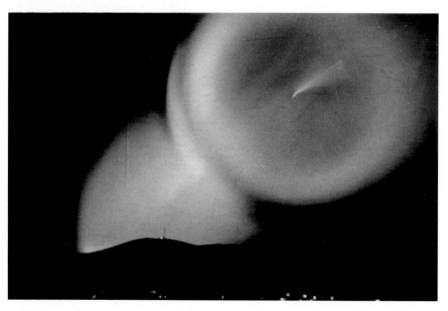

Full bloom, with upper iridescent sphere expanding at around ten thousand feet per second
(over seven thousand miles per hour). *Both photos: Los Alamos National Laboratory photo,
Yang Fujia, August 1991*

Once–Cold Warriors, dining in Healdsburg, California, March 15, 1997. Left to right: German Goncharov, theoretical physics, Arzamas-16; Gennady Gorelik, Sakharov biographer; Lev Feoktistov, deputy scientific director, Chelyabinsk-70; host and co-author Thomas Reed, experimental physics, Lawrence Livermore National Laboratory (LLNL); John Nuckolls, former director, LLNL. *Thomas C. Reed*

The El Salam nuclear reactor, built covertly by the Chinese in the Algerian Sahara, seventy-five miles south of the Mediterranean coast, during the 1990s. For scale, note the human figure between the second and third fence posts. *Global Security.org*

A road-mobile Soviet SS-25 strategic ballistic missile aboard its transporter. Eighty-one of these megaton-class, intercontinental-range weapons remained within Belarus upon the breakup of the Soviet Union in December 1991. Strategic Nuclear Forces, *Russia's Arms & Technologies, Moscow*

Admiral Henry Chiles, CINC STRATCOM, hosting Col.-Gen. Anatoliy Lopata, chief of the Ukrainian General Staff, at Omaha, April 19–20, 1994. This visit took place amidst difficult nuclear weapon removal negotiations between the United States and Ukraine. On June 1, 1996, Russian and Ukrainian officials certified the return of *all* such weapons to Russia. *Bobby Pittard, U.S. STRATCOM*

The entry sculpture at Science City, a nuclear complex built from scratch during the 1980s, near the city of Mianyang, in central China. This laboratory constitutes the heart of the Chinese nuclear weapons program. The fragmented top of the sculpture symbolizes disassembling material in a nuclear explosion; the rods represent emerging gamma radiation. *Dan Stillman*

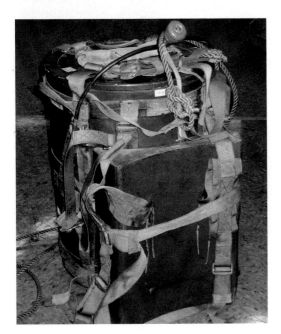

This is a U.S. B-54 backpack bomb. Height: one foot five inches; diameter: one foot; weight: fifty-nine pounds; yield: fractional kiloton. Intended for use in the demolition of critical choke-point facilities in the path of a Soviet advance. Typical of suitcase bombs that might remain within the Russian inventory. *Thomas C. Reed*

President John F. Kennedy, meeting at the University of California at Berkeley, March 23, 1962, with (left to right) AEC Chairman Glen Seaborg, Edward Teller, and Secretary of Defense Robert McNamara. One topic of discussion was the installation of permissive action link locks on U.S. nuclear weapons. *Lawrence Berkeley National Laboratory*

Iranian President Ahmadinejad visiting his uranium enrichment facility at Natanz, April 2008. The short, black cylinder to the left is the carbon fiber rotor, key to the efficiency of this equipment. The taller cylinder to the right is the vacuum casing with cooling coils. The components on the table confirm the development of an indigenous IR-2 centrifuge system modeled on the Pakistani P-2. *Islamic Republic of Iran (government photo)*

that is utter bunk. In 1982, the Chinese leadership made the conscious decision to support the proliferation of nuclear weapon technology into the Third World. Multiple sources confirm this transfer. (See the chapters that follow.)

In 1999, Hu Side told his assembled guests, "We did not need you." That is more bunk. During his ten visits to China, Stillman encountered a vast vacuum cleaner, sucking up American technology and spying on its citizens to a degree that boggles the mind.

During those same travels, the close relationship between the Chinese, French, and Pakistani nuclear programs became abundantly clear. China has now embarked on similar relationships with others in the Third World. Those relationships may be based simply on a need for energy security, or there may be darker motives, but wherever they reach, Chinese ambitions cast a mystic shadow.

China's nuclear weapons program was and remains on a technical par with that of the United States. In some areas, it displays a sophistication unknown in the West. The Chinese nuclear capability matured at a pace unparalleled among the other nuclear powers. It did so with care and precision, coupling overseas technology to native needs with an incredible attention to detail.

There may be room for hope, for in time the younger generation, those who stood up to the tanks in Tiananmen Square, may take over. At Fudan University, heart of the Chinese nuclear incubator, Stillman saw statues of Mao that had been defaced with graffiti. Like Ozymandias before him, the inspirational mottos of the Great Leader had been chipped off, to join the dust of the deserts stretching far away.

One branch of the younger generation, the businessmen of the cities, may peacefully await the end of President Hu Jintao's years in office. The Chinese have developed a respect for legitimacy. The precedent of five-year presidential terms, with a two-term limit, is enshrined in a constitution, and that procedure seems to have become the norm. Unfortunately, these presidential "elections" are completely illegitimate: the vote is limited to the National People's Congress, a flock of Communist Party faithful. Given this stacked deck, these youngsters may seek to pack the Congress, to replace Hu with a true democrat when his second term expires in 2013, but that will not be easy.

Others of the younger generation, the utterly impoverished half in the earthquake-striken provinces, may be more mindful of Chairman Mao's oft-repeated words: "Peasant rebellions have been the driving force of Chinese history." The coming of the Internet has brought an awareness of wealth disparity to rural China. It has also made possible the near-instantaneous assembly of huge crowds to protest dam-building, land-seizures, or simple mismanagement. If one such protest burns out of control, a hundred million Chinese will know about it within an hour. Could the establishment within the cities withstand such spontaneous combustion? Probably not; thus, the efforts by the insiders to muzzle the Internet, to track its users.

Time will tell if the Olympics staged in Beijing during the summer of 2008 were the watershed event, the end of this Chinese government's attempts to make nice to the outside world. Thereafter the insiders may flex China's financial and military muscle, bringing on the defining crisis of this decade. On the other hand, a new generation may make itself felt with a new and better deal for all.

CHAPTER 15

# THE FAKIRS:
# INDIA, PAKISTAN,
# AND NORTH KOREA

*Fakir:* "A Muslim or Hindu itinerant reputed to work miracles"
*Faker:* "One who makes something seem real when it is not"

India, the world's sixth announced nuclear power,[1] does not, by itself, threaten world tranquility. India is, however, the eight-hundred-pound politico-nuclear gorilla. By simply sitting astride the stage of history, India has provided the raison d'être for the blossoming Sino-Pakistani nuclear axis. It is that affiliation which could, in time, destabilize or destroy Western civilization.

India first tested a nuclear device in 1974. That test was conducted under the Rajasthani Desert near the town Pokhran, a village of twenty thousand inhabitants, once a fort astride the Old Silk Road. Pokhran is three hundred miles southwest of New Delhi, but only one hundred miles from the Pakistani border. The West was taken by surprise; India had carefully concealed the test preparations. There was no time for a unified advance protest from the senior nuclear club members, as would preclude similar events in South Africa three years later. The test itself was cloaked in the usual "peaceful purposes" slogans implying the pursuit of science and geophysical exploration. A quarter-century later, however, the term "peaceful purposes" was redefined to mean, "keeping the peace in the face of Chinese and Muslim disrespect."

1. The seventh, if one credits unannounced Israel with having a few nuclear weapons at the time of the Six-Day War in 1967.

At the time of that 1974 test, Indian authorities claimed an energy release of twelve kilotons, probably the design value of the device tested. Western and Soviet analysts concluded the yield was probably half that, and thus those statements from New Delhi became the first in a long line of misrepresentations from Third World nuclear-entrant states.

The Indian device of 1974, known to its designers as Smiling Buddha, was fired at a depth of 330 feet. It produced a "retarc" (*crater* spelled backwards), a non-venting collapsed dome above a nuclear explosion. That surface anomaly reflects a yield that almost, but not quite, blew away the earth overburden.[2] The presence of a retarc, if one knows the depth of device burial, allows a knowledgeable observer to calculate device yield.[3] In the case of Smiling Buddha, the depth of burial and the presence of a retarc led to a calculated yield of about five kilotons, a figure that matches conventional seismic observations and enjoys general acceptance in the Western scientific press. (Some analysts argue for a yield as high as eight kilotons, a figure supported by subsequent scientific comments within India,[4] but there is no convincing basis for yields above that number.) Smiling Buddha used thirteen pounds of plutonium harvested from the CIRUS[5] "Atoms for Peace" reactor. The entire device weighed about three thousand pounds, for a yield-to-weight ratio of 1.7 tons per pound: a little below the first U.S./Soviet plutonium weapons, tested in the 1940s, and far below the results achieved by the more recent nuclear-club initiates in the 1960s.[6] Smiling Buddha was a gadget, not an operational weapon, but as its creator, Prof. Raj Ramanna, admitted twenty-three years later, "The Pokhran test *was* a bomb . . . not all that peaceful."

After the Indian test of 1974, nuclear programs within the Indian subcontinent appeared to run on idle, but appearances can deceive. Nuclear technology began to blossom. In private, the men in charge of nuclear facilities at Trombay, India, and PINSTECH, in Pakistan, were seen as miracle workers, developing (or exploiting) technologies once proprietary to the European world. At the same time, fraud entered the marketplace of nuclear ideas, an approach unthinkable to the Cold Warriors of a generation before. The Seven Deadly Sins sent a delegation to south Asia to aggravate the situation.

First of all, Pride overwhelmed the Indian psyche. That nation had suffered repeated humiliations at the hands of the Chinese. The first took place on the

2. The soil and rock between nuclear cavity and surface.
3. Depth of burial, to preclude venting $= KY^{1/3}$, where K is a constant depending on the geology of the nuclear test site and Y is the device yield, in kilotons.
4. Statements by P. K. Iyengar, one of the device designers and later chairman of the India AEC.
5. Canada India Research United States.
6. The U.S. and Soviet Fat Man gave 2.0 tons of yield per pound of weight, 1945–49. France and China achieved about seven tons of yield per pound of weight with their first shots, 1960–64.

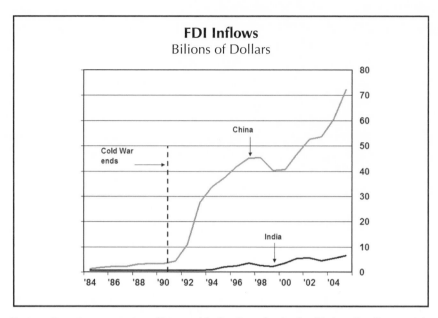

**FDI Inflows**
Bilions of Dollars

Foriegn direct investment into China and India, from the death of Indira Gandhi in 1984 through the end of the Cold War in 1991, to the present time. *UNCTAD*

battlefield, in 1962, during a brief border war in the Himalayan Mountains. The second insult was China's detonation of an A-bomb, its first, in 1964. China and India were antique civilizations, comparable in size and population, but China was moving to the center of the world stage as India stood in the wings. The final insult may have been the financial honors accorded China in the decades to follow as the Cold War ended. Investors began to pour money into China; India was ignored.

In the years that followed the 1974 test, the Indian government weaponized the Smiling Buddha device, undertook the indigenous design and construction of a larger nuclear reactor at Trombay,[7] and began to think about thermonuclear weapons. With China's prior detonation of a multimegaton H-bomb in 1967, it became clear to the Indian leadership that only the firing of a similar Indian device would admit their country to the true inner circle of world powers.

During these same years, Greed infected the mind of A. Q. Khan. Pakistan's one-time boy genius had built a uranium enrichment and liquid-fuelled missile complex from scratch at Kahuta and had seen it renamed the A. Q. Kahn Research Laboratory. By the mid-1980s, Khan's facility was producing enough enriched uranium to facilitate the assembly of A-bombs. At the end of the decade, the Khan Research Laboratory was

7. The 100-megawatt Dhruva reactor.

holding promotional conferences for the benefit of nuclear aspirants. A. Q. Khan began to envision untold riches at the end of his personal proliferation rainbow.

Envy was the affliction of the Pakistani people. In the aftermath of the 1974 Indian nuclear test, leaders in Islamabad could not allow their Hindu-dominated neighbor to enjoy a continuing politico-technical advantage. It was necessary to restore a balance—a tall order, since India enjoyed a wealth and boasted a population that put it in a different industrial league from neighboring Pakistan. India was an English-speaking cousin of the European world. In later years the leaders of government and opposition would join hands to solicit American investment based on India's ties to British custom and law. The Pakistanis had broken those bonds; they would have to turn to India's enemies, principally China, for help.

Anger overwhelmed them all. On both sides of the Indo-Pakistani border, resentment of the bloodbath that followed the 1947 partition, the humiliating loss of East Pakistan in 1971, the continuing bloodshed within the disputed territories of Kashmir, and repeated acts of Muslim terrorism within India pushed the leaders on both sides to pursue a serious nuclear capability.

## INDIA, 1966–1998

Smiling Buddha was the creation of the government of Indira Gandhi. The only child of India's first prime minister, Jawaharlal Nehru, she acceded to the leadership in 1966 after the deaths of her father and his successor.[8] Despite his Third World antinuclear rhetoric, Nehru had extracted a nuclear reactor as a gift from Canada in 1955, had authorized construction of a plutonium reprocessing facility in 1958, and had seen the CIRUS reactor go critical in 1960. The infrastructure for a nuclear weapons program was in place when Ms. Gandhi came to power. Soon after the 1967 parliamentary elections that confirmed her right to govern, Gandhi authorized the re-orientation of India's nuclear research toward such weapons. On June 7, 1972, she authorized the development and assembly of a nuclear device, a decision she did not share with even her closest military advisors.

During those years, the legitimacy of Ms. Gandhi's rule came into question. Opponents alleged that her Indian National Congress Party had resorted to electoral fraud to win the 1971 elections. Balloting subsequent to the Smiling Buddha event generated more questions—and turmoil. On June 12, 1975, the High Court of Allahabad found Ms. Gandhi guilty of misuse of government machinery in her electoral campaign, declared her personal election null and void, and ordered her removed from the parliament. Like many an "indispensable" leader before her, Ms. Gandhi did not care to accept that decision. She requested that the president of India declare a state

8. Lal Shastri, prime minister 1964–66

of emergency; he granted it on June 26. That proclamation gave Gandhi the power to rule by decree, suspend elections, and dispense with civil liberties. Massive riots ensued. Gandhi empowered the police to arrest protesters and strike leaders; opposition political parties were banned; Communist Party leaders were arrested, tortured, and imprisoned; state legislatures controlled by anti-Gandhi parties were dissolved.

To put an end to these difficulties, and perhaps at the urging of a restive army, Ms. Gandhi called for new national elections. They were held during February 1977; she lost. An opposition government held sway for three years, during which time the nuclear weapon program was put on hold, although work on the indigenous plutonium-producing nuclear reactor continued. But then, upon Gandhi's return to power in January 1980, the Indian nuclear locomotive again began to roll. In 1982, she may have authorized a few nuclear tests, such actions only being cancelled in response to international pressures.

Work on the Dhruva reactor reached fruition in 1985; it went critical on August 8, but Ms. Gandhi did not live to see that achievement. She was assassinated on October 31, 1984, by two of her own Sikh bodyguards, seeking revenge for her assault on the holiest Sikh shrine at Amritsar.[9] Rajiv Gandhi was installed by the Congress Party as his mother's successor. He remained in office for a full five years, during which time he perpetuated Ms. Ghandi's vision of a nuclear-armed India.

In 1995, the Nonproliferation Treaty came up for review. The United States enticed the parties to that agreement into an "indefinite extension," with review conferences to be held every five years. To those on the nuclear cusp, such as India, this appeared to be a "permanent entrenchment of an unequal system." The nuclear "haves," the permanent members of the Security Council, were to keep their nuclear franchise. The Third World "have-nots" were to stay that way.

The bomb lobby within India did not think this was fair. They found the NPT indefinite extension to be a de facto agreement that nukes would be around forever. If so, they felt India should join the nuclear club. The Indian government agreed. On June 20, 1996, India's ambassador to the UN Conference on Disarmament announced a reversal of India's long-standing support for a comprehensive nuclear test ban. By implication, India would soon test again; it planned to join the ranks of the nuclear weapon states. Within India the fat was in the fire. Her nuclear weapons program continued to mature, awaiting only the propitious moment to blossom.

9. In May 1984, Sikh extremists occupied the Golden Temple in Amritsar, a city of over a million in the far north of India, converting that temple into a haven for terrorists. At Ghandi's direction, the Indian Army moved in and was met by heavy-weapons fire (machine guns, antitank missiles, and rocket launchers). On June 6 and 7, the Indian army retook control of the temple at a cost of 83 army personnel killed and 249 injured; 493 Sikh insurgents were killed within the temple, and hundreds more in the streets outside. Two Sikhs among Ghandi's security force took revenge four months later.

The elections of March 1998 brought the man of nuclear action to power. A. B. Vajpayee's right-of-center, Hindu-based Bharatiya Janata Party won control of the Indian government. Vajpayee had campaigned on a platform of national strength, intolerance for Pakistani "aggressions" in Kashmir, and the necessity of an Indian nuclear capability. His election resulted in the immediate authorization of Indian nuclear tests. They were to be conducted underground, within two months, using facilities constructed years before.

Three Indian nuclear detonations are alleged to have taken place simultaneously, on May 11, 1998, at the bottoms of three separate holes. The Indians code-named these detonations Shakti 1, 2, and 3. The announced yields of these three tests were forty-five, fifteen, and 0.2 of a kiloton, respectively. Shakti 1 was claimed to be a two-stage thermonuclear experiment. The second was a weaponization of Smiling Buddha, India's 1974 nuclear device. The third event was "to validate new ideas and subsystems."

To understand and perhaps to accredit these claims, one must start with an understanding of the total energy release from the May 11 tests. We turn to three unclassified sources; all of them converge around an estimated total yield of around twelve to sixteen kilotons. The first source is the Federation of Atomic Scientists analysis, last updated in November 2002. From their study of seismic data, U.S. government sources, and the opinions of their own experts, the FAS reported an energy release of twelve to twenty-five kilotons from the May 11, 1998, events.

A second source is Robert S. Norris, of the National Resources Defense Council, reporting in the *Bulletin of Atomic Scientists*, November-December 1998. Based on data from sixty-two seismic stations, Norris concluded the May 11 energy release was twelve kilotons, with a plus or minus three-kiloton band of error (i.e., nine to fifteen kilotons total energy release).

Experts at the United Kingdom's Atomic Weapons Establishment (AWE) took a different approach. They compared total signal strength from the May 11 tests to the signal generated by the first (Smiling Buddha) Indian test, at the same site, in 1974. This approach removes geologic uncertainties, since signal paths from Pokhran to the U.K. recording site would be identical. To calculate the 1998 Indian nuclear energy release, one should decide on the yield of the 1974 event, then multiply by the U.K. factor. The AWE's experts proposed a multiplier of 3.1. Since your authors believe the 1974 test released about five kilotons, this implies a total May 11, 1998 energy release of fifteen or sixteen kilotons. We will use the value sixteen kilotons of total yield in the discussions to follow.

Now let us apportion that energy. The second Indian device tested (Shakti 2), was said to be a weaponization of their 1974 experiment. We believe the design yield in 1974 was twelve kilotons, that the Indians got it right in 1998, and thus the energy release from Shakti 2 was about that number, even though the Indian government claimed a slightly larger yield after the fact.

Shakti 3 was alleged to release 0.2 kilotons. Perhaps it did, although most experts think it was a failed experiment. Subtraction (sixteen kilotons observed, less twelve kilotons for Shakti 2 and zero for Shakti 3) leaves about four kilotons for Shakti 1.

The definitive paper published by the Indian nuclear community after these tests[10] talked knowledgeably about two-stage thermonuclear explosions. That paper claimed a forty-five kiloton yield from Shakti 1, an experiment that "worked perfectly." We doubt that claim. We think the primary went low, delivering perhaps four kilotons, although it might have delivered more, and we doubt the secondary fired at all. We are joined in these views by Dr. P. K. Iyengar, the deputy director of the 1974 Smiling Buddha design team and later chairman of the Indian Atomic Energy Commission. In a 2000 interview,[11] Iyengar stated that "the boosted fission trigger [of Shakti 1] *should* have yielded at least twenty kilotons," and "the secondary (fusion) device burnt only partially, perhaps 10 percent." In other words, a low primary yield failed to light the secondary. That is probably correct.

India claims to have tested two more nuclear devices on May 13 with yields of 0.5 and 0.2 kilotons, respectively. No seismic stations detected these events; the nearest was at Nilore, Pakistan, 450 miles away. The detection threshold at Nilore, for a detonation at Pokhran, would be about twenty tons (0.02 kilotons) of nuclear yield. Thus, these May 13 events may have been safety/engineering tests that worked: that is, the weapons were safe and delivered no yield. Or they may have been failed experiments. Or they may never have happened at all. In summary:

| Test No. | Test Date | Stated Device | Claimed Yield | Indian Scientific Claims | Authors' Conclusions |
|---|---|---|---|---|---|
| 1 | May 11 | Thermo-nuclear | 45 KT | Fission-boosted primary, two-stage thermonuclear, "controlled yield" | Primary went low, ~ 4 KT. The secondary did not light. |
| 2 | May 11 | Fission | 15 KT | Evolved from 1974 test. Smaller and lighter to facilitate weaponization | ~ 12 KT, a boosted fission design, follow-on to the 1974 device. |
| 3 | May 11 | Experiment | 0.2 KT | To validate new ideas and subsystems | Perhaps as stated; more likely a failed experiment. |
| 4 | May 13 | Experiment | 0.5 KT | To validate new ideas and subsystems | No yield detected by others. Perhaps a safety test. |
| 5 | May 13 | Experiment | 0.3 KT | To validate new ideas and subsystems | No yield detected by others. Perhaps a safety test. |

10. R. Chidambaram (former chairman of the Indian Atomic Energy Commission), "The May 1998 Pokhran Tests," paper no. 451 (South Asia Analysis Group, October 2000).
11. *Times of India*, February 12, 2000.

The Indian government made certain other claims in addition to those set forth above:

1. "The need for simultaneous tests was dictated by considerations of convenience and speed." That is probably true, but simultaneity also helps to mask failure.
2. "All tests worked perfectly." That clearly was not so.
3. Shakti 1 "had the purpose of developing warhead yields up to around 200 kilotons . . . a two-stage device of advanced design with a . . . fusion secondary stage which compressed by radiation implosion and ignited." That may have been the purpose of Shakti 1, but we do not see any indication that it happened, and Dr. P. K. Iyengar agrees.
4. "The yield of Shakti 1 was 'controlled' because of the proximity of the Khetolai village nearby." We believe a simpler explanation: Shakti I did not work properly.

Immediately after the Pokhran tests, Prime Minister Vajpayee set forth his reasons for conducting those tests in a letter to President Clinton, with similar messages sent to other national leaders: "We have an overt nuclear weapon state on our borders [China], a state which committed armed aggression against India in 1962. Although our relations with that country have improved in the last decade or so,[12] an atmosphere of distrust persists." Vajpayee then went on to accuse China of helping "another neighbor of ours [Pakistan] to become a covert nuclear weapon state," one that had committed "three aggressions in the last fifty years" along with "unremitting terrorism and militancy sponsored by it in several parts of our country."

Put into simpler words, "China, our rich and aggressive neighbor to the north, and Pakistan, home to Muslim terrorists to the west, are in league against us. We are not going to tolerate that." Perhaps those words were prescient.

## INDIA IN THE TWENTY-FIRST CENTURY

A decade after the emergence of south Asia as a nuclear power, President George W. Bush entered into agreements with India reflecting exactly the concerns expressed by its prime minister in 1998. In the process, the American president attempted to welcome India into the club of nuclear weapon states. Other member states were not pleased. They were appalled at the precedent. The Nuclear Suppliers Group (a group of about fifty industrial nations who banded together in 1975, after the first Indian nuclear test, in an attempt to limit the international transfer of dual-purpose, nuclear-useful materials) was quite reluctant to accept India's accreditation as a recognized nuclear state. Given the impact of such recognition on Western nonproliferation goals, such a

12. Tied to Deng Xiaoping's departure from power in December 1989.

deal with the devil may not be a really good idea.

India now possesses a substantial inventory[13] of nuclear weapons: A-bombs with yields of about twelve to fourteen kilotons each, a yield equivalent to the Hiroshima bomb. The Indian weapon may be reasonably safe, although it is doubtful that any security measures have been built in. Meanwhile, the Indian bomb lobby[14] wishes to resume nuclear testing as soon as possible. These officials joined hands in 2002 to request another round of tests in support of their thermonuclear project. At that time the government declined, but the *Times of India* confirms an ongoing determination. Given the Indian interest in thermonuclear technology and the status arising from such weapons, given her activities in the production of lithium and tritium as well as uranium enrichment, and given the continuing Indian need for parity with China, it is reasonable to expect and assume that India will test again at the next politically opportune time.

The deliberate use of an Indian nuclear weapon, except in the event of a direct military confrontation with another nuclear weapon state, is quite unlikely, but technology leakage is another matter. Two high-level Indian officials, Chaudhary Surendar and Y. S. R. Prasad, both former chairmen of India's state-run Nuclear Power Corporation, are on the U.S. sanctions list for "allegedly passing nuclear secrets to Tehran," and India continues to build on its strategic relationship with Iran. Defense ties with Iran were specifically "deepened" during high-level talks in March 2007 at the same time that the U.S.-Indian nuclear accord was under negotiation. India has many national security interests; they may not all coincide with those of the United States.

## FISSION COMES TO PAKISTAN—IN MORE WAYS THAN ONE

At the time of independence, in 1947, the British colony of India was partitioned into a central mostly-Hindu state, India, and two separated regions with ties to the Muslim religion. The latter parcels, taken together, were to be known as Pakistan. East and West Pakistan were neither contiguous nor compatible, and for years politicians and officers in West Pakistan controlled the government. In 1970, however, the consolidated voters in the east won the Pakistani elections; the authorities in the western capital, Islamabad, did not care to hand over power.

On March 26, 1971, rebellious army officers in East Pakistan declared independence. Prime Minister Gandhi of India, a nation eager to see its Muslim rival dismembered, immediately recognized their legitimacy.

---

13. David Albright (ISIS, May 7, 2005) credits the Indian government with an inventory of almost one hundred nuclear weapons.
14. The Department of Atomic Energy, officials at the Bhabba Atomic Research Center, and the Defense Research and Development Organization.

With a war of independence in the air, the Cold War superpowers promptly took sides. On August 9, India and the Soviet Union executed a twenty-year Treaty of Friendship and Cooperation. As an offset, during that same summer, the Chinese offered material, but not military, support to Pakistan. The Nixon administration, with one eye on its planned rapprochement with China,[15] joined in supporting that country's allies in Islamabad, while the Government of India, having lost a border war with China a decade before, waited for the winter snows to close the Himalayan passes before deploying active support for the rebels in the east.

In preparing for conflict, the generals in Pakistan noted the lessons of the Arab-Israeli Six-Day War of 1967: preemption pays. On December 3, 1971, the Pakistani Air Force staged a preemptive raid on the airfields of northwest India. Those raids were ineffective; the Indian military then struck back.

The United States sent a carrier battle group, led by the USS *Enterprise*, to the Bay of Bengal. The Soviets responded with a trailing naval force, including nuclear-powered submarines, dispatched from Vladivostok. Both forces were on station, armed with nuclear weapons, by the second week of December 1971.

The war itself was a disaster for the overpowered Pakistanis. Within two weeks, Pakistan had lost half its navy in battles off the port of Karachi, half of its air force in the eastern and western skies, and one-third of its army on the ground in East Pakistan. On December 16, the Pakistani Army had no choice but surrender; ninety-three thousand of its troops and camp followers had been taken prisoner. Photographs and videos of Pakistan's Lieutenant General Niazi surrendering his forces to a gloating Indian Lieutenant General Aurora swept the world.

East Pakistan became the independent Republic of Bangladesh. Muslim leaders in Islamabad wept; a young Pakistani scientist in Holland resolved to seek revenge; Brig. Gen. Yahya Khan, the military president of what remained of Pakistan, resigned. On December 20, 1971, a civilian, Zulfika Ali Bhutto, took control of the government. Mr. Bhutto was the leader of the Pakistan People's Party, a newly-organized pro-democracy organization that was supported by the socialist segments of society while opposed to military rule. He was also father to Benazir Bhutto, of whom we shall hear more later. Ms. Bhutto was age eighteen at the time of her father's accession to power.

The lessons imposed on the leaders of the residual nation of Pakistan were clear: a force equalizer was absolutely necessary. Its newly installed president had previously served as minister of fuel, power, and natural resources. As such, the nation's leader was conversant with the possibilities of nuclear power—and weapons. Within three

15. Nixon's surprise trip to China took place six months later, in February 1972.

weeks of his installation, President Bhutto met with about four dozen scientists and bureaucrats at a stately colonial mansion in the town of Multan, Punjab Province, on January 20, 1972, to review the nuclear option.

The usual ebb and flow of graduate students to universities in the West had begun a decade before. In 1965, the Canadian General Electric Company had started work on the Karachi Nuclear Power Plant (KANUPP), a 137-megawatt natural uranium and heavy water reactor that was to be Pakistan's first. KANUPP had already gone critical, in August 1971, and it was to start full-power operation in October 1972. Thus, at the time of his decisive January 1972 meeting, President Bhutto knew he had a plutonium-producing asset in hand.

During the months that followed, Bhutto refocused the work of his nation's Atomic Energy Research Council by taking personal control, renaming it the Pakistan Atomic Energy Commission (PAEC), and installing nuclear engineer Munir Ahmad Khan as its director. It was an inspired choice, though a grim indicator of the fragility of the nonproliferation treaty.

In 1958, Munir Khan had graduated from the Illinois Institute of Technology. He had spent time at the Argonne National Laboratory, the heart of America's nuclear reactor development world, and had then served—for over a decade—as head of the reactor engineering department at the International Atomic Energy Agency, the NPT watchdog in Vienna. In 1972, Munir Khan, the American-trained engineer, was tapped to return to Pakistan for the very purpose of circumventing the NPT, to gain Pakistan's admission to the nuclear weapon club.

Some leading lights in Pakistan's world of physics objected to this goal. Nobel Laureate Abdus Salam was given private assurances of "peaceful intent," then packed off to an academic roost in Great Britain. The uncooperative head of the Atomic Energy Research Council, Ishrat Usmani, was fired and sent to a UN sinecure. Pakistan's nuclear playing field was left to Munir Ahmad Khan. He was the right man for the job.

In 1973, demonstrating his belief in democracy—while building his own scaffold—President Bhutto drafted and brought about the ratification of a new constitution. Henceforward the president was to serve as chief of state; a prime minister was to run the government. Z. A. Bhutto resigned the presidency in August 1973 in order to become the first prime minister of Pakistan; he took the nuclear portfolio with him.

As we have seen, during the year that followed, India tested a nuclear device. With that development, Prime Minister Bhutto directed his PAEC to take Pakistan's nuclear technology "to its logical conclusions"—a nuclear weapon. The project was to be conducted at Wah, near the Pakistan Ordinance Factory, with initial work to be focused on high-explosive lenses driving a plutonium-based weapon design. During that same time period, the Bhutto government signed a contract with the San Gobain firm of France to build a nuclear fuel reprocessing facility within Pakistan, and PAEC Chairman Munir Khan empowered one of his associates, S. A. Butt, to create a component-purchasing network within Europe, to be headquartered in Brussels.

In December 1974, Bhutto met with the young A. Q. Khan, then working (and stealing technology) in Holland. Young Khan (no relation to Munir, head of the PAEC) was recruited into the PAEC fold, but he was instructed to return to Holland, to continue the collection of uranium enrichment technology and to start acquiring the needed physical components. At that time there was no clear need for enriched uranium within the Pakistani nuclear weapon program. Munir Khan already understood centrifuge technology; he had relegated it to secondary status.

In 1975, however, the rules began to change. The international community, in reaction to the Indian test of May 1974, began to embargo the transfer of sensitive technology to potentially nuclear-ambitious states. The Canadians and the French were getting nervous about their support of a reactor and a nuclear reprocessing facility within Pakistan. In response to these pressures, and given the growing suspicions of the Dutch authorities, A. Q. Khan returned to Pakistan in December 1975—nominally on holiday, but in fact never to return (until granted immunity by the Dutch government). Detailed discussions started with President Bhutto. In April 1976, A. Q. Khan started work at the PAEC, headquartered in Islamabad. Tempers flared and egos conflicted as A. Q.'s enthusiasm for uranium enrichment ran up against Munir's plans for a plutonium weapon, but as the year drew to a close, the Canadians formally terminated all support for the KANUPP reactor. (They had been providing fuel rods *and* the heavy water moderator.) The French began to redesign their reprocessing facility to focus on a mixed-oxide product acceptable as a nuclear reactor fuel, but useless in producing plutonium weapon feedstock. Munir Khan's plutonium weapon program was in serious jeopardy. In July 1976, Bhutto hedged his bets by authorizing A. Q. Khan to open his own Engineering Research Center at Kahuta. It was to focus on the enrichment of uranium to weapons grade and, in time, the development of an HEU weapon. With that the die was cast. Prime Minister Bhutto had sent exploratory parties down both paths that could, in time, lead to nuclear club membership.

## BIRTH OF THE ZIA-DENG AXIS

During the previous decade, China had been engulfed in the turmoil and bloodshed of its Cultural Revolution. By 1975, destructive irrationality ruled that land, but amidst this chaos the first generation of communist leadership lay dying. Premier Zhou Enlai had long been considered Mao Zedong's successor, but by that year, both men were terminally ill. Other candidate successors were Jiang Qing, the chairman's wife; ultra-leftist politburo member Wang Hongwen; and the recently rehabilitated pragmatist Deng Xiaoping. Yet much to the surprise of all, upon Zhou's death on January 8, 1976, Mao turned to Hua Guofeng, the fifty-five-year-old party chief of Hunan Province, to serve as premier, first vice-chairman, and thus Mao's hand-picked successor.

Upon Mao's death eight months later, in September 1976, a triangular struggle for power broke out. In one corner stood the Gang of Four, a group led by Mao's widow, who advocated continued revolutionary zeal and terror. The new government, led by Hua Guofeng, advocated a return to central planning along the Soviet model. A third group, led by Deng Xiaoping, wanted to end the mindless terror *and* move to a market-oriented economy.

Within a month of Mao's death, a Hua-Deng alliance brought about the arrest and imprisonment of Jiang Qing and her Gang of Four. During the years that followed, Deng and Hua contested for power within the politburo. As a new constitution was adopted in 1978, Hua retained figurehead status, but he steadily lost control. In 1980, his duties as premier were taken over by Zhao Ziyang, a Deng ally. By 1981, the struggles were over. Hua was replaced as chairman of the Peoples' Republic (i.e., president) by Hu Yaobang and as chairman of the Central Military Commission by Deng Xiaoping. As Mao had observed years before, power comes from the barrel of a gun; Deng's control of the Military Commission, and thus the People's Liberation Army, gave him full control of the state. In time Hua Guofeng moved on into graceful and safe retirement.

The same could not be said for Zulfika Ali Bhutto. As Mao was slipping from his earthly bonds, Pakistan's new democracy was slipping into anarchy. Disputes that started within the National Assembly spread to warfare within Bhutto's own People's Party. In 1976, to help quell disturbances, Prime Minister Bhutto reached into the army's junior officer ranks to appoint a new chief of staff. He chose tank commander Muhammad Zia-ul-Haq. A year later,[19] General Zia staged a coup, deposed Bhutto, and declared himself martial-law dictator.

A year after that, on September 16, 1978, General Zia arranged for the president of Pakistan[20] to resign, with General Zia adding presidential powers to his portfolio. Six months later, on April 4, 1979, Zulfika Ali Bhutto was hanged in the prison at Lahore.

There followed a brief flurry of international indignation, but in December of that year, the Soviets invaded Afghanistan. Pakistan was the only route into that battleground, and General Zia shared the West's hatred of communism. A Western

---

19. On July 5, 1977.
20. Fazal Chaudhry, a member of Bhutto's Pakistan People's Party.

blind eye was turned to Pakistan's other transgressions, which included an ever-expanding nuclear weapons program. During his years in office, 1977–88, General Zia was a reliable supporter of the entire Pakistani nuclear weapons complex.

As the insurgency in Afghanistan wore on, and as General Zia began to impose Sharia law on the people of Pakistan, the administration in Washington changed hands. By 1982, Afghanistan had become a theater of prime interest to President Reagan as well as certain members of Congress. Driving the Soviets out, or, more accurately, turning Afghanistan into a Soviet Vietnam, became an American goal. On December 7, 1982, during co-author Reed's tenure at the White House, General Zia came to visit the American president. Reagan's diary entries for that day reflect the blissful ignorance of the time:

"The weather turned out fine for the official greeting ceremonies for Pres. Zia of Pakistan. We got along fine. He's a good man. (Cavalry) Gave me his word they were not building an atomic or nuclear bomb. He's dedicated to helping the Afghans & stopping the Soviets." The latter sentence was certainly true; the former was an absolute lie. Within three months, Pakistan's Atomic Energy Commission would conduct its first nuclear weapon cold test.

By 1982, having consolidated his power, Deng Xiaoping was ready to remake China. A new national constitution was adopted, and at the same time, Deng published his political roadmap for the future of China. It was a document entitled, *On the Various Historical Issues Since the Founding of the People's Republic of China.*[21] In it, Deng accorded full honors to the departed Mao, while recognizing some of his "mistakes." It then laid out a plan for an economically free but communist-controlled state.

Unfortunately, there was a dark side to the plan: In 1982, Deng's government also began the deliberate proliferation of nuclear and ballistic missile technology into the Muslim and Marxist worlds. China signed a covert nuclear reactor agreement with Algeria, sold CSS-2 missiles to Saudi Arabia, and gave North Korea a full dose of nuclear support, but those events pale in comparison to the help China gave General Zia's Pakistan in that country's attempts to redress the nuclear imbalance within south Asia.

In 1982, prior to General Zia's visit to Washington, China began to assist Pakistani scientists with nuclear weapon design, materials production, and the construction of nuclear infrastructure.[22] A steady stream of Pakistanis were invited to Beijing and the outlying districts of the Chinese nuclear empire for days of briefings, just as Russian professors Negin, Maslov, and Gavrilov had conducted nuclear seminars for their Chinese friends in 1958. (See chapter 4.) During those discussions of 1982 to 1983,

---

21. Adopted by the Sixth Plenum of the Eleventh Central Committee in June 1981.
22. *Proliferation: Threat and Response*, Office of the [U.S.] Secretary of Defense, January 2001.

the Chinese handed over design details for the CHIC-4 nuclear device. Copies of notes and engineering drawings confirming that transfer from China to Pakistan and thence on to Libya, showed up in Tripoli twenty years later. (See chapter 16.) Subsequent actions by Pakistani scientists confirm those events: cold tests of implosion systems began in March 1983. This movement of nuclear technology apparently continued throughout Deng Xiaoping's tenure as chairman of the Central Military Commission, and while Deng lost that job in December 1989, in the aftermath of the Tiananmen Square demonstrations, his successors apparently extended those proliferation policies. During the summer of 1989, Chinese nuclear facilities were awash with Pakistani visitors; we believe they were preparing for the events of May 26, 1990.

General Zia did not live to see that show. On August 17, 1988, his Pakistan Air Force C-130 mysteriously crashed after takeoff from a military airfield in Punjab Province; all passengers and crew were killed. The on-board presence of the American ambassador and his military attaché argue against CIA involvement. Most observers suspect sabotage, motivated either by an internal Pakistani struggle for power or a settling of old scores. The Soviet KGB could have been a player in the latter category. By whatever chain of events, an independent politician, Ghulam Ishaq Khan, immediately assumed the presidency of Pakistan. New elections were set for the fall.

## RAMPING UP

Within a few years of the 1974 Indian nuclear event, the armed services of Pakistan had begun making arrangements for an underground nuclear test of their own. The Special Development Works of the Pakistan Army was formed with the mission of planning, excavating for, and carrying out underground nuclear experiments. The excavation of adits (tunnels with only one open end) began in the mountains of Baluchistan, and at that time the construction of facilities and the installation of cabling started. The design of a bomb was well under way.

In 1997, a publishing house in Lahore, Pakistan, released a collection of mid-1980s to mid-1990s lectures by A. Q. Khan entitled *Dr. A. Q. Khan on Science and Education*. This book discloses some of Dr. Khan's early knowledge about nuclear weapons, including a sophisticated neutron initiation scheme. Initiators are the devices needed to assure an adequate supply of neutrons to the weapon core at the moment of maximum supercriticality. During World War II, the United States achieved this result by mixing beryllium and polonium at the center of an implosion.[23] In

---

23. Polonium 210 is unstable, giving off alpha particles (He4) with a half-life of 138 days. When mixed violently with beryllium, the alpha particles knock neutrons out of the Be9 nucleus and into the assembled supercritical core.

later years the United States and most other nuclear weapon states turned to pulsed neutron tubes, essentially mini-accelerators, to produce a surge of neutrons when needed. But in 1989, at an American Physical Society conference in Albuquerque, the Chinese explained their very different approach to neutron generators.[24] That Chinese initiation scheme appears within Dr. Khan's book, and thus the origins of Pakistan's A-bomb are unambiguously confirmed.

In 1985, the Engineering Research Laboratory in Kahuta, by then known as the A. Q. Khan Research Laboratory, produced its first uranium-enriched to weapons grade, by means of a centrifuge cascade. By 1986, Pakistan had enough HEU for an implosion-type weapon, perhaps a derivative of the CHIC-4 design. With that, Pakistan was nuclear capable. It could have responded to an attack on its vital interests with a nuclear device of its own.

But by then, A. Q. Khan was not the only game in town. Munir Khan had resurrected his moribund plutonium program with a scheme for removing irradiated fuel rods from KANUPP, reprocessing them in-house at PINSTECH.

For at least half a decade after the Canadian withdrawal from KANUPP, that nuclear reactor had not been under serious surveillance by any international organization. Unnoticed, Munir Khan's men had extracted the irradiated materials needed for weapon production. They also built a reprocessing plant, known as the New Labs, to extract the plutonium from within those reactor fuel rods. That facility was based on the technology transferred and then abandoned by the French during the mid-1970s. In later years, the Munir Khan organization also built a heavy component construction shop, known as HMC-3, for the assembly of nuclear reactor vessels and steam supply systems. By the mid-1980s, Pakistan had two viable routes open to a nuclear weapon.

It may be that this challenge to A. Q. Khan's pre-eminence is what drove him to become a merchant of nuclear death. The mid-1980s are the years when he first traveled to Iran.

Amidst these developments, in 1988, General Zia's plane went down and Pakistan was plunged into another political crisis. President Gorbachev had announced his intent to withdraw Soviet troops from Afghanistan, President Reagan was leaving office, and Pakistan was no longer of prime interest to the West. In the election that followed, the Pakistan People's Party, now led by a thirty-five-year-old Harvard and Oxford graduate, Benazir Bhutto, won control of the Pakistani government. The West was enamored of the first female leader of a Muslim nation. At year's end, *People* magazine identified Ms. Bhutto as "one of the world's Fifty Most Beautiful

---

24. Security considerations preclude our discussion of these alternatives.

People." She was also one of the world's most corrupt, but in 1988, her selection as prime minister, serving under tough-minded President G. I. Khan, assured the stability of the country, the continuity of the China connection, and the continued financing of Pakistan's nuclear weapon program. Under Benazir Bhutto's watchful eye, arrangements went forward for the fabrication and testing of those weapons.

## THE FIRST TEST

We believe that during Benazir Bhutto's initial term in office, the People's Republic of China tested Pakistan's first A-bomb on their behalf, on May 26, 1990, at the Lop Nur Nuclear Test Site. We come to this conclusion for a number of reasons:

First, as noted earlier, it is clear that the Chinese began the transfer of nuclear weapon technology to Pakistan in 1982.

Second, we know from documents that turned up in Libya that the Chinese gave the Pakistanis the CHIC-4 nuclear weapon design. That would imply some willingness to see the Pakistani bomb development through "certification" and into production.

Third, co-author Stillman repeatedly saw clear evidence of Pakistani visitors within the heart of the Chinese nuclear complex. They were there throughout the 1980s and certainly in 1989.

Fourth, discussions with Chinese nuclear experts inescapably point to the Chinese nuclear test known as Event No. 35 as the test of a CHIC-4 derivative design. Co-author Stillman, along with many other U.S. nationals, were given briefings within China and again within the United States[25] that disclosed the date, yield, and purpose of every single Chinese nuclear test. Comments regarding the May 26, 1990, event (No. 35) confirm the detonation of an imploded, solid-core, enriched but unboosted uranium bomb that most likely gave ten kilotons of yield, matching the performance of both the CHIC-4 shot and the subsequent May 28, 1998, test within Pakistan.

Next, contemplate the reporting of *Defense and Foreign Affairs Weekly*,[26] entered into the proceedings of the U.S. Senate by John Glenn on May 16, 1989: "It has been further learned that China is making arrangements for a Pakistan nuclear test, most likely at its Lop Nur testing ground."[27]

Now consider the speed and confidence with which the Pakistanis responded to the Indian nuclear tests of 1998. It took only two weeks and three days for the Pakistanis to field and fire a nuclear device of their own. When the Soviets similarly took the U.S. by surprise, on September 1, 1961, it took the nuclear-experienced

---

25. At academic venues.
26. A publication of the International Strategic Studies Association, Alexandria, Virginia.
27. 1989 Congressional Record, S5442

United States a similar seventeen days to get off its first underground shot, but that event was accomplished only by firing a device that had been on hand for years as part of the U.S. nuclear readiness program. The prompt and pre-announced Pakistani response to the Indian test makes it clear that the gadget tested on May 28, 1998, was a carefully engineered device in which the Pakistanis had great confidence. We rely on our discussions with senior members of the Chinese nuclear weapon community, held within the United States during recent years.[28] On one occasion, those conversations turned to the testing of nuclear devices by one nation for other, third-party states. We confirmed to our guests that the United States had conducted such nuclear tests openly and with full disclosure within Nevada, during the 1990s, on behalf of our U.K. allies. We also speculated on Israeli access to U.S. test results. For their part, the Chinese admitted to having conducted hydronuclear and radiation effects tests for France, but most tellingly they also implied—they certainly did not deny—the test of a Pakistani device at Lop Nur.

Last, we rely on a Pakistani source debating the significance of India's May 1974 test. He acknowledged, perhaps displaying the usual desire to one-up the Indians, that by the time of that debate in 1992, the Pakistanis had already tested a nuclear device of their own.

What was tested on May 26, 1990? We believe it was a Pakistani-designed derivative of CHIC-4. It was a fairly crude but reliable enriched-uranium design, unboosted but utilizing the Chinese neutron initiation scheme, all in a configuration that had been successfully cold tested within Pakistan during the 1980s. This was not a cutting-edge experiment any more that was the Soviet test of Joe-1 (RDS-1) in 1949 or the British test of Hurricane in 1952. When states first go nuclear, especially with "transferred" technology, they tend to start off with close copies of the basic "transferred" design. Joe-1 was, internally, an exact replica of the American Fat Man. Hurricane had been designed by British scientists who had worked at Los Alamos and flown the Nagasaki mission in 1945, but who had then been abandoned by their wartime allies. Both tests were intended to give the domestic scientists and their political masters confidence. The test of Pak-1 on May 26, 1990, probably served the same, confidence-building purpose.

## THE DEPARTURES AND RETURNS OF BENAZIR BHUTTO

Ms. Bhutto only lasted for twenty months during her first tour of duty as Pakistan's prime minister. The stench of corruption led to her removal from office on August 6, 1990, but by then her nuclear acolyte, A. Q. Khan, had already privatized the

28. 2005–2007.

transfer of nuclear weapon technology to other Muslim states. He was delivering P-1 centrifuge systems to Iran, under contracts signed during the Zia years, and he was offering to help the disoriented Iraqi government in its search for a nuclear capability as the Desert Storm response to Saddam's invasion of Kuwait took shape.

Ms. Bhutto was replaced by Nawaz Sharif, a Zia follower and the head of the Pakistan Muslim League (Nawaz), or PML (N). The word "party" is often used to describe these political organizations, but the Pakistan People's Party (PPP), the PML (N), the PML (Q), and other such organizations should more accurately be viewed as the personal property of the founders. These syndicates are financed corruptly by the controlling families. That control usually travels with the leader into exile. The party's assets are willed on to successors, and there is little actual democracy within the ranks.

The PPP is a left-of-center organization financed by the Bhutto clan: father Zulfika Ali Bhutto, daughter Benazir Bhutto, and now-widowed husband Asif Ali Zardari. The PML (N) has a more conservative, Punjab-based, pro-military focus. It is the personal property of former Prime Minister Nawaz Sharif. The PML (Q), known as "the King's Party," is General Musharraf's now-failing machine.

Nawaz Sharif held sway for thirty months. During that time, his man Munir Khan started work on a secret, plutonium-producing reactor at Khushab. In 1993, new elections again brought Ms. Bhutto to power. The skimming, kickbacks, and bribes resumed. They only ended when a new president of Pakistan again forced her departure, this time into Dubai exile immediately prior to her fraud conviction. Ms. Bhutto's husband, Asif Ali Zardari, was unable to accompany her, since he was already in custody. He was to spend six years in a Pakistani prison on similar corruption charges.

During Ms. Bhutto's years in office, she entered into arrangements with Kim Jong Il for Pakistan's purchase of North Korean No-Dong ballistic missile technology, presumably in exchange for A. Q. Khan's uranium-enrichment technology. As a farewell she received the heartfelt thanks of the master proliferator. As A. Q. Khan put it in his 1997 book, "She [Benazir Bhutto] has always supported us [at the Khan Research Laboratory] and provided us with every possible patronage and financial support to carry on with our invaluable work for our beloved country."[29]

In later years, Swiss courts found both Zardaris guilty of money laundering; a hundred million Bhutto-Zardari dollars washed through Swiss banks. Polish authorities produced evidence of tractor-purchase kickbacks, while investigators in France unearthed an arrangement whereby the government of Pakistan would purchase only Dassault aircraft in exchange for a 5 percent commission payable to Mr. Zardari. Ten million dollars

29. *Dr. A. Q. Khan on Science and Education* (Lahore, Pakistan: Sang-E-Meel Publications, 1997), 241.

apparently went into Mr. Zardari's Dubai bank account in connection with government controls placed on gold imports into Pakistan. Other in-country depredations went undocumented, but in 1997, Nawaz Sharif and others sympathetic to the generals were returned to power, just in time for the nuclear showdown with India.

## 1998

During the evening of May 11, 1998, the prime minister of India, A. B. Vajpayee, announced the successful completion of India's first nuclear tests since 1974. There had been no forewarning, other than Vajpayee's campaign rhetoric while running for that office, but with the events of May 11, the government of Pakistan was faced with historic choices. Adversary India had strengthened its own nuclear hand but had also provided Pakistan with political cover.

Pakistan's Prime Minister Sharif was traveling in central Asia at the time of the Indian event, but his cabinet and national security advisors seemed to agree that a response was in order. The army advised that it would be ready to test within a week. On Friday, May 15, Pakistan's prime minister met with his cabinet, the military chiefs and leaders of the Pakistani nuclear community. As they discussed their options, nuclear test preparations went into high gear. Cabinet and advisors supported such tests; the prime minister listened without commitment, aware of the international uproar and sanctions sure to follow any nuclear action by Pakistan.

Over the weekend of May 16–17, Sharif came under enormous pressure; military officers communicating with the outside world implied that a decision to test had already been made, by them, if not by the prime minister. At a meeting of the inner cabinet over that weekend, Prime Minister Sharif apparently decided on a "matching and befitting response" to India's test, although execution responsibilities were assigned to the PAEC, not A. Q. Khan's Laboratory. That is because, during the 1990s, Munir Khan's PAEC had returned to a position of pre-eminence within Pakistan's nuclear community. A. Q. Khan's Research Laboratory had never been able to upgrade CHIC-4 into a truly modern nuclear weapon.)[30] On Monday, May 18, Sharif confirmed the order to conduct the explosion to his PAEC chairman. Thereafter, test preparations seemed to run on autopilot, as rehearsed by the military for years.

By mid-week (May 19–20), the necessary nuclear device(s) apparently had been delivered to the Ras Koh test area in the Chagai Hills by air. They were placed in tunnels, instrumentation attached, and the sealing of tunnels began shortly thereafter.

30. Usman Shabbir, "Remembering Unsung Heroes: Munir Ahmad Khan", *Pakistan Defence Journal*, May 2004

That closure was accomplished with six thousand bags of cement put in place by May 27. Certification of test readiness was passed to the prime minister that evening. Given the speed of that response (two weeks after the Indian test) one must conclude that, by 1998, Pakistan was home to a mature nuclear weapons program. At 3:16 p.m. on Thursday, May 28, one Muhammad Arshad, the chief scientific officer at the test site, uttered the words "Allah Akhbar" ("All praise be to Allah") and closed the firing circuits that would give birth to the Muslim Bomb. Shortly thereafter, Prime Minister Sharif advised his nation, and the world, "Pakistan today successfully conducted five nuclear tests. The results were as expected." We believe this to be a massive overstatement, but there undoubtedly was at least one nuclear detonation of significant size.

On Saturday, May 30, Pakistan fired another nuclear device, this one in a test hole, not a tunnel, at Kharan, a desert valley ninety miles to the south of the May 28 test site. Different individuals appear to have been involved, and there are rumors that a second, more conservatively designed, device was ready to go in another hole if the May 30 event had failed.

## EXPLANATIONS

As with the Indian tests two weeks before, Pakistani explanations and claims regarding its tests of May 28–30 did not add up. Initial announcements referred to a matching string of five simultaneous underground nuclear tests and then a sixth "topper." Every Pakistani spokesman said these were "boosted fission devices using highly enriched uranium," but some interesting inconsistencies then ensued.

First, Pakistan's spokesmen after the test(s) could not get their stories straight. The prime minister's initial announcement referred to "five nuclear tests." The foreign secretary then talked about a singular test. Immediate statements by other government officials, carried by the Associated Press of Pakistan, talked about two tests. Then the chorus began to sing in unison: five tests, matching the number fired by India. "Pakistan could do no less."

Second, six full-up nuclear devices, each armed with enough fissionable material to go supercritical, would have eaten up a quarter of Pakistan's nuclear inventory.[31] That is not a rational use for a small nation's weapons-grade materials.

Third, Pakistan claimed that the nuclear yield from the initial five simultaneous events, all allegedly fired within one excavation, was around forty kilotons. Seismic data from many observers in the outside world puts the estimated total yield at nine kilotons.

31. "The Decades Ahead," declassified internal DIA document, 1999.

Finally, the United States has found it quite complex to collect diagnostics from more than two simultaneous nuclear explosions within one tunnel; doing so without years of preparation would be very difficult. Pakistan claims to have fired five nuclear devices simultaneously, within one tunnel, two weeks after the Indian challenge. We find that quite unlikely. A summary of these Pakistani claims follows.

### The Pakistani Nuclear Test(s) of May 28, 1998

| Test No. | Claimed Design | Claimed Yields | Seismic Estimate |
|---|---|---|---|
| 1 | Boosted HEU | The Pakistan Atomic Energy Commission said total yield was 40 kilotons. A. Q. Khan said one device gave 30 to 35 kilotons, with several lower-yield devices fired simultaneously. | Seismic signals suggest a total yield of around 9 +/-3 kilotons for all events, but with probably only one actual nuclear test. |
| 2 | Boosted HEU | | |
| 3 | Boosted HEU | | |
| 4 | Boosted HEU | | |
| 5 | Boosted HEU | | |

In all probability, the Pakistanis made their assertion of five tests on May 28 to match India's similar claim earlier in the month. More likely there was but one true weapon tested, along with an array of engineering or safety tests. We believe the device tested was of an upgraded PAK-1 design, still utilizing highly enriched uranium, but lighter in weight, utilizing boosting, and probably consuming less fissionable material. We shall call this weapon PAK-2, although, by May 1998, Pakistani scientists had studied many alternative designs.

### The Pakistani Nuclear Test of May 30, 1998

| Test No. | Claimed Design | Claimed Yields | Seismic Estimate |
|---|---|---|---|
| 6 | Boosted HEU | "18 kilotons, 60 percent of the first test's yield" | 5 +/-1 kiloton, but still 60% of the actual May 28 yield. |

This final Pakistani nuclear test took place two days after the first, at a different location, under different circumstances, and with a different scientific staff in attendance.

There is no doubt this "sixth" test was a real nuclear event. While its primary political purpose was undoubtedly to one-up the Indians, we believe it was also a true scientific experiment, collecting data on a very different and far more advanced design, PAK-3. The Los Alamos National Laboratory is alleged to have found plutonium in the vented debris. Some observers believe (and we agree) that the May 30 event was Pakistan's first test of a plutonium weapon, fueled by metal illicitly removed from the KANUPP power reactor at Karachi during the unsafeguarded years (1976–82) or thereafter. The modest yield of the May 30 test—five kilotons versus a claimed eighteen kilotons (which was probably the design yield)—suggests a new plutonium design, a lightweight weapon suitable for delivery by Pakistan's growing inventory of ballistic or cruise missiles.

## THE YEARS THAT FOLLOWED

Since well before 1998, the Pakistan centrifuge farms have been spinning out enriched uranium at a steady pace. Most experts[32] now estimate the Pakistani inventory at fifty uranium weapons. At the same time, Pakistan has been running its nominal forty-megawatt nuclear reactor at the Khushab Nuclear Site at full power while refurbishing the French-built reprocessing facility at Chashma . Pakistan will soon have a complete nuclear fuel cycle, capable of producing significant quantities of plutonium, and thus the suspicion of plutonium "fumes" from the May 30, 1998, test give rise to serious concerns for the future. Augmenting this existing plutonium producer, two larger nuclear reactors are under construction at Khushab with the help of the Chinese government. Upon completion, these assemblies could produce hundreds of pounds of plutonium every year: enough for forty to fifty warheads annually.[33]

While the United States has offered to help secure the Pakistani nuclear inventory, the Musharraf government was leery of such intrusions. His scientists were vociferous about the inviolability of safeguards already in place. Musharraf's troops, those charged with enforcing the existing weapon controls, were being stretched thin, physically and intellectually, by the expanding crises within Pakistan. All of these developments lead to some important questions about Chinese intent and ultimate Pakistani safeguards.

First of all, given China's limited uranium supply and unmet energy needs, and given the overwhelming demands on her construction capabilities, why is China helping Pakistan with this major expansion of nuclear infrastructure? Second, who is financing all of this? Saudi Arabia heads the list of suspects, and thus one must ask what the Saudis expect to get in return. And third, what happens upon the collapse of the command-and-control systems surrounding Pakistan's nuclear inventory?

32. Joby Warrick, "Pakistan Nuclear Security Questioned," *Washington Post* (November 11, 2007), A01.
33. Joby Warrick, "Pakistan Expanding Nuclear Program," *Washington Post* (July 24, 2006), A01.

## CHANGES OF MANAGEMENT IN ISLAMABAD

The 1990s were contentious times in Pakistan. Prime Minister Sharif went along with the national mood and authorized the nuclear tests of May 1998, but he may have had little choice. Attempting to refrain might have resulted in his removal from office even sooner than his October 1999 eviction.

The trigger for that change was yet another Indian-Pakistani fight, this one as a result of Pakistani infiltration into the Kargil District of Kashmir in May, 1999. International pressures forced a Pakistani withdrawal, and in the aftermath Prime Minister Sharif decided the army chief of staff, Gen. Pervez Musharraf, had to go. The dismissal was attempted on October 12, while General Musharraf was out of the country. Sharif named Intelligence Director Khwaja Ziauddin to succeed Musharraf, but the army generals did not go along. As Musharraf attempted his return to Pakistan aboard a commercial PIA airliner, Sharif ordered the capital airport closed, leaving the airliner to circle until it ran out of fuel. Musharraf took command of the aircraft, landed safely, and then took over the government. Sharif was arrested and imprisoned. In time he was tried for corruption, tax evasion, embezzlement, attempted highjacking, and terrorism. (Most of these charges will stick to any Pakistani government official.) Sharif's life-in-prison sentence was then commuted to allow a safe exit to Saudi Arabia. He took control of the Pakistan Muslim League (Nawaz) with him.

General Musharraf then legitimized his government with a series of court decisions, referenda, and apparently free and open elections. He pursued better relations with India and has denounced Islamic extremism. He also appeared to be bomb-proof, having survived multiple assassination attempts during his years in office. India and Pakistan appear to seek only parity with, or deterrence of, each other, but governments can change and technology can leak. The principal political parties within India contest for power on the basis of nuclear macho, Pakistani militants wish to depose or kill their president, and the civilians have grown restive under military control. They are now reclaiming power.

These political tides converged at the end of 2007 with General Musharraf turning over control of the army to a fellow officer,[34] with the mass layoff of dissenting judges after Musharraf's "re-election" to the presidency under dubious circumstances. Parliamentary elections were to follow at year's end, but the December assassination of the PPP's Benazir Bhutto[35] delayed that reckoning. In the process, control of her party passed to her even-more-corrupt widower, Asif Zardari.

34. General Ashfaq Kiyani.
35. Apparently by Taliban militants opposed to the appearance of any democracy within Pakistan.

The elections were rescheduled to February 18, 2008. Even though conducted in an atmosphere of widespread vote-rigging, they still resulted in a massive repudiation of Pervez Musharraf's Pakistan Muslim League (Q). Nineteen of his cabinet ministers lost their seats in parliament, and enough opposition candidates were elected to assure Musharraf's removal from the presidency, by impeachment, if those opponents could get their acts together. There followed months of wrangling amongst some of the most corrupt politicians in the world. Second prize, a junior role in the governing coalition, went to Nawaz Sharif and his PML (N). Their primary focus seems to be the reinstallation of judges once sacked by Musharraf in hopes those men would then invalidate Musharraf's 2007 reelection to the presidency. This would settle scores with the man who toppled and exiled Sharif in 1999.

First prize in the parliamentary sweepstakes went to Zardari's PPP. That clique also seeks the replacement of judges, but only with new men who will turn a blind eye to the impending depradations of the Zardari clan. The removal of Musharraf will be a side show. However these struggles turn out, the result could well be the transfer of power to those most willing to sell nuclear weapons, materials, and/or technology on the open market.

Perhaps those sales will be to "responsible" Arab governments, such as Saudi Arabia, thereby triggering offsetting nuclear ambitions by its Shiite neighbor, Iran. Or weapons may be simply sold into the Muslim bazaar, as General Zia wished to do when this program started. In the worst case, the fall of Musharraf and his replacement by radical Muslim elements could open the nuclear floodgates. Nuclear weapons and materials would then surely fall, or be delivered, into terrorist hands. Al Qaida made every effort to achieve this result, acquiring nuclear weapons from the Pakistani stockpile during the years between the 1998 tests and the 2001 attacks on the World Trade Center in New York.[36] The control of Pakistan's nuclear genie is now under assault. The alternatives boggle the mind.

## NORTH KOREA

The Democratic People's Republic of (North) Korea was the third nation to go nuclear, in a half-baked way, at the end of the twentieth century. While not the most dangerous of the nuclear proliferators, North Korea is both puzzling and helpful, because it is the canary in the Chinese coal mine.

The hermit kingdom changed generational leaders on July 8, 1994, but its nuclear ambitions predate that transition by over a quarter-century. In 1965, the Soviets and the

36. George Tenet, *At the Center of the Storm* (New York: HarperCollins, 2007).

North Korean government of Kim Il Sung reached agreement on the construction of a five-megawatt nuclear reactor. It went operational in 1967, with the Soviets supplying the fuel rods. By 1974, the North Koreans had upgraded that facility on their own. It achieved an eight-megawatt power level utilizing indigenous fuel. In the 1980s, and with the coming of Deng Xiaoping in China, serious nuclear weapon developments began to appear, such as high-explosive craters in the sand and the construction of a fifty-megawatt nuclear reactor at Yongbyon. The latter went critical in April 1986. Construction of a reprocessing facility began, in secret, in 1987.

By the end of the 1980s, the plutonium facilities at Yongbyon had delivered enough fissile material to produce one or two A-bombs. In the spring of 1994, just prior to the death of Kim Il Sung and the accession of Kim Jong Il, Secretary of Defense Bill Perry, his assistants, and the Joint Staff developed plans for an Osirak-like strike on Yongbyon.[37] Such an attack would have collapsed the nuclear reactor and entombed all of the plutonium then in production without a Chernobyl-like radioactive plume downwind. That plan was not executed in part because of fears of the North Korean response: an invasion of the South. An opening artillery and missile barrage, aimed at Seoul, might have claimed a hundred thousand casualties. Instead, the Clinton administration, assisted by former President Carter, opted for negotiations. The new North Korean government agreed to an eight-year nuclear truce known as the Agreed Framework. As that time-out ended, as Kim Jong Il established his own priorities, and as U.S. responsiveness slowed, the North Korean nuclear program rose, Lazarus-like, from the dead. Reactor and reprocessing facilities continued to expand; a new high-explosive test facility appeared at Youngdoktong.

During the 1990s, there were also signs of an extensive uranium production program within North Korea. That kingdom enjoys significant deposits of uranium. They are now being mined, with the ore then processed into uranium hexafluoride for use at home or for sale to other nuclear aspirants, such as Libya and Iran. North Korea seems to have built an actual uranium-enrichment facility using technology supplied by A. Q. Khan during his 1990s heyday.[38] North Korea then exports that product to others, a trade that must enjoy the concurrence of the Chinese government, since the use of Chinese airspace is essential to its transfer.

Kim's bomb design? Our Chinese friends tell us he has a descendant of the CHIC-4 design, provided to the Pakistanis more than a decade ago and then franchised by Dr. Khan throughout the proliferant world.

---

37. Ashton B. Carter, "The Korean Nuclear Crisis," *Harvard Magazine* )September–October 2003).
38. Kim Jong Il denies such developments.

## THE TEST AT P'UNGGYE

On October 9, 2006, North Korea conducted a nuclear test underground inside the country's eastern mountains. Within a week of that event, the U.S. Office of Naval Intelligence announced its conclusions, based on vented air samples, that a plutonium device of less than a kiloton yield had been fired near P'unggye. It was probably a plutonium-based derivative of the CHIC-4/A. Q. Khan design, first tested by China in October 1966.

The North Korean device did not achieve its expected twelve-kiloton yield; most evidence points to an energy release of around five hundred tons, 4 percent of the design yield. There are several possible explanations for this misfire. Sloppy machining is one. A nuclear weapon pit must be assembled and then imploded with great precision. The slightest imperfections will result in asymmetry and thus a failure to achieve significant supercriticality. Another explanation might be the lack of an effective neutron initiator; the chain reactions might have started at the wrong time. Or it may be that the North Koreans could not correctly convert the enriched-uranium CHIC-4 design to operate with a plutonium pit. While the North Koreans may have been given the high-explosives chemistry, lens dimensions, and detonator technology for an A-bomb, the neutronics of plutonium is very different from that of highly enriched uranium. Critical masses are different; proper initiation is much more difficult.

A host of other electronic and mechanical inadequacies could have played a role in the North Korean fizzle. Whatever the reasons, North Korea will have to fix the problems and try again if it wishes to claim regular membership in the nuclear club. Whether it does so is up to China, which is why North Korea is so useful as an unambiguous indicator of Chinese intent—the referenced canary in the coal mine.

What was and is Kim Jong Il's objective? Perhaps he envisions North Korea as the Arsenal of Autocracy. With no visible means of support, North Korea may look to sales of enrichment feedstock, crude nuclear weapons, and/or missile technology to support the emperor's lifestyle. The petrodollars are out there. As an example, in 2000, Libya's Qaddafi paid North Korea $600 million for fifty No-Dong intermediate-range ballistic missiles, a lot of money in North Korea, but only two weeks' worth of oil production in Libya. Or Kim may now look to a more focused Iran, to a changing Venezuela,[39] or even to some future government in Mexico[40] grown resentful of its northern neighbor for economic salvation. Any of these petro-patrons could fund an economic recovery in North Korea and a comfortable retirement for its reclusive dictator.

39. The world's fifth-largest oil producer.
40. Number six, right after Venezuela.

Japan, South Korea, Russia, and the United States all have substantial reasons for not wanting North Korea to go nuclear; China is the wild card. It would not seem to be in China's best interest to allow North Korea to continue with its nuclear activities, since Japan, Taiwan, and South Korea might well respond in kind, and if North Korea continues to test, the United States will surely strengthen its ABM deployments along the Asian perimeter.

China could end the North Korean nuclear program with one démarche if it wished to do so. China supplies 80 to 90 percent of North Korea's electric power, 90 percent of its crude oil, and almost all of its diesel fuel. North Korea imports 70 to 80 percent of its foreign goods, including much of its food, from or through China via multiple railway and road crossings from that land. When needed, China provides the military umbrella, the protection that saved Kim's father from the Americans in 1950.

## COUNCILOR TANG PAYS HIS RESPECTS

On October 19, 2006, two weeks after the North Korean nuclear test, a Chinese state councilor,[41] Tang Jiaxuan, visited Pyongyang. His mission: to personally deliver a message from President Hu (and the Chinese politburo) to Kim Jong Il. Did Councilor Tang come to urge restraint? Or was he in Pyongyang to coordinate ambiguous responses to American complaints? There was much economic relief to be gained for the peasants of North Korea if an accommodation with the Americans and their Asian allies could be reached.

The events that unfolded after Councilor Tang's visit suggest a cautious reevaluation within Beijing. Perhaps the Chinese politburo has instructed its North Korean client to discontinue the more visible aspects of its bomb-making and testing. (It is doubtful the Chinese have "gotten religion" on the matter of nuclear proliferation into the Third World. There is too much evidence to the contrary.)

During the year that followed, American and North Korean negotiators, joined during discussions in Beijing with representative of the Chinese, Russian, Japanese, and South Korean governments, may—or may not—have reached some sort of an agreement on a closing down of some parts of North Korea's nuclear program. The American negotiator, Assistant Secretary of State Christopher Hill, was pleased with

---

41. The State Council is one of the three interlocking centers of power within the People's Republic of China, the other two being the Communist Party and the PLA. The State Council is the government's administrative arm. It is led by the premier. Its "upper echelon" is the premier, four vice-premiers, and five state councilors. Thus, a state councilor is among the dozen top administrative officers of the People's Republic of China, two or three levels below the president, but any given councilor may have broader powers if he is also a senior party member.

the "draft agreements" reached in February 2007. The former U.S. ambassador to the UN, John Bolton, remained dubious.

Seven months later, those negotiators met again in Beijing to adopt a "second-phase action plan," but the deadlines at the end of 2007, envisioned when these Six-Party Talks began, all came and went without fulfillment In February 2008, a small delegation of U.S. scientists visited the Yongbyon Nuclear Center and noted "some progress" in the disablement of some nuclear facilities, but at the same time the U.S. director of national intelligence advised the U.S. Senate of his differing views. Director McConnell said that, "While Pyongyang denies a program for uranium enrichment, and they deny their proliferation activities, we believe North Korea continues to engage in both." A few weeks later Secretary Hill hedged his earlier optimism, stating that he was "very concerned" by the lack of progress in his negotiations with North Korea.

As the months rolled by, however, Chinese pressure apparently came to bear. On June 25, the North Koreans delivered a partial Declaration of Nuclear Activities to Beijing. Visible confirmation was provided the next day when the North Koreans blew up the cooling tower at its Yongbyon reactor facility in front of the world's TV cameras.

There may be a nuclear hiatus on the Korean peninsula, but North Korean nuclear experts are quite active elsewhere. It is one thing to close down tangible facilities (if that is what the North Koreans are doing). It is another to erase the memories of those involved, to dissipate the experience gained. North Korean scientists have turned up in Iran, assisting with nuclear test preparations. North Korean engineers may have built a plutonium-producing nuclear reactor for the Syrians. North Korean mines and mills will surely continue to deliver uranium ores and feedstock to the Muslim world. Yet Kim's people continue to starve, potential investors shelve their plans, and the possibility of local hostilities continues to grow.

The North Korean nuclear test of October 2006 brought nuclear club membership, for the moment, to nine. Three of the last four entrants (Israel, India, and Pakistan) never signed the Nonproliferation Treaty. The fourth, North Korea, once did so, and then withdrew.

## QUESTIONS FOR THE NEW MILLENNIUM

In 1982, Deng Xiaoping's China apparently decided to actively support nuclear proliferation into the Third World, specifically the Muslim and Marxist worlds. In the decade that followed, Deng's government then trained scientists, transferred technology, sold delivery systems, and built infrastructure in furtherance of that policy. As a result, two critical questions present themselves:

## Proliferation of nuclear weapon states

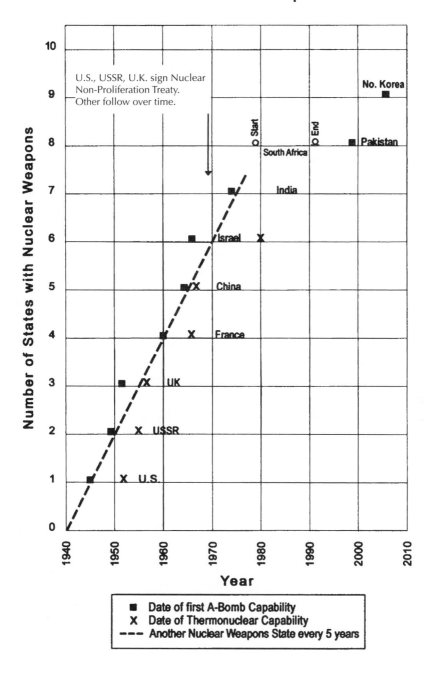

Question One: Did Deng adopt his pro-proliferation policies in pursuit of classical nineteenth-century balance-of-power goals? Were the enemies of China's enemies to become China's friends? Was Pakistan to offset India; was North Korea to unbalance the United States?

Or were Deng's policies tailored to a different set of Chinese "needs," appropriate to the twenty-first century? Would it be in China's best interest to accept, or even encourage, multiple nuclear events (or wars) within the "barbarian" (i.e., Western and Arab) worlds? Would such a chain of events leave China, a land free of Muslim terrorism, as the "last man standing"? And now, twenty years after Deng's departure from power, where are his successors headed?

Question Two: Is anyone truly governing Pakistan? If not, the reader might bear in mind the words of that earlier Pakistani president, Gen. Muhammad Zia-ul-Haq. He helped drive the Soviets out of Afghanistan, but he also executed his predecessor, imposed strict Islamic law, and supported Pakistan's burgeoning nuclear empire. His words in the early 1980s, as that nuclear program got under way: "We should acquire and share nuclear technology with the entire Islamic world." In 1986, when the job was well along and the first Pakistani nuke had been assembled, General Zia proclaimed, "It is our right to obtain the technology [of nuclear weapons], and when we acquire this technology, the Islamic world will possess it with us."

Due process seldom enters into the transfer of power within Pakistan, and with Pervez Musharraf gone, corruption and chaos will surely blossom. It is stunning that a post-Musharraf scenario once cast Benazir Bhutto, one of the great crooks of Pakistani history, as the fairy princess destined to "save" Pakistan from chaos. During her years in office, everything was for sale. Had fate not intervened, nuclear weapons might have made it to the bazaar on her watch. They still may under her husband's guidance.

Alternatively, a radical Islamic successor may arise from the ranks of the army or from its Directorate of Inter-Services Intelligence, the ISI. Might such a newly empowered officer revert to General Zia's goal of sharing nuclear technology with the entire Islamic world, for free? The leaders of al-Qaida certainly hope so.

By the end of the next American president's first term, Pakistan will have produced more than a hundred nuclear weapons. Who will control them? Who will own them?

# FINGERPRINTS

---

Those of us with experience as fathers dread the warning, "some assembly required," but those caveats are important; failure to append them can be burdensome to the firm neglecting to do so. A. Q. Khan should have known that.

In 1986, in response to the American bombing of Tripoli, which was in response to a terrorist bombing of a nightclub in Berlin, which was in response to some other earlier insult, Muammar Qaddafi decided to go nuclear. His initial plan was to breed plutonium; his would-be suppliers were Belgian and Japanese. The latter built and delivered a pilot plant designed to produce natural uranium slugs for use in a heavy water reactor. No product ever emerged from that facility, nor is there any evidence of contracts for the heavy water or the reactor itself. A few million dollars, poured onto the desert sands during the mid-1980s, produced nothing of any practical use.

The next techno-promoter to appear in the desert, in the late 1980s, was German. He was an engineer who advocated centrifuge cascades of his own design. They were to produce highly enriched uranium. Those machines were to be based on technology extrapolated from the designs of others, but none were ever completed. More Libyan petrodollars were wasted, but with those conversations, Qaddafi's interest in centrifuge technology echoed through the Muslim underground.

By the early 1990s, Pakistan's A. Q. Khan was beginning to market the machines and technology born within his laboratory at Kahuta. When he heard of Qaddafi's interest in nuclear weapons, Khan was as happy as a used-car dealer when a newly licensed teenager, awash with trust-fund money, walks onto his lot.

By the mid-1990s, after meetings we now know took place in Dubai, Turkey, and Mali, Colonel Qaddafi had agreed to appropriate $100 million to buy himself nuclear weapons capability from the Khan network. About half of that money may have made it into A. Q. Khan's coffers; the rest appears to have stuck to other fingers along the way. Major sums were simply stolen or were wasted on scientific activities of no practical value to Libya's nuclear weapons program.

As part of the package, Qaddafi was to get engineering drawings of a fairly simple enriched-uranium bomb based on the CHIC-4 nuclear design first tested by the Chinese in 1966. That design was passed on to the Pakistanis after the Indian nuclear test in 1974; we believe a variant was re-tested within China in 1990. If built to specs, Qaddafi's bomb would have worked.

To produce the highly enriched uranium needed for this weapon, Khan proposed to sell Qaddafi a cascade of high-speed isotope-separating centrifuges based on stolen URENCO technology. Like any good used-car dealer, however, Dr. Khan also wanted to move his older inventory. He sold Qaddafi a bank of used P-1 separators, utilizing high-strength aluminum rotors, that had been running at Khan's Kahuta laboratory for several years. They were being replaced by newer P-2 models, utilizing maraging steel, but Khan believed the P-1s would work well enough for Qaddafi's purposes. (In time Qaddafi acquired some P-2s as well.)

Some assembly would be required within Libya, and that is where the trouble began. When selling the Ferrari of fratricidal physics to a young driver, it helps if the buyer knows how to drive. There are not many residents in Libya (six million); few of them have rudimentary mechanical skills; only a handful hold serious academic credentials. The Khan machines were to be installed near Qaddafi's Nuclear Research Center at Tajura, outside Tripoli, but the challenge of unpacking these very sophisticated pieces of rotating machinery, installing them in a secure production facility, connecting them together into a working cascade, and running them around the clock was beyond the ken of the Libyan workforce. No one in Libya really understood the chemistry of uranium hexaflouride; none could manage a 24/7 high-tech engineering operation.

Any sensible car dealer also ought to make sure his customers know where to buy gas. To accompany the used P-1 equipment, Khan sold Qaddafi only a jerry-can equivalent of uranium hexafluoride,[1] the feedstock needed for any uranium-enrichment process. Perhaps Khan was pursuing the marketing strategy perfected by razor-blade makers: sell the centrifuge cheap, then charge full price for a continuing supply of uranium hexafluoride feedstock.

More likely, Qaddafi was to acquire uranium oxide on his own, for processing within Libya. That material, known as yellowcake, can be purchased by legitimate power-generating users from producers in Canada, Australia, or any number of other responsible uranium-mining countries. The International Atomic Energy Agency (IAEA) tracks such purchases, although the production of uranium ore is not within the IAEA's official purview. Upon arrival in the using country, that ore

1. Actually one barrel of UF6, shipped from North Korea in Pakistani containers.

must be converted into uranium hexafluoride prior to use in a centrifuge or gaseous diffusion system. Users not party to the Nonproliferation Treaty (such as Israel) have historically acquired yellowcake in direct deals with producing states (such as apartheid-era South Africa) in covert transactions. The present-day traffic is more obscure (see chapter 18).

Colonel Qaddafi, while operating outside the IAEA, did not have Israel's connections. He could neither purchase yellowcake openly, nor could he trade for it. He had to buy it on the black market. That necessitated dealing with mysterious suppliers in central and southern Africa, some of the most shady businessmen and brutal dictators imaginable. Qaddafi's ultimate supplier of ore turned out to be Niger, his immediate neighbor to the south, but conversion of that ore into useful uranium hexafluoride feedstock was beyond his capabilities. Four hundred tons of yellowcake remain in Libya, awaiting a buyer.

So it came to be that on December 19, 2003, Muammar Qaddafi announced to the world that he had a nuclear weapons program and that he wished to shut it down. That was not a spontaneous announcement. While Qaddafi's men could not properly assemble and run all the equipment he had bought for them, there were other considerations driving this decision.

## ENLIGHTENMENT

The September 11, 2001, attacks on the World Trade Center in New York seem to have been the turning point in Colonel Qaddafi's relations with, and respect for, the United States. Qaddafi was well aware that the newly installed U.S. president had threatened the use of force to preclude the spread of weapons of mass destruction (WMD) even before the 9/11 attacks. After those assaults, and once the ensuing retribution within Afghanistan was underway, Qaddafi contacted Egyptian President Mubarak in an attempt to establish a new relationship with the United States. The U.S. air assaults in Afghanistan started on October 7, 2001, only four weeks after the 9/11 events. By early November, the Northern Alliance was on the move; on November 12, they drove the Taliban from Kabul. On December 17, the last cave in the Tora Bora Mountains was taken by Northern Alliance and U.S. Special Forces. Qaddafi feared he might be next.

As the new year of 2002 dawned, Qaddafi's son, Saif-al-Islam, a resident of Vienna, began his efforts to establish a communication channel with the United States and Great Britain. With his father's apparent approval, Saif wanted to offer a deal: Libya would give up its weapons of mass destruction, with full disclosure; the West would lift sanctions and remove Libya from its "terrorist-supporting" target list. In the fall of 2002, British emissaries appeared in Tripoli to discuss this matter;

in October, communications moved to the highest and most official levels. Britain's Tony Blair wrote to Qaddafi expressing an interest in a mutual rollback of WMD programs and British sanctions.

In the spring of 2003, the American and British armies needed only three weeks to invade and occupy Iraq, to utterly decimate the once best-equipped army in the Arab world, and to demolish Saddam Hussein's emblems of power. The justification for that attack was Saddam's development and alleged possession of weapons of mass destruction. The subsequent occupation was bungled, no nuclear weapons were found, and a long and bloody insurgency would follow, but in the summer of 2003, it was clear that the United States could annihilate any Arab army it wished to take on. It was also clear to Colonel Qaddafi that the American president did not look kindly on Third World states seeking to develop nuclear weapons. Specifically, Qaddafi understood that American marines, landing at the former Wheelus Air Force Base on the Libyan coast, could take control of Tripoli overnight.

Aside from Khan's inoperable machinery and the menacing American troops, there was a third consideration in Qaddafi's decision to fold his nuclear hand: the steady deterioration of Libya's oil industry. When Qaddafi took power in 1969, Libyan petroleum was flowing to market at the rate of three million barrels a day. Within two years, production had dropped by a factor of two, never to recover. Oil in the late twentieth century had become a high-tech business, dependent on the major producers to make it work.

A century before, petroleum had been found seeping to the surface in rural Pennsylvania. In the years that followed, producers dug shallow wells to depths of a few hundred feet. In time, geological studies, subsurface investigations, and rotary drills entered the picture. By the middle of the twentieth century, geophysics and offshore drilling were the norms. By the end of that century, the oil business had gone high tech. Oil scientists studied subsurface geology with three-dimensional digital mapping. Drilling bits were steered, underground, into the desired reservoirs. Pump stations were computer controlled; shipping facilities were marvels of chemical engineering.

Muammar Qaddafi took power in Libya in the midst of this revolution. The conventional wisdom among his lieutenants was that the oil would flow forever. That turned out not to be the case. During the 1970–1973 time period, the first three years of Qaddafi's reign, Libyan oil production fell by half. Qaddafi allowed some European oil firms to continue operations in Libya in hopes of keeping his industry alive, but they were not the heavyweights, and their operations were encumbered by sanctions.

In the aftermath of the 1973 Yom Kippur War, Qaddafi played a major role in the renaissance of OPEC. His domestic crude oil production recovered modestly, and the world price of oil went through the roof, but with the coming of the 1980s,

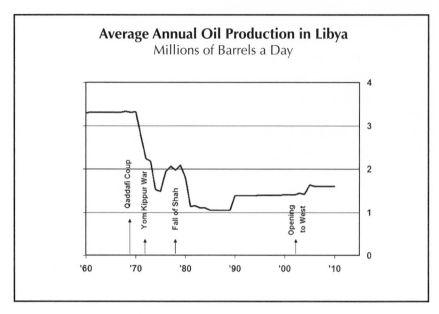

Source: *U.S. Department of Energy*

a decade after the major oil companies had been kicked out of Libya, production had dropped to one-third of pre-Qaddafi levels. Oil industry technology had bypassed Libya, and the younger generation of Libyan leaders knew it.

That younger generation in Libya, specifically Qaddafi's second son, Saif, wanted to rejoin the modern world—to bank in London, not blow it up. While there was adequate oil revenue flowing into Libya, unemployment there was hovering around 30 percent. One of the great oil provinces of the Near and Middle East was stuck in a time warp.

Qaddafi himself had turned sixty. Upon the death of Egypt's Gamal Nasser in 1970, Qaddafi had hoped to inherit the mantle of Arab World Leader, but his eccentricities were too much for his peers. Thirty years later, at the turn of the century, he was an outcast in the Arab world, left to fulminate that he was "more African than Arab."

Amidst these conflicting pressures, and in the aftermath of the second U.S.-Iraqi War, Colonel Qaddafi hosted a pair of interesting visitors. The American worked for the CIA, the Brit for MI-5. Their home agencies had been tracking the activities of Pakistan's A. Q. Khan for twenty years. They had been (covertly) sharing A. Q. Khan's hearth and home for at least three years. The U.S. and U.K agencies knew of the deals afoot with Libya, although not their scope. For much of the summer and fall of 2003, these gentlemen had been making the case to Colonel Qaddafi, his son, and his staff that membership in the nuclear club was not a good idea. Qaddafi had come to the same conclusion.

## THE CRUISE OF THE BBC *CHINA*

The curtain rang down on the Libyan nuclear escapade with an interception at sea. While at first glance that interception appears to have been simply based on good intelligence, there was more to that rendezvous than meets the eye. In the autumn of 2003, probably after intercession from the highest levels, the Central Intelligence Agency decided to act rather than just watch. During the prior three years, the operations directorate had been well aware of A. Q. Khan's nuclear marketing activities, but the ability to report on his travels, his meetings with Muslim-world leaders, and on the progress of al-Qaida's search for nuclear weapons had overshadowed any reflection by management on whether Khan's activities should be stopped. In the spring of 2000, British intelligence ordered their man in the Persian Gulf (Alif Aman) to cease his tracking of A. Q. Khan. In September 2003, however, America's director of central intelligence, George Tenet, met with Pakistan's President Musharraf in New York.[2] The purpose was a disclosure of the U.S. hand, the fingering of A. Q. Khan. Tenet displayed copies of drawings that "were supposed to be in a vault in Islamabad, not a hotel room in New York." He then listed the nuclear technology A. Q. Khan had transferred from Pakistan to Iran and Libya. After those conversations, the CIA's man in Tripoli may have sought Colonel Qaddafi's concurrence in the agency's plan to act, but a few weeks later, the CIA struck on the high seas.

In October 2003, a freighter left Malaysia with suspicious cargo aboard. As the BBC *China* passed through the Suez Canal en route to Libya, the U.S. government made a telephone call to the German owner of that ship, requesting a diversion to Sicily, prior to its landing in Tripoli. The Americans wanted to inspect the cargo. The U.S. Navy stood by to explain this request to the skipper of the BBC *China* if such intercession were needed.

The inspection of the BBC *China*'s hold produced a treasure trove: five containers filled with pumps, centrifuge parts, and key pieces of plumbing, all purchased by B. S. A. Tahir, a Malaysian middleman, as part of the Qaddafi-Khan contract. Any Libyan attempt to explain away this cargo was annulled by a compact disc, given to Qaddafi in November 2003 by his Anglo guests. The disc recorded an intercepted telephone conversation between Libya's nuclear weapons chief Ma'atouq and Pakistan's Khan. Their intent, to develop nuclear weapons in Libya, was inescapably clear from the conversation. Further denial was no longer an option. Full disclosure to the Americans, the British, and the IAEA was the only escape route left.

With the intercept of the BBC *China*, the game was over; or is that what Colonel Qaddafi intended all along? Since he must have known the BBC *China* was en route

---

2. A one-on-one meeting in conjunction with the opening sessions of the UN. See George Tenet, *At the Center of the Storm*, 285.

with illicit cargo, did he allow its capture in order to "burn" A. Q. Khan? Clearly, the Anglo-American allies planned this event as their exposé of the Pakistani merchant of death, but who was in league with whom?

The events of October 2003 remain shrouded in mystery. One cloud is represented by the Pfeiffer Vacuum pumps, discovered in Libya during the early 2004 inspections.[3] These pieces of equipment, designed to operate on 220-volt, fifty-cycle power (the usual European and North African standard) were manufactured in Asslar, Germany, but they did not travel directly from the Pfeiffer Vacuum plant (north of Frankfurt) to Tripoli. Their provenance is most interesting. They were initially shipped to the Los Alamos National Laboratory in New Mexico, which operates on sixty-cycle power. Los Alamos has a strong interest in the nuclear weapons programs of other countries; the United States has a history of intercepting and "adjusting" material en route to dubious recipients. A now-well-known example was the CIA's actions in connection with the Farewell Dossier. "Farewell" was an informant within the Soviet Union, Col. Vladimir Vetrov, who in the 1980s tipped the United States on which technology the Soviet Union planned to steal. Material purchased covertly by Soviet agents within the United States and its allied states was then intercepted by the agency and "adjusted" prior to completing its transit to Russia. Defective computer chips, flawed aerospace drawings, and rewritten software were all injected into an unsuspecting Soviet military-industrial complex. We must suspect the same of vacuum pumps shipped from Germany to Libya via the U.S. nuclear weapons laboratories. Perhaps they had only a GPS transmitter attached to the shipping crates, but perhaps more sophisticated adjustments were being made to equipment headed for Qaddafi's nuclear complex.

It is also strange that a sixth cargo container, filled with more centrifuge parts, was left unexamined onboard the BBC *China*. How could, or why would, the CIA boarding party "overlook" a sixth container? B. S. A. Tahir, in subsequent statements to Malaysian investigators (by whom he is now being held), said the sixth container held parts shipped by a Turkish national via Dubai. Was this shipper a CIA ally, exempt from exposure?

## PROVISIONAL LIBYAN COOPERATION

For a while, during the winter of 2003 and 2004, the Libyans were hospitable and forthcoming to the investigating inspectors. They disclosed the origins of their covert uranium-enrichment program, the details of their nuclear weapons program, and the names of their suppliers. The Libyans provided great insight into Qaddafi's

3. See "Network of Death on Trial," *Der Spiegel* (March 13, 2006).

intentions and his subsequent failures. Inspectors learned the details of A. Q. Khan's travels during the late 1990s as he established his customer base. Dubai was a frequent stopover point. Turkey was the locale of several meetings between Khan; his logistician, Tahir; and the head of the Libyan nuclear weapon program, Ma'atouq. Farther south, however, lay Khan's preferred "second home." He controlled a small hotel in Timbuktu, in northern Mali, named the Handrina after his Dutch wife. In 2000, Khan and his entourage were to be flown to the Handrina in a Pakistani Air Force C-130. He was, nominally, bringing a load of Pakistani wood carvings to the hotel. Oddly enough, Khan was accompanied by Muhammad Farooq, one of his centrifuge experts at the Khan Research Laboratory. En route, "landing problems" developed at Timbuktu; the aircraft put down at Tripoli instead. The cargo was offloaded; some, but not all of it, was then transported by truck on to Mali.

Investigations in 2003 and 2004 also identified the machine shops within South Africa and the manufacturers within Europe who supplied the parts for the Khan machines. These inquiries brought about the indictment of Gotthard Lerch, the alleged European coordinator of this network. Lerch, a resident of Switzerland, was extradited to Germany in 2005 to stand trial on charges of arms-control and export violations. The prosecutors said Lerch was paid more than $30 million to oversee the procurement and circuitous delivery of gas centrifuge equipment. Swiss authorities also arrested members of the Tinner family—father Friedrich and sons Urs and Marco—in connection with the case. Upon his incarceration, Urs Tinner admitted to the possession of A-bomb drawings and specifications within his Swiss office. He claimed to have received them from Kahn's man, B. S. A.Tahir. The prosecutions of Lerch, Tinner, et al., only collapsed when the government was unable or unwilling to produce sensitive documents. In May 2008, the president of Switzerland confirmed the destruction of that evidence—thirty thousand pages of documentation that could have assured the conviction of Lerch and the Tinners. Its disclosure would have unacceptably embarrassed the American CIA.[4]

In addition to exposing the Khan design and fabrication network, the Libyan turnaround resulted in inspectors from the IAEA acquiring two bagfuls of those A-bomb drawings and design specs.[5] Other caches of data included hard disks and DVDs that were A. Q. Khan's sales literature: materials that would have been classified as "secret" within URENCO or the United States. In March 2004, as further evidence

4. Ian Traynor, "Nuclear bomb blueprints for sale on world black market, " *The Guardian* (May 31, 2008).
5. The IAEA turned over the bomb drawings to U.S. and U.K. authorities, since the IAEA charter precludes its involvement in nuclear weapons matters; many of its employees come from non-weapon states.

of its repentance, Libya signed the Additional Protocol to the Nonproliferation Treaty, the only major oil-rich Arab nation to do so.

Amidst this historic nuclear exposé, the American bureaucracy in Washington did its best to effect a derailment. A U.S. aircraft arrived in Tripoli for a lightning extraction of the critical data, drawings, and parts from Libya, but that aircraft lost a lift-enhancing flap on landing. The pilot requested a replacement part from the United States, but the State Department refused. Such an export-controlled item could not be shipped into embargoed Libya. Plane, secret components, and nuclear drawings sat on the ground, and the crew slept in the plane until the bureaucrats relented and the new flap was shipped, days later. In time a naval ship removed tons of the less sensitive material from Libya. Much of it now resides in Oak Ridge within the United States.

By the summer of 2004, Libya's post-disclosure cooperation began to dry up. In part that was because the Qaddafi family had gotten what it wanted: removal from the U.S.-U.K. target list. The Libyan business community also went silent, since it had been welcomed back into the Western world of commerce; the oil companies and tourists were returning. The Libyan scientific bureaucracies stopped talking out of frustration; promises of exciting new work had gone unfulfilled. On top of all that, there was the matter of the money. Libyan bureaucrats grew silent when the accountants began tracking the cash flow. Large sums had been siphoned off; accounting for them could be embarrassing to senior Libyan officials. It was not that the cash disappeared into Swiss bank accounts, although some did. Much of the missing money was spent on the care and feeding of individual Libyan pet rocks: the purchase of impractical scientific equipment or the construction of never-used laboratories and facilities.

## DUSTING THE LIBYAN NUCLEAR CADAVER

As radical Islam began to recover from the invasions of Afghanistan and Iraq, and as the Americans began to appear less invincible, Qaddafi may have reverted to his earlier anti-Western roots. In mid-decade, as Hugo Chavez consolidated his power in Venezuela, the two dictators began to meet regularly in Tripoli. However the Qaddafi years may end, it is clear that the 2003 dusting of the Libyan nuclear cadaver revealed a lot of interesting fingerprints.

That dusting exposed fully the extent of the A. Q. Khan nuclear supply network. The Libyan confession was the smoking gun that forced Khan's patron, Pakistan's General Musharraf, to stage Khan's phony arrest, his public mea culpa, and his confinement to quarters, perhaps for life.

It confirmed the participation of vendors (not necessarily the governments) of Russia, Germany, Malaysia, the United Arab Emirates (Dubai), Switzerland, South

Africa, Turkey, and Holland as suppliers to nuclear proliferators. It also verified the willingness of machine-tool suppliers in Spain and Italy to supply legal but dual-use equipment with no questions asked.

It exposed the role of Turkish nationals (not the Turkish government) in supplying magnets, motors, and electronic parts to the nuclear network, and it reminded the West that while South Africa may have given up its nuclear ambitions, as a nation that country's nuclear experts, machine shops, and high-explosive facilities are still out there on the open market. In 2003, they were working for Khan; today their allegiances are unknown. South African technical mercenaries may be more dangerous that the underemployed nuclear scientists of the former Soviet Union, for the latter, all Russians, have a place to call home. They have family and friends with whom to share the joys and sorrows of life, no matter how impoverished their lives may be. The white Afrikan engineers, refugees from the apartheid-era in South Africa, have no such sense of security. They live in a land that may be sliding slowly into a Zimbabwe-style dictatorship.

The revelations from the BBC *China* and subsequent discussions within Libya also confirmed the opaque role of North Korea in the world's new triangle trade, shuttling gas cylinders made (and stamped with serial numbers) in Pakistan, filled with uranium hexafluoride in North Korea, then delivered to Libya. The denouement in Libya also opened wide a window into nuclear Iran. The IAEA and the Western press came to understand the massive scope of the underground centrifuge farm planned for Natanz (fifty thousand stages), the close links Iran enjoys with uranium sources in Namibia (once controlled by South Africa), and the potential role of those high-tech South African mercenary refugees in the Iranian crisis still to come. Yet, amidst all of these exposures, the Chinese authorities were totally unhelpful, to the point of stonewalling any investigations into Libya's nuclear supply network.

The Libyan exposé only opened a few windows; it did not close any doors. That hard work will be left to others as the Nuclear Express now rumbles on through other Muslim republics and kingdoms of the Middle East.

# STAR AND CRESCENT RISING

The oil shocks of the 1970s signaled the end of the European age. They constituted a double blast from the shotgun of fate that would topple regimes, transfer wealth, and empower leaders whom many would come to call mad. Saddam Hussein was the first. He came to full power in 1979, just as the final oil shock was hitting the Western world. With a well-educated population, a good scientific infrastructure, and the 1973–1979 oil price hikes to pay the bill,[1] Saddam was able to expand a nuclear program started by his predecessor and mentor, Hassan al-Bakr. Central to Saddam's hopes was the Osirak nuclear reactor, built by the French (Saddam's longtime ally and weapons supplier) at the Tuwaitha nuclear complex.[2]

The Israelis saw this project for what it was: a plutonium producer and a threat to their survival. On June 7, 1981, a few weeks before Osirak was to go critical, the Israelis took action. Eight Israeli F-16s bombed Osirak into oblivion with no Israeli losses. There was a great international outcry at the time, but in private, President Reagan was unconcerned. "Boys will be boys," he said.

## IRAQ, 1982–1990

As a result of the raid on Osirak, Saddam learned to be more discreet, but he remained determined to pursue nuclear weapons. On the positive side of his ledger, Saddam was supported by a well-educated middle class. A lot of young men had been sent off to the colleges and universities of America and Britain. Many had received solid educations in physics and nuclear engineering. He also had plenty of cash. On the down side, few of his nuclear apprentices had studied hydrodynamics or materials science, the know-how needed if one is to actually design and build an A-bomb.

1. Iraq was producing oil at the rate of 2.5 million barrels per day in 1980. At $20 per barrel (the 1980 price), that was $50 million per day, or $130 million per day in 2008 dollars.
2. In an amazing display of economic bipartisanship, France had earlier built the Israeli plutonium-producing reactor at Dimona.

Most students returned to Iraq with a silver-spoon mentality and an acquired interest in a pet project. A supportive (and blood-related) cabinet minister would arrange financing for that project, whereupon it would assume a life of its own. With each such appropriation, the Iraqi nuclear complex was becoming a forest of stovepipes, running from treasury to scientist without an overall plan to guide the work.

One classic stovepipe was the continued production of uranium fuel pellets for the Osirak nuclear reactor. That edifice had been blown to bits by Israeli jets; Saddam had decided not to rebuild it. Even so, another part of his nuclear empire continued to produce fuel for that reactor, simply because they had a plant that did that, and no one told them to stop. This would prove to be very confusing to IAEA inspectors later on.

In the aftermath of the Osirak destruction, Saddam's advisors began to reflect on better and less visible routes to a nuclear weapon capability. The breeding of plutonium requires an unmistakably visible and easily attacked nuclear reactor; the enrichment of uranium can be done unobtrusively within very mundane-looking buildings. Saddam's men decided to refocus on the latter approach. In considering the means to achieve highly enriched uranium, the Iraqis took a look at gaseous diffusion, as done by the United States at Oak Ridge; at multiple small centrifuges, as Libya was hoping to do; at laser isotope separation, discussed in Western journals; and at a chemical separation process known as Chemex, proposed by the French. In the end, however, the need to be covert drove the decision. Saddam and his scientific advisors settled on the use of outdated and energy-profligate particle accelerators, first developed by the United States during World War II. They are known as electromagnetic isotope separators (EMIS) or Calutrons (from their development at Berkeley). The inefficiency of these accelerators was not a problem to Saddam. He had plenty of oil with which to generate electricity, and the general-purpose nature of the EMIS components made their purchase unnoticeable in the West. The man he put in charge, Jafar Dhia Jafar, had trained at CERN[3] in Switzerland. Jafar was comfortable with, and knew how to build, large electromagnetic-particle accelerators. He also knew how to keep a secret.

By the late 1980s, Iraq had a first-stage EMIS uranium-enrichment factory in place at Tarmiya. The buildings were huge, and the power lines going in[4] were immense, but inside and out, Tarmiya was a mystery. The Jafar team had maintained secrecy. It had delivered some product, but not much: only a few pounds of low-enriched uranium (3 percent U-235). An A-bomb was not yet in sight.

3. The Conseil Européen pour la Recherche Nucléaire in Geneva, the world's largest particle-physics laboratory.
4. Actually, those cables went underground for the last mile in an attempt to confuse intelligence analysts.

In 1987, Saddam's frustration led him to the proven Arab-world solution: hire a relative. He turned to his son-in-law, Hussein Kamel, to galvanize the uranium-enrichment project, to get it organized, and to produce some results. Hussein Kamel had only a high school education, but he had connections, and he had a sense of purpose. He brought focus and an innovative approach to the enrichment of uranium within Iraq. During those years, A. Q. Khan was visiting other Muslim lands, singing the praises of centrifuge technology at every stop. It may be that in response to that siren song, or perhaps based on independent advice, Hussein Kamel initiated a centrifuge program for the separation of uranium isotopes. The work was to be conducted within Rashidya, a new facility north of Baghdad.

A few German consultants were brought in, nominally as "solar-power experts," to advise on centrifuge technology. German and Austrian industry began to supply the high-strength maraging steel[5] and then carbon-fiber technology needed for the rotors, along with the machinery needed to form them. Swiss industry was supplying the rotor end caps. By 1990, Hussein Kamel had two crude carbon-fiber rotors up and running, but that was the extent of his "success." For comparison, Natanz, in Iran, hopes to have fifty thousand rotors running 24/7.

In the area of nuclear weapon design, Iraqi scientists had thought through the concepts of concentric spheres and done criticality calculations, and they had a polonium-beryllium neutron initiation scheme in mind. In November 1990, after Saddam's invasion of Kuwait, and with Desert Storm in the air, A. Q. Khan sent offers of further help, but at that time Saddam Hussein did not have a working A-bomb in hand.

## DESERT STORM, 1990–1991

For reasons not clear, Saddam invaded Kuwait on August 2, 1990. The invasion and occupation was completed within that one day. A week later, the United States dispatched aircraft to Saudi Arabia. President Bush Sr. extracted immediate support from the UN Security Council (Resolution 660) and a subsequent deadline for Iraq's withdrawal from Kuwait (Resolution 678 on November 29, 1990). The U.S. Congress authorized the use of military force on January 12, 1991.

The air assault of Iraq began on January 17. During the weeks that followed, all the suspected nuclear facilities within Iraq came under attack: the research center at Tuwaitha, the mysterious buildings at Tarmiya and Shaqat that later were found to have been EMIS facilities, the conversion plant at Jazirah,[6] and the uranium

---

5. An essentially carbon-free iron alloy, highly malleable and thus machineable. Maraging steel gets its strength from other alloying elements, e.g., nickle and cobalt.
6. Converting yellowcake into $UO_2$ or $UCl_4$, feedstock for the EMIS machines.

concentrators at Qaim were all hit. The Calutrons were left in smoking ruins.

Postwar inspections by nuclear weapon experts, operating on behalf of the UN, found enrichment hardware and crates of documentation that confirmed the existence of an electromagnetic isotope separation factory, the beginnings of a centrifuge facility, conceptual plans for an implosion device, and an unambiguous Iraqi intent to construct an A-bomb as soon as possible. What they did not find was a coherent management plan for achieving that result. Iraq did not have an Oppenheimer.

In the aftermath of Desert Storm, Saddam tried to hide his nuclear efforts, but his country was soon overrun with inspectors from the IAEA. Their presence was one consequence of the armistice agreement, signed within Iraq in February 1991. Those inspectors had the courage to chase down trucks loaded with nuclear-oriented equipment and documents. Others from IAEA translated and studied the records of Saddam's nuclear staff. The assembled revelations led to the collapse of all Iraqi resistance to full nuclear disclosure. By the end of July 1991, Saddam was instructing his people to "tell the inspectors everything; get them to go away." Follow-up visits to nuclear sites produced buried EMIS equipment, boxes of files on the nuclear program, and the identification of several previously unknown laboratories for handling highly enriched and low-enriched uranium—buildings with concrete walls a meter thick, high-explosive bunkers, and so forth. At the direction of the IAEA, the Iraqi Army demolished, with explosives, eight major nuclear facilities that had escaped destruction by the U.S. Air Force.

In the opinion of those who inspected the Iraqi facilities and files, "Iraq would have achieved a nuclear weapon capability within twenty to thirty months." Others think it might have taken longer, because good management was nowhere to be found, but there can be no doubt that a serious nuclear weapons program within Iraq had once again been nipped in the bud.

## IRAQ, 1992–2000

On the night of August 7, 1995, Saddam's nuclear expediter, Hussein Kamel, defected to Jordan. He wanted postwar Iraq to re-enter the community of nations with a clean slate, and thus he began to talk. Two weeks later, in response to Hussein Kamel's disclosures, Saddam's government turned over, to IAEA and UNSCOM inspectors, seventy steamer trunks of documentation. They disclosed the full extent of Saddam's nuclear, chemical, and biological efforts as well as his ballistic missile ambitions. At the same time, scientists still in Iraq claimed that Hussein Kamel's absence made it easier (that is, safer) for *them* to talk. The net picture that emerged: In 1990 Saddam had a major nuclear weapons program. It had been dismembered by the American bombers during the war, the IAEA inspectors soon thereafter, the ongoing burdens of American reconnaissance overflights, and then UN sanctions as the postwar decade began to unfold. By 1995, there was nothing left. Any attempts by Saddam to re-engineer his nuclear dreams after 1991 would have come to naught.

## IRAQ, 2001–2003

By 2000, Saddam had gotten Iraqi oil production back to pre–Desert Storm levels: 2.5 million barrels per day, in a market where the price of oil had risen sharply. His distortion of the UN Oil for Food program allowed him to pour cash into favored charities and kickback schemes.[7] Some of those funds were used to purchase the conventional arms needed to maintain Saddam's authority within Iraq, but there were no resources left over for the pursuit of nuclear ambitions. Even so, some thought otherwise. One purported indication of Iraqi nuclear intent was the aluminum tubes.

In 2001, American intelligence unearthed the covert and large-scale tender of Chinese-manufactured high-strength aluminum tubes to a Jordanian trading company fronting for an Iraqi business. A CIA analyst concluded, based on the dimensions of the tubes,[8] the alloy involved, and the number of tubes to be ordered[9] that these were intended to be rotors for an Iraqi uranium-enrichment facility. Centrifuge experts at the Department of Energy's enrichment facility at Oak Ridge (the K-25 plant) and other scientists at the Los Alamos and Livermore weapons laboratories disagreed. Some concluded the tubes might be made useable, after cutting and machining, to make a terribly inefficient centrifuge, but most DOE experts said, "No way." Independent consultants from academia were called in. "Unlikely to be used for gas centrifuges" was the response.

The IAEA learned of the aluminum-tube purchase in the summer of 2001. Their experts had spent much of their lives not only inspecting but building uranium-enrichment facilities. They were deeply skeptical of any possible use of those tubes in making an Iraqi centrifuge. Several inspectors did comment, however, on Iraq's purchase of fifty-five thousand similar tubes, during the 1980s, for use in short-

---

7. Saddam and his friends took kickbacks from suppliers, not UN officials. The latter were examining postwar contracts, looking for WMD-related purchases, not overpricing. Thus, Saddam's deliberate overpayment for imports created an immense personal slush fund. The Volcker Commission found more than 2,200 companies from some forty countries colluding with Saddam's regime to bilk the humanitarian program of $1.8 billion. Some of those fortunate suppliers did tangibly "thank" a few UN officials for their "oversights."
8. About three inches in diameter and three feet long.
9. A hundred thousand tubes.

range multiple-rocket launchers. In the late 1970s, Iraq had bought a large supply of Medusa rockets from SNIA Italy; they had been expended in the Iraq-Iran War. Iraq wanted to rebuild its inventory domestically. U.S. Navy experts noted the similarity of the Iraqi-desired tubes to the Navy's Mark 66 rocket motor housing.

Technical and trade-path investigations continued throughout the following year, with the IAEA involved because of its technical expertise. In time, however, U.S. intelligence officials dismissed the opinions of the IAEA that the aluminum tubes were intended for use in rockets. The IAEA was thought to be "under the control of foreigners."

On October 12, 2002, President George W. Bush told the UN General Assembly that "Iraq has made several attempts to buy high-strength aluminum tubes used to enrich uranium for a nuclear weapon." Soon thereafter, the Senate Foreign Relations Committee (Joe Biden, chairman) listened to classified briefings from both sides of the debate; the arguments were intense.

During December 2002, in the run up to Operation Iraqi Freedom, IAEA inspectors were allowed to return to Iraq. They immediately turned their attention to a massive search for the aluminum tubes. Those investigations included many no-notice inspections of suspect procurement offices, but they found no signs of a uranium-enrichment program. Instead, they found a well-documented rocket development effort, one that called for 81-millimeter-diameter (approximately three-inch), high-strength aluminum tubes made to the same specification as the Chinese-tendered tubes.

On January 27, 2003, the IAEA's director, Gen. Mohammed ElBaradei, reported to the UN Security Council that "specifications of the aluminum tubes recently sought by Iraq appear to be consistent with reverse engineering of rockets."

On the other hand, on February 5, 2003, Secretary of State Colin Powell made his memorable presentation to the UN Security Council, with Director of Central Intelligence George Tenet sitting directly behind him. The aluminum tubes constituted the foundation of his case: "Saddam has made repeated covert attempts to acquire high-specification aluminum tubes from eleven countries. Most U.S. experts think they are intended to serve as rotors in centrifuges used to enrich uranium." That statement was incorrect. Only a few CIA analysts and even fewer Department of Energy retirees, all supportive of the administration's political agenda, thought so. DOE and IAEA experts and even the State Department's intelligence staff disagreed, but their views did not matter. Within weeks, the war was on. Six weeks later, after the fall of Baghdad, U.S. forces found no signs of any gas centrifuge program. They declined any involvement with the fifty-five thousand previously ordered tubes still stacked within the Iraqi rocket plant.

The aluminum tubes were but one example of 2003 intelligence myopia. Another involved the alleged correspondence from the president of Niger (the world's third largest producer of uranium) to Saddam Hussein, dated July 27, 2000. It supposedly confirmed Saddam's purchase of five hundred tons of uranium yellowcake ore from Niger. A reference to this "discovery" made it into the president's State of the Union address in January 2003. Unfortunately for all concerned, the letters were phony—obviously so to anyone looking at them or checking them out with a simple Internet search. The alleged signatories had been dead for years; citations were hopelessly outdated. (See chapter 18 for details.)

Alternative theories about a post–Desert Storm (1992–2002) nuclear program continue to circulate. According to one Iraqi scientist stepping forward after the 2003 war, specific documents and centrifuge components lay buried within his garden, hidden for use another day. He dug up one drum for an investigator representing a nongovernmental organization (NGO) and was promptly arrested. Was there really a significant nuclear program within end-of-century Iraq? If so, where is the evidence?

One often-proposed answer: Syria. According to some newspaper reports, Russian Spetsnaz (commando) troops swooped into Baghdad three weeks before the March 2003 American invasion. Their primary mission was to destroy all evidence of the Iraqi-Russian armaments relationship, but once done, the Spetsnaz allegedly turned their attention to relocating the evidence of a nuclear weapons program to Syria, along with Saddam's family's assets. It is true that a lot of trucks carried much merchandise out of Baghdad, but those vehicles were full of gold, rugs, documents, and currency. There is no evidence of weapons materials making that trip.

Another possible sanctuary may have been North Korea. Some in the U.S. nuclear weapons complex view that country as a "safe haven" or "free-trade zone" for nuclear traffickers. Given the opaque nature of Kim Jong Il's society, his country's poverty, and his apparent immunity from American attack, Kim's North Korea may have become a nuclear storehouse, perhaps even a workshop, for the Islamic terrorists. Clearly, he has become a supplier of missiles and uranium feedstock to the Muslim world, but the wholesale movement of an entire Iraqi nuclear complex into that distant land? That seems unlikely. There is no evidence to support that theory.

However the Saddam regime ended, there can be no doubt that he repeatedly sought nuclear weapons prior to 1991. According to Hussein Kamel's 1995 revelations, Iraq also had an active anthrax (biowar) and VX (chemical warfare) program in place at the time of the 1991 war. During that fight, the chemical bunker at Muthanna north of Baghdad was bombed by the U.S. Air Force, although it was not destroyed. In 1992, the UNSCOM sealed the structurally dangerous Muthanna facility, chemical warfare agents still inside, and built an incinerator for disposal of the mustard and sarin agents found elsewhere in Iraq. Anthrax spores were destroyed as well. Thus, Saddam's chemical biological warfare programs came to an end during the 1990s, but in 2003, much of his chemical warfare feedstock remained on hand, within the Muthanna bunker.[10]

It is clear that if left unfettered by sanctions, funded by petrodollars, and free of aerial attack, Saddam's Iraq sooner or later would have become a nuclear weapon state. As it was, Desert Storm ended those dreams in 1991. Operation Iraqi Freedom was an afterthought.

## EGYPT

The Arab Republic of Egypt is by far the most populous nation in the Arab world. It is home to 80 million people with a median age of twenty-four years, but it is also the victim of a bad geologic joke. Amidst an ocean of sand and oil, stretching from Iran in the east to Algeria in the west, Egypt has the people, culture, and location needed to be a major political power. It has the water, flowing profusely down the Nile, and it has a four-millennia tradition of engineering achievement. What it does not have is oil. Egypt produces only 700,000 barrels of petroleum per day, barely enough to fuel its own economy. It is a nation that might have gone nuclear years ago but for the fiscal constraints and its peculiar triangular relationship with Israel and the United States.

The current republic came to life in 1952 with the toppling of King Farouk. Shortly thereafter, the Naguib/Nasser government created an Egyptian Atomic Energy Agency and applied for U.S. assistance under the Atoms for Peace plan. In the years that followed, the Egyptian government then turned on the West, seized control of the Suez Canal, and thereby mobilized the Israelis, French, and British into an alliance that would lead to invasion. The 1956 Israeli-Franco-British attack on Egypt failed in the face of American objections, but an independent Franco-Israeli nuclear weapons program took its place.

During the 1950s, the United States provided Cairo with modest technology assistance in radioisotopes. In 1961, the Soviets built a two-megawatt nuclear reactor for the Egyptians at Inshas, and during those same mid-century years, a lot of young Egyptian students went abroad to study, but at that time there was little practical nuclear work going on within Egypt.

As the 1960s unfolded, the Egyptians watched Israeli nuclear developments at Dimona with concern. They flew reconnaissance missions over the facility, unsuccessfully sought nuclear arms from the Soviet Union and then China, and

---

10. The seals on the Muthanna bunkers were still in place in the spring of 2003, but since then looters have cleaned it out. U.S. troops are now hunting down and destroying those chemical canisters, one at a time.

then planned a ground attack, seeking the destruction of both Dimona and the state of Israel in one fell swoop. Detecting those preparations, the Israelis pre-empted; they won the Six-Day War in June 1967 and then braced for the inevitable Arab counterattack. It ensued in 1973, with Egypt taking the lead and nearly pulling off a victory. Only the logistical intercession of the United States saved the day for Israel. In the aftermath of that Yom Kippur War, the Egyptians turned their attention inward. They signed the Nuclear Nonproliferation Treaty in the vain hope the Israelis would do likewise. A decade later, they signed a full peace treaty with Israel, but given Israel's continuing refusal to accept controls under the Nonproliferation Treaty or to even admit to its nuclear status, Egyptian leaders have rejected any further constraints on their own nuclear activities.

In 1981, with the accession of Hosni Mubarak to the Egyptian presidency, that country's interest in nuclear facilities revived. Egypt acquired a second, twenty-two megawatt nuclear reactor from Argentina,[11] a castoff from an attempted sale to Iran that was halted by U.S. objections. Egypt also bought a pilot fuel reprocessing facility from the French and began its installation in 1989. Strangely enough, that plant was never put into operation. It appears that Pakistan's master proliferator, A. Q. Khan, made his first visit to Egypt about that time. Did he seduce the Egyptians away from the plutonium route with tales of highly enriched uranium? For whatever reasons, by the early 1990s, the Egyptians had refocused their efforts away from the production of plutonium and onto the possibilities of uranium.

It appears that China has also entered into a nuclear cooperation agreement with Egypt, perhaps only focused on the search for uranium, but some think there is much more to the linkage. Starting in the 1980s, with the coming of Mubarak, Egypt began to look for uranium-bearing ore. Those efforts have met with little success, but Egypt continues to pursue those uneconomic ores, low-grade rocks that make no sense from a commercial point of view. They remain suitable only for "sovereign" use, an expression that refers to the use of uranium to support a domestic nuclear weapon program. Today, Egyptian prospectors continue their search while feigning a disinterest in results.

Egypt is probably developing a "breakout capability": a cadre of scientists competent in all aspects of nuclear weapons technology, fully supported by the facilities needed to go nuclear on short order if the politics of the region dictate. Egyptians now enjoy the protection of a tolerant American administration, one that is continually attempting to buy "peace" for Israel, even though the latter is an unfettered nuclear power in its own right.

11. This reactor, also sited at Inshas, went critical in 1999.

## ALGERIA

The People's Democratic Republic of Algeria is another Arabic, mostly-desert nation within North Africa. It hosts half the population but twice the petroleum reserves of Egypt. As a French colony, Algeria was not only the site of the early French nuclear tests; it still "enjoys" a desert landscape littered with souvenirs of those days. Plutonium from the nuclear and one-point safety tests conducted on the surface of the Sahara Desert decades ago still awaits harvesting under the desert sun and sands.[12]

Algeria is also the home of the El Salam (Peace) nuclear reactor and reprocessing facility, both located at Ain Oussera, seventy-five miles due south of Algiers. The facility is remarkable because of the concealment surrounding its conception and construction. In 1983,[13] China and Algeria signed an agreement to build El Salam. This was to be a fifteen-megawatt, heavy water reactor, utilizing 3 percent enriched uranium, sited at the northern edge of the Sahara Desert. Construction began, without notice to IAEA or any Western government, in 1986. At the time of El Salam's construction neither China nor Algeria were parties to the Nonproliferation Treaty. Intelligence agencies only discovered the existence of El Salam in 1991.

During that year, Algeria suffered a parliamentary electoral shock. The Islamist Salvation Front, seeking a national return to Islamic fundamentalism, defeated the National Liberation Front, the protagonists and winners of the war for independence a quarter-century before. The FLN refused to hand over power, a military takeover ensued, the elections were voided, and a new (military) government was installed. During this time, and with that sudden transparency into Algeria, Western intelligence agencies discovered the almost-complete El Salam reactor. That find led to a collapse of the wall of secrecy and to an Algerian acceptance of IAEA inspections and safeguards prior to reactor criticality.[14] Soon thereafter, in 1995, Algeria acceded to the Nonproliferation Treaty, although it has never accepted the Additional Protocol. El Salam has been running for over a decade. It is now surrounded by a battery of long-range SA-5 surface-to-air missiles, designed by the Soviets to attack high-altitude bombers and reconnaissance aircraft. Such a deployment clearly indicates the military importance of this facility to the government of Algeria.

The Spanish intelligence service credits El Salam, in its current configuration, with a capability of producing at least six pounds of plutonium (one Nagasaki-type

---

12. The United States conducted similar tests, usually underground, but always contained, within New Mexico and Nevada.

13. Two years after China began the transfer of nuclear weapon data to Pakistan and other Third World countries.

14. The El Salam reactor went critical on February 17, 1992.

bomb) every year. The problem lies in the size of the cooling towers and the possibility of engineering enhancements. Taken together, those considerations suggest the possibility of a four-fold increase in plutonium production on very short order. Algeria is currently friendly to the United States, but many believe it is another breakout state, developing options to hedge against changes in the political winds.

The earlier secrecy surrounding El Salam and the Chinese involvement raise more questions. Algeria is a major producer of oil and gas;[15] it built the world's first liquefied natural gas plant, at Arzev, in 1964. It may be that China's insatiable appetite for energy led to the construction of El Salam as a quid pro quo. But the timing is odd, coinciding as it does with other Chinese nuclear weapons support to the Arab world. Is there a darker motive here?

## SAUDI ARABIA

The Kingdom of Saudi Arabia, a nation of few people but enormous wealth, has the means to deploy (i.e., acquire by purchase) a nuclear weapon if it wishes to do so. With the ability to produce ten million barrels of oil per day, Saudi Arabia is the elephant in the OPEC living room. The royal family in Riyadh decides how much oil to produce and thus the price all of us pay for gasoline. But Saudi ambitions seem to stretch beyond the oil patch. Saudi Arabia is a Muslim nation of Sunni orientation. By virtue of its wealth and location, if not its population and power, Saudi Arabia may seek the Sunni (anti-Iranian) leadership mantle in the Muslim world.

The Saudis live in a tough neighborhood. The country is 98 percent desert. Israel, Pakistan, and India have more arable land, they can support more people, they have real industries, and all have gone nuclear. Other neighbors have tried to join the nuclear club (e.g., Iraq) or may soon do so (e.g., Iran). Only the Pakistanis can be considered "friendly" neighbors.

There is little evidence of a truly indigenous nuclear weapon program within Saudi Arabia, but so what? Why go to all that trouble when the weapons may be for sale? Money is a surplus commodity in Saudi Arabia. There is some speculation from a high-level Saudi defector[16] that Saudi Arabia has been seeking an A-bomb capability, by means of purchase, since 1975. That was the year when the first wave of petrodollars, arising from the embargoes and price hikes of 1973–1974 hit the Saudi shores. It was also the year when Saudi Arabia opened its first nuclear research center at Al-Suleiyel. Oil revenues tripled again in 1979.

---

15. The equivalent of about 1.9 million barrels per day in 2005.
16. Muhammad Khilewi, second-in-command of the Saudi delegation to the UN. Many in the U.S. Congress and intelligence community are skeptical of his bona fides.

During the 1980s, Saudi Arabia became another Muslim nation entering into a clandestine (but soon discovered) nuclear transaction with Beijing. The Saudis bought fifty aging CSS-2 intermediate range ballistic missiles from China.[17] They are held at two bases south of Riyadh, with each base hosting four to six concrete launch pads and two dozen missiles. This is a 1950s deployment by U.S. standards. The CSS-2 is a single-stage, storable-propellant, liquid-fuelled rocket with a range of about 1,500 miles. It has an average miss distance of well over a mile, making it totally unsuitable for use with explosive or chemical warheads. The launch facilities are soft and cannot accommodate an immediate or salvo launch. They remind us of the Thor IRBM emplacements in Britain during the late 1950s. Why did the Saudis purchase those CSS-2s? What do they intend to use for warheads? Being of Chinese origin, the CSS-2 is *designed* to carry the CHIC-4 A-bomb. And who is the intended target? We assume Tehran, but from Saudi territory, the CSS-2 can also reach Israel, most of the Middle East, much of India, and parts of southern Russia.

That same defector also produced evidence of Saudi support to Saddam Hussein's nuclear weapon program. During the mid-1980s, five billion dollars of Saudi cash allegedly flowed to Saddam, perhaps in exchange for a promise of nuclear weapons when developed. Unfortunately, "friends" do not stay bought for long in the Middle East. In 1991, after the invasion of Kuwait, Saddam's clear intent was to move against Saudi Arabia. Only U.S. and UN intervention precluded such an attack.

## THE SAUDI-PAKISTAN AXIS

The peoples of Pakistan and Saudi Arabia are culturally close, indistinguishable in person. With petrodollars flooding into Saudi Arabia during the 1970s, and with the division of East and West Pakistan in 1971, there blossomed a growing affinity between the surviving West Pakistan and Saudi Arabia.

In 1999, following the Indian and Pakistani nuclear tests of 1998, the Saudis started making "fuel support payments" to Pakistan. These billion-dollar annual bequests, reflected in the Pakistani budgets of 1999, 2000, and 2001, were intended to help Pakistan survive the sanctions imposed by the West after its first nuclear tests. They only ended when the United States replaced them, in 2002, with similar billion-dollar-per-year payments in the wake of 9/11 and the ensuing assault on neighboring Afghanistan.

During 1999, the Saudi minister of defense led a Saudi team in visiting the Pakistani uranium enrichment and missile complex at Kahuta. A. Q. Khan followed up with a return visit to Saudi Arabia that same year. Other exchanges, at lower levels, followed.

---

17. Purchased in July 1985; discovered in April–May 1988. Source: Jim Mann, "Threat to Mideast Military Balance; U.S. Caught Napping by Sino-Saudi Missile Deal," *Los Angeles Times* (May 4, 1988).

That year was also one of transition within Pakistan. General Musharraf seized power from Prime Minister Nawaz Sharif, but instead of execution (the prior fate of Pakistan's deleted civilian leaders), Sharif was exiled to Saudi Arabia—a deal negotiated ahead of time between Islamabad and Riyadh. Sharif remained there for eight years, until the autumn of 2007, when he was allowed to return to Pakistan (along with Benazir Bhutto, returning from Dubai) to participate in the parliamentary elections scheduled for the end of that year. In 2003, Pakistan's President Musharraf visited Saudi Arabia, with multiple follow-up visits by his prime minister. The hospitality was reciprocated later that year when Saudi Arabia's de facto ruler, Crown Prince Abdullah, visited Pakistan. Israeli intelligence claims the topic of discussion was Pakistani warheads, tested in 1998, for placement atop the Saudi's CSS-2 missiles. The Saudis strongly deny that allegation.

In recent years, a major expansion of the Pakistan AEC's classified technical facility at PINSTECH has been noted. It is a major undertaking for a Third World country. Who is financing that construction? Saudi Arabia and/or China are the likely suspects.

After 9/11, Americans noted that fifteen of the nineteen airborne suicide bombers attacking the United States were Saudis. Columnists pointed out the corrosive influence of Saudi lobbying within Washington. American support for the Saudi royal family has weakened, and American determination to deal forcefully with a nuclear Iran may be waning. Politics usually drive the acquisition of nuclear weapons, and thus the Saudis may soon decide to go nuclear on their own. Doing so via the procurement route would obviate the need for the American nuclear umbrella, and it would establish Saudi Arabia's primacy in the Sunni Muslim world. The purchase of enough A-bombs to arm Saudi Arabia's entire CSS-2 missile force might cost only a week's oil production.

## SYRIA

The Syrian Arab Republic has roots in antiquity. It is considered to be a "developing country" of twenty million inhabitants, but to most observers Syria is sliding backward as its oil reserves dwindle and people sink into poverty. Syria currently produces about 400,000 barrels of oil and over 20 million cubic feet of natural gas per day, but that oil production is barely enough to meet domestic demand. Most experts expect the nation to be a net importer within a few years.

Syria is another one-party Arab state, having been run by the Assad family and the Ba'ath party for thirty-eight years. Many members of Iraq's ruling Ba'athist hierarchy fled to Syria at the time of the American invasion in 2003, but there is little indication that any nuclear or other weapons technology traveled with them.

Thus the bewilderment associated with the September 6, 2007, Israeli raid on a mysterious facility in eastern Syria. Early that morning, a squadron of Israeli F-15 aircraft crossed the Syrian coast, flew 250 miles into Syria and completely destroyed a thirty thousand square foot industrial building located near the Euphrates River. Targeting was supported by Israeli special operations forces on the ground. There followed a deafening silence from both Israeli and Syrian governments as each side sought to avoid a further escalation.

Post-strike analyses by some experts, such as David Albright of the Institute for Science and International Security in Washington, D.C., suggest the targeted building contained a partially completed nuclear reactor. The CIA subsequently endorsed that view, claiming the reactor to be of North Korean design, a replica of its Yongbyon facility. If so, that reactor could only have been intended for the production of plutonium; there is no power-generation equipment in evidence. Other analysts have suggested that the mystery building was a warehouse for nuclear materials, for use by Syria, en route to Iran or held in safekeeping for the North Koreans, who are under pressure to dismantle their own nuclear facilities. The Syrian government claims only "a military facility in the process of being built," but it went to great lengths, immediately after the attack, to destroy what was left of the building, to remove any remaining equipment, to bulldoze the site and to bury the rubble. Amidst the conflicting stories, however, one fact is quite clear: North Korean officials and/or scientists were at the site and were involved.

The true story from Dayr az Zawr province will emerge as IAEA inspectors are admitted and Western journalists do their work. But whatever the details, the fact remains that Syria has become one more strand in the nuclear web now spanning the Muslim, petrodollar-empowered Middle East.

## IRAN

The Islamic Republic of Iran, a nation once known as Persia, now hosts a serious nuclear weapon program; there can be no doubt about that. Covert and ominous efforts to enrich uranium continue in a nation that flares its surplus natural gas while pleading an impending energy shortage as a justification for that uranium work. In 2005, the American intelligence community promulgated a finding that "Iran is determined to develop nuclear weapons." In December 2007, the American intelligence community hedged its bets, producing a new national intelligence estimate that found Iran's "nuclear weapons program" halted in the autumn of 2003 in response to "international pressure" while its efforts to enrich uranium have continued apace.

What might those international pressures have been? Most observers include in their lists the rapid destruction of the Taliban regime in Afghanistan in 2001 and the American invasion of Iraq in 2003. The latter, undertaken in an ill-advised hunt

291

for weapons of mass destruction, nonetheless made clear to Third World zealots that the Americans would take harsh steps to stop the spread of nuclear weapons. Libya's Qaddafi so noted and folded his nuclear tent in December 2003. The ensuing collapse and exposure of the A. Q. Khan network must have given the Iranian government further pause. The design of a nuclear weapon is easy to start and stop. It is the enrichment of uranium and the reactor-breeding of plutonium that makes a nuclear weapon state. That work goes forward, in secret and without pause, within Iran.

The foundations for Iran's nuclear capabilities were laid in the days of the shah in the usual way, with the training of students, the search for uranium, and the planning for nuclear power. But during those years Iran was a well-behaved nuclear state. The shah appreciated the need for controls on the proliferation of nuclear weapons; Iran was one of the opening signatories to the Nuclear Nonproliferation Treaty.[18]

After the revolution of 1979, the newly empowered mullahs were at first distracted from nuclear matters, but the outbreak of war with Iraq[19] refocused their attention on the need for equalizing instruments of power. Escalating prices for oil provided the cash; the exodus of talent from the failing Soviet Union would provide the technology. A decade later, when the war with Iraq was brought to a close, the Soviet empire folded, the Iranian coffers were filled, and the Revolutionary Guard had consolidated power, Iran embarked on a serious but covert campaign to develop a nuclear capability of its own.

The revolutionary fundamentalists in Tehran noted well the lessons of Osirak: When developing nuclear weapons, keep a low profile. Spread the facilities out and bury them; otherwise, someone will come blow them up. They also took note of Chamberlain's Law: When faced with difficult decisions, democracies will dither if they possibly can. For twenty years, Iran operated just inside the strictures of the Nuclear Nonproliferation Treaty: claiming nuclear power generation as its only objective, quoting its "inalienable right" to do so under Article IV of the NPT, and disclosing new (and illegal) activities only when caught. It was with the coming of the new century and the inescapable evidence of weapons intent that Iranian engineers and politicians began to stonewall inspectors, break seals, and issue threats. Since then, the development of a nuclear weapon infrastructure has proceeded apace.

## IRAN'S NUCLEAR FACILITIES

An overview of Iran's nuclear complex should start with its uranium mines near Yazd and Bandar Abbas, should include the factories processing yellowcake into uranium

---

18. Iran subscribed on the day the treaty was first opened for signature, July 1, 1968. The NPT went into effect in March 1970, when adequate ratifications were deposited with the UN.
19. In September 1980.

hexafluoride feedstock at the Esfahan Nuclear Technology Center, and should then focus on the centrifuge enrichment plant at Natanz, recently visited (amidst great publicity) by President Ahmadinejad and his national security advisors.

Other uranium-enrichment research, based on laser isotope separation, was undertaken at the Tehran Nuclear Technology Center, without IAEA knowledge. A larger, also secret, laser enrichment facility had been built at Lashkar Ab'ad.

Nuclear reactor construction has been concentrated at Bushehr. Original light water reactors were designed by the Seimens firm of Germany, but the work was taken over by the Russians after the Iran-Iraq War.

A heavy water reactor, more suitable for plutonium production, is under development at Arak. So is a heavy water production facility. Iranian engineers also appear to be planning a deep underground facility appropriate for a nuclear test.

The Iranian nuclear program is funded at a billion-dollar annual level,[20] with its existence confirmed by its suppliers.[21] They constitute the usual suspects.

## WHO ARE IRAN'S SUPPLIERS?

Pakistan's A. Q. Khan first began to transfer uranium-enrichment technology to Iran in 1987. A-bomb design and fabrication plans soon followed. These transactions have been confirmed by Khan's chief logistician, B. S. A. Tahir, from his jail cell in Malaysia. The Russian Federation also provided help large and small: two nuclear reactor frames now sit in Bushehr, awaiting completion by Russian engineers. Fuel rods for these reactors are to come from, and will be reprocessed back into, Russia, a nation that has pledged a ten-year supply of nuclear fuel in an effort to slow the Iranian enrichment program. The Russians also supplied lesser technology, claimed to be legal and above-board but accompanied by refugees from the disintegrating Soviet nuclear empire. Other former Soviet republics are involved as well. The borders between Iran and the Stans are leaky havens to smugglers and black marketeers. France has continued in its role as a supplier of nuclear technology to all comers within the Middle East. Other European industrial states and trading outposts have played their part.

Then there is the Chinese connection, especially worrisome since that nation appears most willing to subordinate ideology, human rights, or most any other political consideration to its commercial interests. A reliable and expandable supply of energy is at the top of China's shopping list. As of now, China imports 14 percent of its crude oil from Iran, but contracts for future purchases include $20 billion

20. Thus consuming about 2 percent of Iran's annual oil revenues.
21. Natalie Nougayrede, "Senior Pakistani Official Says Iran's Nuclear Program is Military," *Le Monde* (May 6, 2007).

dollars worth of liquefied natural gas and a hundred billion dollar joint development of Iran's Yadavaran oil field near the Iraqi border. To balance that trade, China now sells vast quantities of sophisticated arms to Iran and provides significant advice on missile and nuclear technology to that rapidly arming state.

During the 1990s, Iran bought uranium hexafluoride feedstock from European, Chinese, and other suppliers. While the stated use was enrichment to reactor grade (3 percent U-235), there seems to be more to this activity than meets the eye. Environmental samples acquired by the IAEA found traces of highly enriched (weapons grade) uranium within Iran, although the provenance of that material may run to Pakistan, arriving in-country aboard used P-1 machines.

The very large, underground, and once-secret uranium-enrichment facility near Natanz is to accommodate fifty thousand centrifuge machines, running around the clock. This centrifuge hall appears to be built underneath layers of burster slabs: strata of concrete interleaved with soil to defeat penetrating warhead attacks. These bunkers appear to have been designed and built by European contractors.

The list goes on, but the details are less important than the overall message: The Islamic fundamentalists in control of Iran have embarked on a massive but ambiguous nuclear program. It is focused on the development of a nuclear weapon capability, if not the assembly of a weapon itself, within the near future. In its 2007 report on this subject, *Newsweek* magazine condensed the story into four very accurate words: "Twenty Years of Deceit."

## WHO IS RUNNING THIS SHOW?

The government of Iran is complex; at the core it is an Islamic dictatorship. There is a parliament, the Majles, whose members serve four-year terms, but the Council of Guardians must preapprove those candidates. There is a president, also elected to a four-year term, but the Council of Guardians must preapprove his candidacy as well. This council of a dozen men (six clerics and six jurists) are, in turn, appointed by the supreme leader. There have only been two supreme leaders within Iran since 1979: Ayatollah Ruhollah Khomeini and, after his death in June 1989, Ayatollah Ali Khamenei. In essence, the supreme leader calls the shots. Defense, intelligence, and all the other security portfolios are in his hands.

At the time of the 1979 revolution, to achieve and maintain this control, Ayatollah Khomeini created his own security force; it is now known as the Revolutionary Guard. At first that organization's duties were to kill off the shah's men, provide personal security to the leaders of the revolution, and enforce the Islamic codes. (The residue of the shah's army was to defend Iran's territorial integrity.) Iran's Revolutionary Guard bears a striking similarity to the security services of other dictators: Hitler's SS and Stalin's KGB.

Power corrupts, of course. With daily oil revenues of over a hundred million dollars, those controlling Iran, the ayatollahs, have become enormously wealthy. Ayatollah Rasfanjani, the immediate past president of Iran, is alleged to be a billionaire. This wealth is protected and managed by the Revolutionary Guard, which now runs a vast contracting organization known as the Ghorb: the inevitable "winners" of contracts to build state infrastructure.

Over the years, the Revolutionary Guard has expanded its territory. As the "protector of Islam," the Guard now supports terrorist networks throughout the Middle East. As "protector of the revolution," the Guard has organized a volunteer militia, the Basij, to intimidate voters, stuff ballot boxes, and provide cannon fodder when needed for suicide missions. And as the supreme leader's personal instrument of power, the Revolutionary Guard has taken control of the nuclear weapons program of the Islamic Republic of Iran.

## IS THE ECONOMY STABLE?

Iran is awash with oil, but it is also essentially bankrupt. Capital flees the country at every opportunity. Thousands of businesses operate with their offices and bank accounts in Dubai, safely out of the Iranian government's reach. Oil production is stagnant at about two-thirds of the 1974–1976 rate, although price rises have helped mask this effect.[22]

There has been essentially no investment in the domestic oil and gas industry for the past twenty-five years. For one reason, the mullahs have diverted all available cash into a vast and inefficient welfare state. No funds are left for drilling, reservoir development, or refinery repair.[23] Secondly, no sensible Western or Japanese oil firm would try to do business within that erratic land. As a result, little domestic refining capacity remains online. Oil is exported, and gasoline is re-imported, with the government subsidizing its retail sale at twenty to forty cents per gallon. That subsidy alone consumes 17 percent of the Iranian gross domestic product. Such artificially low prices have boosted gasoline demand at a 6 percent annual rate, the highest gasoline consumption growth rate in the world. With the passage of time and the disintegration of the infrastructure, however, such cheap gasoline no longer gets to the consumers within Iran. Smugglers buy it up for clandestine re-export and sale within neighboring countries Turkey, Iraq, and Pakistan at market prices. The

22. Crude oil prices have more than doubled, in inflation-adjusted terms, since the shah's last days in office.
23. Leakage within refineries now consumes 6 percent of total production, according to *Iran Daily* (www.iranmilitary.net/forum/showthread.php?=6469).

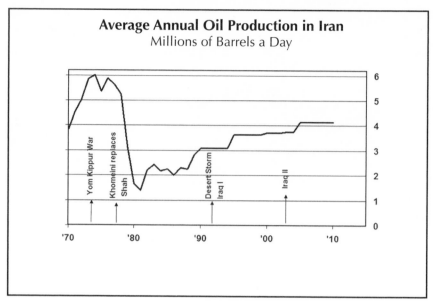

Source: *U.S. Department of Energy*

resulting shortages of gasoline in-country have led to rationing and the fire-bombing of Iranian gas stations by irate drivers. Experts say Iran now needs an injection of about $40 billion to get its oil and gas industry modernized.

Forty percent of the Iranian people live in poverty; inflation runs at about 20 percent per annum; the government admits to 15 percent unemployment, although those who know better say, "double that." It is a country of young people: median age twenty-six, and two-thirds of the population under age thirty. The universities are cranking out female graduates[24] for whom there are absolutely no career opportunities. Many believe these youngsters would vote out their president, Mr. Ahmadinejad, in a flash—if they could. Unfortunately, they cannot. In the run-up to the March 14, 2008, parliamentary elections, the Supreme Leader's Guardian Council barred 1,700 "unacceptable" candidates from the ballot. The survivors of that cut, all totally subservient to the Supreme Leader, won three quarters of the contested seats. The elections of March 2008 only served to confirm and extend the hegemony of Ayatollah Ali Khamenei.

## WHO IS THIS MAN AHMADINEJAD?

Mahmoud Ahmadinejad was elected to the Iranian presidency in 2004 on a platform of economic reform, to "get the country moving again." It was only when he gained power

24. Sixty percent of the classes of 2007.

that he adopted his current and very strident anti-Israeli rhetoric. Perhaps he is doing so to distract the street from the reality of his incompetence. His statement that "the State of Israel should be wiped off the face of the map"[25] is strange, coming as it did from the leader of a nation that has no historical animosity to Israel. Iran is Persian/Azeri, not Arab, and until the fall of the shah, was an ally of Israel, a nation that was most helpful with Iran's early nuclear studies. Perhaps Mr. Ahmadinejad and his Islamic overlords do not represent the thinking of most Iranians. After our discussions with those who live there, those with family or business connections within Iran, or those working in the oil industry, that seems to be a reasonable conclusion. Mr. Ahmadinejad is but a product of the Revolutionary Guard; he is as unbalanced as the rest of the mullahs.

Consider the matter of the plastic keys. The story starts in January 1979, when the shah fled Iran. Within a month, the newly formed Revolutionary Guards had executed the shah's generals, vested power in Ayatollah Khomeini, and otherwise gutted the leadership of a previously strong regional power. Saddam Hussein, in neighboring Iraq, saw an opportunity. He wanted to reclaim rights to the Shatt al Arab waterway, part of the Iran-Iraq border and a key route for the export of petroleum. The shah had forced Iraq to relinquish those rights in 1975.[26] Saddam invaded Iran in September 1980, and for a while things went well. At first, the leaderless Iranian military forces were hopelessly ineffective.

Ayatollah Khomeini then hit upon several theologically correct solutions. One was the creation of the Basij Mostazafan, the "mobilization of the oppressed." These were to be volunteers who would embrace death with religious enthusiasm— forerunners of Hezbollah. The Basiji were to become an arm of the Revolutionary Guard. Mahmoud Ahmadinejad was an early Basij. To this day, he occasionally reappears in his Basij uniform.

In the early 1980s, as the battle lines stabilized, and as the Iranian military got organized, Saddam turned to minefields and chemical weapons to maintain his positions in the face of serious Iranian assaults. To breach the Iraqi lines, the ayatollahs in Iran called on the Basiji for "volunteers," men to march across the minefields. Those responding were the children of Iran, boys from the countryside.

"The purest joy in Islam is to kill and be killed for Allah," Khomeini assured the children. To validate this guidance, the Iranian government purchased half a million small plastic keys from Taiwan. Before each march across the Iraqi minefields, one of the Taiwanese keys would be hung around each child's neck, assuring him of immediate passage to paradise.

25. October 26, 2005.
26. In exchange for calling off Kurdish insurrections in northern Iraq.

Iraqi officers were appalled; barely armed teenagers were marching toward them in straight rows. When one boy was blown apart, the child in back would step over his comrade's remains to continue the advance. If was like the Russians at Stalingrad. "It makes you want to scream, to throw away your weapon," one Iraqi defender cried.

As the *Economist* put it in a September 1983 article, "Iranian boys of twelve, wearing keys to heaven around their necks, are among the most rapidly consumed cannon-fodder in the corpse-hungry Iran-Iraq war . . . Nine out of ten get killed as they march before their elders into the Iraqi minefields."

A half-million Basiji were sent to the front lines. Perhaps only half came home, but Mahmoud Ahmadinejad was one of them. The Iran-Iraq war lasted for eight years, took a million casualties, and settled nothing, but it clarified the role of Allah in the mind of that young survivor, Mahmoud Ahmadinejad.

## WHAT DO THE AYATOLLAHS WANT?

The question two decades later, as a government headed by a Basij veteran now pursues nuclear weapons: Would the ayatollahs, men most willing to use other's children for mine clearing, be deterred by the threat of nuclear retaliation from Israel? The younger citizens of Iran would be horrified at the prospect of a nuclear war, but their opinions do not count. In the mullahs' eyes, the detonation of a few nukes on Iranian soil might be an acceptable price to pay for ridding the Muslim world of the Israeli settlers. In the words of Mr. Ahmadinejad's predecessor,[27] "One nuclear bomb inside Israel will destroy everything, [but] it will only harm the Islamic world. It is not irrational to contemplate such an eventuality."

As with the Soviet leaders from another age, the ayatollahs have probably made arrangements to sit out any nuclear exchange within a safe haven: perhaps on the beaches of the Caspian Sea or within Shiite-friendly Azerbaijan. The ayatollahs may well take actions that will lead to an Israeli nuclear response, but they will also leave it to their countrymen to achieve the "pure joy of Islam, being killed for Allah."

Mr. Ahmadinejad needs confrontation with the United States if he is to keep his hold on power, and he may even believe in nuclear use to eradicate Israel, but the mullahs now have a different agenda; they may be having second thoughts. The mullahs are religious fanatics, but they are also highly corrupt and substantially wealthy politicians, concerned that Mr. Ahmadinejad may be endangering *their* rice bowl. Ideology and religion have become intermixed with property rights in the mullahs' eyes.

Those who know Iran best advise us to look at Iran in 2008 as we looked at the Soviet Union a generation ago. It is a broken country, tightly controlled by a

27. President Hashemi Rafsanjani, December 14, 2001, BBC Monitoring Service.

doctrinaire and dangerous nomenklatura, a military machine floating on a river of oil. Perhaps Ahmadinejad is the Khrushchev of Iran: too unstable for the nomenklatura's tastes. Or perhaps Iran is another China, centrally controlled and exceedingly dangerous. Whatever it is, Iran is *not* a mob of American-hating fanatics. Those who appear in the streets of Tehran are but rent-a-crowds: old-timers, bussed in from the impoverished side of town for stage-managed prayer events. The youngsters are busy shopping and awaiting their next shot at the ballot box, in June 2009.

## WHAT SHOULD WE DO ABOUT
## THE COMING CONFRONTATION?

The Iranian nuclear program is deliberately opaque, but it is also real and clearly focused on the long pole in the tent: the illicit production of nuclear materials. Politicians in the West have turned blind eyes to this fact for thirty years. A half-dozen American presidents have ignored or aggravated the hazards emerging within Iran. European governments have extended, into this new century, the same policy of dithering that empowered the Third Reich. It is now quite late in the game. A U.S. attack on the Iranian nuclear facilities would only solidify the Iranian people behind their erratic president; the Muslim world would unite behind the mullahs in Tehran. Nuclear weapons are as much political symbols as they are military assets. The Iranian people support the idea of going nuclear; it is just that they do not want to see them used.

Unfortunately, there is the dark possibility that Israel may take Mr. Ahmadinejad at his word. Israel's leaders may conclude that the eradication of Israel is truly Iranian state policy. The Israelis may then wish to deal with the Iranian nuclear complex as they did with Saddam's Osirak or with Assad's mystery building on the Euphrates, but that will be hard to do. The flight distances from Tel Aviv to Tehran are more than twice those of Tel Aviv to Baghdad. The Osirak attack in 1981 strained the capability of the Israeli Air Force. An Israeli air attack on Natanz, Tehran, Esfahan, Bushehr, and Arak would require the full cooperation of the United States, and thus a full opportunity to share the blame. Making matters worse, the Iranian nuclear facilities are dug in, their air defenses are far better than those guarding Osirak a generation ago, and we do not really know where they all are.

If survival is thought to be at stake, Israel might make one-way attacks with nuclear-armed aircraft, or it might resort to use of its nuclear-armed Jericho III ballistic missiles with a range well over the one thousand miles needed to attack the nuclear facilities in Iran. Under such circumstances the fat would surely be in the fire. The United States should not get caught up in such activity. Although Mr. Ahmadinejad needs confrontation, he will not be around forever.

Instead, we might reflect on how we defeated the Soviet Union, another evil empire run by a similarly corrupt, nuclear-armed nomenklatura, during the last century. It was accomplished by policies of containment, articulated by George Kennan during the 1940s; by the threat of massive retaliation set forth by Dwight Eisenhower during the 1950s; and by determined pressure applied by the leaders of the Anglo alliance during the 1980s. To paraphrase Mr. Kennan, the dictatorship "holds inside itself the seeds of its own decay"—in this case, the Iranian youngsters.

The West should keep the pressure on. It should impose sanctions, via the UN, as long as Iran's nuclear program operates outside the IAEA. It should stay in touch with Iran's government, as we did with the Soviet leaders during the darkest hours of the Cold War. It should threaten massive retaliation—the incineration of Iran—if any Iranian nuclear weapon is used beyond its borders, but the West should also refrain from acts of war. It should leave the mullahs alone. They are doing a great job of destroying their own economy. Let them continue until the job is done, until the younger generation rises up to say, "Enough!"

## THE CRADLE—AND GRAVEYARD—OF CIVILIZATION?

The cradles of civilization once swung on the Carthage-Tehran axis, but three millennia later, those cities, and many in between, now host different embryos: the dragon's eggs of nuclear disaster. One such shell, in Baghdad, was crushed by repeated Israeli and then U.S. attacks; there can be no doubt about the consequences had we failed to do so.

Cairo represents another fertile nuclear site, with educated people, a reasonable industrial base, and a cultural/colonial heritage conducive to sound scientific work. Israel is the irritating grain of sand within the Egyptian oyster's shell. It would take only the addition of money, like fresh seawater, to produce the nuclear pearl.

Within Algeria and Syria, one reactor does not a weapon state make, but the secrecy surrounding the construction at Ain Oussera or along the Euphrates should give the West pause. Those facilities are prima facie evidence of Chinese and North Korean duplicity when it comes to matters of nuclear proliferation within the Third World.

Saudi Arabia has the money, but not the infrastructure; so what? A half-*billion* dollars of *daily* oil revenue can buy whatever the Saud family wants. Their nuclear tastes may be restrained at the moment, but if that clan is overthrown, replaced by a radical Muslim regime, or if the threat of Shiite encroachment becomes too severe, Saudi Arabia—and thus the Middle East—may become a very different place.

At the northeast end of the axis lies Tehran, home to an educated population, a sound industrial base, and billions of annual oil revenues. Countless layers of technological strata have been laid down on fertile ground by external proliferators. Iran may one day conduct a test of the resulting nuclear product.

None of these eastern states have subscribed to the Additional Protocol of the Nonproliferation Treaty. By declining such participation, all have admitted to nuclear ambitions. One or more of these dragons' eggs are sure to hatch during the administration of the next American president.

# GEORGES-ANTOINE KURTZ IS ALIVE AND WELL

A hundred years ago it was ivory; today it is uranium. Besides that, not much has changed. For much of the twentieth century, uranium was mined in the heart of Joseph Conrad's Belgian Congo, a byproduct of the search for radium, an associated heavy metal that is inherently unstable—that is, radioactive. Radium was discovered by Marie Curie at the beginning of the twentieth century. Its dangers were poorly understood, but its uses were quite unique. When blended with phosphorus, the resulting mixture becomes a luminous paint, glowing in the dark—useful for watch dials, aircraft instruments, and, in time, other tools of war.

With the discovery of nuclear fission in 1938, scientists took a renewed interest in radium's companion element, uranium. Scientists had discovered that metal a century before. It appears near the end of the periodic table, the last of the stable elements, but it remained a scientific curiosity until Hahn and Meitner discovered its tendency to fission. Then, within a year, as the possibilities of nuclear weapons began to dawn on the governments and scientists preparing for World War II, the demand for uranium exploded.

Economically exploitable uranium ores typically contain 0.1 to 1.0 percent uranium; very rich ores contain as much as 15 percent. Extraction and milling are required to produce the bomb-needed metal. During the interwar years, at the time of the Hahn-Meitner discoveries, almost all the world's uranium came from the Union Minière du Haut Katanga.[1] Those ores, known as pitchblende or uraninite, contain uranium in the form of an oxide ($U_3O_8$) which, when separated from everything else, is known as yellowcake: the material that made its way from Katanga to Belgium and

---

1. Within what was then the Belgian Congo, a state that became independent as the Republic of the Congo in 1960, changed its name to become Zaire in 1971, and was then renamed again in 1997, to become the Democratic Republic of the Congo.

thence to the laboratories in Berlin, Paris, and England. Frédéric Joliot-Curie had the foresight to acquire a large supply of yellowcake in 1939 and 1940. He shipped it on to Britain, thence to Canada, as the German army closed in.

With the advent of a serious nuclear weapon program in the wartime United States, the American government sought to acquire uranium tailings from radium and vanadium mines in North America, but the primary source of uranium for America's war machine—the uranium for Fermi's first experimental nuclear reactor, the plutonium-producing machines at Hanford, and the Little Boy weapon—all came from the Shinkolobwe Mine in the Belgian Congo. It was only after the war that mines in Canada, the American Rockies, South Africa, and Australia began to feed the Western appetite for reactor and weapons fuel. At the same time, the Soviets initiated production from the Ore Mountains of East Germany and, in time, from mines within the Soviet Union itself.

The Nuclear Nonproliferation Treaty included uranium mining within its surveillance regime, although without enforcement powers. By the end of the Cold War, Canada, Australia, the former Soviet Union, various states in Africa, and the United States were the world's principal uranium suppliers. Most production is well documented; Australia has strict ultimate-use policies (ernergy, not weapons). As a result, most proliferators seeking to circumvent NPT controls must find their own indigenous uranium supplies (as North Korea has done), trade technology for metal (as Israel has done), or look to the back streets of Africa for suppliers.

## THE URANIUM MINES OF CENTRAL AFRICA

Niger, an African desert republic of thirteen million people, is the world's third-largest producer of yellowcake uranium ore. It is also the world's poorest country, ranking at the very bottom of the UN's human development index. A smuggler's paradise? The president of the United States thought so. In January 2003, he warned of Iraqi nuclear intent based on a suspicion of yellowcake transfer from Niger to Iraq. Unfortunately, the facts were otherwise.[2]

Niger is a former French colony, claimed by Paris in 1922 and declared independent in 1960. It lies astride the Sahara Desert and is 85 percent sand. Only a small southwest extension of arable land astride the Niger River is suitable for the raising of subsistence crops and livestock.

During the closing colonial years, in 1957, geologists from the French Overseas Mining Bureau noted signs of uranium in the northwestern Niger desert. That discovery was of interest to the French government, given its postwar policy commitment to

2. Peter Eisner and Knut Royce, *The Italian Lettery* (Emmaus, PA: Rodale Books, 2007).

nuclear power.[3] An assured supply of uranium to fuel coming reactors was important to the French Atomic Energy Commission. Two years later, the French identified commercially exploitable deposits. Following Niger's independence, the French nuclear fuels agency, COGEMA,[4] organized two uranium-mining companies[5] within that country. Those firms contracted with the Niger government for the development of mines, mills, power-generating stations, and all the other supporting infrastructure needed to exploit these low-grade (0.3–0.5 percent) uranium ores. An important part of that infrastructure was six hundred miles of paved highway, from the mines to the Benin border, allowing connections to ports on the Atlantic coast. The French government, through COGEMA, controls these operations with an iron, though benign, hand. After the American president's statement about an alleged uranium sale from Niger to Iraq, speakers at a World Nuclear Association symposium noted that Niger was "enjoying more than thirty years of safe, efficient, and smooth operations, [providing] a stable supply of uranium, particularly to the European Union." Smuggling uranium yellowcake from the mines in Niger would be an accounting challenge, a logistical impossibility. The French would not tolerate such an inventory disparity; dozens of trucks, loaded with yellowcake, could not traverse the highway to the coast unnoticed.

Untroubled by these facts, in the autumn of 2002, an Italian hustler created a letter and a number of supporting documents, allegedly from President Tandja of Niger to Saddam Hussein. The letter, dated July 27, 2000, purportedly confirmed the sale of five hundred tons (dozens of truckloads) of yellowcake ore to Iraq. In October 2002, an intermediary attempted to sell a copy of this document to an American reporter in Rome. Good journalism soon illuminated the falsity of these papers. (The CIA had been investigating possible Niger-Iraqi links since 9/11, but parts of that bureaucracy had been taken in by the Niger-Iraq scam.) The letters were riddled with misspellings and erroneous names, all clearly evident from the first web search. Further on-site investigations within Niamey[6] confirmed the bogus nature of the July 2000 letter. In early 2003, the director general of the IAEA so advised the UN Security Council. Unfortunately, that is not what the American administration

---

3. Of the electrical power generated within France, 78 percent now originates within nuclear reactors.
4. Compagnie Generale des Matieres Nucleaires, 75 percent owned by the French CEA.
5. The first was the Société des Mines de l'Aïr (SOMAIR), a surface-mining company, established in 1965, with 63.4 percent ownership held by COGEMA and its affiliates, and 36.6 percent by the Niger government. The second, Compagnie Minière d'Akouta (COMINAK), is an underground mining venture, established in 1974, with ownership held by COGEMA, et al. (34 percent); the Niger government (31 percent); and other Japanese and Spanish uranium purchasing entities, 25 percent and 10 percent, respectively.
6. The capital of Niger.

wanted to hear. On January 29, 2003, the president of the United States publicly stated that "The British government has learned that Saddam Hussein recently sought significant quantities of uranium from Africa." That may have been true, but the U.S. government had no such information.

Aside from the tragedy of what followed in Iraq, that statement has led many to discount stories of uranium smuggling within Africa. Nothing could be further from the truth; only the country was wrong. Niger is a poor state, with its uranium supplies tightly controlled, at least until they get to France. It is within other countries, south of the Sahara, where those wishing to build illicit nuclear weapons prowl the streets.

The Katanga mines in what is now known as the Democratic Republic of the Congo (DR Congo) remain the prime proliferation suspect. That nation, once known as Zaire, achieved independence from Belgium in 1960, suffered a three-decade-long dictatorship, and then sank into another decade of civil war. Millions of innocent civilians were killed. As a result of that history, the DR Congo has conflicting constitutions and no effective government. Those nominally in charge, from border guards to ministers, are easily bought off. Minerals illicitly mined find their way to South Africa or Europe via freelance air transport. Some make it all the way to Kazakhstan aboard aging Kazakh and Ukrainian aircraft. Those aircraft return with the arms needed to maintain the miners' writ. In 2004, the DR Congo's mining minister asked for international help in keeping the once-condemned Shinkolobwe uranium mine closed. During that same year, the BBC reported[7] six thousand illegal miners still at work, producing copper and cobalt ores from those highly radioactive mines for delivery to irregular Lebanese, Chinese, and Indian smelters. In August 2005, London's *Sunday Times* alleged that a significant shipment of coltan (the colloquial African name for columbium-tantalum ore, a coveted metal used in the production of consumer electronics such as cell phones, DVD players, and computers) and uranium ores had been made from mines near Lubumbashi to the Islamic Republic of Iran. In March 2007, the head of the DR Congo's Atomic Energy Commission was arrested on suspicion of "orchestrating illicit contracts to produce and sell uranium."[8]

The heart of the Katanga mining industry is Kolwezi, a hundred miles west of Shinkolobwe. The premier mine is the Musonoi, producing copper and cobalt ores with assays of 1.5 percent and 0.32 percent, respectively.[9] The uranium found

7. On March 25, 2004.
8. The issues involved in Professor Fortunat Lumu's arrest were economic, not proliferation. He enjoyed too many comforts of life after signing an agreement, on behalf of the DR Congo government, with Brinkley Mining, a London-based uranium exploration company.
9. According to the statements of the mining companies involved.

within the associated pitchblende ore has a much higher assay, but the mining companies deny any production. They do admit their ores are "hot," and they confirm diversion and sequestering of uranium from the mining operations "for health reasons." Where does it go?

Or consider the Rössing mine, located in the heart of the Namibian desert. Rössing, "one of the most controversial single mining projects anywhere on the globe," is the world's largest open-pit uranium mine. It was conceived in 1976, during the years of South African colonial control of what was then Southwest Africa, a key piece on John Vorster's nuclear chessboard. The Rio Tinto Group, a British firm, manages the mine, and appears to own a controlling interest, but the minority ownership is vague, and its customer lists are opaque. A 10 percent ownership appears to run to the Namibian government, another 10 percent to the French energy firm Total, 5 percent to Germany's Urangessellschaft, with another 5 percent sprinkled among various South African interests, but the most interesting part-owner of the Rössing mine is the government of Iran.

The shah's government took a 15 percent interest in Rössing at the time of its start-up, in 1976. During the late 1970s, substantial shipments of yellowcake went to Iran. Upon seizing control, the ayatollahs suspended the shah's nuclear power program, but, from current appearances, they did not end it. The present government of Iran denies receiving any uranium from Rössing, but accuracy is not an Iranian stock in diplomatic trade. Namibian mine managers refuse to divulge customer lists; the nation's minister of mines furnishes few reports. In the newly independent nations south of the Sahara, "controls" seem to be negotiable. Based on third-party reports, Rössing's other customers include Japan (although shipments to that nuclear-knowledgeable state went undocumented for years), Taiwan, and—since 2004—the People's Republic of China.

A third interesting source of African uranium lies within Zambia, a landlocked nation of enormous mineral wealth. Zambia was once known as the British colony of Northern Rhodesia. Its mining center at Kitwe is home to the Mopani mine, one of Africa's most prolific copper and cobalt producers. Ores within the central African copper belt usually run 2 to 3 percent copper and perhaps 0.2 to 0.3 percent cobalt. The latter is an important alloying element in the steel, aerospace, and nuclear industries. Cobalt prices have doubled in the past year to more than $30 per pound, but one interesting aspect of the African copper-belt mining industry is seldom discussed. Those copper-cobalt ores are also rich in uranium.

When Zambia achieved independence from Great Britain in 1964, it was the third-largest copper producer in the world. It was an island of prosperity in Africa, but three decades of political turbulence, mine takeovers by the state, one-party rule, and slumping copper prices dropped copper production by a factor of three. It also dropped Zambia into poverty.

With the end of the Cold War, socialism became passé, and privatization was in. As the oligarchs swept through Russia, Chinese interests[10] began buying up the defunct Zambian copper-belt mines. Cultural conflict ensued as the Chinese population within Zambia soared. China's President Hu Jintao visited Zambia in 2007, in an attempt to smooth over these relations and to celebrate the reelection of a China-friendly incumbent president. But the Dow-Jones Newswires more accurately captured the spirit of twenty-first-century Africa: "The privatization of Zambia's copper industry has left the fate of [its] miners in the hands of highly dubious Chinese, Swiss, and U.K.-registered companies [along with their] negligent contractors."

## THE CHINESE LEND A "HELPING HAND"

The mining districts of northern Zambia and southern DR Congo lie well within the African interior, seriously isolated from the trade routes of the world. The DR Congo has only one port; Kinshasa and its delta communities lie 1,200 miles to the northwest of Kolwezi, at the mouth of the Congo River. Zambia is landlocked. To get copper-belt ores to market during the 1960s required the use of rail lines transiting the then-apartheid states of Rhodesia and South Africa.

As Third World solidarity became fashionable during those years, and as the Peoples' Republic of China entered the nuclear club,[11] Chinese planners took note of this geopolitical opportunity. They offered to finance the construction of a new railway, from copper belt to the sea, through more politically correct territory. It was to run northeast from central Zambia, through the Muchinga Mountains, across the African Rift, and over the Tanzanian countryside to the port of Dar Es Salaam on the Indian Ocean.

In the late 1960s, the Tanzania-Zambia Railway Authority was created to execute this project. Work started in 1970. The Chinese shipped in everything needed to do the job, from nuts and bolts to track, construction machinery, food, and thousands of Chinese workers. More than sixty Chinese two-thousand-horsepower diesel hydraulic locomotives were brought in to ferry the crews, parts, and equipment to the construction sites, but those engines were a disaster. They were terribly underpowered for the eight-hour haul up a continuous 2-percent grade from the coast to Mbeya. Invariably, one engine ended the day by dragging another one home, trailing a half-empty string of railcars behind.

10. The China Non-Ferrous Metal Mining Company.
11. In 1964.

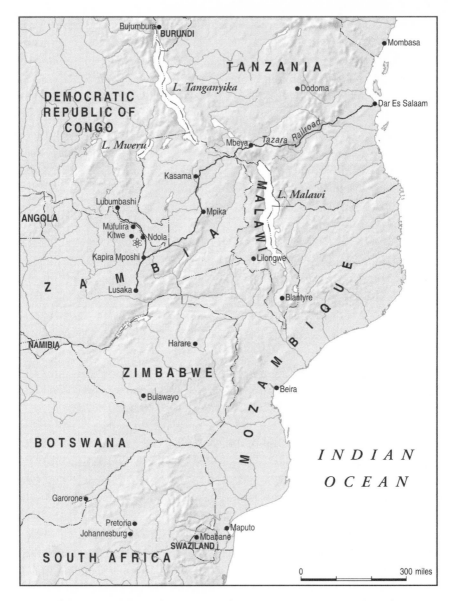

Route of the Tazara Railroad, from Dar Es Salaam, on the Indian Ocean, through
Tanzania, crossing the border into Zambia between lakes Malawi and Tanganyka,
proceeding southwest through Zambia to connect with the north-south rail system at
Kapiri Mposhi. *Meridian Mapping*

The railroad, known as the Tazara, commenced operation six years later. The project cost $500 million in 1976 dollars.[12] From the beginning, it was a political success, delivering ores from mines to the sea without transiting apartheid territory, but the Tazara was also an operational failure. Throughout the railroad industry it became known as a white elephant, never operating at more than 20 percent of capacity. In the early 1980s, the original, underpowered Chinese locomotives had to be replaced. Thirty General Electric three-thousand-horsepower, diesel electric locomotives, manufactured under license by Krupp in Germany, took their place.

Investing based on politics, not economic reality, is seldom wise. With the coming of the 1990s, the politics of southern Africa changed. Apartheid ended in both Rhodesia and South Africa. The old trade routes returned to life. Traffic on the Tazara Railroad, already an inefficient operation, dropped by another factor of two. The line is now bankrupt. Strangely enough, however, the Chinese have offered to step in, buy the company and continue its operations. Why should they do this: for the sake of Third World solidarity? Not likely; the Chinese seldom invest hundreds of millions on that basis. A more likely answer is to maintain access to the supplies of copper, cobalt, and other minerals that the Chinese need. They need access to their "Multi-Facility Economic Zone" in Chambishi (near Kitwe), to which the Chinese have committed nearly a billion dollars of new capital. But one must also ask if copper and cobalt are the only minerals of interest.

## MARLOW'S RETURN

A century ago, Joseph Conrad wrote about his first trip up the Congo River, in the 1890s, aboard a paddlewheel steamer. He fictionalized this odyssey as *Heart of Darkness*, the tale of British sailor Charles Marlow, who accepts a job as a ferryboat captain and proceeds up the Congo River through conditions of growing brutality, to rendezvous with the company's evil but most productive ivory hunter, Georges-Antoine Kurtz.

Let us imagine a rewrite of this story, placing it at the *end* of the twentieth century, with our protagonist riding the rails, rather than a steamer, as he pushes into the Heart of Darkness. His trip might be faster, but he would still find the native residents exploited, the ivory hunters at work, and the objective at the end of his travels malevolent.

Marlow II would depart the modern but hot, humid, and crowded Dar Es Salaam railway station at dawn. He, a mob of fellow passengers, and a long string of mostly empty freight cars would proceed across the coastal hills of Tanzania to enter the

12. Almost two billion in 2008 dollars.

Kilombero River valley at midday. By nightfall, after an arduous climb up the long grade to the top of the African Rift, Marlow II would make it to Mbeya, a regional capital, hidden in a narrow valley at an altitude of five thousand feet. The view out the window would look like Scotland. During the night, if the train were running functionally, Marlow II would pass the village of Tunduma, cross the African Rift, enter Zambia, and proceed on to Kasama by sunrise. Kasama is the capital of Zambia's Northern Province. It is a semi-industrial city of two hundred thousand souls, and a major crossroads, with waterfalls, a lake, and an apparent ocean of corrugated metal roofs. A few more hours of travel would bring the traveler to Mpika, past more waterfalls and into the Muchinga Mountains. By nightfall of the second day, Marlow II's journey on the Tazara would end at the cow town of Kapiri Mposhi, a dusty wide spot on the North-South "Highway." After a good night's sleep, Marlow II would board the Zambian Railway for the last leg of his trip into the copper belt.

The trip from Kapiri Mposhi to Kitwe should take a few hours. Marlow II's fellow passengers might include a number of Chinese engineers and a clutch of resentful Zambians—workers and their families returning to the Mopani mine. Along the way they might pass the graves of the forty-nine miners killed in the Chambishi mine explosion in 2005 or of the half-dozen others killed by police during the 2006 wage protests. Armed men seen outside the window would not be cause for immediate alarm; they would be the poachers, hunting rhinoceros and elephant into extinction in pursuit of the last ivory tusk. Marlow II would not see many old people; perhaps one or two. AIDS has ravaged the countryside; the average Zambian is only seventeen years old. He can look forward to a few years at the mine, earning $1 per day; an evening shower from the acidic rainfall originating with the smelters; and an occasional civil war as corrupt dictators struggle for control of Zambia's mineral wealth.

The Mopani ores assay at 2 percent copper and 0.5 percent cobalt. Uranium is never mentioned in the company reports, but experts estimate a 1 percent uranium content as well.[13] Where does it go? And who owns the Mopani mine? The Zambian government controls 10 percent; an investor in Vancouver, B.C., holds a 17 percent interest; but the majority, a 73 percent stake in the Mopani mine, is held by the Glencore Corporation, a multinational headquartered in Baar, Switzerland. Upon his arrival in Kitwe, Marlow II might head for the offices of the Mopani Mining Company on Central Street, but when inquiring as to the whereabouts of the Head Man he would get a very different answer from the one Marlow I received a century before.

13. *Rush and Ruin: The Devastating Mineral Trade in Southern Katanga, DRC,* Global Witness Publishing, September 2004, is an excellent guide to current mining activities in central Africa (www.globalwitness.org/media_library_detail.php/125/en/rush_and_ruin).

"Mistah Rich not here; he live in Switzerland."

The Glencore Corporation was once known as Marc Rich and Company, AG. The Marc Rich family appears to have been the sole owners of Glencore. They live in Zug, Switzerland. This is the same Marc Rich who received a notorious and well-funded pardon from President Clinton on that president's last morning in office. That pardon was issued without benefit of Justice Department review or comment by the responsible U.S. Attorney.[14]

Readers should not think for one moment that they understand life within the web of the African uranium dealer; neither do we.

14. Mr. Rich, a Belgian by birth, fled the United States and renounced his citizenship in 1983 at the time of his indictment for income tax evasion and illicit trading with Iran. He paid a $200 million tax settlement to the IRS. Both the prime minister of Israel and the head of Israel's Mossad formally supported Rich's clemency appeal, citing his invaluable assistance to Israeli intelligence and societal needs. Those needs likely included help with Israel's nuclear weapons program.

# CHAPTER 19

# WHY?

The days of our age are three score years and ten, . . .
[Yet they] so soon passeth away, and we are gone.
—Psalm 90

On December 21, 2008, the biblical three score and ten will have passed since Lise Meitner and her nephew took their historic stroll in the Swedish woods. During a few hours of that winter solstice, Meitner and Frisch accounted for the barium in Otto Hahn's experimental flotsam: nuclear fission. With that, the clock began to run.

In the decades that followed, the industrial superpowers converted Meitner's theory to practice; a resurgent Middle Kingdom broke the European nuclear cartel; the West unintentionally funded the spread of that technology into the Third World. Then, with end of the twentieth century, the chickens came home to roost. Thousands of engineering students, trained in the West, returned to their native lands to assist aging zealots in forging the weapons of nuclear terror needed to settle old scores.

Most of those zealots now advocating a new world order actually seek a return to older ways, to a mythical time of universal order, of state-defined "virtue," of rule by an all-seeing wise man. Within that vision there is no place for human rights, democracy, or the consent of the governed.

In the case of China, this vision implies a unified Confucian empire with no competing sovereignties on the world stage. Virtue is defined by the writings of Mao, as interpreted by the mandarins, to retain their control. The "barbarian" non-Chinese are to be subject to that rule. If there is strife, including nuclear strife beyond the Middle Kingdom, so be it.

Radical Muslims envision a return to the tenth century. Virtue is set forth in the Koran. Within Iran, the supreme leader interprets those writings to mean, "The purest joy in Islam is to kill or be killed for Allah." Elsewhere, Islamic kings and dictators lean on the Koran as the nomenklatura of the Soviet Union leaned on the writings of Marx—to justify their monopoly on power. Nuclear weapons may be handy for bringing about this Islamic joy and/or for expanding the reach of the ayatollahs.

With the passage of seventy years, with the metastasis of nuclear technology into the minds of the aggrieved, and with the wealth needed to support nuclear terror now spread into the Muslim world, the mandarins and the ayatollahs are ready to strike back. They wish to settle old scores: to reverse the crusades, to shred the unequal treaties, to retract the decisions of colonial officers and CIA operatives taken without the consent of the Chinese and Muslim elite. They want nothing less than for the Westerners to "passeth away and be gone."

It is important to understand this goal as we reflect on the Long War now underway. We are not facing a swarm of bumblers wearing ski masks. While the word "terrorist" conjures images of hate-filled lunatics eager to spill blood—people who often blow themselves up by mistake—reality is more complex. Terror is but one weapon in our opponents' arsenal, and some of them have very rational objectives. We are facing a clever coalition of enemies with a broad cultural agenda. Our opponents are knowledgeable in the use of media, they understand the role of economics in this war, and they have more than one historical precedent on their side. In many cases, nuclear explosives are simply a means to an end.

In thinking through how to respond to the threat of nuclear terror, we need to have an accurate picture (or collection of pictures) of how the radical Islamists, Third World fascists, and/or Chinese mandarins envision the coming of their new world order.

## THE IRRATIONAL HATER

Our most immediate concern must be the Irrational Hater. This is the leader of the network conjured in the popular press, the terrorist driven by hate and nominally operating without a long-range plan. In September 2001, a handful of such people hit New York, but they missed their key targets in Washington: the White House and Capitol. Those people detest the current president of the United States, and they will loathe his successor. They will try again. There is little we can do in the short term to defuse that hatred; we can only identify such conspirators, deal with them overseas, secure our borders, and plan for our defense and recovery if they gain entry to the United States.

The Irrational Hater hopes to collect a few pounds of weapons-grade fissionable material from inside the former Soviet Union (or some other willing vendor); assemble it into a weapon, using old but readily available technology; and deliver it for detonation within an iconic U.S. city or institution. The Irrational Haters may assemble their bomb overseas, shipping it up the Anacostia or Hudson Rivers on a yacht, or they might transport only components into the United States, assembling the resulting weapon in-country for delivery by truck. Alternately, the Irrational Haters may acquire an assembled nuclear weapon from a destabilized Pakistan or a cash-hungry North Korea.

That is exactly what al Qaeda sought to do in 2000. During that year, in the run-up to 9/11, al Qaeda contacted a Pakistani charity nominally run for the benefit of Afghan refugees. That charity's founder and most of its leaders worked at Pakistan's nuclear weapons agency. Negotiations were under way for the Pakistanis to "share" one or more nuclear weapons with the leaders of the Taliban in Afghanistan. (Pakistan had tested two devices successfully in 1998 and, by 2001, clearly had a modest inventory of nuclear weapons on hand.) Osama bin Laden and the Taliban leader, Mullah Mohammed Omar, met with a Pakistani nuclear delegation in Afghanistan in August 2001 to discuss these matters.

Sharp American intelligence and decisive action by the Musharraf government defused that plot. Upon interrogation, the Pakistani scientists confirmed their meetings with the Taliban. The government of Pakistan improved its weapon security procedures, and the plot was neutralized, but that will not be al Qaeda's last try.

Should a nuclear device detonate by surprise anywhere in the world, the forensic scientists of the nuclear weapons community will be able to identify the source of the fissile material within a few hours. The nuclear weapon states and the IAEA have built an excellent library of nuclear fingerprints that precludes anonymity, but the Irrational Hater may not care. Once his weapon is delivered and detonated, the Irrational Hater has achieved his goal: revenge.

Whatever the weapon's provenance, a few kilotons detonated off the Washington Navy Yard or next to the Mall would take out the Capitol and White House. It would kill, maim, or incapacitate hundreds of thousands of innocent civilians. What remained of the U.S. government would be driven to bunkers and trailers scattered throughout the Appalachian Mountains.

Only in the longer term is there any hope for curing this hatred and thus precluding such an event. Islamic young men must be offered respect and opportunity, weaning them from their radical leaders. The female half of Islamic society must be empowered, thus allowing them to take control of their own lives. Only then will a broadly based Islamic middle class have a vested interest in peace. Awaiting those days, for our safety we must rely on good intelligence, decisive action, and recovery planning.

## THE RETURN OF LENIN

Another model for nuclear use might arise from the ambitions of those who seek to dissolve and replace the U.S. government with a dictatorship of the proletariat:

something similar to the events that collapsed Imperial Russia. Lenin was able to succeed in 1917 only because Russia had been starved, decimated, and demoralized by World War I, a struggle still grinding on when he arrived at the Finland Station. As Alexander Kerensky later wrote about those times, "A whole world of national and political relationships [was gone]; all existing political and tactical programs hung uselessly in space." Amidst that exhaustion, St. Petersburg was fertile ground for a small band of well-organized conspirators. Lenin and his associates were able to seize power, kill their competitors, and, after a bloody civil war, impose their will on an entire nation. In 1917, there was no civil authority left to oppose Lenin's acts.

Could a few nukes, planted around the United States, produce a similar exhaustion and chaos? Envision a first strike on Washington, decapitating our democratic government, followed by a pair of blasts outside Chicago then Los Angeles.

A hit on the nuclear reactors and fuel storage facilities southwest of Chicago would rain fallout throughout the Midwest and all across the East Coast. Immediate fatalities in the greater Chicago area might approach a million, but the casualties from radiation effects stretching a thousand miles downwind would be far greater. The chaos would overwhelm the first responders within much of Indiana, Ohio, Pennsylvania, the Virginias, and the Northeastern Metroplex.

A few kilotons then delivered to the Los Angeles Marina would devastate Santa Monica, Inglewood, and the beach cities. Inland, the sick and dying staffs at the network anchor stations in Hollywood and Burbank would surely report on that bedlam. They would relay images of the death and destruction within Los Angeles all across the land, as long as their physical condition allowed.

Could the U.S. government continue to command respect and maintain order under those circumstances? Or would American society start to devour itself, hunting for further bombs-in-hiding, pursuing the perpetrators, and rioting for food, medical care, and protection—the Hurricane Katrina aftermath, times ten million? Could al Qaeda sleeper cells then take advantage of the chaos, as did Lenin in 1917, to impose Sharia law on what remained of the United States? Or would the "well-regulated militias" so carefully protected by the Second Amendment to the Constitution of the United States rise up to seize control? In either case, constitutional government as envisioned by the Founding Fathers in 1787 would be gone.

Thoughtful former defense officials have written about these possibilities and about the actions needed to prepare for life "After the Bomb."[1] They set forth the

1. William J. Perry, Michael M. May, and Ashton Carter, "After the Bomb" *New York Times* (June 12, 2007, with subsequent publications by Stanford University's Center for International Security and Cooperation).

federal authority and planning needed to take charge, save lives, maintain order, and guide evacuations in the event of a malevolent nuclear detonation (or detonations) within the United States. These gentlemen know what they are talking about; we should take heed.

## THE THIRD WORLD DICTATOR

A third route to nuclear Armageddon might be triggered by a Kim Jong Il, a new Saddam, or a royal family gone paranoid. Any of those individuals might wish to achieve a local hegemony or religious primacy via the use of a nuclear device. North Korea has already sold No-Dong theater ballistic missiles to multiple Middle Eastern states. China has peddled its CSS-2 intermediate-range missile to the Saudis. Pakistan is now producing the nuclear warheads needed for sale to the owners of those rockets.

To establish his authority, an ambitious dictator might launch an armed rocket straight up, firing a nuclear device fifty miles over his own territory. He could then claim the shot to be "scientific research," properly conducted over his own sovereign lands while not polluting the atmosphere. The result would be highly visible evidence that he had joined the nuclear club: his weapon works, he has the ability to deliver it at the time and place of his choosing, and he merits respect. In the process he would have shut down countless reconnaissance satellites.

If Saddam Hussein had waited to invade Kuwait until his nuclear capability was in hand, and had then pulled off such a demonstration in the mid-1990s, would London and Paris have been willing to go to bat for Kuwait City and Riyadh? Perhaps not. A Third World dictator's follow-on shot onto Riyadh, Seoul, or Tehran might not be necessary, but a reflexive nuclear exchange could follow. As U.S. leaders plan the future support of Middle Eastern allies, or as they reflect on military expeditions into that world, they must bear in mind this possibility.

## THE CURRENCY TRADERS

A fourth objective of nuclear use might be to bring about a chain of events similar to, but much broader than, those that nearly closed down Southeast Asia in 1997. During a few days that summer, when the custodians of the hot money lost confidence in the currencies of Thailand, Taiwan, and Malaysia, the market capitalizations of those nations fell by half overnight. That summer of 1997 might be the terrorist's template for forcing the fire sale of U.S. assets, ending the role of the U.S. dollar as the preeminent world currency, and thus fulfilling the dreams of Auric Goldfinger.

Consider the huge U.S. trade imbalance now pouring dollars and gold into the Chinese and Persian Gulf treasuries. Every day, when the secretary of the U.S.

Treasury comes to work, he must arrange to borrow another two billion dollars, simply to finance that day's increased debt. He must do so while continuing to roll over another nine *trillion* dollars of existing national debt. Foreigners now hold a quarter of that debt,[2] with China our leading overseas creditor.

In September 2007, foreshadowing threats to come, the Chinese government hinted at the possible "nuclear option of dollar sales" if Washington pursued trade sanctions. As one wire-service story put it, "Beijing may use its $1.33 trillion of foreign reserves as a political weapon to counter pressure from the U.S. Congress [to devalue the yuan]." The U.S. Dow-Jones dropped three hundred points on that announcement alone.

Before leaving work at the end of his busy day, the treasury secretary must also recognize that within the United States the boomers are retiring. Their Social Security and Medicare payments will soon exhaust the government's so-called "trust fund" earmarked for OASDI[3] payments. In the face of rioting by the seniors and/or a tax revolt by the juniors, will the United States, be able to continue to borrow overseas? What happens when the Chinese and the Saudis refuse to accept any more American IOUs? What happens if they deliberately stage a run on the U.S. dollar?

Much of the American financial infrastructure was relocated well out of New York City after 9/11, but a single nuclear detonation in Washington or New York could be the trigger that destabilizes the U.S. financial system. Relocated structures, vaults, and financial databases might survive, but confidence is a fragile thing. If America's overseas creditors lose faith in the U.S. currency, or if they turn malevolent, the results could be fiscally fatal. Holders of American assets could be pushed to discounted sales. The overseas assets of the major oil companies could be seized, impounded, or nationalized with impunity, just as the United States once froze Iranian and North Korean assets held in U.S. banks. Operations remaining within the contiguous American forty-eight states might only endure within a Chinese financial protectorate. The collapse of the German currency in the 1930s played a major role in Hitler's rise to power; al Qaeda well understands that fact.

To deal with this possibility, the United States must get its fiscal house in order. Multiple administrations and congresses have spent twenty-five years living beyond their means, tolerating the flow of petrodollars to now-terrorist states, and ignoring the coming tsunami of old age and medical entitlements. The piper will soon demand payment; he may be wearing a robe.

---

2. The rest is held by U.S. citizens and their governments, as "savings." Some presidential candidates have estimated the foreign holdings of the U.S. national debt to be as high as 44 percent of the total.
3. Old age, survivors, and disability insurance.

## DETERRENCE

Another twenty-first-century role for nuclear weapons might be a simple continuation of Cold War practices: deterrence. Third World nuclear states may well wish to deter the major powers from interfering as they settle local scores, by conventional or nuclear means.

China is not developing a sophisticated nuclear capability, quiet submarines, and a reconnaissance satellite to facilitate an attack on the United States; those assets are meant to deter the United States from involvement when the government in Beijing feels it is time to repossess Taiwan.

Iran, no matter how irrationally managed, is not likely to strike the United States out of the blue. Hezbollah sleeper cells may transport nuclear devices into the United States, but the mullahs will then only advise the United States to mind its own business as they turn their attention to Israel or some other local grievance.

In the event of a local nuclear counter-threat, will the mullahs back down? Recent history suggests otherwise. It was the mullahs in Tehran, after all, who were willing to use Iranian children to clear Iraqi mines in the Iran-Iraq war. There may well be a Middle Eastern nuclear firefight. Should the United States get involved? We had best think that one through ahead of time.

## THE MANDARINS

The most challenging questions to arise from the preceding chapters are these: Why did the government of China, during the reign of Deng Xiaoping (1981–1989), aggressively promote the transfer of nuclear weapon technology into the Third World? And why do they continue to do so now?

The original reasons may have reflected a simple balance-of-power argument: arm the Pakistanis to offset the Indians; arm the North Koreans to keep the United States busy. But your authors suspect more than that. We believe that, at least in the 1980s, some factions within the Chinese government thought a nuclear detonation, sometime in the future within the West, could be helpful in restoring China's global preeminence, so long as such a device was assembled and fired by other hands. There must be no Chinese fingerprints.

If New York were hit with a terrorist nuclear device, the Chinese would be the first to offer medical assistance, blankets, and toys, but the fact is, with New York down and the dollar discredited, the mandarins of China would be the last men standing. China would emerge as the world's preeminent economic power, with the clout to allocate energy resources as it saw fit. It would still have to deal with Russia, Japan, and India, along with an aging and Muslim Europe, but Mao's dream of a return to greatness would have been fulfilled.

We doubt succeeding generations of leadership within China share those ambitions, although some factions (the People's Liberation Army) may still do so. It is clear the youngsters within China, those born after the Great Leap Forward, view the United States as a key market, not an adversary. But the old guard is still in charge. In 2007, the Communist Party Congress[4] re-installed Hu Jintao as party leader with a writ running to 2012, and it recognized the party leaders in Shanghai and Liaoning as heirs apparent thereafter. The mandarins do not plan to relinquish their power any time soon.

## SEVENTY YEARS LATER

Many societies and states have much to gain from a nuclear detonation on U.S. soil. The Irrational Haters might feel justice had been done, while their patrons might welcome the rise of a new economic and/or religious order in the world. The mere threat of such a detonation may allow the settling of old scores in a manner that will cost the lives and freedoms of millions.

In 1938, the Nuclear Express pulled out of Berlin. For half a century it picked up speed, but it never came off the rails. Rational people, concerned about the well-being of their children, held differing views about the social system that would best assure their future, but the initial use of nuclear weapons was never an option. The Cold War cost blood, toil, sweat, and tears, but it was settled without a nuclear exchange.

There then ensued the usual postwar interregnum. During those inattentive years, as the Europeans celebrated, men from different cultures boarded the Nuclear Express. Like masked bandits in old-time Westerns, the Third World raiders seized control of the locomotive as the passengers snoozed.

As Edward R. Murrow reported from London during Britain's darkest hours in the dying days of the Chamberlain administration in early May 1940,[5] "The people here feel the machine is out of control, that we are all passengers on an express train traveling at high speed through a dark tunnel toward an unknown destiny. The suspicion recurs that the train may have no engineer."

The Nuclear Express now hurtles into a new century with a boxcar of nuclear technology, a hopper filled with fissile materials, a mail car packed with cash and millions of sleeping passengers. The engineers driving this train seem unconcerned about the safety and well-being of those passengers, even their own children. A massive train wreck, defying all previous human experience, could lie ahead.

---

4. Meeting in Beijing in October 2007.
5. Edward R. Murrow, *This is London* (New York: Simon & Schuster, 1941), 52.

# EPILOGUE

As the Nuclear Express rolls into the twenty-first century, it is only the new American president who can deal with the engineers at the throttle. Without his intervention, the proliferation freight cars—filled with weapon feedstock, nuclear technology, and Muslim animosity—will surely come off the rails. Millions will die, and more than one democratic society will be consigned to the dust-heap of history.

The hazardous waste in the hopper car must be our immediate concern. The Soviet Union produced more than a thousand tons of very dangerous weapons materials—plutonium and highly enriched uranium—during the Cold War years. The ensuing governments of Boris Yeltsin and Vladimir Putin have worked diligently, with U.S. assistance, to find it. Perhaps 99.9 percent has been located, but that leaves 0.1 percent unaccounted for: more than a thousand pounds of weapons-grade fissile matter. The raw material for dozens of nuclear weapons remains out there, somewhere, in the Soviet wasteland.

Second, nuclear technology has spread; the European monopoly has been broken. Westerners once held *all* the honors in the fields of nuclear physics and the associated engineering domains, but others now lead the way. Chinese theoreticians thought through thermonuclear technology faster than any of their predecessors. Russian weapons designers are innovating in a manner surprising to the West. Muslim engineers built a network of nuclear suppliers that is available to anyone with the cash to subscribe. A subcontinent once thought to be nonaligned fired a nuclear device without warning. And all of these networks are interconnected and unstable. As master proliferator A. Q. Khan put it a decade ago, "There was a Christian bomb, a Jewish bomb, a Buddhist bomb, and a Hindu bomb. Now there is a Muslim bomb!" A Pakistan ruled by a different government, backed by Saudi money and infused with Chinese technology, could well become the supplier of nuclear weapons to al Qaeda and the aggrieved Muslim world.

Third, when the nuclear age opened, the Middle East and the Muslim worlds were impoverished backwaters. The United States was a net exporter of oil, and it was the world's leader in the technology of finding and producing that fuel, but conflicts within the last quarter-century have shuffled the deck. The events of 1973 to 1979 triggered the biggest transfer of wealth in the history of the world. Some of this wealth was wisely invested, in petrochemical industries within the host countries. Some was

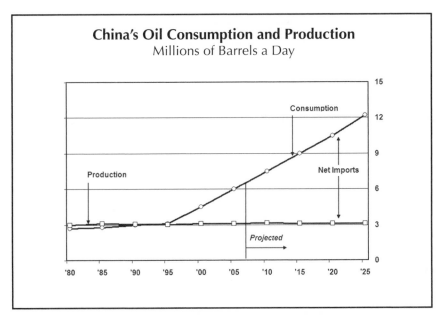

**China's Oil Consumption and Production**
Millions of Barrels a Day

China's historic and projected energy demands. These claims now determine the monetary and social cost of the world's energy supplies. *U.S. Department of Energy*

spent with compassion, improving the lot of the poor. But most of those petrodollars went to stabilize illegitimate governments, empower dictators with nuclear dreams, or enrich royal families who bought off their dissidents with madrassa schools and creature comforts. It is the graduates of those madrassa schools who now seek to inflame the world.

The West has not cared to adopt energy policies that would staunch this flow of riches, and with the end of the Cold War, China is raising the price of energy in monetary, social, and environmental terms. While China's prosperity is building a middle class, and while that generation may, in time, rein in China's nuclear irresponsibility, the oil shocks of the 1970s and the Chinese prosperity of the 1990s are, at the moment, funding the engines of cultural hate within the Third World. Petrodollars, directly or indirectly, are procuring the weapons of Armageddon.

Most important, we must consider the engineers driving this train. With the coming of Mao, or perhaps just the end of World War II, China awoke from five centuries of somnolence. The society that once invented gunpowder and compass, and then turned inward, has once again come to life. By the end of the twentieth century, China had become highly competitive in terms of nuclear weapons, business, technology, and its aggressive search for energy.

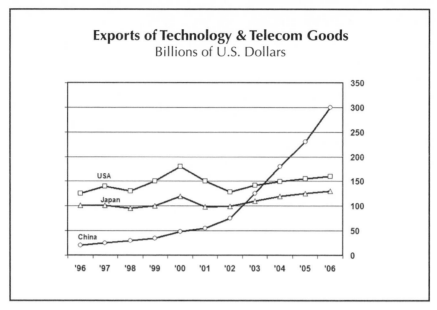

**Exports of Technology & Telecom Goods**
Billions of U.S. Dollars

Technology is no longer an American, European, or Japanese monopoly. China has taken the lead in high-tech manufacturing for the export market. *OECD Information Techonology outlook, 2006*

As fissile materials, petrodollars, and diffusing technologies converge, and if we are to avoid a massive train wreck, the governments of Western civilization might wish to take five constructive steps:

## FISSIONABLE MATERIALS

First of all, we must make the securing of Soviet fissionable materials a top national priority. That is not a simple job. Those materials need to be located and inventoried. Formal portals and informal networks need to monitor their movement. Electronic, physical, and political controls must confirm custody. Surplus materials must be affirmatively rechanneled into the commercial energy sector. Retired weapons must be protected en route to disassembly. And all of these safeguards, once in place, must continue to operate in the face of endemic corruption after American support ends. Beyond that, the Soviet scientists, engineers, and technicians once involved in the nuclear weapons industries must be assured of a safe and prosperous future. They must turn a deaf ear to the siren songs of the terrorist Lorelei.

The American Congress once did its part in this campaign; it created the Nunn-Lugar legislation needed to finance the redeployment of Soviet nuclear talent. Non-governmental organizations (NGOs) such as the Nuclear Threat Initiative (NTI) and the Institute for Science and International Security (ISIS) have taken up the crusade. But congressional support has dwindled, and the new Russian government no longer welcomes the assistance of NGOs. The presidents of the United States and Russia must return this problem to the top of *their* agendas. It must become the business of the Russian *people* to enforce these controls. They must not allow their bureaucrats or bandits to interfere or obstruct. The stakes are too high.

## SAFEGUARDS AND INSPECTION

Second, responsible governments must strengthen the international safeguards against nuclear proliferation. The Nuclear Nonproliferation Treaty of 1970 was the intended vehicle for this. The International Atomic Energy Agency (IAEA) in Vienna was to be the instrumentality of enforcement, but the concept of "enforcement" was very different a quarter-century ago. Nonproliferation examiners of the 1970s were to fulfill the role of bank examiners: people who assured fellow members of the establishment that no one was cooking the books. Industrial heavyweights of the Second World (industrial states of Germany, Japan, Sweden, Switzerland, Brazil, Argentina, et al.) wanted assurances from their peers that nuclear weapon matters were to be left to the permanent members of the UN Security Council, that everyone else could go about their business without the hazards and costs associated with nuclear weapon production. The host countries welcomed auditors; full disclosure was the order of the day. Inspectors from the IAEA became accountants; they spent their time weighing, counting, and confirming shipping documents. Just as bank examiners do not look for counterfeiters (a job left to the Secret Service), so has the IAEA averted its gaze from the possibility of nuclear break-ins.

Today the IAEA still inspects only "declared" facilities, those offered up for inspection by treaty signatories who wish to assure their neighbors (sometimes fraudulently) of peaceful intent. Contrary to popular belief, the IAEA's statute does *not* run to the investigation of illicit proliferators, nor does it include the surveillance of uranium mining.

If we are to make it through the twenty-first century, better enforcement will be necessary. The IAEA must be empowered to seek out and identify nuclear weapon cheaters. Such a change would require an amendment to the Nonproliferation Treaty; that will not be simple. Many Third World states, such as Pakistan, consider the NPT to be highly discriminatory, protecting the nuclear "haves" from competition by the "have-nots." This group, known as the Nonaligned Movement, enjoys a large majority within the IAEA member states. They would prefer to foreclose, not expand, the NPT's reach.

As a first step in strengthening the NPT, two-thirds of the signatories to that treaty have agreed to an Additional Protocol, a document that gives the IAEA far broader proliferation-monitoring powers. Unfortunately, aside from the Big Five, most of those who have signed the Additional Protocol are not serious players in the nuclear world; none of the dangerous Middle Eastern and Asian states have subscribed. Algeria, Egypt, Iran, India, Israel, North Korea, Pakistan, Saudi Arabia, and Syria all remain unbound by the Additional Protocol. Even worse, most of those states are working diligently to preclude any further surveillance of proliferation activities. The United States must use all the leverage at its disposal to achieve universal acceptance of the Additional Protocol to the NPT.

We also must do better at playing the cards we have been dealt. At one time Western intelligence services had a close and mutually respectful relationship with the International Atomic Energy Agency, but that is no longer the case. Inspectors from the IAEA knew, in 2003, there were no illicit uranium shipments from Niger to Iraq, but U.S. officials did not care to listen. The United States operates the world's best overhead surveillance systems, and the IAEA is empowered to utilize commercial space imagery, but doing so is an expensive undertaking. The intelligence services and commercial interests of many First and Second World countries image interesting targets every day, but the IAEA receives few images, perhaps one or two per year. The IAEA's imagery exploitation capability is quaint and ineffective when compared to that of the United States. To rectify this situation, the larger IAEA member states must provide imagery and analysis to that agency on a timely basis.

Finally, dedicated IAEA inspectors must be supported in their efforts to get the facts. Armed with their findings, we must then enforce realistic controls on the production of fissionable materials, on the development of nuclear weapons, and on the transfer of technologies and hardware to proliferant states. While we must address the legitimate energy needs of possible proliferators, the UN Security Council must act when weapons development appears on the horizon.

## ENERGY

Third, the United States must adopt energy and fiscal policies that will seem Draconian in their scope. The United States alone can no longer staunch the flow of petrodollars to the radical Muslim states. The growth in petroleum demand from the industrializing world now precludes such a unilateral solution. The time for that was 1973–1974, but energy independence for the United States—whatever that term means—is still a possibility should the nation and its political leaders have the fortitude.

A first step would be the movement of American gasoline prices to European levels. As of this writing gasoline costs about $9 (U.S) within the European Community, $4 in the United States. Burdensome as the American price may be, market forces must be brought to bear to encourage further conservation efforts and a conversion to alternative fuels. A federal gasoline tax is the logical route to such parity. Such a tax would have to be offset with tax reductions elsewhere to ease the impact on those hardest hit and to keep the federal government on a tight fiscal leash, but every penny of gasoline tax brings in $1 billion per year of tax revenue. Raising U.S. prices to $9 per gallon would, in the near term, and after offsetting tax reductions, bring hundreds of billions of dollars per year into the federal treasury. Presto! The federal deficit disappears. If the proceeds are earmarked for the OASDI trust fund, Social Security and Medicare might just survive. The purpose of such a tax increase would not be revenue production, however. An increased gasoline tax would force an immediate reduction in the domestic demand for gasoline and would provide a strong incentive for alternative sources of mobil power. A companion to increased gasoline taxes should be broad and mandatory gasoline conservation measures. American vehicles currently average 21.5 miles per gallon. Those in the European Union average 42 miles per gallon; in Japan it is 47 miles per gallon. CAFE[6] standards, fleet incentives, and taxation are the tools needed to effect conservation, again with offsets to preclude a further bloating of the federal government. The provisions of the Energy Independence and Security Act of 2007 are steps in the right direction.[7]

To address the supply side of the gasoline equation, the United States must pursue new technologies for the production of motor fuels, technologies that are both cost-effective and that are net energy producers: for example, the refining of cellulosic biomass to produce ethanol. Cellulosic biomass is the technical term for plants or grasses grown for the purpose of being refined in toto. They could produce about seven gallons of fuel for every gallon consumed by the farm equipment and refineries needed to manufacture the product. This approach must not be confused with the current (and politically popular) fermentation of ethanol from corn, a process that consumes at least seven gallons of fuel for every eight gallons produced, in the process driving the price of every corn product, from cattle feedstock to tortillas, through the roof. The use of agricultural products to fuel transportation is not a new concept. A century ago, half the land given over to cereal production in Great Britain was planted to oats, to feed the horses.

We cannot produce our way out of this energy problem, but every barrel of oil pumped in North America is over $100 less sent to the OPEC world. We should allow and encourage crude oil production within the United States and its immediate neighbors, and we should encourage other non-Muslim, non-OPEC producers to expand their oil production as well. Russia and the former Soviet Republics are the primary candidates for such support.

6. CAFE = Corporate average fuel economy standards, enacted by the Energy Policy and Conservation Act of 1975.
7. These include imposing a new CAFE standard of thirty-five miles per gallon by 2020.

Electricity generation is not a primary consumer of oil within the United States, but we should lighten the demand for all carbon-based fuels by expanding our use of wind turbines and solar power where it is economically feasible to do so, by converting from incandescent to fluorescent lighting, and by recognizing that nuclear power is about to enjoy an interesting renaissance. Developing nations, those with a desperate need for electrical power, may install up to a thousand new nuclear power plants within the next thirty years, and the industrialized world must decide on replacements for its first round of nuclear power plants. They are now reaching their half-life.

The new nuclear power plants will be environmentally friendly (no carbon dioxide), of modest size (three hundred megawatts), and—if we do not care to compete—will be built by the worlds' nuclear power experts: France, Japan, Russia, and perhaps South Africa. The Russian Federation is already retooling its Severodvinsk nuclear submarine shipyard to produce these medium-size reactors on an assembly-line basis.

## THE INTELLIGENCE COMMUNITY

As a fourth step in preparing to face the challenges of nuclear terror, the new president must address the leadership, structure, and focus of the U.S. intelligence community. Today it is broken: disconnected at the top, arrogant at the bottom.

Documentation now coming to light[8] makes it clear that, a half-century ago, the CIA was well aware of Lee Harvey Oswald's Cuban connection. It simply chose to withhold this crucial information from the Warren Commission as that group was investigating the Kennedy assassination. In time Lyndon Johnson angrily learned the truth. As he put it at the end of his administration, "Kennedy was trying to get Castro, but Castro got to him first."

During the early 1980s, President Reagan decided to support the anti-Soviet insurgents within Afghanistan, but it took a senior member of congress[9] and the passage of four years to move the hardware around the CIA, past the obstructing Pakistani ISI, over the ineffective expatriates, and into the hands of the mujahideen who were actually doing the fighting. Only in September 1986 did the mujahideen start killing Soviet helicopters and tanks.

During the current decade, the CIA blatantly withheld interrogation tapes from the 9/11 Panel as that group considered the causes, perpetrators, and lessons learned from the September 11, 2001, attacks on the World Trade Center. This arrogance was brought home to your authors as we submitted this manuscript to the intelligence

8. Tim Weiner, *Legacy of Ashes* (New York: Doubleday, 2000), 235.
9. *Charlie Wilson's War*, Universal Studios, 2007.

community for comment, as we felt obligated to do, given our years of intelligence-oversight activities. The Defense Intelligence Agency made every effort to suppress our observation (in chapter 8) that, in 1964, the intelligence community was astonished to find no plutonium in the first Chinese nuclear test. The open literature is full of references to that missed call.

The intelligence community needs to refocus its efforts away from Cold War instruments aboard satellites and other platforms to human intelligence on the scene. Overhead photography and signals intelligence gave the United States great insight into the Soviet war machine, but today's challenge is different. We need insight into the radical Muslim and isolated North Korean mind. That can only be accomplished on the ground, with great effort, training, and by the recruitment of Muslim and North Korean agents in place.

The American intelligence community has only served the country well when the man in charge is competent, awash with integrity, and enjoys the full confidence of the president of the United States. John Kennedy set the example, turning to rock-ribbed Republican John McCone as his first director of central intelligence because McCone, as Eisenhower's AEC Chairman, had stood up to that president and gone public when Eisenhower ignored every indication of an Israeli nuclear program. During Kennedy's watch, McCone identified the Cuban crisis of 1962 in its formative stages, even though the president would not act until he saw photographic confirmation of the missile buildup during October of that year.

William Casey is another example of a CIA director who changed American history. Casey was a World War II intelligence hand. In many ways, he was the proverbial bull in the China shop: a dreadful manager, but a determined Cold Warrior. Having directed Reagan's campaign for the White House, Casey enjoyed the president's full confidence, reflected in Casey's being the first director of central intelligence to benefit from cabinet rank. Casey also enjoyed access—the president and his national security advisor listened, in private, when the director of central intelligence spoke. Casey, in turn, recruited outsiders. He brought into the intelligence community, and thence into National Security Council deliberations, the non-CIA economists[10] who could and would identify the terminal condition of the Soviet economy—a confrontational opportunity the national security establishment did not wish to exploit.

On the other hand, President George W. Bush violated a primary ground rule for any new administration: pick your own team. Lyndon Johnson stuck with Robert McNamara as secretary of defense and paid the price. George W. Bush stuck with Bill Clinton's George Tenet as director of central intelligence, with disastrous results.

10. Specifically, Henry Rowen, chairman of the Intelligence Council, an outsider from Stanford.

Newly inaugurated presidents must choose their own man or woman to lead and restructure the entire intelligence community and then pay attention to the results.

## CHINA

Finally, we must get serious about China. There is every indication that during the Deng years, 1981–1989, China became highly supportive of nuclear proliferation into the Third World. China transferred technology to Pakistan, attempted to build a secret plutonium-producing nuclear reactor in the Algerian desert, and sold to Saudi Arabia intermediate-range missiles suitable only for the delivery of nuclear weapons. Further, China has tolerated a nuclear weapons program within North Korea and has catered to the nuclear ambitions of the Iranian ayatollahs in a blatant attempt to secure an ongoing supply of oil.

China has also become the leading supplier of other WMD technology into the Third World. China declined to join the Proliferation Security Initiative (PSI), an international legal framework adopted in 2003 for interdicting the shipment of chemical, biological, and nuclear weapons and materials around the globe. The PSI consists of fifteen core countries;[11] another sixty have agreed to cooperate on an ad hoc basis. This latter group includes those nations most often used for ship registration, such as Panama. In October 2006, even after the North Korean nuclear test, the Chinese ambassador to the UN stated that, "China does not approve of inspecting cargo to and from the D.P.R.K."[12] That is not surprising. China has allowed many a proliferant state to overfly China when picking up illicit goods in North Korea.

In May 2007, the Congressional Research Service (CRS) published a bill of particulars. Among other transgressions, that report noted that, immediately prior to the 2003 Iraqi Freedom War, China supplied Iraq with critically needed missile components. China also supplied Iraq with missile-guidance software disguised as "children's computer software."

In the early 1980s, China transferred a nuclear weapon design package to Pakistan's A. Q. Khan. The latter then reconveyed that information on to Libya, Iran, and others. In 1996, China shipped five thousand ring magnets to the A. Q. Khan Research Laboratory in Pakistan. They were used in the rotator suspension system of A. Q. Khan's enrichment centrifuge machine. In 1996, China sold a special industrial furnace,[13] along with associated diagnostic equipment, to unsafeguarded nuclear

---

11. Which include the United States, United Kingdom, Russia, France, Germany, Japan, Spain, Italy, and Australia—but not China.
12. The Democratic People's Republic of Korea, *i.e.*, North Korea.
13. Operating at very high temperatures, suitable for the casting of uranium and plutonium weapon shapes.

facilities within Pakistan. "P.R.C. officials planned to submit false documentation as to the final destination of the equipment," the CRS advised. In the late 1990s, China transferred ballistic missile blueprints, equipment, and complete missiles to Pakistan in full violation of the Missile Technology Control Regime (MTCR).

Since 1991, China has been assisting the raw-materials side of the Iranian nuclear weapons program with the shipment of uranium (from world sources), advice on the mining of uranium within Iran at Saghad, instructions on the design of an ore-to-hexafluoruide conversion facility at Eshfahan, and construction of an EMIS enrichment facility at Karaj. In 2002, China's NORINCO transferred missile technology to Iran, again in violation of the MTCR.

China has been using North Korea as the re-transfer point for the sale of nuclear and missile technology to Iran, Syria, Pakistan, Egypt, Libya, and Yemen. China has overseen the North Korean–Pakistani trade of missiles for nuclear equipment. Chinese and North Korean military officers were in close communication prior to North Korea's missile tests of 1998 and 2006, even though the PLA denies having any knowledge of those tests.

Until the Libyan retrenchment of 2003, China was training Libyan missile experts at Beijing University while transferring other missile data directly to Tripoli.

What emerges from all this is a pattern of Chinese misrepresentation (i.e., lying) as well as a support for Axis of Evil states that, since the end of the Cold War, has cost American lives.

Your authors are of the view that some within the government of China might not object to the nuclear destruction of New York or Washington, followed by the collapse of American financial power, so long as Chinese fingerprints could not be found at the scene of the crime. Radical Muslim terror is not a problem for China; to some in Beijing, it may be seen as the route to China's hegemonic future.

On the other hand, within China there is more than a generational gap—it is a canyon. While the old timers, with the exception of a few who have noted the human cost, revere Mao's "achievements," the younger generation (those born after the Great Leap Forward) are scornful of Mao's follies. Those "youngsters" are turning fifty now, and they are building a new society via the Internet and their world markets. Their turn may soon come, a generational clash that may make the 1960s in the United States seem tranquil. We must continue to support human rights within Chinese society, not just as an American export, but because it is the dream of the Tiananmen Square generation. In time those youngsters could well prevail, and the world will be a less contentious place.

## CONCLUSIONS

The United States is now engaged in a new Cold War on two fronts. It will be long and hard. There is the confrontation with the radical Muslim world, and there is the struggle for economic survival vis-à-vis China. We believe those foes are in league. Fortunately, our problems are with the mullahs, not the younger generations within the Middle East, and with the government of China—the communist old guard and the anti-American military establishment—not the burgeoning middle classes. The people of China are waking up to the possibilities stretching out before them; there is a growing awareness of the perks reserved for the insiders.

The obstructions on the rail bed of history—finding the fissionable materials, strengthening the IAEA, getting realistic about energy policy, rebuilding the American intelligence community, and taking China seriously—will be difficult, but we might keep these needs in mind as we empower our next generation of national leaders. A unified effort might just keep the Nuclear Express on track. Divisive efforts will surely bring about the greatest train wreck in the history of mankind.

# GLOSSARY

**atom bomb (or A-bomb):** A nuclear weapon in which the splitting (fission) of atomic nuclei results in an explosion of devastating force, heat, and light. The destructive energy of an atomic bomb is measured in kilotons of TNT-equivalent energy. That energy release derives from the nearly instantaneous and uncontrolled successive fissioning of uranium or plutonium atoms in a chain reaction.

**bhangmeter:** An optical sensor used to detect and quantify the yield of atmospheric nuclear detonations. These detectors record the distinctive double pulses of light emitted by an atmospheric nuclear burst: a sharp initial maximum, a transition valley, and then a broad second pulse. The first observed signal, a short and intense flash lasting for around one millisecond, comes from the surface of the fireball. The second, longer, and less intense signal lasts for a second or so. It emerges from the ionized gasses at the front of the shock wave moving away from the detonation. These signals, taken together, are quite unambiguous. The time between the lowest point in the intermediate valley and the second pulse maximum can give an early estimate of device yield.

**bomb-grade uranium:** See "HEU."

**boosting:** Boosting within a nuclear weapon takes place when a shell of fissionable material is imploded to supercriticality, begins to fission, and thus initiates fusion within a small amount of deuterium-tritium gas placed within the weapon core. That thermonuclear burn creates a flood of high-energy neutrons that significantly boosts the fission yield.

**CEA:** The French Atomic Energy Commission: le Commissariat à l'Énergie Atomique.

**CEP:** Circular error probable, a measure of missile accuracy. Specifically, the radius of a circle within which half the incoming projectiles are expected to impact.

**chain reaction:** A self-sustaining nuclear reaction occurring when a fissionable nucleus, usually uranium or plutonium, absorbs a neutron and splits in two, thereby releasing energy and two or three more neutrons. These neutrons go on to cause yet more fissions, each step requiring about $10^{-8}$ seconds, or ten nanoseconds.

**China Academy of Engineering Physics (CAEP):** The organization responsible for the design and testing of Chinese nuclear weapons.

**critical mass:** A mass of fissionable material just large enough to sustain a chain reaction. Critical mass is a function of the enrichment of the fissionable material, its geometry and density, and its (reflective) surroundings.

**Curie:** A measure of radioactivity; $3.7 \times 10^{10}$ spontaneous nuclear transitions per second. One gram of radium-226 has a radioactivity of one curie. The radioactivity of any material will decline over time at a rate measured by its half-life.

**DEFCON:** Defense Condition, or alert status of the U.S. Armed Forces. In peacetime most U.S. forces are at DEFCON 5; when at nuclear war, DEFCON 1. Raising alert status shortens reaction time in the event of an attack on U.S. interests, but elevated DEFCON conditions become more costly and are difficult to maintain for extended periods of time. United States forces went to DEFCON 3 at the time of the Yom Kippur War; SAC went to DEFCON 2 at the time of the Cuban Missile Crisis.

**depleted uranium:** The residue from the separation of uranium isotopes: i.e., the material left behind (mostly uranium-238) when most of the uranium-235 has been removed.

**deuterium:** An isotope of hydrogen whose nucleus consists of one proton and one neutron. Deuterium has twice the mass of ordinary hydrogen, and thus water made from oxygen and deuterium is known as heavy water, an essential moderator in certain types of nuclear reactors.

**electron:** An elementary particle having a very small mass ($\sim 9 \times 10^{-28}$ gram) and a unit charge of negative electricity. In every atom a cloud of electrons surround the nucleus within various orbital shells. The hydrogen atom has one electron; the uranium atom has ninety-two electrons.

**equation of state:** An equation that relates the temperature, volume, and pressure of a gas, taking into account the forces between the molecules and elementary particles within that gas. At the temperatures and pressures involved in nuclear weapons, all metals have become gasses.

**Fifth Academy:** The organization responsible for China's satellite, missile-range, and other space activities. It was established in 1956 by Qian Xuesen, a Caltech scientist who had been deported from the United States.

**fission:** The splitting of an atomic nucleus into two parts, usually when bombarded by a neutron, but sometimes spontaneously. The fission of heavy elements releases substantial energy.

**Force de Frappe:** The French "Striking Force," a triad of strategic nuclear forces, independent of the United States, first envisioned by Charles de Gaulle in the 1960s.

**fusion:** The combining of two light atomic nuclei to produce a nucleus of greater mass. The fusion of light elements, especially isotopes of hydrogen, releases substantial amounts of energy. These are known as thermonuclear reactions because they will not take place except at very high temperatures and densities.

**half-life:** The time required for half of any quantity of unstable nuclei or particles to disintegrate. The half-life of a particular nucleus is always the same, independent of temperature, pressure, or chemical combination. Half-lives are used to measure radioactivity and to distinguish one nuclide from another.

**HEU:** Highly enriched uranium, uranium metal wherein the U-235 isotope content has been raised by any one of several enrichment technologies from the natural 0.7 percent to over 80 percent (usually 93.5 percent) U-235. Sometimes referred to as bomb-grade uranium, weapons-grade uranium, or Oralloy (Oak Ridge alloy). This is in contrast to reactor-grade or low-enriched uranium (LEU), containing only 2–3 percent U-235.

**hydrogen bomb (thermonuclear or H-bomb):** A nuclear weapon in which a significant portion of the released energy comes from the fusion of hydrogen isotopes: i.e., deuterium and tritium. These are often called thermonuclear weapons because exceedingly high temperatures and densities are needed to initiate these fusion reactions.

**isotope:** Different forms of the same element, an element being matter with the same atomic number (number of protons) and chemical characteristics. Isotopes of any given element have different atomic weights because they have different numbers of neutrons within the nucleus, and thus they have different physical properties.

**isotope separation:** The process of separating specific isotopes of a given chemical element. Most isotope separation techniques are based on the atomic weight of each isotope or on the small differences in chemical reaction rates produced by different atomic weights. All large-scale isotope separation schemes employ a number of stages that produce successively higher concentrations of the desired isotope after each stage. Separation techniques include diffusion, centrifugal effects in a centrifuge, vortex tubes, electromagnetics, lasers, and chemistry.

**JPL:** Jet Propulsion Laboratory.

**Manhattan Project:** The American A-bomb program during World War II. The name was chosen to be misleading; once under way it had little to do with the island of Manhattan. The work was managed by the Manhattan Engineering District of the U.S. Army Corps of Engineers.

**megawatt:** The rate at which energy is produced or consumed, in electrical, mechanical ,or thermal form. A typical U.S. home requires about one kilowatt (0.001 megawatt) of power. A diesel-electric locomotive delivers three to five megawatts. Reactors aboard the aircraft carrier *John F. Kennedy* produce around two hundred megawatts in total.

**moderator:** A material placed within a nuclear reactor to slow down neutrons emerging from one nuclear fission, thus making them more susceptible to capture by the next nucleus. An effective moderator must absorb only kinetic energy, not neutrons, and thus the chemical purity of the moderating material is extremely important.

**natural uranium:** Uranium emerging from the mining and smelting process, before enrichment: 99.3 percent uranium-238, 0.7 percent uranium-235. Uranium oxide ore is known as yellowcake.

**neutron:** An elementary particle with no electric charge that has about the same mass as a proton. Neutrons are found within the nucleus of every atom except the lightest isotope of hydrogen. They are used to bombard nuclei to produce fission and other nuclear reactions because neutrons are unaffected by the electromagnetic forces within the nucleus.

**neutron bomb (enhanced radiation weapon):** A nuclear weapon designed to maximize its production of neutrons (for disabling troops or other weapons) while minimizing fission effects of blast, heat, and radioactive contamination. While neutron bombs deliver more radiation per unit yield compared to standard weapons, they still inflict devastating physical damage on their surroundings.

**neutron initiator:** The mechanical or electronic device intended to deliver a burst of neutrons to the core of an imploding fission weapon at the exact moment of maximum supercriticality.

**Ninth Academy:** The early name given to the Chinese nuclear weapons developers. In time the Ninth Academy was renamed the China Academy of Engineering Physics.

**nuclear cross section:** The probability of interactions between particles, usually between a neutron and an atomic nucleus, expressed in units of area. Nuclear cross sections are measured in barns, a barn being $10^{-28}$ square meters. These cross sections, as a function of the incoming nuclear particle's velocity, were one of the early secrets of the A-bomb.

**nuclear device:** A device, be it an experimental structure or portable capsule, intended to release vast amounts of nuclear energy. Some nuclear devices are no more than elaborate physics experiments, while others are prototype weapons. A "nuclear device" is not a "bomb" until it has been weaponized: that is, engineered for reliability, produceability, safety, and security as well as for compatibility with the intended delivery vehicle and environment.

**nucleus:** The central part of an atom, consisting of protons and neutrons. The nucleus carries a positive charge and forms a core containing most of the mass of an atom around which electrons orbit.

**one-point safety:** The assurance that, in the event of a detonation occurring at any one point within a weapon's high-explosive system, the probability of a nuclear fission yield of more than four pounds of TNT equivalent will be less than one in a million. This is an important threshold in the event of an aircraft accident, small-arms fire, terrorist attack, or other unexpected event.

**permissive action link (PAL):** An electro-mechanical assembly within a nuclear weapon intended to preclude its detonation without the insertion of some outside information, usually a string of digits, held by the National Command Authority. PALs can also add to the safety of the weapon in the event of lightning strike or other accident.

**plutonium:** A silvery-white, slightly radioactive, metallic element, atomic number 94, that has fifteen different isotopes with atomic weights ranging from 232 to 246. Most have short half-lives; the most stable is plutonium-239, with a half-life of 24,200 years. Even so, that longevity is short compared to the lifetime of our planet, and thus very little plutonium is found in nature. The highly fissionable plutonium-239, most often used in A-bombs, is produced within nuclear reactors by bombarding uranium-238 with neutrons. Such a bombardment produces some of the other, undesirable plutonium isotopes as well, which poses severe timing and chemical challenges to any weapon proliferator.

**pre-initiation:** The initiation of nuclear fission before achieving the intended supercritical configuration within a nuclear weapon. Pre-initiation will result in a nuclear yield substantially lower than intended.

**P.R.C.:** The People's Republic of China, the government of mainland China, installed in Beijing by Mao Zedong on October 1, 1949.

**proton:** A subatomic particle charged with one unit of positive electricity, found in the nuclei of atoms and having a mass about 1,836 times that of an electron. The number of protons in each nucleus is the atomic number of the element. An atom of ordinary hydrogen contains one proton and one electron.

**radiation case:** The outer case of a thermonuclear weapon. It must be thick, dense, and opaque enough to contain the radiation emitted by the primary stage of the weapon for the time required for that radiation to travel the length of the capsule, usually on the order of tens of nanoseconds.

**R.O.C.:** The Republic of China, whose nationalist government, led by Chiang Kaishek, took refuge on Taiwan in 1949.

**RV:** Reentry vehicle, the front end of a ballistic missile, designed to protect the warhead inside from heating or other damage during reentry into the atmosphere, en route to its target.

**shake:** The unit of time used in the design of nuclear devices, being $10^{-8}$ seconds or 10 nanoseconds. This is one nuclear-fission generation time. The name arose from the expression, "a shake of a lamb's tail."

**SIGINT:** Signals Intelligence, the collection of intelligence from any electronic transmission, be it radio, radar, or other.

**spontaneous fission:** Naturally occurring fission arising from the instability of a nucleus without any external neutron bombardment.

**subcritical mass:** An amount of fissionable material insufficient to maintain a chain reaction under the specific conditions of geometry, density, etc.

**supercritical mass:** A mass of fissile material so configured that, once the fission chain reaction starts, it can end only in the rapid (or explosive) disassembly of the material involved.

**thermonuclear device:** See "hydrogen bomb."

**tritium:** A radioactive isotope of hydrogen with a nucleus containing one proton and two neutrons; thus, it is three times as heavy as ordinary hydrogen. Tritium plays a key role in H-bomb design. It is manufactured for storage and weapon use by bombarding lithium with neutrons within a nuclear reactor. It is also produced in real time during the thermonuclear burn of lithium. Tritium has a half-life of 12.5 years.

**yield:** The energy released during a nuclear explosion, measured in pounds, tons, kilotons (KT), or megatons (MT) of TNT equivalent.

# THE PHYSICS OF NUCLEAR WEAPON DESIGN

Physical matter is made up of atoms. Each atom consists of a nucleus—a bunch of tightly bound protons and neutrons—surrounded by a cloud of electrons, orbiting in clearly defined shells. Protons in the nucleus carry a positive charge; they tend to repel each other. They are held in place by the neutrons, which carry no electrical charge at all. Think of neutrons as sticky marbles, holding the nucleus together in the face of the repelling charge on each proton. The number of protons in a nucleus is known as the atomic number. That number determines the chemical properties of that atom, and all atoms with the same atomic number are known as an element. The element hydrogen has one proton, iron has twenty-six, uranium has ninety-two.

Neutrons then join the nucleus, in numbers usually exceeding the number of protons, to keep the nucleus stable. The total number of protons and neutrons, taken together, is known as the atomic weight. Basic hydrogen has no neutrons, because no "glue" is needed to hold a one-proton nucleus together, but sometimes a neutron does attach itself to an isolated hydrogen nucleus anyway. Such a nucleus, made up of one proton and neutron and thus with an atomic weight of two, and is known as deuterium. If another neutron is attached, hydrogen-3 is known as tritium.

Iron, with twenty-six protons, is usually found with thirty neutrons, for a total atomic weight of fifty-six. Some iron atoms can exist briefly with only twenty-six neutrons; other iron atoms are found with as many as thirty-four neutrons. These different varieties of iron, all with twenty-six protons but with atomic weights ranging from fifty-two to sixty, are known as isotopes. An isotope is one variety of an element; every element has several different isotopes. Iron is one of the most stable of the elements, which is why it is found at the core of our planet.

Uranium, at the upper end of the table of elements, has ninety-two protons. It takes between 138 and 148 neutrons to hold the uranium nucleus together, but even so, many isotopes of uranium are unstable. Adding another neutron will often split

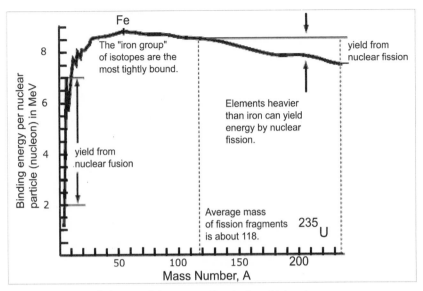

Source: *Department of Physics and Astronomy, Georgia State University*

the uranium nucleus in two, a process known as fission. Adding a neutron to an "overweight" uranium nucleus, one with an atomic weight of 238 (U-238), will sometimes lead to the breeding of new elements, the most stable of which is plutonium (Pu-239). Plutonium is not stable on our geologic time scale, but it will last for thousands of years before decaying into lighter elements. Because of this marginal stability, plutonium is easier to fission than the more stable uranium. That's why A-bomb makers like it.

As protons and neutrons assemble to form a nucleus, they lose a little bit of mass. That mass turns into energy, known as the binding energy for that element. The element with the highest binding energy is iron, which is why it is so stable. The curve of binding energy for all the elements is shown above.

As is evident from the above, uranium, at the right end of the chart, will give off energy when splitting into fission fragments. Some uranium isotopes fission more easily than others; uranium 235 (U-235), with 92 protons and 143 neutrons, is the easiest. It is this reaction that provides the energy released from the weapon known as an A-bomb.

The left end of the chart poses an even more intriguing possibility: the *fusion* of hydrogen into *heavier* elements. This is very hard to do, because the single proton in the hydrogen nucleus will fight off other positively charged protons. With the addition of a few neutrons, however, and if the nuclei can be made to impact each other with enough velocity (accomplished by means of very high temperatures), fusion will occur. This fusion of hydrogen into the two-proton element helium is the source of energy from our sun as well as within the weapon known as the hydrogen or H-bomb.

## WEAPONIZING THE PHYSICS

To make a uranium fission weapon work, one must assemble enough U-235 to sustain a chain reaction; neutrons emerging from one fission must go on to trigger others. This requires a large enough mass of U-235 to achieve supercriticality; that was the concept employed in Little Boy, the bomb dropped on Hiroshima in 1945.

In that weapon, a subcritical mass of U-235 was located at one end of a gun barrel; another subcritical mass was placed at the other end. When over its target, the propellant in back of the first piece of U-235 was ignited, projecting it down the gun barrel at high speed. When it met the second piece of U-235, supercriticality occurred. When flooded with initiating neutrons, the weapon exploded, giving a yield of fifteen thousand tons of TNT equivalent.

When the Allied scientists first met at wartime Los Alamos, the element plutonium had just been discovered—artificially created, actually, within an accelerator at Berkeley. They thought about the possibilities of using this new element within a weapon, as it should be much easier to fission than uranium, but plutonium-239 is only marginally stable. As it decays it gives off neutrons, and they, in turn, will lead to a premature detonation and thus a degraded yield in any gun-type weapon, as described above. Thus, the second American A-bomb, designed to utilize plutonium, was of a different concept. At the center of Fat Man lay a sphere that would be imploded, compressing and more rapidly assembling a plutonium ball. Fat Man was first tested in the New Mexico desert on July 16, 1945, because success was not assured. That test, known as the Trinity event, was heavily instrumented; it was a giant physics experiment, not just a fireworks display. With adjustments, Fat Man was then dropped on Nagasaki three days after the Hiroshima attack. Japanese scientists apparently could tell the difference; the war in the Pacific ended a week later.

Both Little Boy and Fat Man weighed about five tons, but as time went by, fission weapons became more compact. Within two decades it was possible to package fission devices into artillery shells, rocket warheads, and backpack bombs. Five decades after Trinity, World War II nuclear yields of twenty kilotons could be delivered within man-portable warheads.

Unfortunately there is no longer any "secret" to A-bomb design. There are only two factors now limiting membership in the A-bomb club. The first is the availability of fissile materials. U-235 and Pu-239 are difficult to make; they require very large and expensive production facilities. However, once produced, those lethal metals do not go away. They do not deteriorate on the human time scale; they are with us for all (human) time unless burned up in power reactors or otherwise destroyed.

The second constraint on A-bomb development does not actually preclude bomb construction. The problem is simply one of efficiency. Any terrorist organization or nuclear-aspiring state can get kiloton-size yields, using World War II technology, from a contraption the size and weight of an automobile. Sophisticated designers, from the United States to China, will get the same results from a suitcase. To the terrorist, that may not make much difference.

## GOING THERMONUCLEAR

While A-bombs are devastating enough, the energy available at the fusion end of the binding energy curve has long been of greater interest to weapon designers. It was the temperatures and pressures required to achieve fusion that seemed unattainable. Then, five years after the Trinity test, Los Alamos scientists Edward Teller and Stanislaus Ulam came up with the solution: a two-stage approach, compressing and then igniting a separate or secondary pod of thermonuclear fuel. The igniter, or primary, would be an A-bomb. The radiation energy emerging from that bomb would compress a second stage, an opaque capsule containing hydrogen in various forms, to achieve ignition. All of this compression and ignition would occur within a few nanoseconds, that being the time available before the secondary was hit by the exploding primary. A schematic diagram of an H-bomb is shown below.

Thermonuclears cannot be designed by hit-or-miss experiment. They must be conceived and tested conceptually, by computer. Only when a design is complete can a nuclear weapons laboratory conduct a proof test of the finished product; such tests have taken place only in remote arctic, oceanic, or desert havens. Thus, sophisticated computer codes and vast digital machines have become the new objects of nuclear espionage.

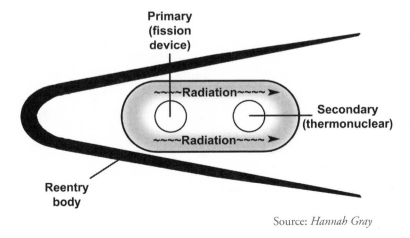

Source: *Hannah Gray*

The original debate about H-bombs focused on the huge energy emerging from such weapons, enough to destroy entire cities in one shot, but history has turned out differently. H-bomb technology has moved in the direction of miniaturization, not larger yields. Even in the world of nukes, enough is enough. Thermonuclear technology has allowed "adequate" yields to be packaged within very compact weapons, and thus the American strategic deterrent has gone to sea. Most of the world's nuclear deterrent forces now ride aboard submarines, reasonably immune to surprise attack and thus quite stable in times of crisis.

## Bombing Missions Over Japan by the 393rd (Nuclear) Bombardment Squadron of the U.S. Army Air Force's 509th Composite Group, July 20–August 14, 1945

| Mission | Date | No. of Aircraft | Target[1] | Bomb Type |
|---------|------|-----------------|-----------|-----------|
| 1 | 20 July 1945 | 3 | Koriyama | Pumpkin[2] |
| 2 | 20 July 1945 | 2 | Fukushima | Pumpkin |
| 3 | 20 July 1945 | 2 | Nagoaka | Pumpkin |
| 4 | 20 July 1945 | 3 | Toyama | Pumpkin |
| 5 | 24 July 1945 | 3 | Sumitomo | Pumpkin |
| 6 | 24 July 1945 | 4 | Kobe | Pumpkin |
| 7 | 24 July 1945 | 3 | Yokkaichi | Pumpkin |
| 8 | 26 July 1945 | 4 | Nagoaka | Pumpkin |
| 9 | 26 July 1945 | 6 | Toyama | Pumpkin |
| 10 | 29 July 1945 | 3 | Ube | Pumpkin |
| 11 | 29 July 1945 | 3 | Koriyama | Pumpkin |
| 12 | 29 July 1945 | 2 | Yokkaichi | Pumpkin |
| 13 | 6 Aug. 1945 | 3 | Hiroshima | "Little Boy" atom bomb |
| 14 | 8 Aug. 1945 | 3 | Osaka | Pumpkin |
| 15 | 8 Aug. 1945 | 3 | Yokkaichi | Pumpkin |
| 16 | 9 Aug. 1945 | 3 | Nagasaki | "Fat Man" atom bomb |
| 17 | 14 Aug. 1945 | 4 | Nagoya | Pumpkin |
| 18 | 14 Aug. 1945 | 3 | Koroma | Pumpkin |
| (surrender) | 15 Aug. 1945 | | | |
| (cancelled) | ~ 18 Aug 1945 | | unknown (possibly Nagoya) | |

Source: *Gordon Thomas and Max Morgan-Witts,* Enola Gay: Mission to Hiroshima *(Loughborough, England: White Owl Press, 1995).*

The Fat Man dropped on Nagasaki was the only complete nuclear weapon remaining in the U.S. inventory. Bomb casings, electronics, and other components were all on Tinian, but enough plutonium for a bomb pit would not have been available until a week after the August 9 attack on Nagasaki. A third drop, in the area of Nagoya, was planned for August 17–18.

After bombing Nagasaki, the United States discontinued the pumpkin flights, awaiting a Japanese surrender, but after five days there was no response. On August 14, the 393rd Bomb Squadron restarted practice runs with a seven-pumpkin attack on Aichi Prefecture in hopes the Japanese would notice, to incentivize a Japanese surrender and to prepare for the August 17–18 drop.[3]

At noon on August 15, 1945 (Tokyo time), the emperor of Japan broadcast his acceptance of the Allied surrender terms. There had been an attempted coup the night before as elements of the military tried to find and destroy the emperor's message, recorded the previous evening.

**Notes to Appendix B table:**

1. To maximize surprise, and thus protect the precious atomic payloads from interception, planned A-bomb targets were omitted from the initial pumpkin bombing lists.

2. Crews of the 393rd Bombardment Squadron practiced by dropping ten-thousand-pound "pumpkins," painted orange and shaped like Fat Man, onto Japanese targets. Each contained 5,500 pounds of explosives. They were weighted and balanced to simulate a Fat Man.

3. After the planned August 17–18 drop on another major Japanese city, if there had been no surrender, the American army chief of staff, Gen. George Marshall, was planning to use the next-available A-bombs as "tactical nuclear weapons" in preparation for the assault on Kyushu. He would have had available, and was planning to use, one A-bomb per week during September and October 1945. The invasion was scheduled for November 1. An increased flow of weapons would have been available thereafter, during November and December, to support that landing and then to support the invasion of Honshu that was to follow. It would have been quite a mess.

# U.S. AIRCRAFT ACCIDENTS WITH NUCLEAR WEAPONS ABOARD

Table I

**U.S. in-flight military accidents during 1950 involving
propeller-driven aircraft with early, separate-capsule
A-bomb components on board**

| Date | Event | Nuclear materials involved | Contamination | Fatalities |
|------|-------|----------------------------|---------------|------------|
| Feb. 13, 1950 | B-36 engine failure over Canada. Ejected a dummy bomb over the ocean, which exploded on impact. Crew then bailed out over Canada. | One weapon, no capsule, on board | None evident | None |
| Apr. 11, 1950 | B-29, ferrying components, crashed three minutes after takeoff from Kirtland AFB, New Mexico. Some high explosive burned, none exploded. Capsule aboard, not in weapon. | One weapon and capsule on board; capsule recovered | None | Entire crew |
| Jul. 13, 1950 | B-50 developed flight control problems over Lebanon, Ohio. Flew into the ground. Explosive in weapon detonated on impact. | One weapon, no capsule, on board | None | Entire crew (16) |
| Aug. 5, 1950 | B-29 developed mechanical problems on takeoff from Travis AFB, California. Crashed and burned. Explosive in weapon detonated. | One weapon, no capsule, on board | None | Crew and fire fighters (19) |
| Nov. 10 1950 | B-50 developed an in-flight emergency over the open ocean. Jettisoned weapon to save aircraft. High explosive in weapon detonated upon ocean impact. | One weapon, no capsule, on board | None evident | None |

## Table II
## In-flight U.S. military aircraft accidents,
## 1956–1957, involving bombers and transport aircraft
## with separate-capsule A-bomb components on board

| Date | Event | Nuclear materials involved | Contamination | Fatalities |
|---|---|---|---|---|
| Mar. 10, 1956 | B-47 from MacDill AFB, Florida, failed to meet its tanker over Mediterranean; disappeared and was never found. No weapon detonation possible. | No weapons, but two capsules on board | None evident | 3 |
| Jul. 27, 1956 | B-47 with no weapons on board lost control on landing, hit a weapon storage igloo, damaged several weapons. | One detonation in igloo, no capsule involved | None | None |
| May 22, 1957 | B-36 landing at Kirtland AFB, New Mexico, accidentally released a weapon on approach. Weapon exploded on impact. | Capsule in aircraft, not inserted | Only within bomb crater | None |
| Jul. 28, 1957 | C-124 ferrying weapons from Dover, Delaware, lost power and jettisoned two weapons over the Atlantic. No detonations upon water impact. | No capsules in any weapons | None evident | None |
| Oct. 11, 1957 | B-47 suffered a tire explosion after takeoff, crashed, with one weapon aboard. Detonations after crash, in fire. | One weapon on board, no capsule inserted | None | 3 |

Table III

## U.S. military aircraft accidents involving
## B-47 jet aircraft flying airborne alert missions during 1958
## with a live thermonuclear weapon on board

| Date | Event | Nuclear materials involved | Contamination | Fatalities |
|---|---|---|---|---|
| Jan. 31, 1958 | B-47 with one operational weapon crashed overseas on takeoff, burned for seven hours. | High explosive in weapon did not detonate | Asphalt under aircraft removed | 3 |
| Feb. 7, 1958 | B-47 collided with F-86 over Georgia, jettisoned one weapon off Savannah before landing. | No detonation on water impact | None evident; weapon not found | None |
| Mar. 11, 1958 | B-47 accidentally jettisoned one unarmed weapon over South Carolina. That weapon exploded on impact. | No capsule aboard or in weapon | None | None |
| Nov 4, 1958 | B-47 caught fire on takeoff from Dyess AFB, Texas, and crashed. | One weapon detonated; no nuclear yield | Limited to crash site | 3 |
| Nov 26, 1958 | B-47 with one weapon on board caught fire on the ground at Chennault AFB, Louisiana. | One weapon destroyed; no nuclear yield | Limited to aircraft wreckage | None |

## Principal Soviet Nuclear Production Facilities

| Facility Name | Location | Function | Employees in 1989 | Comments |
|---|---|---|---|---|
| Angarsk | Angarsk | Uranium enrichment | — | Proposed international enrichment facility |
| Arzamas-16 | Sarov | First nuclear weapons research and development facility (the Soviet Los Alamos) | 25,000 | Also a weapons production facility, Avangard |
| Chelyabinsk-65, a.k.a. Mayak | Ozersk | Six reactors producing plutonium and tritium, and reprocessing fuel | 18,000 | Also manufactures weapon components |
| Chelyabinsk-70* | Snezhinsk | Second nuclear weapons research and development facility | 15,000 | Analogous to Livermore in the U.S. |
| Krasnoyarsk-26* | Zheleznogorsk | Three plutonium production reactors and one reprocessing plant, all underground | 11,000 | Last two nuclear reactors to close in 2011 |
| Krasnoyarsk-45* | Zheleznogorsk | Second largest HEU facility (diffusion and centrifuge) | 10,000 | Now producing enriched uranium for power plants |
| Sverdlovsk-44 | Novouralsk | Largest uranium enrichment facility (diffusion and centrifuge) | 15,000 | — |
| Sverdlovsk-45 | Lesnoy | Materials production and nuclear weapons assembly, now discontinued | 10,000 | Currently disassembles weapons |
| Tomsk-7* | Seversk | Uranium enrichment, five reactors producing plutonium and tritium, plutonium parts fabrication | 20,000 | Last plutonium production reactor to close in 2008 |
| Zlatoust-20* | Zlatoust | Second nuclear weapons assembly facility | — | — |

*These plants constitute the second, parallel network of Eastern nuclear facilities.
Source: Oleg Bukharin, "Conversion in Russia's Closed Nuclear Cities," delivered at a workshop at Princeton University, November 2000.

# NOTES ON D. B. STILLMAN'S TEN VISITS TO THE CHINESE NUCLEAR WEAPON COMPLEX, 1990–2001

In China, ideas for new nuclear weapons originate in the CAEP.[1] Their proposals go to the General Armament Department of the PLA[2] and COSTIND,[3] who jointly decide on a course of action. If the design concept is approved, the actual number of nuclear device tests conducted in support of that weapon depends on the resources available within the national budget of China.

## NUCLEAR TESTS

The Chinese Nuclear Weapons Test Base (CNWTB) is a six-hour drive south of Urumqi in the Xinjiang Province near the city of Wushihtala (or Uxxaktal). The living area for the test-site workers and military cadre is known as Malan, but that name does not appear on any maps of China. When I was there in 1990, the population of Malan consisted of around two thousand PLA personnel and perhaps eight thousand civilians, including families. Those numbers grew, temporarily, during final test preparations. The CNWTB now reports to the General Armament Department of the PLA through an organization known as Base 21. The Chinese test site area is seven times larger than the U.S. Nevada Test Site. It is an electronically secure facility.

1. China Academy of Engineering Physics, the equivalent of Los Alamos, Livermore, and Sandia in the United States.
2. The People's Liberation Army.
3. Commission on Science, Technology, and Industry for National Defense. This commission reports to the State Council, i.e., the cabinet.

The Chinese nuclear diagnostics were every bit as good as those used in American nuclear tests, if not better. For example, consider the frequency response of their oscilloscopes. The Northwest Institute of Nuclear Technology (NINT) scientists showed us several Chinese-built five-megahertz oscilloscopes, with their fastest oscilloscope able to record 1.5 gigahertz signals.

Scientists at NINT also had developed and fielded a dual-axis PINEX (pinhole neutron experiment) to provide dual images within the deuterium-tritium burn region of a boosted primary during implosion, at exactly the desired moment. What made this PINEX detector unique was its dual-axis capability. This feature allowed the Chinese to image either two time-sequenced events in a specific region of burn within the nuclear device or to record events at two separate locations within the nuclear device at any given time.

During evenings in our barracks, the Chinese showed us videotapes of some of their earlier nuclear effects experiments. One such test, the twelfth Chinese shot conducted on November 18, 1971, surrounded the nuclear explosive with a variety of targets at a distance: submarine-pen doors, underground military command bunkers, military aircraft, tanks, and even animals, caged in place with instruments attached. I noted with interest that Chinese procedures were identical to those followed at the U.S. Nuclear Weapons Test Site.

The NINT personnel are all PLA people; they are responsible for recording nuclear test diagnostics data, then performing the radiochemical analysis of the bomb debris to ascertain device performance. The NINT headquarters is located about fourteen miles east of Xian, in Shaanxi Province.

## NUCLEAR TECHNOLOGY

The Chinese were very interested in the development of a neutron bomb. In their quest for a successful design, they met with failure four times. On December 19, 1984, they finally achieved a credible enhanced radiation performance from a device yielding two to five kilotons. They conducted a final proof test on September 29, 1988. That device produced two kilotons of energy release and a lot of neutrons. Out of the forty-six device tests in the entire Chinese nuclear program, six (or, one out of eight) were devoted to neutron bomb development.

On my first trip to Mianyang, in April 1990, just as I had concluded an unclassified briefing to several Chinese scientists at the China Academy of Engineering Physics, one of those present made a reference to a highly classified project then under way at Livermore. He even identified it by its specific Livermore code name, asking if that project involved pumping a laser with fission products. I ignored his question, continuing on as if the question had never been asked.

On my first trip to visit the Institute of Applied Physics and Computational Mathematics (IAPCM), I learned that because the Soviets had withdrawn all support from the Chinese nuclear program in 1959, plutonium played no role in early Chinese nuclear tests. Plutonium production and processing had come to a standstill; enriched uranium was China's only route to its first nuclear weapon. Until the 1998 nuclear tests in Pakistan, China was the only country to initiate a nuclear weapon program without plutonium. They started with what they had: enriched uranium-235. The first Chinese test using plutonium did not take place for another four years, December 27, 1968. By then they had already tested an H-bomb.

Based on my ten trips to the Chinese nuclear weapon facilities, spread over an eleven-year time span, I am convinced that Chinese nuclear weapons technology is on a par with that of the United States. The Chinese achieved this rapid success with nuclear tests numbering only 4 percent of the U.S. total.

## ORGANIZATION OF THE
## CHINESE NUCLEAR WEAPON PROGRAM

When my travels were over, I put together a "wiring diagram" to explain this most puzzling Chinese nuclear weapon complex. My conclusions are reproduced on the page that follows; an explanation of some of the institutes' locations and duties are on the pages that follow that chart.

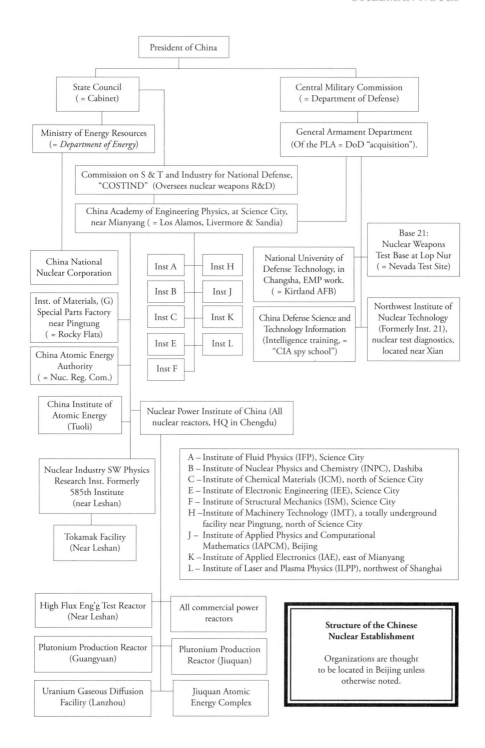

President of China

State Council
( = Cabinet)

Central Military Commission
( = Department of Defense)

Ministry of Energy Resources
(= *Department of Energy*)

General Armament Department
(Of the PLA = DoD "acquisition").

Commission on S & T and Industry for National Defense,
"COSTIND" (Oversees nuclear weapons R&D)

China Academy of Engineering Physics, at Science City,
near Mianyang ( = Los Alamos, Livermore & Sandia)

Base 21:
Nuclear Weapons
Test Base at Lop Nur
( = Nevada Test Site)

China National
Nuclear Corporation

Inst A   Inst H

Inst B   Inst J

National University of
Defense Technology, in
Changsha, EMP work.
( = Kirtland AFB)

Northwest Institute of
Nuclear Technology
(Formerly Inst. 21),
nuclear test diagnostics,
located near Xian

Inst. of Materials, (G)
Special Parts Factory
near Pingtung
( = Rocky Flats)

Inst C   Inst K

Inst E   Inst L

China Defense Science and
Technology Information
(Intelligence training, =
"CIA spy school")

China Atomic Energy
Authority
( = Nuc. Reg. Com.)

Inst F

China Institute of
Atomic Energy
(Tuoli)

Nuclear Power Institute of China (All
nuclear reactors, HQ in Chengdu)

A – Institute of Fluid Physics (IFP), Science City
B – Institute of Nuclear Physics and Chemistry (INPC), Dashiba
C – Institute of Chemical Materials (ICM), north of Science City
E – Institute of Electronic Engineering (IEE), Science City
F – Institute of Structural Mechanics (ISM), Science City
H – Institute of Machinery Technology (IMT), a totally underground
      facility near Pingtung, north of Science City
J – Institute of Applied Physics and Computational
      Mathematics (IAPCM), Beijing
K – Institute of Applied Electronics (IAE), east of Mianyang
L – Institute of Laser and Plasma Physics (ILPP), northwest of Shanghai

Nuclear Industry SW Physics
Research Inst. Formerly
585th Institute
(near Leshan)

Tokamak Facility
(Near Leshan)

High Flux Eng'g Test Reactor
(Near Leshan)

All commercial power
reactors

Plutonium Production Reactor
(Guangyuan)

Plutonium Production
Reactor (Jiuquan)

Uranium Gaseous Diffusion
Facility (Lanzhou)

Jiuquan Atomic
Energy Complex

**Structure of the Chinese
Nuclear Establishment**

Organizations are thought
to be located in Beijing unless
otherwise noted.

**The Commission on Science, Technology, and Industry for National Defense** (COSTIND) is headquartered in Beijing, as is the General Armament Department (GAD) of the PLA. Those organizations oversee the China Academy of Engineering Physics (CAEP), which is located in Science City, about four miles north of the city of Mianyang in the Sichuan Province. The CAEP oversees the development of all nuclear weapons, doing so currently through ten institutes spread throughout China. These include:

**A:** The Institute of Fluid Physics (IFP) reports to the CAEP and is also located within Science City. The IFP has six high-explosive test chambers located there and three more high-explosive outdoor test sites within a two-hour drive northeast of Science City.

**B:** The Institute of Nuclear Physics and Chemistry (INPC) reports to the CAEP and is located near the town of Dashiba, about a two-hour drive to the west of Science City. Two prompt-burst reactors and a three-megawatt research reactor are located there.

**C:** The Institute of Chemical Materials (ICM) reports to the CAEP and is located about a ninety-minute drive to the north of Mianyang just beyond the town of Zitong. Two high-explosive test sites are also located there.

**E:** The Institute of Electronic Engineering (IEE) reports to the CAEP and is located in Science City. The mission of the IEE is similar to that of the Sandia National Laboratories in Albuquerque, New Mexico (i.e., weapon-arming and firing sets).

**F:** The Institute of Structural Mechanics (ISM) reports to the CAEP. Its headquarters is now located in Science City, but the majority of its activities are located within a rectangular basin about a ninety-minute drive north of Mianyang.

**G:** The Institute of Materials, which includes the Special Parts Factory, was reassigned to the China National Nuclear Corporation in early 1998. It is located a two-and-a-half-hour drive north of Science City, near the city of Pingtung.

**H:** The Institute of Machinery Technology (IMT) reports to the CAEP. It is probably co-located with the Special Parts Factory (SPF) in an underground facility near Pingtung.

**J:** The Institute of Applied Physics and Computational Mathematics (IAPCM) reports to the CAEP and is located in Beijing. This institute is home to the Chinese nuclear weapon designers.

**K:** The Institute of Applied Electronics (IAE) reports to the CAEP and is located about a seventy-five-minute drive to the east of Science City. A relativistic electron beam accelerator is located at the IAE.

**L:** The Institute of Laser and Plasma Physics (ILPP) reports to the CAEP and is co-located with the Institute of Fine Mechanics in the Jiading section of northwest Shanghai. Inertial confinement fusion experiments are conducted at the ILPP.

The **China National Nuclear Corporation** (CNNC) was formed in 1988 as a corporation to oversee the research, development, and operation of China's nuclear industry. That industry includes the production of nuclear weapons as well as the operation of nuclear reactors and uranium-enrichment plants. The CNNC is headquartered in Beijing and reports to the State Council (the Cabinet) through the Ministry of Energy Resources. The CNCC oversees the following organizations, among others:

**1. The Special Parts Factory**, transferred from CAEP to CNNC in early 1998, is now known as the Institute of Materials (IM). Its mission remains the same—the fabrication of nuclear weapons.

**2. The China Atomic Energy Authority**, located in Beijing, is charged with managing China's relations with the International Atomic Energy Agency in compliance with the Nonproliferation Treaty.

**3. The China Institute of Atomic Energy,** located in Tuoli, twenty miles south of Beijing, is the main research arm of the CNNC, conducting work in physics, radiochemistry, reactor engineering, and materials processing.

**4. The Nuclear Power Institute of China** is the comprehensive base for the design, engineering, testing, construction, and operation of China's nuclear reactors. With headquarters in Chengdu, it oversees operations of the following entities, among others:

- The High-Flux Engineering Test Reactor (HFETR) Facility, which is the largest engineering test reactor in Asia. It is located about a six-hour drive south of Mianyang, near the city of Leshan.
- The Chinese plutonium production reactors, located near Guangyuan in northeast Sichuan Province and near Jiuquan in the northwest part of Gansu Province.
- The first Chinese gaseous diffusion plant (GDP), located near Lanzhou in the southeast part of Gansu Province. This facility separates uranium-235 from uranium-238.
- A second-generation GDP, located near the city of Heping in the south central part of Sichuan Province.

## THE CHINESE NUCLEAR AGENDA

From my discussions with Chinese nuclear weapons personnel, I perceived their interests to lie in the following areas:

**Nuclear Design** (Of primary interest, but most discussions were out of bounds)
• Hydronuclear testing
• The measurement of primary-emitted neutron effects on other weapon components

**Weapon Vulnerability** (The effects of one nuclear detonation on another weapon)
• Nuclear hardening of materials and electronics
• The response of ablative-type materials to high levels of gamma and neutron flux
• Structural response of materials to X-rays of different energies
• Prompt-burst reactors

**Nuclear Testing Diagnostics**
• Shock-mounting of instrumentation trailers
• Sub-nanosecond diagnostic techniques
• Picosecond photodetectors
• The proper calibration of streak cameras
• Determining nuclear yield from gamma detector data
• Spatial resolution in gamma ray detection
• Adjusting the dynamic range for fiber optics
• Compton diodes
• Materials for the conversion of gamma or X radiation to light

**Advanced Systems**
• Inertial Confined Fusion
• Relativistic Electron Beam Accelerators
• X-ray lasers
• Directed energy weapons

**Safety and Security**
• Plutonium aging in their stockpiled nuclear weapons
• Nuclear-test verification of other countries
• Arms-control issues
• All forms of diagnostics to detect nuclear detonations
• Means to assure the safety and security of their weapons

## HU SIDE CLOSES THE DOOR

Academician Hu Side, a 1958 graduate of Fudan University in theoretical physics, had been instrumental in arranging my visits to the Chinese nuclear community. During my ten trips he was serving as the deputy director, and later as the director, of the

China Academy of Engineering Physics, the organization with overall responsibility for Chinese nuclear weapon development.

On May 17, 1999, after a decade of enjoying Hu's hospitality, my U.S. traveling companion (fluent in Chinese) and I were present for a meeting at the IAPCM with Hu Side and a few of his scientific associates. At the end of the day, we assembled for a small banquet, and as we sat down, without further ado, Hu launched into a long, well-rehearsed, and clearly intended diatribe, delivered without notes, to the two of us.[4] Without doubt it closed the door on any further relationships between the U.S. and Chinese nuclear weapons communities.

"There has been a sharp decline in U.S./China relations. They are at the lowest point in years and are likely to remain bad for some time. There are many reasons for this, and the number of reasons has been steadily growing over the past year. You predicted that U.S./China relations would enter a difficult period when we met with both of you in Science City in December 1998. However, we had no idea that the deterioration would be so swift and so dramatic.

"The most immediate provocation was the bombing of our embassy in Belgrade on May 8, 1999.[5] We do find it hard to believe that this was a mistake! With all the CIA's resources, how could it be possible that you would have used a four-year-old map and misidentified an embassy building that is so prominent? Some of us will wait to make a judgment on this until after the U.S. or NATO releases its report, but we will be in the minority.[6] It will also be important to see what the U.S. or NATO does to those who were responsible for this mistake. If no one is held to be responsible, then we will reach the judgment that the bombing was deliberate.[7]

"More important for us in the CAEP is the matter of the accusations of espionage. You have overestimated the scientific and technical capability of the U.S. and seriously underestimated that of China. You have insulted us! You must have made these charges for political reasons and not on the basis of evidence of what we

4. Understanding the import of what we were hearing, my traveling companion and I were able to take copious notes. Since the talk was given in Chinese, the presence of an interpreter repeating the message facilitated that process. We were able to transcribe our notes into a record of that talk a few hours later, in our hotel room.

5. During the previous week, an American B-2 hit the embassy, along with other targets in Belgrade, with smart weapons. Three Chinese journalists were killed, and twenty others were injured.

6. Hu believed that the majority of the Chinese people would *not* accept the report; they would always believe the bombing was on purpose.

7. Investigations were completed in April 2000. They found that the CIA supplied erroneous targeting information which was not adequately reviewed by Pentagon and NATO officers. One mid-level CIA officer was dismissed and six others were reprimanded. There were no Department of Defense or other military reprimands.

have done. We never learned anything from you! I never asked you for anything, especially from Stillman, and you never told me anything. We did not need you [Americans]! [Wen Ho Lee] is a scapegoat.

"You have seriously and probably permanently damaged the scientific and lab-to-lab exchanges. Don't you know that no one loses anything in mutually beneficial exchanges? Exchanges help both sides understand each other and build trust. This is why we started the exchange, and we are agreeing to [continue] work with Stanford University. We believed that at the end of the Cold War we needed to change direction and become more cooperative.

"With regard to the level of our nuclear weapons development, we don't need anything from the U.S. We began development of thermonuclear weapons beginning with our third nuclear weapons test and had solved all of the problems by the sixth nuclear weapons test in 1967. What the U.S. did for us and the whole world was to prove that atomic and thermonuclear weapons worked. That is what you gave us and everyone else. That was the main secret that you gave away. Everything else we did on our own."

With Hu stopping for a breath of air, I spoke up to compliment him on his contribution to the development of sophisticated thermonuclear primaries, since a few years earlier I had learned that he had been the designer of China's first such primary.

Hu resumed his peroration: "Yes, but we did not come to the idea of those sophisticated primaries from you [the United States]. This was the only logical way to reduce the diameter of a nuclear weapon in order to fit it into smaller diameter reentry vehicles for the next generation of nuclear warheads as well as third-generation weapons in particular.[8] In the late 1970s, China realized that we must reduce the diameters of our next generation nuclear weapons. We understood the general principles involved in sophisticated primaries and the physical laws involving criticality and diameter [as a function of geometry]. We then began to test our nuclear weapons using different shapes based on these principles. The reason we did not successfully design these sophisticated primaries earlier in our program was because we did not have the computer capability needed to design such things. We only began to get this computing capability in the early 1980s. However, even then, that capability came slowly. There was no big jump even though we were getting new, more capable computers. We had to learn how to use the computers as well as how to design these shapes.

"By the late 1980s and up to the mid-1990s, we expanded our knowledge of the nuclear weapon design requirements step by step. We came to agree with your scientists that we had mastered 80 percent and then 90 percent of the full potential

8. For example, artillery shells.

[i.e., efficiency] of the nuclear weapon design. The ability to get the last 10 percent would be of very little military value and also very expensive to acquire. We did not see the military requirement for further nuclear weapons tests, nor were we able to justify the expense. So we agreed with you to enter into a CTBT.[9] And we thought that, by doing this, we could cooperate with you [the United States] on ending the nuclear arms race. But that apparently was not your [American] idea.

"This is why we will postpone our planned meeting with Stanford University for July to October. Working together with you [Americans] will be more difficult. The hosting of foreign visitors will become almost impossible, and all work with your nuclear weapons laboratories will stop. We will wait to see how the atmosphere develops. I wish I could testify before your U.S. Congress to tell them how much damage has been done![10] They have turned cooperation into conflict. I could tell them, that is, I could tell them the truth that we never found it necessary to steal any U.S. nuclear weapon secrets."

That is a strong statement. When considering Hu's disclaimer, your authors would prefer to rely on the words of Prof. Qian Xuesen, patriarch of the Chinese missile and space programs.[11] In addressing a Chinese National Defense Science and Technology Intelligence Working Conference in Beijing, in July 1983, Professor Qian said: "I maintain that the matter of intelligence collection is a science and technology; we should put our best efforts into researching intelligence collection."

Or perhaps the words of advisors to the U.S. director of National Intelligence twenty-five years later: "[Today] there are forty thousand Chinese hackers who are collecting information off U.S. information systems and those of our partners. How many of them can read English? Almost every one of them."[12]

9. Comprehensive Test Ban Treaty.
10. He was referring to the Cox Committee report to the U.S. House of Representatives, March 1999, which said, in summary:
    a. The People's Republic of China has stolen design information on the most advanced U.S. thermonuclear weapons.
    b. The Committee judges that the People's Republic of China's next generation of thermonuclear weapons will exploit elements of stolen U.S. design information.
    c. P.R.C. penetration of our national weapons laboratories spans several decades and continues today.
11. Huo and Wang, *Sources and Technologies of Obtaining National Defense Science and Technology Intelligence* (Huo & Wang, 1991).
12. Ed Giorgio, former NSA cryptographer, as quoted in Lawrence Wright, "The Spymaster," *New Yorker* (January 21, 2008).

# CHRONOLOGY

|                    | **1938**                                                                                                                                                                                                                                                   |
|--------------------|---------------------------------------------------------------------------------------------------------------------------------------------------------------------------------------------------------------------------------------------------------------|
| **November**       | Hahn and Meitner meet in Copenhagen, discuss the results of neutron bombardment experiments.                                                                                                                                                                |
| **December 22**    | Meitner and Frisch (in Sweden) write to Hahn (in Berlin) proposing "nuclear fission" as an explanation for Hahn's experimental results.                                                                                                                      |
| **December**       | Hahn and Strassman publish their findings.                                                                                                                                                                                                                  |

|                    | **1939**                                                                                                                                                                                                                                                   |
|--------------------|---------------------------------------------------------------------------------------------------------------------------------------------------------------------------------------------------------------------------------------------------------------|
| **March**          | Joliot-Curie in France and Fermi and Szilard in the United States note with interest the Hahn/Meitner discovery of nuclear fission. They replicate those experiments and observe the release of additional neutrons, implying the possibility of a chain reaction and thus a bomb. |
| **April**          | Flerov and Rusinov, in Moscow, make similar observations.                                                                                                                                                                                                   |
| **Summer**         | Khariton and Zeldovich, in Leningrad, publish papers (internally and in secret) on the steps needed to develop a Soviet A-bomb.                                                                                                                              |
| **September 1**    | Hitler invades Poland; World War II begins.                                                                                                                                                                                                                 |

|                    | **1940**                                                                                                                                                                                                                                                   |
|--------------------|---------------------------------------------------------------------------------------------------------------------------------------------------------------------------------------------------------------------------------------------------------------|
| **May 10**         | Hitler invades the Low Countries (Belgium, Holland, and Luxembourg). The invasion of France follows. All fall to the Germans within a month.                                                                                                                 |
| **May 10**         | Churchill takes power in the United Kingdom, soon encourages serious investigations of nuclear weapon possibilities.                                                                                                                                         |
| **Summer**         | With the United Kingdom in danger of invasion, the British nuclear weapons program is relocated to Chalk River, Canada, then to New York and Los Alamos.                                                                                                     |
| **August–September** | The Battle of Britain is fought in the skies over England. The United Kingdom wins; Hitler calls off a German invasion and turns his attention to the Soviet Union.                                                                                        |
| **October**        | In Tokyo, Colonel Suzuki and Professor Sagane produce a fission-weapon study for the Japanese Army general staff.                                                                                                                                            |

**1941**

Late Winter      Khariton and Zeldovich, in the U.S.S.R., calculate the critical mass of U-235 to be twenty-two pounds.

March      Discovery of plutonium by Glenn Seaborg in Berkeley.

June      MAUD Committee reports to the British War Cabinet "On the Use of Uranium for a Bomb." Critical mass of U-235 is estimated at 25 pounds.

June 22      Germans invade Soviet Union, thereby initiating a two-front war.

September 16      The United Kingdom and the U.S.S.R., now allied in the war against Hitler, install the young Mohammed Reza Pahlavi as shah of Iran, deposing his pro-Nazi father.

Autumn      U.S. officials formalize their serious interest in A-bomb development.

December 7–8      Japanese attack Pearl Harbor; the United States declares war on Japan; Germany declares war on the United States.

**1942**

June      German Armaments Minister Speer convenes his nuclear advisors in Berlin; Professor Heisenberg urges bomb development, others do not.

June 23      Hitler decides to pursue rockets and jet aircraft rather than nuclear weapons.

September      General Leslie Groves put in charge of the U.S. Manhattan Engineering District; acquisition of land for Oak Ridge facilities begins.

December 2      Fermi's "nuclear pile," the world's first, goes critical in Chicago.

**1943**

January 31      German General Paulus surrenders at Stalingrad; the turning of the tide in the Soviet Union's war with Germany.

February 28      Norwegian Special Forces destroy Norsk Hydro heavy water facility. Soon thereafter, German Armaments Minister Speer confirms the end of all nuclear weapons work within Germany.

February      Soviets open Laboratory No. 2 in Moscow to pursue nuclear weapons development.

March      J. Robert Oppenheimer arrives in Los Alamos to open the scientific laboratory there.

March 10      Igor Kurchatov put in charge of Soviets' Laboratory No. 2.

May      Japanese nuclear weapon project, the "N Project," starts at the Aviation Technology Institute in Tokyo with Professor Nishina in charge.

Autumn      Japanese start a second, centrifuge-based nuclear program, the "F Project," at Imperial University of Kyoto.

November      Professor Takeuchi's uranium isotope separator is first tested in Tokyo.

**1944**

July      General de Gaulle visits North America, meets with French refugee nuclear scientists in Montreal, learns of their weapons work, and urges their immediate return to France.

August 25      Liberation of Paris by Allied armies.

September 27      The world's first plutonium-producing nuclear reactor goes critical at Hanford, Washington.

| | |
|---|---|
| **October** | The United States, United Kingdom, and U.S.S.R. recognize Charles de Gaulle as leader of the Provisional French Government. |

### 1945

| | |
|---|---|
| **April 12** | Franklin Roosevelt dies; Harry Truman becomes U.S. president. |
| **May 8** | End of World War II in Europe. |
| **June 1** | Truman's interim committee on bomb use meets and recommends against a demonstration. "The A-bomb is too intricate . . . operation far from routine." |
| **July 16** | Fat Man, world's first A-bomb, is tested in New Mexico as the Trinity event. |
| **July 22** | Truman and Churchill, at Potsdam, decide to use the A-bomb on Japan. |
| **July 24** | Truman advises Stalin of the Trinity test. Stalin urges its use against Japan. |
| **July 26** | Clement Attlee becomes prime minister of United Kingdom. The United States, United Kingdom, and China issue the Potsdam Declaration, calling on the Japanese to surrender or face "prompt and utter destruction." |
| **August 6** | Little Boy A-bomb attack on Hiroshima. |
| **August 7** | Japanese General Arisue, with staff drawn from N and F Projects, is directed to investigate the Hiroshima bombing. |
| **August 9** | Fat Man attack on Nagasaki. |
| **August 10 (a.m.)** | Emperor Hirohito breaks with history and actively participates in a Japanese cabinet meeting. U.S. code breakers immediately learn of this fact. |
| **August 10 (p.m.)** | General Marshall withdraws General Groves' authority to use A-bombs without prior presidential approval. |
| **August 14** | Second cabinet meeting with Hirohito actively participating. He ends debate, directs war termination, and records an acceptance of the Potsdam Declaration. An attempted coup fails. |
| **August 15** | The Hirohito acceptance of the Potsdam Declaration is broadcast at noon, Tokyo time. The war in the Pacific ends. |
| **August 18** | A third A-bomb attack is planned on Aichi Prefecture but never executed. |
| **October 18** | Charles de Gaulle, having been recognized a year before as the leader of the Provisional Government in France, creates the world's first atomic energy commission. Eminent physicist and Communist Party member Frédéric Joliot-Curie becomes its first high commissioner. |
| **October 21** | First postwar elections in France. Socialists and communists gain control of parliament, but de Gaulle remains as prime minister. |
| **October 24** | UN Charter ratified by World War II victors. |
| **November 9** | The United Kingdom's Attlee comes to Washington and meets with U.S. President Truman and Canadian Prime Minister King to promote UN control of atomic energy. U.S. Congress objects. |

### 1946

| | |
|---|---|
| **January 26** | Faced with continuing parliamentary obstructions, de Gaulle resigns as prime minister of France. |

| | |
|---|---|
| **February** | Igor Gouzenko, a code clerk in the Soviet embassy in Ottawa, having defected during the previous September, reveals the extent of Soviet nuclear espionage within the United States and Canada. |
| **March 5** | Churchill, as a private citizen, delivers his Iron Curtain speech in Fulton, Missouri. |
| **April** | Soviet nuclear weapons R&D moves to Sarov, 240 miles east of Moscow. Installation to be known as Arzamas-16. |
| **April** | Soviets decide to build their plutonium production facilities at Mayak (Chelyabinsk-40). |
| **August 1** | McMahon bill signed in United States, precluding the sharing of any nuclear information with any other countries and establishing the U.S. Atomic Energy Commission. |
| **November 5** | Republicans win a sweeping victory in U.S. congressional elections, picking up fifty-five seats in the House, twelve seats in the Senate. The Republicans thus gain legislative control for the first time since the prewar years. To the British political leadership, the election of 1946 implies a return to American prewar isolationism. |
| **December 25** | Soviets' first experimental nuclear reactor, F-1, goes critical at Laboratory No. 2 in Moscow. |

### 1947

| | |
|---|---|
| **January** | Gen 163 Committee of the British Cabinet meets, decides to proceed with development of a British nuclear weapon. The decision is not announced publicly for over a year. |
| **May 22** | President Truman signs legislation funding the support of anticommunist military activities, thus giving muscle to the Truman Doctrine. |
| **July 12** | Marshall Plan adopted by the recovering European states. |
| **August 15** | India gains independence from Great Britain, and the former colony is partitioned into Hindu India and Muslim Pakistan. |

### 1948

| | |
|---|---|
| **Spring** | Los Alamos weapon physicist Joan Hinton moves to China. |
| **May 14** | British Mandate in Palestine expires; British forces leave; David Ben-Gurion proclaims the independence of the State of Israel, Truman immediately recognizes the Ben-Gurion Government as the *de facto* authority in that state. |
| **June 10** | Soviet plutonium production reactor A goes critical at Mayak. |
| **June** | The Soviet Special Committee approves a work plan for the development of a Soviet thermonuclear weapon. |
| **June 21** | Soviets announce the Berlin Blockade, effective June 24. |
| **Summer** | Qian Sanqiang, future father of the Chinese A-bomb, returns to China after a ten-year stint in Paris as a student of Frédéric Joliot-Curie. |
| **December 15** | The first French experimental nuclear reactor, F-l, goes critical at Fort de Chatillon. |

### 1949

| | |
|---|---|
| **April 4** | The North Atlantic Treaty Organization (NATO) is formed. |
| **May 11** | Soviets lift the Berlin Blockade. |

| Summer | Ben-Gurion sends six top Israeli physics students to study in Zurich, Amsterdam, England, and the United States. |
| --- | --- |
| August 29 | Soviet Union tests first nuclear weapon, RDS-1, internally an exact replica of U.S. Fat Man, in eastern Kazakhstan. The event is not publicly announced, as Stalin is fearful of a pre-emptive U.S. response. |
| September 23 | Truman announces the detection and analysis of the Soviet nuclear test. |
| October 1 | Mao Zedong's communists formally take power in China. |
| December | Mao visits Moscow, meets with Stalin. |
| December 16 | The Sino-Soviet Treaty of Friendship, Alliance, and Mutual Assistance is signed in Moscow. |

### 1950

| January 23–27 | Klaus Fuchs, a resident in Britain, is uncovered as a Soviet spy. His confession cools U.S.–U.K. nuclear collaborative efforts and is probably a factor in Truman's decision to proceed with the H-bomb. |
| --- | --- |
| January 31 | Truman authorizes work on a thermonuclear weapon. |
| February | Fuchs is sentenced to fourteen years in Britain's prisons. |
| March | North Korea's Kim Il Sung visits Moscow, meets with Stalin. They agree on a plan for the North's invasion of South Korea. The Soviets are to assist in the planning, but they are to play no role in ground combat. |
| June 25 | North Korea invades the South. |
| July | First U.K. nuclear reactor goes critical at Windscale. It will begin to produce plutonium in early 1952. |
| September 15 | U.S. forces land at Inchon, turn the tide of war in Korea. |
| October 16–19 | Chinese forces enter the Korean War. |
| December | Eisenhower named Supreme Commander of NATO forces in Europe. |

### 1951

| March | Teller and Ulam publish, internally and secretly at Los Alamos, the correct solution to H-bomb design. |
| --- | --- |
| April 11 | President Truman relieves General MacArthur of command in Korea. |
| October 26 | Winston Churchill returns to power as prime minister of the United Kingdom. |

### 1952

| July 23 | Officers of the Egyptian army overthrow King Farouk. Nasser soon takes power. |
| --- | --- |
| October 3 | United Kingdom tests its first nuclear device, Hurricane, off the Monte Bello Islands in Western Australia |
| October 31 | United States tests its first thermonuclear device, a two-stage experiment with ten megatons of yield, at Eniwetok Atoll in the Pacific. |

### 1953

| January 20 | Dwight Eisenhower assumes the U.S. presidency. |
| --- | --- |
| March 5 | Josef Stalin dies; Malenkov and Khrushchev assume positions of premier and general secretary of the Communist Party of |

| | the Soviet Union (CPSU), respectively. |
| **July 27** | Ceasefire in Korea. |
| **August 12** | Soviets detonate RDS-6s, a layered, single-stage thermonuclear device. |
| **December 8** | Eisenhower proposes "Atoms for Peace" plan at UN. |

## 1954

| **March** | United States conducts the Castle nuclear test series in the Pacific. Portable, high-yield thermonuclear weapons are first tested, with the radioactive debris sampled by other nuclear-aspirant states. |
| **April** | Zeldovich (internally and secretly) announces "discovery" of radiation as the means to implode a Soviet thermonuclear secondary. |
| **May 7** | French fort at Dien Bien Phu falls, inspiring the French to think more seriously about nuclear weapons. |
| **June 16** | The Defence Committee of the British cabinet decides to pursue the thermonuclear option. |
| **November 1** | Algerian rebels declare war on the French government and attack multiple police stations in Algeria. |
| **December 2** | United States and Taiwan sign a mutual defense treaty. This is the "last straw" in Mao's decision to go nuclear. |
| **December 26** | French cabinet decides to develop nuclear weapons, although without providing adequate funding. |

## 1955

| **January 15** | Mao, at a meeting of his Central Secretariat, makes the formal decision to pursue the development of a Chinese nuclear weapon. |
| **February 8** | Malenkov is forced out as premier of the Soviet Union. Khrushchev achieves full control. |
| **April 18–24** | Afro-Asian governments meet in Bandung, Indonesia, to organize a formal antinuclear-weapon alliance. |
| **November 22** | The Soviets detonate RDS-37, a true two-stage thermonuclear weapon with a derated yield of 1.6 megatons. |

## 1956

| **January 7** | France's first plutonium-producing reactor, G-1, goes critical at Marcoule. |
| **February 25** | Khrushchev delivers anti-Stalin speech to his Twentieth Party Congress of the CPSU. Mao is not pleased. |
| **June 22** | France and Israel sign a comprehensive armament- technology, and intelligence, sharing agreement. |
| **June 28–30** | Uprising in Poznan, Poland, the first against a communist government. 400 tanks, 10,000 troops disperse a crowd of 100,000 gathered outside secret police headquarters. |
| **July 26** | Nasser nationalizes the Suez Canal. |
| **August** | Israeli, French, and British representatives meet at Sèvres (France) to plan Operation Musketeer—the joint invasion of Egypt and repossession of the Suez Canal. |
| **October 23–**<br>**November 10**<br>**October 29–** | Uprisings in Hungary are crushed brutally by Soviet troops. |

| | |
|---|---|
| **November 15** | The Suez crisis: Israel invades Egypt; the United Kingdom and France then follow. The United States, caught unaware, opposes the invasions. France, the United Kingdom, and eventually Israel withdraw and lose confidence in the United States as an ally. |
| **November 8** | Israel's Foreign Minister Golda Meir and Director-General of the Ministry of Defense Shimon Peres travel to Paris to ascertain what help they might expect from the French in the event of a military showdown with the Soviets in Egypt. Answer: not much assistance now, but help with the nuclear bomb later. |
| **November 30** | The French Army agrees to fund fully a French nuclear weapons program. |

## 1957

| | |
|---|---|
| **April** | Soviet government assigns E. D. Vorobiev the job of "bringing China into the nuclear age." His team departs for Beijing the following month. |
| **May** | The French Cabinet approves construction of a large nuclear reactor, under contract, for the Israelis at Dimona. |
| **October 7** | The Soviets launch Sputnik. This was the high point of Soviet-Chinese relations. |
| **November 8** | The United Kingdom detonates its first H-bomb, Grapple X, at Christmas Island in the Pacific, with a yield of 1.8 megatons. |

## 1958

| | |
|---|---|
| **January** | Mao unleashes the Great Leap Forward in China. |
| **June 1** | Charles de Gaulle returns to power as prime minister of France, a consequence of the grinding rebellion in Algeria. |
| **June 18** | Soviet nuclear weapon experts Negin, Maslov, and Gavrilov arrive in Beijing to instruct the Chinese on the details of A-bomb construction. |
| **July** | Khrushchev visits China. Meetings do not go well. Khrushchev concludes Mao is mad and rethinks his support of Chinese nuclear ambitions. |
| **Autumn** | De Gaulle dissolves the French Fourth Republic, creates the Fifth Republic, and takes office as its first president in January 1959. |

## 1959

| | |
|---|---|
| **Spring** | U.S. photo interpreter Dino Brugioni briefs the Eisenhower White House on the Israeli nuclear reactor apparently under construction at Dimona. He notes its similarity to the French plutonium producer at Marcoule. |
| **June 20** | Khrushchev formally advises the Chinese that the Soviets will no longer help China with its development of nuclear weapons. |
| **June 24** | Klaus Fuchs is released from his British prison and emigrates to East Germany. |
| **Summer** | Fuchs meets with Qian Sanqiang, leader of the Chinese nuclear weapons program. U.S. nuclear secrets are undoubtedly transferred. |

## 1960

**February 13**  The French test their first nuclear device at Reggane in the Algerian Sahara.

**August**  Decimated by the Great Leap Forward and dismayed by the Soviet withdrawal of support, the Chinese stop work on their plutonium production reactor at Jiuquan and concentrate on enriched-uranium production at Lanzhou.

**August**  The first Corona satellite photography of the Soviet Union becomes available to the United States, several months after the discontinuation of U-2 overflights of the U.S.S.R., following the shoot-down of of Francis Gary Powers on May 1, 1960.

## 1961

**January 14–18**  At the Ninth Plenum of the Chinese Communist Party, Liu Shaoqi and others begin to dismantle the Great Leap Forward. Mao loses control.

**January 20**  John Kennedy assumes the U.S. presidency.

**March 4**  First successful Soviet ABM test.

**September 1**  Soviets break nuclear test moratorium. Radiochemical analysis of the resulting test debris confirms shocking improvements in Soviet nuclear weapon technology.

## 1962

**January 13**  First U-2 overflights of mainland China, flown by Republic of China (R.O.C.) pilots. They had been approved by Kennedy in 1961.

**June 6**  Kennedy signs National Security Action Memorandum 160, directing the installation of permissive action links (PALS) on U.S. nuclear weapons, starting with those positioned overseas.

**October 20– November 21**  Chinese-Indian border war in the Himalayan Mountains. Chinese win.

**October 24–28**  The Cuban missile crisis brings the United States and U.S.S.R. to the brink of nuclear war.

## 1963

**Summer**  Kennedy initiates discussions with Soviets on limiting or precluding Chinese A-bomb development. Those discussions come to naught.

**August 5**  The Limited Test Ban Treaty is signed in Moscow.

**November 22**  John Kennedy assassinated, Lyndon Johnson becomes U.S. president. Documents made available decades later implicate Cuba in the shooting.

**December**  Israel's plutonium production reactor goes critical at Dimona.

## 1964

**January**  Lanzhou begins the delivery of highly enriched uranium to the Chinese nuclear weapons machine shops.

**October 14**  Khrushchev is removed from Soviet power, retires within Moscow, and is replaced by his protégé Leonid Brezhnev as first secretary of the CPSU.

**October 16**  China tests her first nuclear weapon at Lop Nur in Sinkiang Province.

## 1965

| | |
|---|---|
| **February 7** | The United States begins the regular bombing of targets within North Vietnam. |
| **March 8** | 3,500 U.S. Marines go ashore at Da Nang, South Vietnam, the first American combat troops dispatched into that country. |
| **July 30** | Medicare and Medicaid are signed into U.S. law. These entitlements may lead to the insolvency of the U.S. government during the height of the war on terror a half- century later. |

## 1966

| | |
|---|---|
| **May** | Mao regains full power in China. On May 16, he initiates the Cultural Revolution, which again paralyzes his country for over three years. The internal strife continues until Mao's death in 1976. |
| **July 2** | France initiates nuclear testing at Mururoa Atoll in French Polynesia. |
| **September 6** | John Vorster, a Nazi sympathizer during World War II and the architect of apartheid, becomes prime minister of South Africa. |
| **Autumn** | Israeli scientists conduct an important underground experiment in the Negev Desert, probably a hydrodynamic test of their initial A-bomb design. |
| **October** | China's first plutonium production nuclear reactor goes critical at Jiuquan. |

## 1967

| | |
|---|---|
| **June 5–11** | Israel's Six-Day War, a pre-emptive attack on Egypt and Syria. Israel apparently has at least two nuclear weapons in inventory. The United States is not seen as providing immediate help to the Israelis. |
| **June 17** | China detonates its first thermonuclear weapon, with a yield of 3.3 megatons. |

## 1968

| | |
|---|---|
| **July 1** | First signatures on the Treaty on the Nonproliferation of Nuclear Weapons. |
| **August 24** | France detonates its first thermonuclear device, with a yield of 2.6 megatons, in French Polynesia. |

## 1969

| | |
|---|---|
| **January 20** | Richard Nixon assumes U.S. presidency. |
| **September 1** | Muammar al-Qaddafi mounts a successful coup in Libya. |
| **November** | The ARPANET, predecessor of the Internet, starts operation as a Defense Department data-sharing network. |

## 1970

| | |
|---|---|
| **January 16** | Qaddafi takes full power as prime minister and minister of defense in Libya. |
| **April 24** | China's first satellite, *Dong Feng Hong 1*, is launched into orbit. |
| **July** | The Nuclear Nonproliferation Treaty enters into force. |

## 1971

| | |
|---|---|
| **March 27** | Rebel officers in the eastern zone of Pakistan declare independence. Both civil war and a war with India ensue. |

| | |
|---|---|
| **October 25** | At the UN, the People's Republic of China replaces the Republic of China (Taiwan) as the recognized government of China. Beijing thus gains a permanent seat (and veto power) within the Security Council. |
| **December 16** | Pakistan's army in the east surrenders. East Pakistan, with Indian military support, gains independence as the Republic of Bangladesh. A new government takes power in the residual western Pakistan. |

### 1972

| | |
|---|---|
| **January 20** | Pakistan's President Bhutto convenes a conference with his scientific advisors to discuss the possibility of developing a Pakistani nuclear weapon. |
| **February 21** | Nixon visits China. |
| **May 26** | U.S.-Soviet ABM Treaty signed in Moscow. |
| **June 7** | Indira Ghandi, prime minister of India, authorizes the construction of an Indian A-bomb. |
| **October** | KANUPP nuclear reactor commences operation, a potential source of plutonium for Pakistan's nuclear weapons program. |

### 1973

| | |
|---|---|
| **October 6–22** | Yom Kippur War. Egypt and Syria attack Israel. The United States clearly and unambiguously saves the Israelis from defeat by Arab armies. OPEC first flexes its muscle and triples the price of oil. |
| **November 30** | UN adopts Resolution 3068, chastising the government of South Africa and identifying apartheid as a "crime against humanity." |

### 1974

| | |
|---|---|
| **Early in year** | Israel's Moshe Dayan visits South Africa after the Yom Kippur War. |
| **April 25** | The Carnation Revolution in Portugal ends the Salazar-Caetano dictatorships and thus sets in motion the independence of her colonies in Africa. These include Mozambique and Angola, states that will, in time, become havens for South African ANC guerillas. |
| **May 18** | India tests a plutonium-based nuclear device underground in the Rajasthani Desert. The fissionable material comes from an Atoms for Peace Candu reactor. |
| **August 8** | Richard Nixon resigns, Gerald Ford becomes U.S. president. |
| **Summer** | Israeli Minister of Defense Peres meets with South African Prime Minister Vorster in Paris. Soon thereafter, Israel and South Africa exchange diplomatic recognition and ambassadors. |
| **Autumn** | A. Q. Khan spends sixteen days at the URENCO facility in Holland, covertly collecting technology. |
| **December** | A. Q. Khan and Pakistan's President Bhutto first meet in Karachi. They discuss the advantages of HEU technology. |

### 1975

| | |
|---|---|
| **April 30** | Fall of Saigon. U.S. helicopters evacuate remaining civilians from embassy rooftop. End of U.S. military involvement in Vietnam. |

| | |
|---|---|
| **December** | A. Q. Khan permanently relocates from Europe back to Pakistan. |

### 1976

| | |
|---|---|
| **March** | Peres visits South Africa. |
| **April** | South African Prime Minister Vorster visits Israel. |
| **Spring** | Pakistan's President Bhutto authorizes A. Q. Khan to organize and build the uranium-enrichment facility at Kahuta as an alternative to Munir Khan's stalled plutonium program. |
| **July 30** | Soviet reconnaissance satellites notice nuclear test preparation in South Africa's Kalahari Desert. The United States soon confirms; preparations are cancelled. |
| **September 9** | Mao dies in Beijing at age eighty-two. |
| **October 6** | China's newly empowered chairman, Hua Guofeng, arrests the Gang of Four (Mao's widow plus three), thereby ending China's Cultural Revolution. A half-decade of political realignment begins. |
| **December 23** | Canadians terminate all support for Pakistan's KANUPP reactor. The plutonium option becomes endangered. |

### 1977

| | |
|---|---|
| **January 20** | Jimmy Carter assumes U.S. presidency. |
| **July 5** | General Zia ul-Huq overthrows Prime Minister Bhutto to take power in Pakistan. He imposes Islamic law in 1978, hangs Bhutto in 1979. |
| **Late in year** | French industry (San Gobain) withdraws from the construction of Pakistan's reprocessing facility. |
| **November 4** | UN imposes a complete arms embargo on South Africa. |

### 1978

| | |
|---|---|
| **January** | South Africa's Valindaba enrichment facility produces its first sample of uranium enriched to 80-percent U-235. |
| **October 6** | Ayatollah Khomeini expelled from Iraq, moves to Paris. |

### 1979

| | |
|---|---|
| **January 2–February 11** | Overthrow of the shah of Iran; Ayatollah Khomeini takes power; the world price of oil again triples. |
| **July 16** | Saddam Hussein takes full power in Iraq. |
| **September 22** | Mysterious, apparently nuclear, event in the South Atlantic near South Africa's Prince Edward and Marion Islands. |
| **November 20** | Grand Mosque at Mecca seized by Saudi insurgents, but royal family regains control. |
| **December 24** | Soviets invade Afghanistan. |

### 1980

| | |
|---|---|
| **April 18** | Zimbabwe (formerly Rhodesia) gains independence from Great Britain and soon becomes another haven for ANC guerillas operating in South Africa. |
| **October 16** | Last atmospheric nuclear test by any nuclear power (China). |

**1981**

| | |
|---|---|
| January 20 | Ronald Reagan assumes presidency of the United States. |
| During year | Deng Xiaoping consolidates power within China, assuming the chairmanship of the Central Military Commission. Hua Guofeng is relieved of all powers but retires gracefully. |
| During year | Pakistan's indigenous New Lab reprocessing facility is completed at PINSTECH. Munir Khan's plutonium-oriented nuclear program returns to life. |
| June 7 | Israeli Air Force attacks and destroys the Osirak nuclear reactor in Iraq. |

**1982**

| | |
|---|---|
| May 5 | Ronald Reagan adopts his plan for ending and winning the Cold War (NSDD-32). |
| November 10 | Leonid Brezhnev dies. Yuri Andropov assumes power in Soviet Union on November 12. |
| December 4 | The People's Republic of China adopts a new constitution. During the year, the Deng government also adopts a policy of actively supporting nuclear proliferation within the Third World. |

**1983**

| | |
|---|---|
| During year | Pakistani scientists receive nuclear weapon training in Beijing; China and Algeria sign agreement to build El Salam nuclear reactor (covertly) in Algeria; North Korean nuclear developments begin in earnest. |

**1984**

| | |
|---|---|
| February 9 | Yuri Andropov dies. |
| February 13 | Konstantin Chernenko assumes power in the Soviet Union. |
| During year | Construction of North Korea's 50-megawatt nuclear reactor starts at Yongbyon. |

**1985**

| | |
|---|---|
| March 10 | Konstantin Chernenko dies. Mikhail Gorbachev assumes power in the Soviet   Union the next day. |
| During year | Pakistan's Engineering Research Laboratory in Kahuta produces its first weapons-grade highly enriched uranium (HEU). |

**1986**

| | |
|---|---|
| April 15 | American air raids on Tripoli and Benghazi, Libya. |
| April 26 | Explosion and fire at the Chernobyl nuclear reactor in northern Ukraine. The resulting fallout seriously pollutes neighboring Belarus and fully discredits the Soviet *nomenklatura*. |
| Summer | In response to the April 15 raids, Libya's Qaddafi decides to go nuclear and seeks equipment suppliers within Europe. |
| By end of year | Pakistan has enough HEU to fabricate a CHIC-4–type nuclear weapon. |

**1987**

| | |
|---|---|
| During year | A. Q. Khan begins to transfer uranium-enrichment technology to Iran. |

| | |
|---|---|
| **December 8** | INF Treaty signed by Presidents Reagan and Gorbachev in Washington. |

## 1988

| | |
|---|---|
| **May 15** | The Soviet army begins its withdrawal from Afghanistan. |
| **August 17** | General Zia al-Haq of Pakistan dies in a mysterious airplane explosion that also takes the life of the U.S. ambassador. In December, General Zia is succeeded by a civilian, Benazir Bhutto, daughter of the president that Zia had replaced and executed a decade earlier. |
| **August 20** | Iran-Iraq War ends after nine years of hostilities and more than a million deaths. |
| **December 1** | The Supreme Soviet (parliament) of the Soviet Union adopts new election laws that provide for contested elections and secret ballots. |

## 1989

| | |
|---|---|
| **January 20** | George H. W. Bush assumes U.S. presidency. |
| **February 15** | Last Soviet troops leave Afghanistan. |
| **April 15–June 4** | Protests originating in Tiananmen Square spread throughout China. Deng Xiaoping wins a 3–2 vote in the Chinese politburo authorizing force to deal with these riots. |
| **September 14** | F. W. de Klerk elected to the presidency of South Africa, succeeding P. W. Botha. Upon his election, de Klerk discloses plans to end apartheid as well as the South African nuclear weapons program. |
| **During year** | Pakistan's A. Q. Khan delivers the first P-1 centrifuge to Iran. He also begins to offer nuclear technology to other nations. |
| **December** | Deng Xiaoping is removed as chairman of the Chinese Central Military Commission, replaced by Jiang Zemin. Deng's role is thereafter limited to economic policy. |

## 1990

| | |
|---|---|
| **May 26** | Chinese apparently test a Pakistani nuclear device at Lop Nur. |
| **August 2** | Saddam Hussein's Iraq invades Kuwait, seizes control in one day. |
| **October 6** | A. Q. Khan offers to help Iraq with nuclear weapons, although too late, as Desert Shield is already under way. |

## 1991

| | |
|---|---|
| **January 17– February 27** | UN forces, led by the United States, successfully assault Iraq and liberate Kuwait. |
| **February 9– March 3** | In separate referenda, the citizens of Estonia, Latvia, and Lithuania vote for independence from the Soviet Union. |
| **December 7** | The newly elected presidents of Russia, Ukraine, and Belarus meet at the Bison Forest hunting lodge outside Brest. They agree to dissolve the Soviet Union and create a Confederation of Independent States. |

| | |
|---|---|
| **December 22** | The leaders of all the Soviet republics except Georgia meet at Alma Ata to sign the Commonwealth Declaration, which abolishes the Soviet Union. |
| **December 25** | Soviet President Gorbachev resigns the presidency of a no-longer-existing Soviet Union, handing the nuclear keys to Boris Yeltsin, president of Russia. |

## 1992

| | |
|---|---|
| **During year** | North Korea begins the transfer of missile technology to Pakistan, presumably in exchange for uranium-enrichment assistance. Delivery of the latter skills starts in the late 1990s. |
| **May 23** | Representatives of the United States, Belarus, Kazakhstan, Russia, and Ukraine meet in Lisbon to sign a protocol to the START I Treaty of 1991, wherein those successor states agree to be bound by that treaty, with nuclear weapons to be "maintained under the safe, secure, and reliable control of a single unified authority." |
| **By end of May** | All tactical nuclear weapons within the non-Russian Soviet states have been transferred to Russia. |

## 1993

| | |
|---|---|
| **January 20** | William Clinton assumes U.S. presidency. |
| **February 23** | First attack on New York's World Trade Center, by Iraqi-born terrorists, delivering a "fertilizer bomb" within a Ryder truck. Six people killed, more than a thousand injured. |
| **March 24** | President F. W. de Klerk discloses details of South Africa's abandoned nuclear weapons program to his parliament. |
| **Late in year** | Pakistan's Benazir Bhutto visits North Korea, opens the door for the trade of A. Q. Khan's uranium-enrichment technology for North Korean ballistic missile designs. |

## 1994

| | |
|---|---|
| **January 14** | The presidents of Russia, Ukraine, and the United States meet in Moscow to sign the Trilateral Agreement, facilitating the return of nuclear weapons within Ukraine to Russia in exchange for reactor fuel from Russia and financial assistance from the United States. |
| **July 8** | Kim Il Sung, dictator of North Korea dies. His son, Kim Jong Il, takes power. |
| **November 8** | Republicans win control of the U.S. House of Representatives for the first time in forty-six years. |

## 1995

| | |
|---|---|
| **Spring** | A. Q. Khan begins the shipment of advanced (P-2) centrifuge components into Iran. |
| **May** | Russian and Kazakh officials confirm that all nuclear warheads once within Kazakhstan have been returned to Russia. |

## 1996

| | |
|---|---|
| **June** | Russian and Ukrainian officials confirm that all nuclear warheads once within Ukraine have been returned to Russia. |

| | |
|---|---|
| **July 3** | Boris Yeltsin is re-elected to the presidency of the Russian Federation in the face of a powerful challenge by resurgent communists. |
| **November** | Russian and Belarusian officials confirm that all nuclear warheads once within Belarus have been returned to Russia. |
| **During year** | North Korea begins delivery of No-Dong missiles to Pakistan. |

### 1997

| | |
|---|---|
| **May 1** | Tony Blair elected as the U.K. prime minister. |
| **July 1** | Hong Kong reverts to Chinese rule after 156 years as a British colony. |
| **During year** | A. Q. Khan begins to transfer centrifuge components into Libya. |

### 1998

| | |
|---|---|
| **March 2–7** | Elections within India oust the Gandhi-led Congress Party, producing a plurality for the BJP party and resulting in the installation of A. B. Vajpayee as prime minister. |
| **March 28** | The Vajpayee government wins a full vote of confidence in the Indian Parliament. At about this time, India decides to conduct nuclear tests. |
| **May 11** | India claims to test three nuclear devices. Apparently only two work, and only one as designed. |
| **May 13** | India claims to test two more nuclear devices. No seismic signals detected outside India. |
| **May 28** | Pakistan claims to have fired five nuclear devices; more likely one actual test of an advanced HEU design. |
| **May 30** | Pakistan fires a second nuclear device at a different location and under different circumstances from the May 28 event. It appears to be an advanced, plutonium-based design. |

### 1999

| | |
|---|---|
| **March 12** | NATO admits Poland, Hungary, and the Czech Republic to membership, thus moving NATO's borders to the Russian frontier. |
| **March** | The Saudi minister of defense visits the Khan Research Laboratory in Pakistan, the first foreigner to do so. |
| **August** | Vladimir Putin assumes the presidency of the Russian Federation. |
| **October 12** | General Pervez Musharraf seizes power in Pakistan, toppling Nawaz Sharif in a bloodless coup. |

### 2000

| | |
|---|---|
| **March 26** | Vladimir Putin elected president of Russia in his own right. |
| **September** | Libya receives its first two P-2 centrifuges from A. Q. Khan, along with 50 kilograms of uranium hexafluoride, and orders more of both. |

### 2001

| | |
|---|---|
| **January 20** | George W. Bush assumes U.S. presidency. |
| **September 11** | World Trade Center in New York and Pentagon in Washington, D.C., are attacked by terrorist-hijacked commercial airliners; three thousand are killed. |

| | |
|---|---|
| **October 7–**<br>**December 17** | U.S. and Northern Alliance forces route the Taliban from control of Afghanistan. |
| **December** | The Khan network provides Libya with a nuclear weapon design that originated within China. |

## 2002

| | |
|---|---|
| **April 30** | Pakistan voters give Perez Musharraf a five-year presidential term. |
| **May 21** | The U.S. State Department names Iran, Iraq, Cuba, Libya, North Korea, Sudan, and Syria as "state sponsors of terrorism." |
| **August** | National Council of Resistance, an Iranian exile group, discloses the existence of Iran's uranium-enrichment facility at Natanz. |
| **November 15** | Hu Jintao becomes general secretary of the Communist Party of China. |
| **November 21** | NATO invites Bulgaria, Estonia, Latvia, Lithuania, Romania, Slovakia, and Slovenia to join its ranks, thereby further irritating the Russian government. |

## 2003

| | |
|---|---|
| **March 15** | Hu Jintao assumes the presidency of China, while outgoing president Jiang Zemin retains chairmanship of the Central Military Commission. |
| **March 20–April 9** | United States, United Kingdom, and other coalition forces invade and take nominal control of Iraq. |
| **October** | Freighter BBC *China*, sailing from Malaysia and bound for Libya, is intercepted in the Mediterranean Sea. She is rerouted to Sicily, where she is boarded by U.S. and U.K. intelligence officers. Five containers filled with nuclear production machinery are found. |
| **Autumn** | According to an unusual National Intelligence Estimate (made public in December 2007), "In the fall of 2003, Tehran halted its nuclear weapons program." This statement refers to a pause in weapon design, not uranium enrichment. |
| **December 19** | Libya's Qaddafi reveals, and announces the abandonment of, his nuclear weapon program. |

## 2004

| | |
|---|---|
| **January** | A. Q. Khan confesses to the management of a clandestine, international nuclear technology network. It had been selling nuclear weapons technology to Libya, Iran, and North Korea, among others, for years. |
| **February 5** | General Musharraf, president of Pakistan, pardons Khan, while subjecting him to house arrest, and thus inaccessibility to Western intelligence investigators. Khan remains a national hero. |
| **March 11** | Islamic extremists from North Africa with ties to al Qaeda attack trains in Madrid: 191 killed and 2,050 injured. The Aznar government falls in elections three days later. Subsequently, the new Spanish government withdraws its troops from Iraq. |

| September | President Hu Jintao takes full power in China, adding the chairmanship of the Central Military Commission to his portfolio. |

**2005**

| April 23 | A. Q. Khan admits to selling gas centrifuge technology to North Korea. |
| August 6 | Mahmoud Ahmadinejad assumes presidency of Iran, with a four-year term. |
| July 7 | Terrorists in London with ties to al Qaeda attack three underground trains and one bus, killing 52 and injuring more than 700. |

**2006**

| April 11 | Iran's President Ahmadinejad confirms that Iran has produced a few ounces of low-grade enriched uranium. |
| October 9 | North Korea conducts a low-yield (probably a fizzle) nuclear event underground. High Chinese officials visit Pyongyang two weeks later. |

**2007**

| February | As part of the Six Power Talks, Americans reach "draft agreements" with North Koreans that may (or may not) close down the North Korean nuclear weapon program. |
| March 9 | During the run up to his re-election campaign, Pakistan's Musharraf removes the chief justice of Pakistan's supreme court, Iftikhar Chaudhry. Major demonstrations ensue. |
| June 29–30 | Terrorists attempt to bomb central London with fuel, gas canisters, and nail bombs. A day later, a second attacker drives a bomb-laden vehicle into the entry doors of the Glasgow air terminal. All involved are medical students, practitioners of Islamic fundamentalism. |
| July | The price of crude oil reaches $66 per barrel, for the first time surpassing the inflation-adjusted price at the peak of the 1980 Iranian crisis. |
| October | The National People's Congress re-elects Hu Jintao as leader of the Communist Party of China, thus assuring his election as president. He is not expected to retire until 2012. |
| October 6 | Musharraf is indirectly re-elected to a five-year presidential term by Pakistan's electoral college. On November 19, a stacked supreme court rejects all challenges to that election. On November 28, Musharraf resigns his army commission. |
| December 27 | Benazir Bhutto, General Musharraf's leading domestic political opponent, is assassinated in Rawalpindi. |
| December 31 | North Korea fails to meet its deadline for "disablement" of its nuclear weapon program. |

**2008**

| February 18 | Parliamentary elections in Pakistan. Musharraf's party wins only 16 percent of the seats; nineteen of his ministers lose. Opposition parties win enough seats to impeach, but alliances |

to do so are unlikely. Islamist parties are obliterated, dropping from fifty-nine seats to just three.

**March 2**   Dmitry Medvedev elected president of Russia, replacing Vladimir Putin, who is immediately appointed prime minister. A double-headed government appears to ensue, but its stability is in doubt.

**March 14**   Legislative elections in Iran confirm the hegemony of Supreme Leader Ayatollah Ali Khamenei. His Guardian Council had barred 1,700 "unacceptable" candidates from the ballot; surviving conservatives, subservient to the Supreme Leader, win three-quarters of the seats. Reform appears nowhere on the Iranian horizon.

**March 22**   Presidential elections in Taiwan return Chiang Kaishek's Kuomintang Party to power after eight years of pro-independence "adventurism" by the Democratic Progressive Party. Better relations with mainland China may ensue.

**April 2**   The American negotiator with North Korea, Christopher Hill, expresses his "concern" over the lack of progress on nuclear disablement.

**June**   The price of crude oil reaches $132 per barrel, twice the constant-dollar price during the 1980 Iranian crisis.

**June 26**   North Korea publicly destroys a nuclear reactor cooling tower at its Yongbyon nuclear complex one day after delivering a long-delayed declaration of nuclear activities to the Six Party office in Beijing.

**August 11**   Pakistan's ruling coalition parties agree to commence impeachment proceedings against President Musharraf.

**August 18**   Pervez Musharraf resigns as president of Pakistan.

**September 6**   Pakistan's provincial-based Electoral College elects Asif Ali Zardari to the presidency of Pakistan. Zardari's credentials include marriage to slain former prime minister Benazir Bhutto and eleven years in prison on corruption charges.

**November 4**   The United States elects a new president. The American people hope for an era of competence, since the Nuclear Express may well come off its rails during the forty-fourth president's term in office.

# ACKNOWLEDGMENTS

Your authors are children of the U.S. Atomic Energy Commission, a marvelous institution that achieved so much in the way of science with so little in the way of bureaucracy. We are deeply indebted to those old timers for their insight into what really happened on Tinian Island and a hundred other places as nuclear history was born and as that technology began to spread, often by surreptitious means. We are equally indebted to their successors, the men and women with whom we worked in preparing a complex manuscript that would be both accurate yet not helpful to those wishing to proliferate nuclear weapons into the wrong hands. Jim Greening and Joe Vital at the Department of Energy's Office of Security each held one end of that tightrope.

Co-author Reed is indebted to the nuclear historians of Western Europe, the men and women who welcomed him to London and Paris. His conversations with Lorna Arnold and Katherine Pyne, along with a review of their subsequent writings, opened doors into the heroic British nuclear program. Their advice led to important inquiries of others and thus, in time, an understanding of the decision cycles and technology transfers within the British nuclear world. Henri Conze convened a meeting of the grand old men of the French nuclear program. He did so at the University of Paris, but the leads emerging from those conversations spread around the world. They illuminated a complex web still emerging from the shadows.

Co-author Stillman traveled a harder road, from Moscow to Beijing. Academician Yuliy Khariton, the Cambridge-educated mastermind of the first Soviet A-bomb, invited and then arranged for Stillman's 1991 visit to the inner sanctum of the Soviet nuclear world—the weapons laboratory known as Arzamas-16. Khariton then stood by Stillman's side, day after day, to assure full disclosure of Soviet nuclear achievements—while sometimes masking their sources. Stillman's ten trips to China were organized by academics Hu Side and Yang Fujia, both well-connected technocrats who arranged visits to offices, nuclear laboratories, and test sites never before seen by Western eyes. Over the years, Hu and Yang have stayed in touch, updated our findings and become close personal friends.

Both of us are indebted to the senior hands within the American intelligence community. Arnold Kramish, a former U.S. AEC intelligence officer, helped pick the locks on doors not easily opened, Israel being a prime example. Former directors of

American central intelligence (John Deutch and James Woolsey) guided our searches. Lieutenant General Eugene Tighe, a one-time director of the Defense Intelligence Agency, added encouragement and perspective.

Beyond these luminaries, there are a host of other sources, experts on the energy supplies and nuclear intrigues of the Mideast, North Korea, and Africa. We would like to express specific thanks to these people, but we cannot easily do so. Their careers and perhaps even their personal safety could be forfeit. Our sources include retired engineers now living on the west coast of Africa, retired ambassadors commuting from Trombay to San Francisco, physicists blogging from Islamabad, inspectors headquartered in Vienna, commuters from the U.S. weapons labs to North Korea and other nascent nuclear states, and retired oil executives to whom Ghawar, Azadegan, and Tengiz are second homes. Their numbers are legion; they know who they are; their insights into the realities of the twenty-first century have been indispensable.

In addition to those flesh-and-blood resources, we are indebted to the Internet web sites maintained by responsible nuclear watchdog entities: The Natural Resources Defense Council, the Federation of American Scientists, the Nuclear Threat Initiative, the American Physical Society, Global Security, and the Hoover Institution. Their accounts are the bane of the American intelligence community, but their reports do constitute "publication" in the open literature. At the same time, we are also indebted to those who helped evaluate other "revelations." In this era of web-provided data, the credentials of every researcher, columnist, and blogger must be checked and re-checked.

To return to an earlier time, we would like to thank the men who first opened our eyes to the beauty and symmetry of nuclear physics during the late 1950s and early 1960s: Prof. Richard Scalettar at the University of Southern California and Prof. John Blair at the University of Washington. We thank our mentors at Livermore (Edward Teller) and Los Alamos (Harold Agnew) who had faith in our creative talents when those talents were well hidden by youth. Returning to this century, we would like to thank a few of those who urged and enabled us to write and to persevere in the publication of this history. That list would include Rodney Barker, Bill Broad, Steve Coll, Al Heiman, David Hoffman, Richard Honsinger, Tom Jordan, Bob Kane, Sara Pasqualoni, Bradley Rowberry, and Libby Watch as well as all the Reed and Stillman children who have been so supportive over the years.

In the practical world, we owe the greatest thanks to our publisher, Richard Kane of Zenith Press, who first appreciated the significance of this tale; to our meticulous editor at Zenith Press, Steve Gansen; and to our most talented copyeditor, Tom Kailbourn. We thank Ballantine Books, publisher of Reed's *At the Abyss* for permission to use the epilogue of that book as the starting point for this one, and we thank Steve Benka and the American Institute of Physics for their support in publishing the technical details of the Chinese nuclear tests in the September 2008 issue of *Physics Today*. Susan Spaulding provided wise legal counsel. Hannah Gray was responsible for our secretarial work and much more: the preparation of graphics, production of the manuscript in electronic form, and its repeated delivery to co-authors, agent, and publisher. Phil Schwartzberg of Meridian Mapping created our maps. Presiding over all of this was our most patient literary agent, Phyllis Wender of The Gersh Agency. We appreciate, beyond words, her early encouragement, the countless hours devoted to shaping this work and her patience in contracting for its publication.

Oddly enough, we thank each other, because the production of *Nuclear Express* has been a classic literary partnership. We hope Danny Stillman's bulging scientific rolodex and his dedication to accuracy, Tom Reed's political network and his literary talents, along with both authors' lifetimes of nuclear weapons experience have brought to the reader a better understanding of the nuclear crises soon to descend.

Most importantly, we thank our dear wives, who are also our dear friends—Kay Reed and Ruth Stillman. Their early encouragement, patience over the years, and understanding of the demands on our time made this work possible.

# INDEX